English Literature from 1785

HARPERCOLLINS COLLEGE OUTLINE

English Literature from 1785

Kathleen McCoy, Ph.D.
Seton Hall University

Judith Harlan

HarperPerennial
A Division of HarperCollins*Publishers*

This book is dedicated to Jack, Jimmy, and Maggie Nachlin
and to
Joellen Valley, Hugh, Tannis, and Rachel McCammon,
and to Lawrence H. Cooke

An American BookWorks Corporation Production

Editor: Thomas Quinn

Library of Congress Catalog Card Number: 91-58271

ISBN: 0-06-467150-X

94 95 96 ABW/RRD 10 9 8 7 6 5 4 3 2

Contents

Preface

The HarperCollins Outline text *Introduction to English Literature from 1785* presents what great English men and women thought and felt, and then wrote down in good prose and striking poetry in the English language. In its broadest sense, English literature is simply the written records of a people, including its history and sciences as well as its poems, plays, essays, and novels. As a written record of the human spirit, it both preserves the ideals of a developing civilization and is one of the most important and delightful subjects that can occupy the human mind.

The outline offers both the student and the general reader a historical and cultural context within which the authors and their works may be examined and appreciated in relationship to their different periods. The reader should find their understanding and appreciation enhanced by the detailed time lines and the introductions which precede each chapter as well as by the clear, concise text. Content summaries and selected references appear at the end of each chapter and emphasize both recent scholarship and classic studies. The Glossary is an important and integral part of the book.

The book is designed to be useful to the student or reader as a ready reference tool whether as a review book in conjunction with any of the standard college anthologies, or as a textbook for initial study with individual selections. The amount of detail devoted to each form, author, or writing is in proportion to the difficulty or complexity of the subject. We have not tried to give subtleties of interpretation or enter into any controversy, but it is not possible to describe a literary work without some implied interpretation. We have tried to be mainstream at the risk of stating the obvious.

It is a pleasure for us to acknowledge the scholarly contributions and constructive editorial assistance of those who have done so much to make this book possible. We thank each person.

Mikos Grieco assisted with the research, while Tom Quinn, Susan McClosky, Tannis McCammon, and M. R. Kline reviewed and edited the manuscript with keen eyes and great skill. Each made useful suggestions, "good catches," and offered continuing encouragement to us. Our friend, Noreen Morin, again prepared the endless drafts and the final manuscript, but most important, she offered her constant support, encouragement, and enthusiasm throughout.

English Literature
from 1785

1

The Romantic Age (1785 to 1832)

1760–1762	MacPherson publishes Ossianic *Fragments of Ancient Poetry Collected in the Highlands of Scotland*
1760–c. 1785	*Sturm und Drang* movement in Germany
1760–1820	Reign of George III
1762	Rousseau, *Social Contract*; child prodigy Mozart begins tour of Europe
1764	Walpole, *Castle of Otranto, A Gothic Story*; Percy, *Reliques of Ancient English Poetry*
1765–1769	Blackstone, *Commentaries on the Laws of England*; Hargreaves refines "spinning jenny"; Watt invents steam engine
1774	Goethe, *The Sorrows of Young Werther*
1774–1778	Warton, *History of English Poetry*
1775–1783	War with American colonies
1776	Smith, *Wealth of Nations*
1777–1820	Blake's poems written
1778	Deaths of Rousseau and Voltaire
1779–1781	Johnson, *Lives of the Poets*
1781	Kant, *Critique of Pure Reason*; Schiller, *The Robbers*
1783–1789	Day, *Sanford and Merton*; Blake, *Poetical Sketches*
1784	Death of Samuel Johnson; John Wesley founds Methodism

1785	Cowper, *The Task*
1786	Mozart's *Marriage of Figaro* has first performance
1786–1796	Burns's poems written
1789	The Bastille stormed, French Revolution begins; George Washington becomes first president of the United States
1790	Burke, *Reflections on the Revolution in France*
1791	Boswell, *Life of Johnson*; Paine, *Rights of Man*
1792	Wollstonecraft, *Vindication of the Rights of Woman*
1793	Godwin, *Enquiry Concerning Political Justice*; Louis XVI beheaded; France declares war on Britain and Holland
1794	Radcliffe, *Mysteries of Udolpho*
1795	Napoleonic Era begins
1798	Wordsworth and Coleridge, *Lyrical Ballads*; Malthus, *Essay on Population*; Irish rebellion led by Wolfe Tone
1798–1817	Coleridge's poems and essays written
1798–1850	Wordsworth's poems written
1800	Edgeworth, *Castle Rackrent*; Bill of Union of Great Britain and Ireland
1801	First census of England and Wales taken, subsequently every ten years thereafter
1802	Cobbett founds "Political Register," a forerunner of political reviews; Australia colonized
1803–1805	Beethoven composes opera *Fidelio*
1804	Napoleon crowned emperor
1805	Nelson defeats French fleet in Battle of Trafalgar
1805–1817	Scott's poetry period
1807	Lamb, *Tales from Shakespeare*; abolition of slave trade
1807–1823	Byron's poems written
1808–1810	Physicist and chemist John Dalton introduces theory of atomic structure of matter
1812	Napoleon's invasion of Russia fails; United States and Great Britain go to war
1813	Austen's *Pride and Prejudice* published; Robert Southey named poet laureate
1813–1821	Shelley's poems written
1814	The Treaty of Ghent ends the War of 1812

1815	Final defeat of Napoleon by British and Prussian forces at Battle of Waterloo; Congress of Vienna reorganizes Europe for post-Napoleonic period
1816	Rossini, *Barber of Seville*
1817–1820	Keats's poems written
1818	Mary Wollstonecraft Shelley, *Frankenstein*
1819	First transatlantic steamship; Schopenhauer, *The World as Will and Idea*
1820–1830	Reign of George IV
1821	De Quincey, *Confessions of an English Opium Eater*; Constable paints *The Hay-Wain*
1826	Disraeli, *Vivian Gray*; Cooper, *The Last of the Mohicans*; first Temperance Society
1828	Webster, *An American Dictionary*
1829	Catholic Emancipation Act
1830	Tennyson's first poems; Berlioz begins *Symphonie fantastique*; first railroad begins the railroad era
1830–1837	Reign of William IV
1831	Scott's last novel
1832	Reform Bill

*S*ocial, political, and economic changes in England had gradually been increasing during the second half of the eighteenth century. England was becoming industrialized before any of the other major European powers. While France stagnated under a bankrupt monarchy, England was growing up around new centers of manufacture and mining. From its beginnings as a basic agricultural economy, England was becoming urban, and its trade was increasingly international. With its navy dominating the seas, England was able to exploit the untold wealth of new lands, establishing colonies, or "ports of trade," in markets throughout the Old and the New World while slowly spreading worldwide the empire of the Anglo-Saxons. Under a constitutional monarchy, the modern form of "cabinet government" responsible to Parliament and to the people had been established. Political progress was slow, but not so slow as to provoke the type of revolutionary outbreak that was wrenching France by the end of the century.

THE ROMANTIC PERIOD

To many cultured English people, these changes were seen less as progress than as the end of the good old days. Urbanization brought city squalor; the newly rich industrialists seemed to lack a paternal interest in the countryside and in the common people. Farmers were displaced by the enclosure of common lands and by the purchase of small farms, which reorganized agriculture on a larger scale. Many farm and village families relocated to towns, where they became factory laborers, employed for long hours doing tedious and often dangerous work in the mills. The concentration of poverty in industrial towns, along with the increasing affluence of factory owners, created a new type of class division. It became apparent that poverty was not just a universal and inevitable part of the human condition. It could be seen that economic arrangements created poverty and thus could also, presumably, be altered to help the poor. The old hierarchy of nobles, gentry, and commoners no longer seemed a just and necessary structure. The class made up of "commoners" experienced remarkable economic mobility: upward mobility among traders and factory owners of the new middle class and downward mobility among menial factory workers. In the poetry of Wordsworth, for example, simple rural folk are often portrayed as displaced or abandoned by a society that had become careless of its people. Wordsworth, however, never explicitly made the connection between the condition of the individual and the economy.

Ideas of the Enlightenment thinkers, especially of the "philosophes" in France, led to new perceptions of human nature and of the individual's role as a member of the state. The human being was seen as having "natural rights" rather than being the servant of the state. On the contrary, it was thought that the state was created to serve and protect the individual. The revolution in the British colonies of America helped reaffirm these ideas. When in 1789 the French people stormed the Bastille (the prison that had come to symbolize political oppression) in Paris, English liberal thinkers became fired with enthusiasm and with the expectation that a new political order would make freedom more widespread. English writers such as William Godwin and Mary Wollstonecraft responded to the political excitement. Each wrote political tracts and works of fiction to express new visions of freedom and to propound that the social injustices had been caused not by individual weaknesses but by a corrupt system of authority in which power was unfairly concentrated.

The electoral system of England was based on land ownership, and the allocation of parliamentary seats had not been adjusted to reflect the shifts of population. Some of the new industrial towns of the north were practically without parliamentary representation, despite their having great financial power. At the same time, small rural towns that had lost population (later referred to as rotten boroughs) still sent to Parliament representatives chosen by the very few voters. A town in which the election of a member of Parliament was controlled by a single local lord or by his family was called a "pocket borough." Voters in all the boroughs had to be men who owned property or leased it for at least ten pounds a year. Freeholders or small nonagricultural workers in the counties had to have incomes of at least forty shillings a year; very few small farmers could meet the economic qualifications. Most industrial workers owned no land at all. The inequalities of the distribution of political power were so glaring that public demonstrations resulted. Therefore, when the French Revolution demonstrated the danger of depriving the masses of representation, pressure for election reform began to build in England. It was not until 1832 that the first Reform Bill was passed. Although the act did not give everyone a vote, it did lower the property requirement so that most of the male middle class became eligible and redistributed parliamentary representation in favor of the industrial cities. Ordinary workers, however, still did not qualify to vote. It was assumed that the workers' interests would be protected by their employers, the factory owners, who could now vote. A second Reform Bill, which passed in 1867, further broadened the voting base to include most male workers, and a third, passed in 1884, broadened the base to include all adult males except criminals and lunatics.

Still, conditions at the beginning of the nineteenth century did not look bright. The first impulse of the ruling aristocracy and gentry of "Old England" was to resist the social and political pressures for change. They held on all the more tightly to their inherited privileges and authority. The poets and novelists tended to identify with the interests of the disenfranchised, and often dislocated, poor. Celebration of the "free individual" and condemnation of the social system that held the individual down were two of the most pervasive ideas in literature at the turn of the century. Civilization was no longer represented as the height of human accomplishment. On the contrary, civilization was shown as a collection of rules and institutions designed to withhold liberty and thus to blight the individual's inherent good nature.

Poetic Forms

In poetry the landscape was the "natural" setting and subject. Whereas the poets of sensibility, who wrote in the middle decades of the eighteenth century, had described a picturesque rural scene as the setting and background of their meditations and feelings, the turn-of-the century poets put themselves above the scene and surveyed the vista that lay below. These poets expressed feelings of terror, melancholy, or nostalgia provoked by the scene. The new poets tended to view from close up the natural subject: the flower, the animal, the tree. They drank in their sensations of the vivid natural subject, receiving from it the ideas and feelings that provided their poetic material.

The primary mode of "romantic poetry" was the *lyric*. The poet spoke in the first person, present tense, saying "I see, I hear, I feel." Early romantic poets used the forms of the folk song and ballad, writing poems consisting of simple stanzas with short lines and much repetition. The great romantics, however, also developed longer lyrics, forms of the ode, to encompass their more complex and ambitious expressions. All the poets experimented with varieties of forms, using irregular stanzas and varying line length. Their less successful efforts tended to be the longer narrative poems, with mythical or visionary characters and situations. Because these poems were less unified and less spontaneous, they tended to lose focus. Many such poems were left unfinished. The sonnet form was revived, but not the long cycle of sonnets that had been so popular during the Renaissance. Keats in particular tried to revive some of the other stanzaic forms of the Renaissance poets, especially the Spenserian sonnet. In general, though, the romantic poets sought a rich melodious effect for their most impressive works.

For all the romantic poets, poetry involved the re-creation of sensation. These poets' main goal was to arouse an immediate feeling in the reader. They stressed the power of the imagination that was involved in a joyful, active, and creative way with the materials of the natural world. The poets thought of the imagination as a power, a capacity of the mind to make new images by combining and reordering sensations. One recurrent theme was the poet's lament that his creative imagination seemed to have lost some of its power, leaving melancholy and regret.

Because the individual poet's imagination was held to be so central to the creative process and was so fully revealed in his poetry, romantic poetry appears at times to be egotistical. Often the poem seems to revolve around the poet's own personal condition of mind. The exploration of the poet's self, however, was a means of approaching the truth of the whole human condition. Wordsworth asserted, "the poet is a man among men," perhaps more sensitive than most but certainly not fundamentally different. There-fore, in exploring his own mind, feelings, memories, and shifts of mood, the poet shows what is essential to all minds and thus creates a poetry that arouses a sympathetic response in his reader. One important image in this poetry is the eolian harp or lute. The eolian harp is a musical instrument consisting of strings inside a frame. As the wind blows across it, music is produced. The analogy is made to the poet, who thus is an instrument played upon by winds of sensation, creating a music that is his poetry.

Dramatic Forms

The romantic era was not an important age in the history of English drama. The Theatre Licensing Act of 1737, which provided for systematic censorship of all plays, was still in effect. This meant that plays of satire or political comment were unlikely to be approved for performance. Melodramas portraying middle-class domestic life and sentimental comedies were still standard theatrical offerings, along with revised and adapted versions of Shakespearean plays. The two licensed or legitimate theaters of London—the Drury Lane and the Covent Garden—became arenas for the display of sensational acting. Actors rather than playwrights became the main attractions that drew crowds to the theater. Still, a large portion of the middle class rejected the theater as an art form and scorned actors as disreputable or immoral. Meanwhile, lower-class audiences patronized various music halls, where they were entertained by songs and dances of a more rowdy sort.

The major poets of this era were not interested in the theater as an outlet. The poets focused on their inner states of mind and on the nuances of their feelings and did not see the stage as an appropriate setting for their ideas. A few poets wrote "closet dramas," that is, plays intended for reading rather than for presentation on the stage. But generally the complex plot structures and social situations of drama were outside the mainstream of romantic literary development.

The Novel

Prose fiction, well established as a popular form during the middle of the eighteenth century, continued to be widely read. The novel that traced an individual's adventures as he or she entered into adult society and found the right niche was still produced. This type novel had an increasingly didactic tone and purpose, stridently seeking to show that the right education of the child would produce an upright and happy adult. One such "novel of purpose" was Thomas Day's *Sanford and Merton* (1783–1789). In this widely read work, Day tried to illustrate the educational theories of Rousseau by contrasting rich, spoiled Merton with poor, virtuous, sensitive Sanford. Still another type of novel of purpose was represented by the works of Maria Edgeworth, whose *Castle Rackrent* (1800) showed the ill effects of the greedy absentee landlord not only on his tenants but also on his own family.

THE GOTHIC NOVEL

The form of novel that most flourished toward the end of the eighteenth and the beginning of the nineteenth century was the novel of romance and terror called the *Gothic novel*. Gothic novels were set in remote times and distant places, such as medieval Italy. They did not purport to show realistic life scenes. These novels included dark castles with gloomy dungeons and mysterious passageways. Spirits of ancestors and displaced heirs usually came back to haunt the living.

Castle of Otranto, A Gothic Story. One of the first of such novels was Horace Walpole's *Castle of Otranto, A Gothic Story* (1764), an incredible story that begins with a startling scene wherein a gigantic helmet suddenly drops into the courtyard of the castle, killing the castle's usurper. The true heir is a prince, who comes to the castle disguised as a peasant. After a suitable amount of intrigue, the prince regains his birthright and marries the usurper's intended bride. This novel established the general formula of sensationalism and suspense, mystery, and terror that was expounded by a large number of novelists during the next few decades.

Mysteries of Udolpho. The most famous English Gothic novel was *Mysteries of Udolpho* (1794), by Anne Radcliffe. The sentimental heroine is an orphan who is confined in an old Italian castle and threatened by all sorts of supernatural terrors. The gloomy villain, the heroine's aunt's husband, seems to want her destruction, but she escapes and marries the hero, who has helped her flee the castle. This novel, typical of the Gothic style, has characters who are either very good or very evil, and complex, unpredictable action in a bizarre setting. Mrs. Radcliffe's novel was later satirized by Jane Austen in *Northanger Abbey*. Austen's heroine is a young girl who has read too many Gothic novels and thus imagines that fantastic and terrible crimes have happened in an ordinary English country house where she is a guest.

The Gothic novel was very successful. Some of the best known were Clara Reeve's *Old English Baron* (1778), Matthew Gregory Lewis's *Monk* (1796), and Charles Maturin's *Melmoth the Wanderer* (1820). The climax of the development of Gothic fiction is represented by Mary Wollstonecraft Shelley's *Frankenstein* (1818).

Frankenstein or The Modern Prometheus. The character Frankenstein is a scientist who discovers the secret of giving life to lifeless material and creates a living being. The huge, strong, and horrible-looking creature he creates is lonely and tormented, seeking only a female partner. Eventually the creature murders his creator and then destroys himself. This novel not only climaxes the Gothic mode in fiction but also reflects some of the philosophical concerns of the novel of purpose. The monster created by Frankenstein is portrayed as a noble and benevolent being who becomes wild and terrible because of the neglect and mistreatment he suffers in the world.

Major Novelists   The two outstanding novelists of the romantic period were Jane Austen and Sir Walter Scott. Their novels were very different in style and subject matter: Austen refined and simplified the novel—developing the satire on manners in a series of courtship novels, while Scott, using a much broader range of subjects and settings, developed the historical novel.

SIR WALTER SCOTT (1771–1832)

Scott was born just north of England, in the border country of Scotland. His literary work began with translations of German romantic ballads, but he soon discovered that there was romance enough in his own Highlands. During 1802 and 1803 he produced the three volumes of his *Minstrelsy of the Scottish Border*, for which he had been collecting old ballads for many years. Scott's earliest poetry consisted of narrative verse based on the history and culture of his native region. His first original work, *The Lay of the Last Minstrel*, appeared in 1805 and was an immediate success. *Marmion*, written in 1808, and *The Lady of the Lake* (1810) aroused Scottish and English readers to intense enthusiasm and brought unexpected fame to the author. But Scott grew to feel that his poetic romances were overshadowed by the work of Byron, and so after 1810 he turned his attention to prose.

Scott is credited with the development of the historical novel—that is, with the novel that does not merely use an historical setting as background but that shows the lives of the main characters being shaped or determined by discrete historical events. Scott introduced historical persons into his novels, who then became minor characters. Between 1814 and 1819 Scott wrote his Waverly novels, based on the history of Scotland. The best known of these are *Waverly* (1814) and *The Heart of Midlothian* (1818). After 1815 Scott found himself heavily in debt because of the failure of a publishing concern in which he had been a partner. He wrote intensively, some say heroically, in order to pay off the debt. The novels of this later period are set in medieval England and include his most famous novel, *Ivanhoe* (1819). Scott also wrote critical reviews of books for the Tory journal *The Quarterly*, which he had helped start. He was an admirer of the novels of Jane Austen, though they were very unlike his own, and realized early the high quality of her talent.

JANE AUSTEN (1775–1817)

A clergyman's daughter, Jane Austen grew up in a Hampshire village amid a lively household of six brothers and sisters. Her life was remarkably uneventful. Austen was an avid reader and began to write fiction in her teens. In 1801 the family moved to the more cosmopolitan setting of Bath, a resort city for the gentry. After her father's death in 1806 the family moved again, first to Southampton and then back to Hampshire. Austen did not marry. She spent her life making visits to the homes of relatives, maintaining an active correspondence with her sister Cassandra and with her nephews and nieces, and, of course, writing her novels. She died at the age of forty-two of Addison's disease.

Jane Austen deliberately restricted the scope of her novels to the realms of her own rather limited experience. She dealt with the social relationships among families of the small-town gentry, whose lives were taken up with visiting, walking in the countryside, and attending parties and picnics. The action of each novel involves a problem of courtship; the heroine must avoid unwanted suitors and, without violating the restraints of modesty, attract the right marriage partner. The tone of each novel is ironic; Austen satirizes the pride, snobbishness, and foolish sentimentality of her characters. But Austen does not address questions of social justice or political inequality; in this respect, she is an author more of the classical age that had just ended than of the romantic age. Jane Austen was modest about her own literary accomplishments. In a letter to her nephew Edward she describes her novels as "that little bit [two inches wide] of ivory, in which I work with so fine a brush as produces little effect after much labor." She met with scanty encouragement in her own generation. Her greatest novel, *Pride and Prejudice*, finished in 1797, went without a publisher for sixteen years. Austen extensively revised her novels, and none of them was published in the order of its composition. For example, *Northanger Abbey*, her first complete novel, was not printed until after her death, in a combined volume with her last novel, *Persuasion* (1818). The four novels published during her lifetime were *Sense and Sensibility* (1811), *Pride and Prejudice* (1813), *Mansfield Park* (1814), and *Emma* (1816). All of these novels were published anonymously.

Many critics have believed that Austen chose to limit the scope of her novels as a way to achieve a more finely focused, delicate, and artistic structure. She refined the rather loose and episodic prose form of the novel, cutting away the excessive digressions, interpolated stories, and rambling commentaries of the narrator. Austen's reputation has grown steadily since the first reception of her works, and it remains high today.

Minor Novelists

Other novelists active in the romantic period included Fanny Burney, whose successful early novel *Evelina* (1778) was followed by *Cecilia* (1782), *Camilla* (1806), and *The Wanderer* (1814); and Thomas Love Peacock, who wrote a parody of the Gothic novel, *Nightmare Abbey* (1818), and *Crotchet Castle* (1831). However, the major novelists of the nineteenth century—Dickens, Thackeray, the Brontës, and George Eliot—belong to the Victorian period.

The romantic period in England was a time of intense social and political change. The spirit of liberalism and the call for individual freedom loosened many of the traditional restraints, and the resulting social unrest brought about a redistribution of power as well as a new awareness of the effects of economic inequalities. In literature, this new spirit came as a release from the weight of the past, permitting bold and imaginative poetic experimentation. Political revolution in France seemed to liberate the romantic poets to treat the subjects of nature and the common person with intense new feelings. The manifesto of the new poetic spirit was the statement by Wordsworth and Coleridge in the preface to Lyrical Ballads. *They asserted the possibility of a freer and more personal type of poetry. Although each poet took up the challenge in his own way, not one was unaffected by it.*

Selected Readings

Abrams, M. H. *The Mirror and the Lamp: Romantic Theory and the Critical Tradition.* New York: Norton, 1953.

_____, ed. *English Romantic Poets.* New York: Oxford University Press, 1960.

Beers, Henry A. *A History of English Romanticism in the Eighteenth Century.* New York: Holt, 1916.

Cockshut, A. O. J. *The Achievement of Walter Scott.* New York: New York University Press, 1969.

Devlin, D. D. *The Author of Waverley: A Critical Study of Walter Scott.* Lewisburg: Bucknell University Press, 1971.

Fletcher, Richard M. *English Romantic Drama, 1795–1843: A Critical History.* New York: Exposition, 1966.

Gaull, Marilyn. *English Romanticism: The Human Context.* New York: Norton, 1988.

Houtchens, Carolyn, and Lawrence H. Houtchens, eds. *The English Romantic Poets and Essayists: A Review of Research and Criticism.* New York: New York University Press, 1966.

Reiman, Donald H., ed. *The Romantics Reviewed: Contemporary Reviews of British Romantic Writers.* New York: Garland, 1972.

Sabin, Margery. *English Romanticism and the French Tradition.* Cambridge: Harvard University Press, 1976.

2

Early Romantics: Blake, Burns, and Wollstonecraft

c. 1760	Beginning of Industrial Revolution
1760–1765	MacPherson publishes Ossianic *Fragments of Ancient Poetry Collected in the Highlands of Scotland*
1760–1820	Reign of George III
1765–1769	Hargreaves refines "spinning jenny"; Watt invents steam engine
1775–1783	War with American colonies
1777	Burns goes to Kirkoswald to study surveying
1781	Kant, *Critique of Pure Reason*
1783	Blake's *Poetical Sketches* set in type
1784	Death of Samuel Johnson
1786	Burns, *Poems, Chiefly in the Scottish Dialect* (Kilmarnock Edition); Wollstonecraft, *Thoughts on the Education of Daughters*
1787	Burns begins collecting and editing for *The Scots Musical Museum*
1788	Wollstonecraft, *Mary, a Fiction*; Blake begins experimenting with relief etching; Burns marries
1789	Blake, *Songs of Innocence*; Wollstonecraft, *Original Stories from Real Life*; French Revolution begins; George Washington becomes president of the United States
1791	Boswell, *Life of Johnson*; Paine, *Rights of Man*

1791–1793 Blake, *Vision of the Daughters of Albion*

1792 Blake, *The Marriage of Heaven and Hell*; Wollstonecraft, *A Vindication of the Rights of Woman*

1794 Blake, supplemental poems added and editions printed as *Songs of Innocence and of Experience*

1795 Napoleonic era begins

1796 Burns dies

1798 Godwin, *Memoirs of the Author of "A Vindication of the Rights of Woman"*

1800 Blake moves to Sussex under patronage of William Hayley

1802 *The Edinburgh Review*, first literary review, established

1803 Blake acquitted after arrest and trial for sedition

1804–1820 Blake develops major prophetic books, *The Four Zoas*, *Milton*, and *Jerusalem*

1816 Coleridge, *Christabel* and *Kubla Khan*

1827 Blake dies

Even those English writers who had begun to write before the shock and exhilaration of the French Revolution were influenced by the growing spirit of rebellion and the developing urge to reject the restraints and rationalism of mainstream eighteenth-century thought. These writers did not, however, form a group. Blake, Burns, and Wollstonecraft evolved a highly individual approach through which each expressed his or her own desire for freedom. For a variety of reasons, each writer was isolated. Only Burns enjoyed a popular following. What these first-generation romantics had in common was neither ideas nor style but great originality that allowed each to follow a fresh course.

WILLIAM BLAKE (1757–1827)

Blake's background was very ordinary; his father was a tradesman in London, a dealer in clothing and knitted goods. Blake's education was in art, although he was widely read in the English poetry of the Renaissance. At the age of fourteen, already an art student at the Royal Academy, Blake became apprenticed for a term of seven years to the engraver James Basine. (An engraver etches an image on a wood or metal surface and then applies inks and prints multiple copies of the image.) During this period, Blake also began to write poems. After his apprenticeship, Blake earned his living by engraving book illustrations. In 1782 he married an illiterate young woman named Catherine Boucher, whom he taught to read and to help him make engravings of his own poems. Meanwhile, Blake had made friends with other artists; some of these helped him publish *Poetical Sketches* (1783), the only one of Blake's literary works to be printed. Blake later set up his own engraving shop, where he produced *Songs of Innocence* (1789), embellishing it with marginal engravings colored by hand. In 1800 Blake left London for the town of Felpham in Sussex to be near his friend and patron, William Hayley, a popular poet whose works he was employed to illustrate. Blake was intensely productive in the 1790s and the early years of the new century.

During this period he worked out an extensive and complex visionary and mythical system. In 1803, however, Blake became involved in a strange incident that caused him great distress. In the garden of his house in Felpham, he got into a bitter argument with a soldier. Blake ordered the man to leave, but the soldier refused and threatened Blake and his wife. Blake pushed the soldier out and continued to push him until they reached the village inn. In retaliation, the soldier accused Blake of sedition, saying that Blake had "damned the king." A trial was held and Blake was acquitted, but the experience left him with a lasting fear and bitterness, making him suspicious even of his own friends. He came to feel that he would never find a sympathetic audience for his difficult and complex poetry. Blake continued to work as an illustrator and to write poetry, but not as abundantly as before. He died in obscurity at the age of seventy.

Of all the romantic poets Blake was the most independent and probably the most original. He was a poet of inspiration alone, obeying no voice but the one he heard in his own mystic soul. As a poet, he set out to create his own mythology to counteract what he perceived as the deadening rationalism of the European Enlightenment. He was deeply familiar with the Bible and made use of biblical lore, but he also created his own dynamic allegorical figures. He did not accept the conventional orthodox interpretation of Christianity; he saw himself as a prophet called upon to release the "Divine Vision of the Bible" from the limiting distortions of history. He looked back to Milton as the last great visionary poet of English culture. Blake saw humankind as confined by nature and society: "Man in a divided state, violated by moral restraints and by the weight of authorities." He felt that the individual could regain wholeness only by freeing the intellect and achieving a visionary ecstasy. Los is the figure of imaginative power who says, "I must create a System or be enslaved by another Man's" while Urizen (your reason) acts to limit and distort. Blake's mythology continued to develop, and he created many other mythical figures. This pantheistic conception seems to have been not merely a creed but the very essence of Blake's life. He never attempted to found a new religious cult but rather followed his own way despite discouragement and failure. Blake said of his work, "That which can be made Explicit to the Idiot is not worth my care."

Poetical Sketches (1783)

This is a collection of lyrics, most of which Blake wrote between the ages of twelve and twenty. The poems show the influence of Shakespeare, Spenser, and Milton. "To Spring," for example, imitates the rich sensuous detail of Spenser's style, creating bridal images of the coming of the season. In "To Autumn" the season is personified as a masculine figure, singing a song of joy and leaving, as he goes, a load of golden fruit. By contrast, the Song that begins "How sweet I roam'd" delights the reader with the conventional Renaissance imagery of love—roses and lilies, gold and silk— then shows the lover, in the final stanza, as a caged bird, mocked by the prison of love. This dire turn at the end is very Blakean. Blake also wrote lyrics based on situations in Shakespeare's plays, such as the "Mad Song" for the fool in *King Lear*. The fool depicts the "frantic pain" that has seized his brain.

All Religions Are One; There Is No Natural Religion (a); And There Is No Natural Religion (b)

These three brief prose tracts from 1788 each consist of six or seven statements opposing the Enlightenment idea that people know God through their perception of the natural world that is God's creation. Blake finds this "natural religion" too limited because it ignores the "Poetic Genius" of the individual, his or her essence. If people rely only on the knowledge provided by the senses, as Enlightenment philosophy taught, then they could never rise above mere sense to grasp the Infinite.

Songs of Innocence and of Experience, Showing the Two Contrary States of the Human Soul

SONGS OF INNOCENCE

These poems were originally engraved on illustrated plates in 1789. They were mostly joyful and sweet lyrics creating images of childhood in a happy natural setting. The titles "Laughing Song" and "Infant Joy" illustrate the tone; the children are angelic and are compared with lambs. In a few of these Songs, however, Blake suggests that the innocent child is caught in an exploitative and harsh world that is beyond his or her understanding.

"The Chimney Sweeper." In this poem a child who has been "sold" into a dreary life of dangerous, dirty work is consoled by a happy dream.

SONGS OF EXPERIENCE

In *Songs of Experience*, added in 1794, Blake takes a darker, sadder tone. These lyrics depict a world of sickness and tyranny. Children are poor and deprived of joy; love has become a type of bondage. Many of the *Songs of Experience* correspond to specific *Songs of Innocence*; some even have the same title. For example, two are called "Holy Thursday"; the lyric from

Songs of Innocence shows radiant, lamblike children singing angelically; the poem from *Songs of Experience* shows poor and hungry children whose song is a "trembling cry." Likewise, the second song of "The Chimney Sweeper" emphasizes the abandonment of the child and the false, restrictive piety of the adult world.

"THE LAMB" AND "THE TIGER"

Two of Blake's most famous lyrics, "The Lamb" and "The Tiger," are from these two groups of Songs. In the first poem, the innocent child speaks to the lamb, his counterpart, and says that they are both the creations of God as Christ. In the second poem, the speaker raises questions about the nature of the creator; in fact, the poem consists entirely of a series of rhetorical questions. The tiger's beauty or "symmetry" is fearful. It suggests a creator who is powerful and daring; the image of a blacksmith working upon metal with fire and hammer suggests the creator's nature. The crucial question "Did he who made the Lamb make thee?" links the two poems and suggests the range or contrary powers of the creator.

SOCIAL EVILS

Blake also addresses the evils of society in *Songs of Experience*. In "The Sick Rose" and "The Garden of Love," venereal disease and the tyranny of organized religion are shown as corruptors of spontaneous love and joy.

"London." The poem "London" contains a more explicit treatment of the same theme. In this poem the speaker, walking through the city streets, sees a populace full of grief and fear, restrained by "mind-forged manacles," the bonds of modern society. In the third stanza, the child as chimney sweeper and the man as soldier are both abused by the powers of church and state. The final stanza presents the young girl as a harlot, corrupted by a society that she, in turn, corrupts with disease.

THE MARRIAGE OF HEAVEN AND HELL

After the French Revolution, Blake foresaw a new release of energy in the world; people had been freed of the old restraints of orthodoxy and reason. In this ironical book composed and hand-engraved in 1792, Blake apparently reverses the usual values of good and evil. Evil becomes linked with energy, freedom, and action while good is merely passive reason and restraint. The opening poem introduces the poet/prophet Rintrah. Rintrah's anger drives the work, which is written in biblical style and rhythm prose. Rintrah has briefly surveyed the historical progress of the just person from meekness to rage. In the following sections, each corresponding to a "plate" or illustration, the poet/prophet states his satiric proverbs and "Memorable Fancies."

Plate 3. In plate 3 Blake states the controlling ideas: "Without Contraries is no progression." The basic contraries are Good and Evil. "Good is the passive that obeys Reason. Evil is the active springing from Energy."

Plates 5 through 10. The prose sections reiterate the same ideas, now celebrating energy and desire. In plate 5 Blake reinterprets Milton's *Paradise Lost*, identifying the Messiah with Reason and Satan with Desire. Blake asserts that "Milton . . . was a true Poet and of the Devil's party without knowing it." In the first Memorable Fancy, the poet pictures himself walking in Hell. He lists the ironic Proverbs he has gathered there, continuing through plate 10. They are perverse and shocking; for example, "The tygers of wrath are wiser than the horses of instruction" is directly contrary to the traditional Christian condemnation of wrath as a deadly sin. The tyger image suggests will and energy, in contrast to the dull restraint of "horses," mere domestic beasts of burden.

Plates 12 and 13. The second Memorable Fancy, in plates 12 and 13, parodies a tale by the philosopher Emanuel Swendenborg, whom Blake read with interest but ultimately found to be inadequate. In these plates, Blake dines with the biblical prophets Isaiah and Ezekiel, who hold up Poetic Genius as the authentic origin of all ideas about God.

Plates 14 and 15. In plates 14 and 15 Blake discusses his own role as poet: he cleans and heals people's perceptions with the acid of his wit (and with the acid of his engraving technique).

Plates 16 and 17. Plates 16 and 17 repeat the Proverb of Hell that "the weak in courage is strong in cunning" and again develops the idea of the two contraries: the Prolific who makes and the Devourer who consumes. Blake stresses that the two cannot and should not be reconciled.

Plates 17 through 20. This Memorable Fancy, extending from plate 17 through plate 20, is a visionary journey, a parody of the epic hero's trip into the underworld. Blake is taken by an Angel to see the fearful image of his eternal damnation. Blake is guided through the stable, the place of Jesus' birth; through the church and down into the vault, the place of Jesus' burial under the church; and into a mill, which represents the rationalism of the Enlightenment. The poet and the Angel finally hang above an abyss, viewing a chaotic scene of fire and tempest, with monstrous spiders and serpents. As soon as the Angel retreats, the scene changes to one of peace, showing only a harper singing in the moonlight. The horrible vision was the creation of the Angel of theology. The poet then shows the Angel a vision of his eternal fate. This vision involves a babbling debate among chained monkeys representing theologians devouring each other with analysis. When the Angel protests, the poet replies with the motto: "Opposition is true Friendship."

Plate 21. In plate 21 Blake again criticizes Swendenborg as superficial and as a mechanical analyzer. In the final Memorable Fancy the Devil speaks, praising Jesus as the greatest man, one who mocked the restraints of rules and commandments and acted on impulse, virtuously.

After the first engraving of *The Marriage of Heaven and Hell*, Blake added plates 25, 26, and 27. These contain the Song of Liberty, a celebration of revolution. Liberty is portrayed as a fiery figure stalking the earth and causing the ruin of kings, warriors, and other figures of repression. Thus out of destruction comes joy.

After this prose work, Blake went on to develop further his ideas of contrarieties in mystical and complex prophetic books. These poetic works, full of mythological giant figures, include *The Book of Urizen* (1794) and ultimately *The Four Zoas* (1797–1804). It was while working on this last poem that Blake underwent the trial for sedition that seemed to exhaust his energies.

ROBERT BURNS (1759–1796)

Burns came from an impoverished background in Ayrshire, Scotland. His father, a tenant farmer, wanted his sons to have the best education possible, and had them taught by a local tutor. Young Burns was an enthusiastic reader of both Scottish and English literature. Even as a young farmer and plowman he was known to bring a book to the table and to read as he ate his meals. Aside from reading, his main interest, from his middle teens onward, was romancing young women. By the time he was twenty-six his affairs had become so notorious that in despair over his poverty and personal habits Burns decided to leave his home and seek his fortune in the West Indies. Needing to earn money for such a trip, Burns gathered some of the poems he had written and in 1786 had them published in the nearby town of Kilmarnock under the title *Poems, Chiefly in the Scottish Dialect*. These, known as the Kilmarnock poems, were so successful that a second edition was published the following year in Edinburgh, the Scottish capital. In the capital, Burns was welcomed and feasted by the best of Scottish society, who celebrated him as a natural genius, an untaught plowman with a gift for spontaneous poetry. Burns played this role for his own advantage. But his unexpected triumph lasted only one winter. His fondness for taverns and riotous living shocked his cultured entertainers, and he received scant attention during a second winter in Edinburgh. Burns went back to Ayrshire, where he married Jean Armour, one of his old sweethearts, who had already borne him twins. He was given a local government post as a tax inspector and settled in the town of Dumphries. Meanwhile, he continued to write.

Burns began to collect, revise, and publish the folk songs of Scotland. He died at the age of thirty-seven.

Although Burns was a believer in republican government and a champion of the rights of the individual, he was not a revolutionary in poetry. He expressed no new theory of poetry, but instead used the rich literary materials of his heritage to speak straight from the heart to primitive emotions. His best works are in the Scottish dialect, but he was aware that using both Scottish and English words enriched his poetry. Burns wrote both lyrics and satires. His tender love lyrics, such as "A Red, Red Rose," and his drinking songs, such as "Auld Lang Syne," are some of the best-known works in all British literature. As a satirist, Burns built upon the tradition of Pope and Swift, using irony, mock-heroic events, and self-revealing characters representing folly and corruption.

Burns's Satire

"TO A MOUSE"

One of the original Kilmarnock poems, the satire "To a Mouse" is an address by the plowman to a mouse whose nest he has torn apart with his plow. The six-line stanza form is a standard of the Scottish elegy. The speaker slips out of dialect when stating an abstract idea ("man's dominion / has broken nature's social union") and then returns to dialect when addressing the specific problem of the "poor beastie." The speaker enters sympathetically into the problem of the mouse whose little house and supply of food, carefully and laboriously stocked for the winter, are destroyed. In the last two stanzas, the poet compares the mouse's predicament with that of humankind, both deciding that people and beasts find that their "best laid plans" are often ruined by unexpected disasters. However, the speaker goes on, the mouse has this advantage over humans: it does not anticipate future problems nor lament the problems of the past.

"TO A LOUSE"

"To a Louse," another satire, is also from the Kilmarnock edition. *Louse* is the singular of *lice*, common pests before the days of frequent bathing and insecticides. The satiric situation has the speaker observing a vain young woman wearing a fancy new bonnet in church, tossing her head to show off the hat. She is unaware that a louse has crawled out of her hair and is climbing up her bonnet, among the ribbons and lace, to the top. The first six stanzas are addressed to the louse itself. The speaker scolds the louse for its impudence and advises it to go bother some poor old woman or ragged boy, which the speaker believes are more appropriate hosts. Besides, the speaker advises the louse, it won't find much to eat on this bonnet. The last two stanzas are silently addressed to Jenny, the wearer of the bonnet. The speaker suggests that she not make such a display of her hat. If we could only see ourselves as others see us, he thinks, we would avoid the mistake of showing off. The mockery is mild; the speaker is basically sympathetic to both the girl and the louse and, in the final stanza, to all humankind.

"HOLY WILLIE'S PRAYER"

"Holy Willie's Prayer" was written for Burns's friend Gavin Hamilton, who had been accused of faults of behavior by an elder of the Scottish Kirk, or church, and was tried for these minor crimes in a church court. The accuser was William Fisher, the Willie of the poem, who is portrayed by Burns as a drunken, lecherous hypocrite. Hamilton was acquitted of the charges, and Burns celebrated his friend's victory with this poem. The poem was circulated in manuscript form but was never printed during the poet's lifetime.

The poetic form is a dramatic monologue; the speaker is Willie himself as he prays to God after Hamilton's acquittal. Willie believes in the doctrine of "predestination" and he believes that he is one of the elect whom God has chosen for prosperity during life and salvation after death. In the first five stanzas, Willie congratulates himself on his exalted spiritual status. He admits that he is really subject to the sins of lust and drunkenness, but he ironically supposes that these are burdens God has given him to bear, and he accepts them as a curb to his pride. About the middle of the poem Willie turns his attention to his recent public defeat by Hamilton in the church court. Willie asks God to revenge the shame he feels and to put a curse on Hamilton. The prayer turns into a sour, almost violent invective. God is asked not only to curse Hamilton but also to damn his lawyer, Robert Aiken, who had mocked Willie and his supporters in the court. The final stanza turns back from curses to prayer; Willie asks prosperity for himself, for the glory of God. The prayer reveals Willie not as a pious or charitable man of God but as a self-righteous and jealous person. There is an ironic contrast between Willie's self-satisfaction and the disgust the reader feels as Willie reveals himself.

"TAM O'SHANTER"

The narrative poem "Tam O'Shanter," written in tetrameter couplets, retells a local folk story about how witches congregate at Alloway Kirk, an old ruined church near Burns's home in Ayr. It is mock-heroic in that the central character, Tam, or Tom, emboldened by his drunkenness, dares to ride past the perilous ruin and escapes the monstrous witch. It satirizes the false courage of the drunkard while mocking the superstitious belief in witches.

The first twelve lines describe the pleasures of the alehouse where men meet to drink at the end of market day, delaying the tedious journey home to their impatient wives. Tam himself is introduced in line 13 as one who neglects his wife Kate's warnings and lingers too long over friendly drinks whenever he goes away from home. The Tale begins at line 37, with Tam enjoying a cozy social evening at the village tavern while a storm rages outside. Eventually Tam must get up and ride home through the dark, wet night. He mounts his mare, Meg, a stout horse, and starts out singing as he rides. As he approaches the ruined Alloway Kirk he passes the places where many previous folk have met disasters—smotherings, broken necks, murders, and suicides. Suddenly he sees that the old church is full of light. Drawing closer, he looks in upon a scene of wild dancing by witches and warlocks. Old Nick, the devil himself, is present in the shape of a beast. The dance is fast and crazy; corpses watch from open coffins. As the fun grows "fast and furious" Tam wishes it were pretty young girls dancing, not ugly old witches. One witch, Nannie, wearing only her "cutty sark," a short shift or slip, captures Tam's fancy so that he calls out to her, "Well done, Cutty Sark" (line 189). At that moment the witches realize they are being watched. The eerie light goes out and all the ghostly dancers start to chase Tam. His horse, Meg, puts on all speed to reach the mid-point of the next bridge, because, as Burns points out, evil spirits cannot follow a person over a running stream. Just at the last moment, Nannie reaches out and grabs Meg's tail. Though horse and rider escape, Meg's gray tail is left behind. In the conclusion, the poet asserts the truth of his story and warns the reader in a mock moral against drinking too much.

Burns's Lyrics

Burns was interested in the preservation and revival of the folk songs of Scotland. In his last years he participated with publishers in compiling and editing collections of these songs. His own songs, though original, drew upon the phrases and images of the folk tradition.

"A RED, RED ROSE"

Of Burns's love lyrics, the most famous is "A Red, Red Rose." This lyric captures the essence of simple love songs. It starts with two common similes: love is like a rose and like a melody. The lover boasts in the second and third stanzas that his love will last until the seas dry up and the rocks melt.

The final stanza is a farewell and a promise to return. None of these ideas or similes is new, but Burns puts them together flawlessly, with perfect placement of each term, so that the result feels like an individual declaration of feeling by a sincere lover.

"A FOND KISS"

Similarly, "A Fond Kiss" is a song of parting in which the lover expresses his regret and reveals his broken heart. Again, the sentiment is not new, but the simple, straightforward words give an impression of honest, manly grief. There is no incident or suggestion of why the lovers must part; the poet focuses on the feelings only, thus making it applicable to any situation in which lovers part.

"AFTON WATER"

The song "Afton Water" is in praise of a beautiful girl asleep by the river Afton. It is full of the sights and sounds of the local countryside, which provides a fit setting for the beloved Mary. The song was written in 1786 for Mary Campbell, a young woman whom Burns loved and wooed that year. It was set to music by Alexander Hume and became a sentimental favorite among popular singers. It remained a favorite well into the twentieth century.

**Burns's
Drinking Songs**

In addition to these sweet love lyrics, Burns wrote drinking songs and songs of Scottish patriotism. Some of the drinking songs were Burns's cleaned-up versions of ribald or bawdy native songs. Two such songs were very popular: "Comin Thro' the Rye" and "Green Grow the Rashes." The most universal of all drinking songs is Burns's "Auld Lang Syne," sung around the world on New Year's Eve, wherever British influence has been felt.

**Burns's
Patriotic Songs**

Burns's patriotic feelings are expressed in "Scots, Wha Hae," a battle call in which the hero, Bruce, rallies his troops to defeat the English at the great battle at Brannockburn (1314). A more general song of republican, antiauthoritarian feeling is "For A' That and A' That," which celebrates in rousing stanzas the integrity of the poor, honest Scots and mocks the pretensions of the English aristocracy. It concludes by predicting the coming brotherhood of humankind. The song is a response to the early stages of the French Revolution, which Burns realized was spreading its influence all around the world.

MARY WOLLSTONECRAFT (1759–1797)

Like Burns, Mary Wollstonecraft was born into the family of a poor farmer. Unlike Burns's father, however, hers had pretensions to gentility. As his farm ventures failed, her father descended into violent drunkenness. Even as a young child, Wollstonecraft had to defend both herself and her submissive mother from his bouts of drink-induced rage and physical abuse. Nevertheless, with the help of a local clergyman and his wife, and with the friendship of a neighbor girl, Fanny Blood, she was able to educate herself through reading. At the age of nineteen she hired on as a lady's companion and left home. Later (1783–1785), with two of her young sisters and her good friend Fanny, she established a school for girls at Newington Green, near London. There she became acquainted with several liberal thinkers, including the Reverend Richard Price, a leading radical author. He helped influence Wollstonecraft's social and political ideas. Meanwhile, Wollstonecraft's friend Fanny had married and then died in childbirth, and the school at Newington Green had failed. Mary found herself in debt and in despair. To repay her debts she wrote her first book, *Thoughts on the Education of Daughters* (1786), a conventional series of essays. After working as a governess for a while she went to London, where she worked as a reviewer and translator for the radical publisher Joseph Johnson. Johnson printed Wollstonecraft's first novel, *Mary, a Fiction* (1788), the story of a persecuted woman. She also published a book for children, *Original Stories from Real Life*. The children's book was such a success that it was translated into German. The second edition of the book was published with illustrations by William Blake.

In London, Wollstonecraft became a member of a liberal group that sympathized with the French Revolution. When the revolution was attacked by Edmund Burke in his *Reflections on the French Revolution* in 1790, Wollstonecraft and several others, including Tom Paine, wrote rebuttals. Hers was entitled *A Vindication of the Rights of Men*. In 1792 Mary wrote *A Vindication of the Rights of Woman*, a defense of underprivileged women. Later that year she went to Paris to observe the French Revolution firsthand. There she met an American, Gilbert Imlay, with whom she had an affair that resulted in the birth of a daughter. Imlay's subsequent neglect of Wollstonecraft drove her to despair; she made two attempts at suicide but was rescued each time. Wollstonecraft eventually established a relationship with the radical philosopher William Godwin, whom, despite both their convictions against marriage, she married when she became pregnant. Wollstonecraft died at age thirty-seven of complications following the delivery of their child, a daughter, Mary Wollstonecraft Godwin, who was to marry the poet Percy Bysshe Shelley and write the classic novel *Frankenstein*.

Wollstonecraft's ground-breaking argument in *A Vindication of the Rights of Woman* did not start a movement toward women's rights. As her life became known through Godwin's book *Memoirs of the Author of "A Vindication of the Rights of Woman"* (1798), in which he details her affairs, her suicide attempts, and her liberal positions on religion and sexual matters, she came to be seen as a notorious figure by even the most progressive thinkers of Victorian England. Thus the force of her ideas was lost in disapproval of her behavior until recent decades of this century.

A VINDICATION OF THE RIGHTS OF MEN

This book explores the plight of the lower classes in both France and England. Wollstonecraft then extends the implications of her argument to show more specifically how the social system affects women, illustrating that they were always an oppressed group, no matter what their class status. The book was sensational and original; few of the Enlightenment philosophers had analyzed the situation of women.

A VINDICATION OF THE RIGHTS OF WOMAN

Although Wollstonecraft had already postulated the basis for individual rights in her *Vindication of the Rights of Men* in 1790, the immediate occasion for writing the *Rights of Woman* was the 1791 report that the French revolutionary Charles Maurice de Talleyrand had called for a system of free education for all boys throughout France. Wollstonecraft realized that the new society envisioned by the revolutionaries would continue to leave women in the same disadvantageous position they presently suffered. She insisted that women be included in the new order, basing her argument on her own life and the lives of the middle-and upper-class women she had known and observed. Wollstonecraft assumed that poor women had more independence because they earned their own livings; she did not realize how such women were economically exploited.

Women's Mental Abilities. Wollstonecraft first attacks the idea that women have inherently inferior mental ability. She agrees that women often act less rationally and responsibly than men, but she points out that all women's training and education is focused on attracting and pleasing men. Not being educated to think for themselves, women necessarily are occupied with trivia and devoid of active virtue. Following the psychology of John Locke, Wollstonecraft asserts that anyone who is badly educated will become corrupt. Freedom, she went on, must be linked to responsibility. Too much power leads to abuse, so she theorizes that a more equal sharing of power between the sexes will bring about more general virtue and happiness.

The Status of Women. In the second chapter Wollstonecraft turns to the particular status of women. She states that women are encouraged to be idle and to get their way through cunning. Innocence is regarded by her not as a virtue but, except in children, as a weakness.

Education. Wollstonecraft states her belief that the basis for a good education is the same for both sexes. Here she begins to refute the position of Rousseau, who argued that women should always be trained for the pleasure of men. She sees this as a sensuous, libertine argument. She argues that passionate love is necessarily of short duration; therefore, husbands and wives should ideally become friends. Further, she states, weak women are not good wives; they cannot even behave like rational creatures.

Wollstonecraft develops her arguments with specific references to how women lived at the time. Her treatise is repetitious and tends to digress, but she argues with great energy and force. The reader feels her exasperation and impatience with the condition of women's lives. She describes conventional marriage based on property considerations as "legal prostitution" and exclaims "What nonsense!" to some of Rousseau's opinions. She cites the bad effects of property laws that discourage independence by denying women the right to the profits of their own labor, and she suggests that women should have their own representatives in government. Wollstonecraft also makes several suggestions as to what women can do for themselves. She believes that women should behave modestly among themselves without being prudish, that they should give their children honest information about procreation, and that they should nurse their own children instead of putting them out to a wet nurse. She feels also that they should not consult astrologers or read sentimental novels but instead should study the proper education of their children and act for the general public good.

Wollstonecraft advocated state-sponsored day school for both boys and girls in the same schools, believing that the best educational arrangement was for children to meet together for study and play during the day but to return to their own homes for parental supervision every evening. Her plan avoided both the overindulgence of the private tutor or governess and the bullying and moral corruption of boarding schools. Interestingly, the Wollstonecraft plan of public education first became common in the United States, where small communities set up coed day schools as the frontier moved westward.

Ideas about individual freedom and hopes for a better social system were stirred and intensified by the start of the French Revolution in 1789. In England a group of radical thinkers including Blake, Wollstonecraft, and their associates created in their poetry and prose visions of a new order that would liberate men and women from the restraints of conventional moral authorities and economic exploitation. The common, ordinary man or woman was the center of interest. Even Burns, who relied on the poetic materials of his national culture, celebrated the folk and satirized the false and rigid restrictions of the "Kirk." Most writers laid the groundwork for a revolution in poetry, which was to put the feelings of the individual at the center of poetic expression.

Selected Readings

Crawford, Thomas. *Burns: A Study of the Poems and Songs.* Stanford: Stanford University Press, 1960.

Damon, S. Foster. *A Blake Dictionary: The Ideas and Symbols of William Blake.* Providence: Brown University Press, 1965.

Jack, R. D. S., and Andrew Noble, eds. *The Art of Robert Burns.* London: Vision, 1982.

Lister, Raymond. *William Blake: An Introduction to the Man and to His Work.* London: Bell, 1968.

Newmann, Bonnie Rayford. *The Lonely Muse: A Critical Biography of Mary Wollstonecraft Shelley.* Salzburg: University of Salzburg Press, 1979.

3

The Major Romantic Poets

1789 French Revolution begins

1791 Paine, *Rights of Man*; Boswell, *Life of Johnson*; Wordsworth makes first trip to France

1792 Wordsworth makes second visit to France

1793 Wordsworth, *Descriptive Sketches*; Louis XVI beheaded

1794 Southey, *Wat Tyler*

1795 Napoleonic era begins

1796 Coleridge, "Ode to France," "The Watchman," and "Ode to the Departing Year"

1797 Wordsworth, "The Borderers"; the Wordsworths and Coleridge move to the Lake District of Sussex

1798 Wordsworth and Coleridge collaborate on *Lyrical Ballads,* which includes "The Rime of the Ancient Mariner" and "Lines Written a Few Miles Above Tintern Abbey"

1799 Wordsworth composes the "Lucy" poems

1800 Wordsworth and Coleridge produce second edition of *Lyrical Ballads*; Union of Great Britain and Ireland

1802 Coleridge, "Dejection: An Ode" published; *The Edinburgh Review*, first literary review, established

1805 Scott, *The Lay of the Last Minstrel*; Battle of Trafalgar

1807 Wordsworth, *Poems in Two Volumes*; Byron, *Hours of Idleness*; gaslights introduced in London; British slave trade abolished

1809–1810 Coleridge publishes periodical *The Friend*; quarrels with Wordsworth

1813 Coleridge, *Remorse* presented at Drury Lane Theatre; Southey, poet laureate; Shelley, *Queen Mab*; Austen, *Pride and Prejudice*

1814 Wordsworth, *The Excursion*; first use of steam in printing; Congress of Vienna

1815 Wordsworth, *The White Doe of Rylstone*; Battle of Waterloo; end of Napoleonic War

1816 Coleridge, "Christabel" and "Kubla Khan"; Coleridge moves into Highgate under supervision of Dr. James Gillman, who controls his addiction

1817 Coleridge, *Biographia Literaria*

1819 Wordsworth, "Peter Bell": "The Waggoner"; first transatlantic steamship

1820 Coleridge's journal *A Tour on the Continent* written

1825 Coleridge, *Aids to Reflection*; Pushkin, *Boris Godunov*

1828 Coleridge and Wordsworth reconciled; Shubert, *The Great Symphony* (in C Major)

1834 Coleridge dies; Berlioz sets *Harold en Italie* to symphonic music

1843–1850 Wordsworth, poet laureate

1849 Coleridge, *Lectures on Shakespeare* published posthumously

1850 Wordsworth dies

*W*hile reactions to the new ideas about the rights of the individual and to the new movements to extend political power invigorated some English writers during the last decades of the eighteenth century, it remained for the poets themselves to develop a new theory of the sources and purposes of poetry. In England such a new theory grew out of an unusual collaboration between two great poets who, while very different in personal style, stimulated each other and encouraged each other's creativity. Together, William Wordsworth and Samuel Coleridge set in motion a new train of poetic thought that produced one of the richest eras of lyric poetry in the history of English literature. Their interaction helped each define more clearly what poetry should be about and how it should achieve its goals. This friendship, though brief, lasted long enough to generate the romantic movement in English literature. Wordsworth and Coleridge were aware that they were doing something new, and they were exhilarated by the feeling of being poetic "revolutionaries." One of the most important dates in the history of English poetry is 1798, the year Wordsworth and Coleridge's Lyrical Ballads was published.

WILLIAM WORDSWORTH (1770–1850)

Wordsworth was born in Cumberland, in the northwest region of England, an area of lakes and hills. This rural setting became an important part of his poetry. Wordsworth's father was a law-agent employed by Lord Lonsdale; his mother died when he was eight. During the years that Wordsworth and his brother attended Hawkshead School, they lived in a rural cottage. Young Wordsworth spent much of his time rambling about the neighboring fields, woods, and streams. His involvement with nature and with the simple country folk beginning from this time generated relationships and observations that became central to his later poetry. When Wordsworth was thirteen his father died, leaving most of the family inheritance tied up in the debts of Lord Lonsdale. The children's inheritance was not paid until after the lord's death in 1802, when the poet was thirty-two. Still, young Wordsworth was able to attend Cambridge University, taking an A.B. degree in 1791. During the summer vacation before his last year at Cambridge, Wordsworth and a friend took a walking tour through France. The fall of the Bastille had filled the French people with jubilation, inspiring them with hope for a new, more democratic form of government. Wordsworth became caught up in the enthusiasm. His political idealism was reinforced when he returned to France the following year. That same year he had an affair with a middle-class French girl, Annette Vallon, who later bore him a child. Having run out of money, Wordsworth returned to England to seek funds. While he was away England declared war on France, making a reunion with Annette impossible. For a period, Wordsworth suffered from feelings of guilt, frustration, and even from divided political loyalties.

At this point Wordsworth received a small legacy from a friend, enabling him to live independently. He settled in a cottage in the Lake District with his younger sister Dorothy, who became his lifelong caretaker, companion, and collaborator. They lived near the poet Samuel Taylor Coleridge, whom Wordsworth had known at Cambridge. The two poets met every day to discuss their work and together developed new ideas about the forms and subject matter of poetry. This close association culminated in their joint publication of *Lyrical Ballads* (1798). This publication was a milestone in poetic theory; readers felt that something radically new was being put forth. For the second edition, published in 1800, Wordsworth wrote a preface explaining their objections to the diction and poetic forms of the past century and articulating their new romantic poetic principles.

Shortly after the publication of *Lyrical Ballads*, Lord Lonsdale's estate finally settled the debt to the Wordsworth heirs, allowing William and Dorothy to move into a more comfortable cottage. William, having finally come to an understanding with Annette Vallon, whom he had not seen for ten years, decided to marry his childhood friend Mary Hutchinson. The couple had five children, of whom three survived to adulthood.

About 1810 Wordsworth and Coleridge argued; their quarrel resulted in many years of estrangement. Though they eventually reconciled, they were never again the close friends and poetic collaborators they had been. As Wordsworth continued to publish poetry, his reputation grew. In 1813 he was given a government position as tax collector.

Wordsworth's earliest poetry was his best. The next generation of romantic poets—Byron, Shelley, and Keats—found Wordsworth rather dull and egotistical. By then Wordsworth had lost his political radicalism and had become a political conservative, just as his poetic originality by then had yielded to a more bland and somewhat repetitive style. In 1843, when Wordsworth was in his mid-seventies, he was named poet laureate. By then he was considered a sort of national treasure, a monument to the great age of poetry past. For some he was even a tourist attraction as he greeted visitors at his last cottage home at Ambleside.

Wordsworth's Lyrics and Odes

Wordsworth's poetry has as its basic subject his own youthful feelings and experiences. He attempts to recreate sensations and to link these remembered sensations not only with emotional states but also with moral ideas. Nature is the great nurse and teacher of the poet, who is most open to her influence in childhood. Therefore, age moves the poet farther away from his sources of inspiration.

Lyrical Ballads, with a few other Poems

Wordsworth's contributions to this volume deal with the nature images and the people of the Lake District where he grew up. As Coleridge later explained in *Biographia Literaria*, Wordsworth intended "to give the charm of novelty to things of everyday." Using simple forms, short lines, and everyday vocabulary, Wordsworth focuses on and dignifies the emotions of the folk, especially the old and the very young.

"SIMON LEE"

In "Simon Lee," for example, Wordsworth gently mocks the reader for expecting some exciting tale, when all the poem offers is the image of a broken old man, once an active huntsman but now a feeble worker of the soil. The only incident the poem describes is when Simon, unable to dig out a stubborn tree root, is helped by the poet and, to the grief of the poet, gives him too many thanks.

"WE ARE SEVEN"

In "We Are Seven" the poet discourses with a child, a simple girl who explains to the poet that among the seven children of her family she includes the two that "in the churchyard lie." That is, she does not recognize death as a separation or loss; she resists the logic of the poet who counts only five living children. Insisting on her own count, she makes the more adult view of the poet seem ultimately less wise than her own.

"LINES WRITTEN IN EARLY SPRING"

A central concept of the *Lyrical Ballads* is simply stated in "Lines Written in Early Spring." Here the poet sits passively in a grove, enjoying birds, trees, and flowers. These "fair works" of nature, he feels, are linked to the "human soul," giving rise to thoughts about the disharmony among human beings, which contrasts with nature's harmony.

"EXPOSTULATION AND REPLY" AND "THE TABLES TURNED"

Similarly, in "Expostulation and Reply" and "The Tables Turned," the poet defends a position of "wise passiveness" in which we allow the powers of nature to act upon us and teach us. The poems present the opposing points of view of Wordsworth and his friend. The friend insists that books are the source of wisdom, but Wordsworth argues, "Let Nature be your Teacher." The intellectual pursuit of knowledge, he argues, distorts "the forms of things," but Nature has "sweet love."

"TINTERN ABBEY"

The final poem in *Lyrical Ballads* is an ode titled simply "Lines" and subtitled "Composed a Few Miles Above Tintern Abbey, on Revisiting the Banks of the Wye During a Tour, July 13, 1798." This awkward title is usually shortened to "Tintern Abbey." Because of the poem's loose structure, Wordsworth did not call it an ode but developed it as an extended lyric meditation on memory, guiding the reader through a series of emotional states.

Background. Some biographical background helps clarify the poem. Wordsworth had first seen Tintern Abbey, an old ruin, in 1793. At the end of 1792 he had returned from France full of enthusiasm for the Revolution but grew dejected when England went to war against France. His friend William Calvert had asked Wordsworth to join him in a walking tour of southern England, but the two separated at Salisbury Plain. Near Stonehenge, Wordsworth experienced a mystical restoration of faith as he saw visions of the ancient Britons. In a new mood of confidence and hope for the French republic, Wordsworth walked on alone to the valley of the Wye River where for the first time he saw Tintern Abbey.

When Wordsworth began to write the poem, almost five years later, matters in France had deteriorated. In the meanwhile, he had read Godwin's *Political Justice* and written poems such as "The Cumberland Beggar" and "The Ruined Cottage" in sympathy with the poor. He had made a home with his sister Dorothy near Alfoxden and had started working with Coleridge. In June of 1798 William and his sister had just spent a week with Coleridge at Stowey, preparing poems for the printer. Then the Wordsworths took a "four-day ramble" to the Wye valley, where they viewed the abbey from the same vantage point Wordsworth had enjoyed five years before. In the poem Wordsworth recalls the scene and his formerly enthusiastic state of mind. He feels the poem arise spontaneously as he and his sister leave the Wye and continue their tour.

Forms. In the first twenty-one lines, Wordsworth describes the scene as unchanged during the past five years. The poet emphasizes the lapse of time, saying, "again I hear," "again do I behold," and "again I see." The landscape is rich, green, and peaceful, suggesting the seclusion of a hermitage.

In line 22, the poet shifts his attention from the present scene to recapitulate his memories of it. These memories have comforted and consoled him in the intervening years spent in less beautiful, more urban settings; they have also generated moods of calm awareness that have mystically enlightened him. In such moods, he feels, another kind of perception comes to us, so that "we see into the life of things" (line 49). He had often returned in spirit to the Wye for escape from the busy and fretful world.

In line 58, the poet begins a transition back to the present moment. He enjoys the pleasure of this time and also anticipates that he will enjoy it again in future memories.

But at line 66 he starts to recapitulate his life as a series of stages in the development of a relationship with nature. At first he roamed as freely as an animal, but as he grew he felt joy and rapture and passionate involvement with his own youth. Now he is involved with human concerns. He has become more thoughtful and sees nature in the light of those thoughts. He still loves nature, but in a more mature and more emotionally subdued way.

In lines 106–107 Wordsworth suggests an important romantic conception: the mind not only receives sensations from the outside world, but it also half-creates, by its own operations of memory, imagination, and perception, the scene before the eyes. The "mighty world of eye and ear" is based on nature but is also shaped by the poet's mind.

In the final section of the poem, from line 111 to the end, Wordsworth turns to his sister who stands beside him, enjoying the view. (Her presence has not been previously mentioned in the poem.) Addressing her as his "dearest Friend," he compares her simple, intense pleasure with his own at the earlier stage of his life. He prays that she will benefit from the love of nature as he has done and find in it solace from the "dreary" scenes of adult life. He suggests that if they are separated in the future (perhaps by death?), she will find comfort in the memory of this moment of shared experience.

Although the manuscript for *Lyrical Ballads* had been already worked out in cooperation with Coleridge, Wordsworth added "Tintern Abbey" at the end. It was one of the outstanding poems of the collection.

PREFACE TO *LYRICAL BALLADS*

Although it had a mixed critical reception, the first edition of *Lyrical Ballads* was a "sellout." Two years later, in 1800, Wordsworth and Coleridge prepared a new, two-volume edition with additional poems, including the long narrative poem "Michael." Wordsworth also added an explanatory preface in which he defended the new type of poetry that he and Coleridge had put forth.

A New Poetic Standard. The preface argues for a new poetic standard. Wordsworth rejected the neoclassical theory of poetry, which arranged the different kinds of literature in a hierarchy, each with its own appropriate subject matter and level of diction. Wordsworth particularly rejected the elevated poetic diction of eighteenth-century poets such as Thomas Gray, whose language was artificial and whose style was unnatural, based on reading rather than on speech. Wordsworth proposed making poetry through the selection and arrangement of the sincere and simple language of the ordinary individual, adapting prose language to poetic uses. Thus Wordsworth undermined the dignity of poetry, but he also gave it a newer, broader scope that included a range of persons and situations never written about before—the humble and rustic life taken seriously.

A New Role for the Poet. Wordsworth also redefined the role of the poet. The poet is merely "a man speaking to men," albeit one who has a greater than average sensibility and "knowledge of human nature." The poet's main qualifications are not in matters of craft or technique; he is a poet because his feelings allow him to enter sympathetically into the lives of others and to translate passions into words that please. "The poet thinks and feels in the spirit of the passions of men." It follows, says Wordsworth, that poets must use the language of other men.

A New Definition of Poetry. Poetry itself is redefined as "the spontaneous overflow of powerful feeling: it takes its origin from emotion recollected in tranquility." That is, poetry is the outcome of a creative process. The poet thinks about an emotional experience "in tranquility," after the original moment of feeling has passed. But as he thinks, the emotion returns, and while under the influence of this renewed feeling, the poet begins to write the poem. Pleasure is the state in which the poetic composition is written, and pleasure is also found in the result. Wordsworth assumes that the reader of such poetry will share the poet's pleasure. At least, said Wordsworth, that is what he aims for in his poetry.

THE "LUCY" POEMS

Traveling in Germany with his sister Dorothy in 1799, Wordsworth composed a group of five poems about a young woman, Lucy, who dies just as she reaches maturity. She is described as a lovely maiden, raised simply in the English countryside. The speaker of the poems is her lover. No particular person is known to have inspired these poems. Wordsworth seems to have merely savored the romantic situation of the death of a pretty young woman.

"Strange Fits of Passion Have I Known." In this poem the speaker describes a mystifying moment when, as he rode toward Lucy's house to visit her, he gazed at the moon and was suddenly struck by the fear of her death. In the other poems, Lucy is already dead and he laments the loss of her.

"Three Years She Grew." In this poem, written after Lucy's death, Lucy is seen as returning to Nature just at the moment she reached perfection.

"She Dwelt Among the Untrodden Ways." The poet celebrates Lucy's beauty, remarkable because of the obscure life she lived.

"A Slumber Did My Spirit Seal." Here the lover envisions Lucy as having returned to earth "with rocks, and stones, and trees." She has rejoined nature.

"I Traveled Among Unknown Men." In the last of the Lucy poems the speaker/lover is away from England, remembering his native land with all the more nostalgia because Lucy lived and died there.

"LUCY GRAY," OR "SOLITUDE"

Despite its name, this is not one of the Lucy poems. It is based on an actual incident of a child who became lost in a snowstorm in Yorkshire. (Wordsworth had heard of the tragedy while in Germany in 1799.) Wordsworth transformed the incident, following first the child's point of view as she wanders lost in fields of snow, then shifting to the grief of the parents as they search for her, following her footprints to the stream where she apparently drowned. In the last two stanzas the poet imagines that her spirit still lives about the countryside, roaming and singing a "solitary song."

"MICHAEL" AND "THE RUINED COTTAGE"

These are two blank-verse narrative poems about the grief suffered by rural folk whose loved ones must depart for the alien world beyond the local village. In each poem the suffering of the central character is paramount. The unfinished sheepfold and the deteriorating cottage symbolize the loss of all hope and pleasure in the lives of the folk who are left behind. Their long years of waiting are dramatized by the futile gestures they make to keep up a home for the one who will never return.

"Michael." In this poem the old shepherd loses his son, who goes to the city. Although the son vows to return, he is never seen again.

"The Ruined Cottage." This poem is about a wife whose husband has joined the army as a way to lift them out of grinding poverty. The husband does not return, and the wife's poverty only increases, as the wreck of her cottage shows.

"RESOLUTION AND INDEPENDENCE"

This poem was first called "The Leech Gatherer." The central figure, as in the narrative poems just described, is a poor abandoned country person whom Wordsworth both admires and pities. The poem is written in rhymed stanzas of seven pentameter lines. The incident on which the poem is based was described by Dorothy Wordsworth in her entry in the *Grasmere Journal* for October 3, 1800.

As he starts out for a pleasant walk on the moors, the poet's joyful mood changes to one of dejection as he thinks about the uncertainties of a poet's life. He remembers Thomas Chatterton, an early romantic poet who committed suicide, and he thinks of Robert Burns, who suffered poverty. In this more gloomy mood, the poet meets a very old man, "his body . . . bent double," standing propped on his staff at the edge of a pond. The poet questions the old man and finds that he gathers leeches from ponds and sells them for medical use. (At that time leeches were widely used for bloodletting.) In a reflection of his own anxiety about the future, the poet questions the gatherer about the future of his livelihood. The old man explains that leeches are now more difficult to find, but still he perseveres. Comparing his own relative youth and comfort with the weary and difficult life of the leech gatherer, and seeing how cheerfully patient the old man remains, the poet feels his own troubles diminished. "I could have laughed myself to scorn," he says, admiring the firm mind of the poor old man.

This poem provides a clear example of the dignified though simple speech of the man of humble social station, the sort of speech Wordsworth designated in his preface to *Lyrical Ballads* as the most appropriate language for poetry. In stanza 14 the leech gatherer's words are described as "a lofty utterance" and as "choice word and measured phrase." The old man seems almost to have appeared supernaturally to warn the poet against shallow self-pity and useless fears.

"I WANDERED LONELY AS A CLOUD"

This short lyric is one of Wordsworth's most famous. The poem includes in brief form Wordsworth's central idea of the creative process—"emotion recollected in tranquility"—as he had outlined it in the preface to *Lyrical Ballads*.

The initial experience of emotion occurs when the poet comes upon a field full of blooming daffodils, bright yellow spring flowers, "tossing their heads" in the breeze. As he gazes he feels great joy. In the final stanza the poet shows himself as removed from the original scene in both time and place. But as he remembers it, his "vacant or . . . pensive mood" is replaced by a pleasure that is like the joy he felt on seeing the flowers. He says that "they flash upon that inward eye," meaning the eye of memory and imagination. Recalling the daffodils, he has seen them again in his mind's eye and has again felt the joy of his earlier experience.

"MY HEART LEAPS UP"

This single lyric stanza expresses Wordsworth's continuing joy in nature and his persistent belief in the sacredness of that joy. His statement that "the Child is father of the Man" suggests that childhood is superior to adulthood because the child has a more natural and complete response to the beauty of nature.

This early love of nature leaves a legacy of a "piety" or belief that sustains the adult. Wordsworth used three lines of this poem as a motto for his great ode "Intimations of Immortality," which explores more fully the child's glorious intuition of divinity.

"ODE: INTIMATIONS OF IMMORTALITY FROM RECOLLECTIONS OF EARLY CHILDHOOD"

This irregular ode in eleven stanzas is Wordsworth's most thorough treatment of his concept of the child's intense sympathetic relationship with the natural world and the gradual fading of the relationship as it is replaced by the ordinary restraints and distractions of adult life. Like "Tintern Abbey," this poem contrasts an earlier free and joyous state of mind with a present state that is more sad and thoughtful. The word *intimation* in the title means a hint or an implied revelation. Wordsworth's point is that the immortality of the human soul begins before birth. Though Wordsworth found this notion useful and appealing, he later stated that he had not meant to offer it as an item of belief. The mood of the ode shifts between joy and grief as the poet focuses on childhood and adult life, the past and the present, pleasant memory and melancholy regret.

Stanza 1. This stanza states the general idea that time has taken away a sense of "glory" and "freshness."

Stanza 2. In stanza 2, the poet realizes that the scenes of nature are just as beautiful as ever and that it is he who has changed. He no longer feels the "glory" that he once did. The earth seems to have faded because he is less sensitive to it.

Stanza 3. This stanza describes the gaiety of the earth. The poet puts aside grief and indulges in a holiday mood. He addresses a celebrating shepherd boy as "Thou Child of Joy." The boy represents the intense natural pleasure of childhood.

Stanza 4. The poet says that since he himself was once such a happy child, he understands and shares the child's joy. However, his present joy is not the same as it was when he was a child. Sensing that something is gone, he asks "Whither is fled the visionary gleam?" This question and the one in the next line ("Where is it now, the glory and the dream?") end the first draft of the poem; Wordsworth later went on to try to answer the questions.

Stanza 5. Stanza 5 outlines the process of human growth. At birth, the child emerges from a state of glory that he immediately begins to forget as he becomes immersed in earthly life. But even as the "shades of the prison house" of day-to-day life begin to close in on him, he still remembers the splendid visions of his earlier existence. He remains "Nature's Priest" until he becomes an adult.

Stanza 6. This stanza presents earth as a mother or a nurse who replaces the fading visions of glory with her own natural pleasures.

Stanza 7. In stanza 7 the child pursues the occupations of ordinary existence; he imitates in his play the rituals and business of earthly life, learning to play the roles of an adult.

Stanza 8. Here the poet again addresses the child directly, calling him the "best Philosopher" and "Mighty Prophet" because he still retains a sense of immortality. The poet then asks the child why he so perversely seeks the yoke of maturity. The tone of this stanza is mournful, in contrast with the joy of the opening stanzas.

Stanza 9. The mood of the ninth stanza shifts abruptly back to one of joy. That emotion gradually builds, though with some hesitations, throughout the rest of the ode. Looking back on his childhood, the poet gives thanks for those early feelings and ideas, even though they are now only dimly remembered. The poet finds that these faded recollections can still comfort and console him. As a man, he is now far inland from the sea of immortality out of which the child was born, but he can still, in imagination, travel back and recapture some of the feelings he had then.

Stanza 10. In stanza 10, the final stanza, the poet rejects grief and regret, taking pleasure instead in the qualities of a mature mind. These qualities— "sympathy," "faith," and "the philosophic mind"—the poet feels are the products of human sympathy. The stanza is addressed to Nature itself, whom the poet still loves, though in a more somber way. Now that he knows about death, the world is different, but it is still good.

"ODE TO DUTY"

This is a Horatian ode, calmer and more regular in form than "Intimations of Immortality." Here Wordsworth personifies duty, forgetting for the occasion the dislike of abstract personification he had expressed in the preface to *Lyrical Ballads*. He praises duty as the best guide to a happy life. Stating that he formerly had neglected duty for "smoother walks" in the past, he now dedicates himself to duty, hoping to find security, repose, and pleasure. Just as the stars obey laws of motion, so the more humble function of duty is to guide by moral law. The poet asks for the guidance and the strength that come from being duty's "Bondsman."

Wordsworth's Sonnets

Wordsworth wrote occasional sonnets from 1802 until late in his career. The best are on various subjects and so do not form a sonnet cycle. He used the Italian sonnet form, comprised of an octave and a sestet, rather than the English form of three quatrains and a couplet. Many of the sonnets describe the feeling of a moment, the beauty of a dawn or a sunset, or the feeling of joy that turns back into grief. Other sonnets are philosophical meditations on the state of English society.

"LONDON, 1802"

This sonnet denounces the stagnation and selfishness of English society, whose leadership has abandoned its responsibilities. The poet calls upon Milton, saying that England needs his spirit of "cheerful godliness" and his devotion to duty.

"THE WORLD IS TOO MUCH WITH US"

Similarly, this sonnet makes a broad, general condemnation of English society. People are interested only in "getting and spending." Wordsworth states that they have become insensitive to the force and beauty of Nature and says that rather than live such a life of materialism, he would prefer to be a pagan savage who sees the ancient gods in motion when he looks at nature.

Wordsworth's Autobiographical Poem

THE PRELUDE, OR THE GROWTH OF A POET'S MIND

Wordsworth worked on this long autobiographical poem from 1798, the period of *Lyrical Ballads*, almost to the end of his life, expanding and revising it frequently. The poem was originally planned as a preface to a long philosophical poem that was to have been titled *The Recluse*. That poem was never written. A mature version of *The Prelude*, containing fourteen books, was published in 1850. Wordsworth continued to revise the work until his death later that year.

The Main Theme. Wordsworth develops and expands to epic proportions the theme of his own development from a child of nature into a poet. He traces the influence of various experiences on the growth of his imagination, starting from infancy. It is partly a confessional poem, that is, a revelation of the poet's spiritual life as he passes through periods of doubt and anxiety and achieves moments of affirmation and vision. Full of miscellaneous segments that vary in tone, the poem is unified by Wordsworth's sense of his destiny as a poet and of the loftiness of the poetic vocation. Thus the poet is a new kind of hero, and becoming a poet is an epic journey. The essential heroic quality is imagination, the power of poetry. The poet's life is presented as a pilgrimage of the soul.

The Friend. Wordsworth addresses the poem to a sympathetic listener whom he calls Friend. The Friend was originally Coleridge, to whom Wordsworth had read the first two-part version of the poem in 1799. Even after the poets' estrangement, however, Wordsworth kept the "Friend" as the audience to whom the poet's life history is revealed and explained.

Book 1. One typical incident from childhood is described in lines 357 to 414 of Book 1. On a summer evening the boy Wordsworth stealthily takes a small boat and rows toward the middle of the lake. As he rows the boy uses a distant mountain top to guide him. It begins to seem that the mountain rears up before him in a threatening gesture of disapproval. The boy turns back and returns the boat. The effect of the experience lingers for many days, darkening his imagination and troubling his dreams. Thus the Spirit of the Universe (line 401) moves the boy and inspires feelings and thoughts that become part of his being.

Book 14. The climactic episode of *The Prelude*, the vision of Mount Snowdon, the highest peak in Wales, occurs in Book 14. Wordsworth saw the mountain while on a walking tour with Robert Jones, a Welsh friend with whom he had previously visited the Alps. With a local shepherd as guide, the two friends set out on a summer evening to climb the mountain. It grows dark and foggy. Wordsworth, who is in the lead, suddenly notices a brightness around him. He looks up to see the moon shining clearly. Around and below him the fog and the mist are spread out like a great ocean. He and his companions seem to be standing in an "ethereal vault" above the hidden world. Wordsworth compares their position with that of "majestic Intellect," or with "the power of the Imagination," standing above the world and transcending mere sensory experience to create ideal forms in the mind. The Imagination holds communication with the spiritual world. At this moment Wordsworth feels powerful and free, as if his whole life had been preparing him for this transcendent experience.

The Prelude. This poetic personal narrative recapitulates and explores the main themes of Wordsworth's poetry:

> the glory of infancy;
>
> nature's benevolent influence on the soul;
>
> the creative power of the imagination;
>
> the poet's importance as interpreter of all these things to the rest of humanity.

DOROTHY WORDSWORTH (1771–1855)

After the death of her parents, Dorothy Wordsworth lived with various more or less sympathetic relatives until William made a home for her in her twenty-fourth year. She was a part of his household from that time until his death. He valued her companionship as a fellow observer and lover of nature, especially during their many ambles and walking tours during the decade of his greatest productivity, from 1795 to 1805. Although, as her journals show, Dorothy had a strong emotional attachment to her brother, she displayed no jealousy and encouraged him to marry Mary Hutchinson, their mutual friend from childhood. Dorothy participated in the work of the household and in the care of her nieces and nephews.

Dorothy did not enjoy robust health. In 1835 she became seriously ill and never wholly recovered. Her decline was both physical and mental. She lived another two decades as an unhappy invalid.

Wordsworth's Journals

Dorothy's own creative energies were expressed mainly in a series of journals. This literary occupation aided without rivaling her brother. Both Wordsworth and Coleridge benefited from details and descriptions in her journals, which were not secret diaries but were written for the use and pleasure of others.

None of Dorothy Wordsworth's journals was published during her lifetime. The *Alfoxden Journal*, covering the crucial year of 1798, the year of the *Lyrical Ballads*, has, except for the entries from January to April, been lost. These entries had been transcribed in 1897 by William Knight. Dorothy also wrote a journal covering her years with William at Grasmere (1800 to 1803), and she wrote records of the tours they made to Germany in 1798 through 1790 and to Scotland in 1803. She also wrote chronicles of their excursions in the Lake District, where they lived. Her last journals include *A Tour on the Continent* (1820), accounts of tours of Scotland (1822) and the Isle of Man (1828).

GRASMERE JOURNALS

The Leech Gatherer. The entry for October 3, 1800, opens typically with an account of some ordinary domestic events and activities—the weather, who came to visit, what walks were taken. Then it turns to an extended description of a poor old man, a leech gatherer, whom William and Dorothy met as they walked toward their cottage. She describes the old man's appearance, relates his account of his background, and even cites the scarcity of leeches and the subsequent rise in price. Her account is factual and even includes an account of the old man's wounds from a recent accident with a cart. Later, in the journal entry for May 4, 1801, we find Dorothy occupied in making a copy of the poem "The Leech Gatherer," which William has just composed. After Wordsworth made further revisions, the poem was published in 1807 under the title "Resolution and Independence."

A Field of Daffodils. Similarly, Dorothy's entry for April 15, 1802, describes coming upon a wide field of daffodils on the margin of a lake. Her description is reflected in her brother's poem "I Wandered Lonely as a Cloud," which includes the same details of the flowers tossing their heads and seeming to dance with joy. Coleridge also occasionally took a detail or a phrase from Dorothy's journals.

Biographical Details. The *Grasmere Journals* cover the meeting in Calais, France, with Annette Vallon and her daughter, William's child, and the journey to Yorkshire with William for his marriage to Mary Hutchinson. The intensity of Dorothy's reaction to the wedding raises some question about her acceptance of the marriage, but she does not show in her journal, as she did not show in her life, any anger at having to share her brother's attention.

SAMUEL TAYLOR COLERIDGE (1772–1834)

Coleridge was born in Devonshire, the thirteenth child of a country clergyman. His father died when Coleridge was nine, and the boy was sent to a charity school in London called Christ's Hospital. He was a good scholar. While at this school he met the future essayist Charles Lamb, who became a lifelong friend. At nineteen Coleridge went as a charity student to Cambridge University, where he gradually ceased being a serious scholar and drifted into a life of idle dreams and dejection. Finding himself seriously in debt, Coleridge left the university and enlisted in a cavalry unit of the Light Dragoons. This attempt to start a new life resulted in failure because he was unable to stay on a horse. Coming to his rescue, his older brothers paid his way out of the Dragoons and sent him back to Cambridge, where he remained until 1794, never earning a degree.

Soon thereafter, Coleridge met the young poet Robert Southey, who had been expelled from Oxford University for his unorthodox opinions. Coleridge was attracted by Southey's radical ideas. Together they planned a "pantisocracy," a utopian community that they hoped to establish on the Susquehanna River in central Pennsylvania. According to the plan, each member of the community was to marry a good woman and take her with him. In his enthusiasm for the scheme Coleridge married Sara Fricker, the sister of Southey's wife. However, the poets' utopian dreams never materialized because they did not even have enough money to pay their traveling expenses to the United States. Thus Coleridge found himself with a wife who turned out to be less than suitable. They lived together amicably at first, but by 1806 the couple had separated.

Meanwhile, there were several positive developments in Coleridge's life. He became friends with William Wordsworth, who encouraged his own poetic efforts. While Coleridge and his wife were living in the village of Nether Stowey, William and his sister Dorothy moved to Alfoxden, only three miles away. Such close proximity led to frequent visits. Perhaps not coincidentally, this was Coleridge's period of greatest productivity.

After the poets' 1798 collaboration on *Lyrical Ballads*, a tragic weakness took possession of Coleridge. Despite all his genius and learning, it became impossible for him to hold himself steadily to any one work or purpose. Since about 1800 Coleridge had been using laudanum, a liquid form of opium, for relief from the pain of neuralgia. He soon realized that the drug was addictive. Coleridge decided to travel to Germany, where he spent almost a year studying the works of the German philosopher Immanuel Kant. On returning to England, Coleridge moved to Keswick, thirteen miles from Grasmere, where the Wordsworths had established a household. Coleridge's financial situation had been eased by an annuity of 150 pounds a year from his friends Thomas and Josiah Wedgwood, whose family owned a china business. Meanwhile, his relationship with his wife had been deteriorating, and he fell in love with Sara Hutchinson, Wordsworth's sister-in-law. Then Coleridge's health began to fail. He sought relief by traveling to Rome and Malta, where he hoped the milder climate would enable him to work. The change of climate did not help, and by 1806 he was increasingly dependent on laudanum. After his return to England he separated from his wife and moved to London to start a new career as a lecturer and journalist. He lectured on poetry and the fine arts to enraptured audiences until his frequent failures to meet his appointments diminished his popularity. He became irritable and depressed and in 1810 he quarreled with Wordsworth. Despite attempts at reconciliation two years later, the friendship was permanently damaged. Through all his travails Coleridge continued to write, producing occasional poems, essays, and even a tragic drama.

The major work of his mature years was his *Biographia Literaria,* or literary biography.

In 1816 Coleridge went to live in the household of his physician, James Gillman, who brought Coleridge's drug addiction under control without entirely curing it. Coleridge lived with Dr. and Mrs. Gillman for the rest of his life. He became a grand old man of English literature and philosophy. He was a brilliant conversationalist and a stimulating intellectual who inspired his friends by his ideals and his cheering message of beauty and hope.

Coleridge's "Conversation" Poetry

Coleridge developed a form of meditative poetry in blank verse called "conversation" poetry. It was used to convey the unspoken remarks of the poet to another person.

"THE EOLIAN HARP"

This poem was written before Coleridge's close association with Wordsworth. The harp of the title was an instrument designed to be placed in an open window. As a breeze blew through it, the strings of the harp vibrated, creating a musical sound. The harp was named after Aeolus, the Greek god of the winds.

"The Eolian Harp" is a "conversation" poem. Here, the addressed person is Coleridge's wife, Sara. The poem was first composed soon after their marriage, but Coleridge revised it several times. The poem reflects the disparity between their points of view. In the poem, Coleridge enjoys the idea that the harp can represent "all of animated nature," that is, that the natural world is like an instrument played upon by "one intellectual breeze" that is God. But once he has expressed this idea, he reacts to her unspoken but assumed "reproof." Sara represents the more orthodox Christian concept of God that focuses on Christ as the savior of sinners. This contrast between the free, imaginative play of his mind and the more humble, dutiful faith of his wife suggests one of the incompatibilities that would eventually cause the couple's separation.

"THIS LIME-TREE BOWER MY PRISON"

This conversation poem arose out of an unfortunate domestic incident. During a visit from his old school friend, the essayist Charles Lamb, Coleridge made plans to go walking with Lamb and with William and Dorothy Wordsworth. He was prevented from going when his wife had accidentally poured some boiling liquid on his foot.

In this blank-verse poem, Coleridge is seated in a small grove, or "bower," of lime trees while the others take the planned walk across the heath to a particularly delightful dell, a small valley with a waterfall.

The first part of the poem, lines 1 through 20, depicts Coleridge sitting alone and complaining of the lost opportunity to go with his friends and to store up sweet memories of the occasion. He has been to the dell before, and he describes detailed memories of the scene his friends will be enjoying.

In the second part, lines 21 to 42, Coleridge imagines his friends emerging from the dell into the open fields. In his imagination he participates in the pleasure that Lamb must feel, especially since his friend is usually confined to the city and has lately suffered "calamities" in his own family. Speaking to his absent friend, Coleridge says that he too has gazed at the beautiful scene, feeling in it the "Almighty Spirit."

A change in feeling marks the third and final part of the poem, which begins at line 43. The poet now says he is glad he could not go with his friends, because sitting alone has also been a rich experience. From his little bower he has watched closely the effects of the changing light upon the foliage. He has enjoyed the shifting patterns of light and darkness as the sun moved across the sky. The insects, birds, and bats have kept him company. He has realized that even the humblest aspect of nature is stimulating and can fill the imagination with "Love and Beauty." He has decided that it was better not to have gone with his friends, because in solitude the soul is lifted by a contemplation of "joys we cannot share." Coleridge finds enjoyment in this solitude by imagining that perhaps both he and Lamb are looking at the same bird (a rook), gazing at it from their two different vantage points. Starting with a sense of loss and abandonment, the poem ends in pleasure; the last word is "Life."

"FROST AT MIDNIGHT"

This, the most famous of the conversation poems in blank verse, was written at Nether Stowey in 1798 and was included in the first edition of *Lyrical Ballads* later that year.

The first twenty-three lines set the scene. It is a cold and silent night in February. Everyone in the household is asleep except the poet, who is sitting by a dying fire. His infant son sleeps in a cradle nearby. The only thing moving in the room is a film of soot flapping in the grate of fire. This black film, called a "stranger," was commonly believed to indicate that an absent friend would arrive soon.

In the second part of the poem (lines 24 to 43), the sight of the "stranger" reminds Coleridge of seeing the same phenomenon in the fire when he was a lonely school boy in London. At that time the "stranger" had made him think of the village where he was born. These memories had stayed with him the next day, interfering with his study and arousing hopes that someone from his village might come to visit him at school. It is an image from a lonely boyhood.

In lines 44 to 64 the poet addresses his sleeping son, admiring the beauty of the infant and predicting that instead of growing up in a crowded city, as he did, the boy will grow up in the freedom of the countryside, close to nature and benevolently affected by the spirit of God that is in nature. Therefore, the poet concludes, his son will find all seasons sweet. The poem returns at the end to the cold and frosty moonlit night that inspires the poet's meditations.

"Frost at Midnight" is a typical romantic poem in that it unites the present scene with memories of a similar scene and looks ahead to the future, ending in joy or, at least, calm. It can be compared with Wordsworth's "Tintern Abbey," for example.

Coleridge's Narrative Poems and Odes

"THE RIME OF THE ANCIENT MARINER"

This long narrative poem in rhymed stanzas started as a collaborative effort with Wordsworth. Wordsworth, however, soon abandoned the project, leaving it to Coleridge to produce one of the outstanding poems of *Lyrical Ballads*. The basic story of sin and redemption is set within the framework of a wedding. As three jolly young fellows approach the wedding hall, one is stopped by a weird old man, the Mariner, who captures the youth's attention with a "glittering eye" and insists on telling his story.

Part 1. The story begins with the wedding guest trying in vain to get away and join the party, while the Mariner insists on telling his story. He was a seaman on a ship that was driven by storms to the Antarctic, where it became locked in ice. In this predicament, the ship was visited by an albatross, a great sea bird, that seemed to befriend the men. They were glad to see the bird; they hailed it "in God's Name." Then their luck improved; the ice broke up and a breeze from the south pushed them north through the fog. But suddenly, in what seems an act of perverse cruelty, the Mariner shot the benevolent bird.

Part 2. Part 2 describes how the Mariner was criticized by his shipmates for killing the bird that made the wind blow. When the fog cleared, however, they decided that he was right to kill the bird that brought the fog and mist. When the ship reached the southern Pacific Ocean, the breeze stopped and the ship was becalmed under a hot, baking sun. In the midst of an ocean of water, the ship dried out and the men became parched from thirst. They turned against the Mariner again, saying that his killing the bird caused their misery. As a sign of his guilt they hung the corpse of the albatross around the Mariner's neck.

Part 3. The calm and drought went on and on. Suddenly the Mariner saw a ship approaching, even though there was no wind. The sailors rejoiced, thinking they would be saved, but the ship turned out to be a ghostly skeleton of a ship, her timbers like ribs through which the setting sun could be seen. There were only two on the ship: Death and Life-in-Death. They were playing with dice for the fate of the Mariner, and Life-in-Death won. The sun went down abruptly and the moon came out. All the sailors dropped down dead, their souls passing by the Mariner like the whiz of a crossbow. Only the Mariner was left alive.

Part 4. At the beginning of Part 4 the young wedding guest breaks into the story, expressing his fear that the Mariner is really a ghost. The Mariner assures his listener that he did not die. Indeed, he confesses that he felt cursed and wished for death when he was alone, under the moon, with only the company of the water snakes who swam in the shadow of the ship. In a moment of intense loneliness, the Mariner saw the beauty of these water snakes and spoke a blessing on them. Immediately the albatross, the sign of his guilt, dropped from his neck.

Part 5. In Part 5 the Mariner tells how he finally slept and woke to find the buckets on the ship filled with rain. He felt a breeze and saw strange lights in the sky (the aurora australis). Even while the moon shone, it rained again. Then, weirdly, the dead sailors all arose and began to sail the ship. Again, the wedding guest interrupts the Mariner with his fears, and again he is reassured. The corpses of the sailors had been animated by angel spirits. The sun came out, and the ship sailed up to the equator. But before the Mariner was allowed to leave the southern hemisphere, the Polar Spirit required revenge for the death of the albatross. In a swoon the Mariner heard two demons discussing the penance that the Mariner must do for killing the albatross.

Part 6. Part 6 opens with a continuation of the dialogue of the demons. Soon the Mariner awakened from his trance and found the ship still being sailed by the animated corpses. A swift breeze drove the ship back home. Once inside the harbor, the spirits departed from the sailors, leaving them mere corpses as before. A pilot boat was rowed out to the ship to take the Mariner to shore; it carried a pilot, his son, and a good Hermit, a holy man who would hear the Mariner's confession.

Part 7. Just as the pilot boat reached the Mariner's ship, the latter split up and went down "like lead." The Mariner was rescued, but his rescuers sensed that he was somehow a cursed being. The pilot's boy lost his wits in fright. When the Mariner asked a blessing from the holy man, the Hermit demanded that the Mariner tell what happened, that is, that he confess. Then, for the first of many times, the Mariner told his story. Since then, he periodically feels a great agony that can be relieved only by telling his story again.

At the end, the wedding party comes out of the church, but the wedding guest, finally released from the Mariner's hold, finds he has no heart for the celebration. The story has made him "forlorn: A sadder and a wiser man."

The Marginal Notations. The tale's mysteriousness perplexed many readers, so in later editions Coleridge added a set of explanatory marginal notes. But even these notes do not fully explain the significance of each force or spirit in the story. Some readers track the appearance of the sun and moon as symbols of evil and good. Whatever interpretation is applied, the appeal of the tale lies partly in the feeling that no simple, rational explanation can ever fully elucidate such bizarre events; the appeal is to the imagination.

"KUBLA KHAN; OR, A VISION IN A DREAM"

According to Coleridge, this fascinating fragment was inspired in 1797 or 1798 by a dream he had after taking "two grains of opium" as medicine. He had fallen asleep while reading of Kubla Khan. When he awoke, a complete poem of several hundred lines was fully formed in his head. But, after he had written fifty lines, he was interrupted "by a person on business" who kept him about an hour. When Coleridge returned to write, the poem had faded, leaving only a few "scattered lines and images." Coleridge said that he published the partial poem in 1816, at the suggestion of Lord Byron, only as "a psychological curiosity."

The Place. As it stands, the poem is more suggestive than coherent. It begins with a description of Xanadu, where the great Mongol ruler Kubla Khan has built a "pleasure dome" on the river Alph. This "sacred river" arises from a violent waterfall in a deep chasm in the side of a hill. After descending from its tumultuous beginning the river winds for about five miles "through wood and dale" and alongside the palace of the Kubla. It then disappears into underground caverns.

The Sounds. Starting at about line 29 the description focuses on sounds: first the mysterious "ancestral voices" that prophesize war to the Kubla, then the voice of the maid from Abyssinia who plucks a dulcimer, a small stringed instrument, as she sings a song. The maiden's song is associated first with a vision, then with memory. The poet feels that if he could recapture that song he could himself compose a song or poem about the pleasure dome and all his listeners would be struck with "holy dread."

The poem is rich with suggestion. The place names—Xanadu, Alph, Abyssinia, Mount Abora—are associated with several places in the ancient world. The lush description contains great emotion, as if some momentous or violent event were about to happen. But since it remains a brief fragment, the poem's mystery can never be unraveled. It is wide open to interpretation; perhaps that is at the heart of the pleasure it offers the reader.

"CHRISTABEL"

This poem, the first part of which was written in 1797, is also a fragment. Coleridge had wanted to include it in the 1800 (second) edition of *Lyrical Ballads*, but it was not yet finished; it was still incomplete when he finally published it in 1816. As it stands, the poem is the beginning of a medieval tale about a demon or witch. It is written in a strange meter of four stresses to a line, and a varying number of unstressed syllables. (Such a meter was used in medieval Anglo-Saxon poetry.)

Part 1. At the poem's opening, it is midnight in Langdale Castle. Everyone is asleep except Christabel, the lovely daughter of Sir Leoline, the lord of the castle. Christabel is roaming in the woods, thinking about her lover, a knight to whom she is betrothed but who is now far away. Hearing a moaning coming from the other side of an oak tree, Christabel discovers a beautiful pale lady, barefoot and with jewels in her hair, who begs for help. Her name is Geraldine. She tells Christabel that she was abducted from her home by five warriors, who tied her to a white horse and brought her to this oak tree and left her, vowing to return. Geraldine begs Christabel for help. They walk back to the castle of Sir Leoline, at the entrance to which

Geraldine falls down and must be lifted over the doorstep. This is the first of several hints that Geraldine is an evil spirit, because such beings cannot pass on their own through a doorway that has been blessed. Likewise, when Christabel utters a prayer of thanks to "the Virgin" that they are safe inside, Geraldine cannot join in the prayer. The old watchdog does not bark at this stranger; he only mutters in his sleep, and the ashes in the fireplace suddenly flame up as Geraldine passes by.

In Christabel's chamber the two ladies undress for sleep. They lie down together, Christabel wrapped in the arms of Geraldine. As Christabel sleeps, the guardian spirit of her dead mother is driven away by Geraldine. Thus, by the end of the first part, the poet has led the reader to the conclusion that Geraldine is entrapping Christabel or trying to seduce her, to capture her soul. But he reminds us that "saints will aid if men will call."

Part 2. It is morning. Geraldine and Christabel rise and dress, but Christabel retains an uneasy sense of the sinister influence of Geraldine. They visit Sir Leoline, to whom Geraldine introduces herself as the daughter of Lord Roland de Vaux, a man who had once been Sir Leoline's closest friend but had since become a bitter enemy. Captivated by the beauty of Geraldine, who embraces and kisses him, Sir Leoline tells his bard Bracy to travel to the castle of Lord Roland and invite him to come back to Langdale Castle.

Meanwhile, Sir Leoline challenges the five scoundrels who abducted Geraldine to appear at a tournament one week later to defend, if they can, their honor. But, seeing Geraldine's influence over her father, Christabel asks that the guest be sent home at once. Sir Leoline, captivated by Geraldine and in a fury at this breech of hospitality, responds angrily to his daughter. Christabel cannot explain her fears because her tongue has been bewitched by Geraldine. The second part ends with the poet's meditation about the irrational anger of a parent toward an innocent child.

An Explanatory Note. Where the story might have led is anyone's guess. Certainly the fragment is full of sexual innuendo and suggestions of seduction, jealousy, and betrayal. But Coleridge, who claimed to have had the whole plot worked out in his mind, was never able to put the remainder into verse. In 1816 he published the fragment and a preface, in which he insisted on the poem's originality despite its similarities to other verse tales by both Byron and Scott.

"DEJECTION: AN ODE"

This poem is often compared with Wordsworth's "Ode: Intimations of Immortality." Coleridge started writing this ode as a response to Wordsworth's. Both poems lament the fading of poetic power and imagination and the loss of a creative and energizing relationship with nature.

The Quoted Stanza. "Dejection" begins with a stanza from an old folk ballad that tells of the courage of Sir Patrick Spence in confronting a murderous storm. In the quoted stanza the speaker predicts a storm because the night before he saw "the new Moon/ With the old Moon in her arms"— that is, a crescent moon that dimly illuminated the rest of the moon.

Stanza 1. Like a conversation poem, the ode starts on a quiet note, commenting on the weather, which is calm now but is soon to be stormy. The poet longs for the wind to start blowing; he feels dull and hopes that the buffeting of the wind will arouse him and enliven his soul. Thus, as well as being a natural force, the wind also represents the creative energy or power that the poet has felt before but now lacks.

Stanza 2. In stanza 2, the poet describes his present grief and blankness. He addresses a lady (the poem was originally inscribed to Sara Hutchinson), telling her that he has spent the evening gazing at the sunset. He describes it but complains that he is merely seeing it, not *feeling* it. He is detached from nature, emotionally dead to its influence.

Stanza 3. The poet continues his lament that mere "outward forms" cannot generate the passion that drives his creativity.

Stanza 4. Stanza 4 explains that the creative imagination makes nature beautiful. A "glory" in the poet's soul animates the "cold world" of material objects. Coleridge uses the metaphor of a marriage to explain the relationship of poet and nature. The poet is the bridegroom.

Stanza 5. Still speaking to the lady, the poet wishes her the joy that results from the wedding of nature and the soul. This heavenly joy is a special gift that makes the natural world beautiful and glorious.

Stanza 6. In stanza 6 the poet looks back on his youth as a time of joy and hope. Now he feels bowed down by care (perhaps resulting from his failed marriage) and by a loss of imaginative power. This is the cause of his dejection.

Stanza 7. The poet rouses himself to cast off "viper thoughts" of depression. He becomes aware that the calm weather described at the beginning of the poem has been replaced by a wild storm. The wind is shrieking through the landscape and is creating a crazy music in the eolian harp that is framed in a window of his cottage. He imagines that the wind is telling a sad, violent story, perhaps of an orphan girl lost in a storm. The sounds alternate between screams and moans, inspiring terror and pathos.

Stanza 8. The final stanza brings us to midnight. The dejected poet cannot sleep. He prays for sweet sleep for the lady and wishes her joy. He hopes she will enjoy the uplifting, joyful spirit that has abandoned him. The closing lines of the ode restore the calm of the opening, but the calm has been transferred to the lady.

Coleridge's Prose Works

Of Coleridge's prose works, the *Biographia Literaria*, or *Sketches of My Literary Life and Opinions* (1817), his *Aids to Reflection* (1825), and the posthumously published *Lectures on Shakespeare* are the most interesting from a literary viewpoint.

BIOGRAPHIA LITERARIA

The Latin title means "literary biography." This prose work started as a preface to a collection of Coleridge's poems but grew into a two-volume work.

In the first part Coleridge describes his early years, his friendships with other writers, his school years, his relationship with Wordsworth, and his study of philosophy. In the second part he examines poetic theory. He now disagrees with much of Wordsworth's discussion in the preface to *Lyrical Ballads*, but he believes that the poetry is better than the theory. In particular, Coleridge does not agree that the best diction for poetry is the "language of ordinary men."

Coleridge also explains his own theory that the imagination as a creative force interacts with the perceptions of the senses. Imagination, Coleridge believes, is primarily the power of perception and secondarily the creative capacity to reexpress perceptions. Fancy is the mere mechanical ability to call up memories or impressions. Coleridge suggests that the creative imagination is located in the nonrational part of the mind. Thus, he suggests a psychology of the unconscious, which since his time has been a fruitful source of study of the creative process.

*W*ordsworth *and Coleridge together generated a revolution in English poetry. Their combined volume, the* Lyrical Ballads *of 1798, marked a significant turning away from the restraints of the classical tradition in poetry and a turning toward a freer, more experimental, and more emotionally charged lyricism.*

Wordsworth's preface of 1800 and, later, Coleridge's Biographia Literaria *were the manifestoes of a new aesthetic sense. Everything written before seemed suddenly old-fashioned or stale.*

Wordsworth and Coleridge inspired a rising generation of lyric poets, especially Keats, Shelley, and Byron, to write in this new manner and to experiment even further.

The reading public's taste in poetry was shaped for the rest of the century by the ideas of "what poetry really is," as stated by Wordsworth and Coleridge. The images and phrases of their poems passed into the common poetic discourse of the nineteenth century, bringing about such a change in taste that earlier poets were largely ignored or devalued.

Selected Readings

Barfield, Owen. *What Coleridge Thought*. Middletown, CT: Wesleyan University Press, 1971.

Byatt, A. S. *Wordsworth and Coleridge in Their Time*. New York: Crane, 1973.

Coburn, Kathleen, ed. *Coleridge: A Collection of Critical Essays*. Englewood Cliffs, NJ: Prentice-Hall, 1967.

Halliday, F. E. *Wordsworth and His World*. New York: Viking, 1970.

MacClean, Catherine MacDonald. *Dorothy Wordsworth: The Early Years*. New York: Viking, 1932.

Marchant, Robert. *Principles of Wordsworth's Poetry*. Swansea, Wales: Brynmill, 1974.

Sherry, Charles. *Wordsworth's Poetry of the Imagination*. Oxford: Clarendon, 1980.

4

Second-Generation Romantic Poets: Byron and Shelley

1800 Wordsworth and Coleridge produce second edition of *Lyrical Ballads*; Union of Great Britain and Ireland

1802 *The Edinburgh Review*, first literary review, established

1805 Scott, *The Lay of the Last Minstrel*; Nelson wins Battle of Trafalgar

1807 Byron, *Hours of Idleness*

1808 Goethe, *Faust*, Part 1

1809 Byron, *English Bards and Scotch Reviewers*; Byron begins tour of Europe and Asia Minor

1812 Byron, *Childe Harold* (cantos I and II)

1813 Byron, *The Giaour* and *Bride of Abydos*; Shelley, *Queen Mab*; Southey, poet laureate

1814 Scott begins historical novels with *Waverley*; first use of steam in printing; Congress of Vienna

1815 Battle of Waterloo; end of Napoleonic Wars

1816 Byron, *Childe Harold* (Canto III) and *Prisoner of Chillon*; Byron leaves Britain; Shelley, *Alastor*; Coleridge, "Christabel" and "Kubla Khan"

1817 Byron, *Manfred*; M. Shelley, *Frankenstein*; Keats, *Poems*; Coleridge, *Biographia Literaria*; Gericault painting, *The Raft of the "Medusa"*

1818   Byron, *Childe Harold* (Canto IV) and *Beppo*; Shelley, *Revolt of Islam*; Keats, *Endymion*

1819   Byron, *Don Juan* (cantos I and II); Shelley, "Ode to the West Wind" and *The Cenci*; Keats, *Hyperion*; Peterloo Massacre at Manchester

1820   Shelley, *Prometheus Unbound*; Keats, *The Eve of St. Agnes and Other Poems*; Scott, *Ivanhoe*

1821   Byron, *Don Juan* (cantos III through V) and *Cain*; Shelley, *Adonais*; Delacroix paints *Dante and Virgil in Hell*; Greek War of Independence from Turkey

1822   Byron, *Vision of Judgment*; Shelley, "Hellas"; Shelley drowns

1823   Byron, *Don Juan* (cantos VI through XIV); Beethoven, *Symphony No. 9* and *Missa Solemnis*

1824   Byron, *Don Juan* (cantos XV and XVI); Byron dies

The new tone and definition of poetry that Wordsworth and Coleridge had created was stimulating to younger poets, who felt that unexplored areas of poetic subject matter had been opened up to them. The heavy hand of the past, especially that of English classicism, had been removed, or at least lightened. The young poets looked to Wordsworth as their poetical father.

Even Byron, who admired the eighteenth-century poet Alexander Pope and who mocked Wordsworth in his satires, still benefited from the more introspective and confessional style of poetry. Wordsworth had prepared the way; he had educated the reading public to expect new things and to read with a more open and sympathetic attitude. Byron and Shelley, each in his own way, were rebels who rejected the institutions of contemporary society and longed for the more perfect worlds of the past and future.

GEORGE GORDON, LORD BYRON (1788–1824)

George Gordon was born into an aristocratic but highly eccentric and unconventional family that was known for its daring and violence. His father was a dissipated spendthrift; his mother, a Scottish heiress, was passionate and unbalanced. His father died when Byron was only three years old and the boy was raised in comparative poverty by his mother, a woman of more rigid principles and a narrow, sour outlook on life. Byron's life changed when, at the death of an uncle, he, at age ten, became George Gordon, Lord

Byron. He inherited a title, moderate wealth, and an old castle in poor condition. With his inheritance Byron was sent to Harrow school and then to Cambridge University.

One other important factor influenced Byron's childhood and youth. He was born with a malformed foot (called a clubfoot). He threw himself into fencing and swimming, where he could demonstrate that this defect was not a real handicap. Still, he walked with a limp, despite his energetic athletic exercises.

In 1807, while at Cambridge, Byron published his first volume of poetry, *Hours of Idleness*. He was only nineteen. The poems were savagely attacked by a critic for the *Edinburgh Review*, provoking a response by Byron titled *English Bards and Scotch Reviewers*. Byron attacked not only his enemies, the critics, but also Scott, Wordsworth, and nearly all the literary men of his day, satirizing them in heroic couplets after the manner of Pope's *Dunciad*.

In 1809, after finishing Cambridge, Byron and a friend set out on a tour of Europe and Asia Minor. Deciding to go off the beaten track, they visited Malta, Greece, and the Near East, rather than just the heavily toured cities of Italy and France. The literary results of this tour were the first two cantos of *Childe Harold*. The work made Byron instantly popular, and his fame began to overshadow that of Sir Walter Scott. His descriptions of romantic scenery as well as some adventurous verse tales set in the Near East increased his fame. Byron took advantage of his popularity to make several speeches in the House of Lords supporting liberal causes.

The Byronic Hero

In his narrative verse tales, Byron introduced a distinctive type of hero, a young man of striking appearance who, despite deep and sensitive feelings, maintains a public attitude of pride and cynicism. The Byronic hero conceals his inner misery behind a careless facade. Many of Byron's readers, especially women, equated the poet with his romantic characters. Byron was sought after, flattered, and almost besieged by women. As a kind of escape, he married a woman with a temperament very different from his own. She was Annabella Milbanke, an English heiress and an intellectual interested in mathematics. A legal separation ended the marriage a year later. One child resulted from the marriage—a daughter, Augusta Ada, who became a mathematician and a pioneer in computers.

Meanwhile, Byron's fame was turning to notoriety. His relationship with his half-sister Augusta was rumored to be incestuous. Society turned against Byron, so he left England in 1816 and never returned.

Byron went first to Geneva and then to Venice. He added more cantos to *Childe Harold*; wrote a tragedy, *Manfred;* and began *Don Juan*, a long narrative satire. After a period of general debauchery in Venice, Byron formed a stable relationship with Teresa Gamba Guiccioli, an activist in Italian nationalistic politics. The two moved to Pisa, where the English poet

Shelley was already established with his wife and a circle of friends. In 1822 Shelley's death by drowning and Byron's departure for Genoa caused the circle to break up.

Soon afterward, the restless Byron traveled to Greece, where Greek patriots were mounting a rebellion against their rulers, the Turks. Enlisting in the cause of Greek independence, Byron equipped, at his own expense, a troop of Greek patriots, intending to train them and lead them into battle. But Byron became ill with a fever and died shortly after his thirty-sixth birthday.

Byron was a fascinating person. He won a much more immediate and widespread fame than any of his contemporaries. The idea of the Byronic hero, a role he played as well as a character he created, was captivating. The German poet Goethe was among many European admirers of Byron. His rejection by English polite society made him all the more alluring to liberal thinkers among the artistic and intellectual community of Europe. Thus Byron's influence derived not so much from his poetry as from his personality and his reputation.

Byron's Poetry

ENGLISH BARDS AND SCOTCH REVIEWERS

This satire in heroic couplets is a protest against what Byron considered the weakness and bad taste of the older generation of English romantic poets, including Wordsworth, Coleridge, Scott, Southey, and many other lesser and now-forgotten writers.

Style. Imitating Alexander Pope, Byron adopted the pose of one driven to write satire out of a desperate revulsion against the low level of poetic achievement in those poets admired by the dull public. Byron was bored by the soft and sentimental strain of romanticism that tended to focus on the weak and the simple. He preferred "Pope's pure strain" rather than "simple Wordsworth," whom he called "that mild apostate from poetic rule." He mocked "gentle Coleridge" for his obscurity and his "turgid ode and tumid stanza." He saw Wordsworth and Coleridge not as great innovators but as timid, mediocre poets who wrote about character and incidents too commonplace to merit poetic treatment.

Byron also attacked the major critics of the day, especially Francis Jeffrey, the tough and sour editor of *The Edinburgh Review*. This long satire (1,070 lines) was first published anonymously in 1809.

Later regretting his personal attacks, in 1816 Byron wrote in the margin that "the tone and temper are such as I cannot approve."

"WRITTEN AFTER SWIMMING FROM SESTOS TO ABYDOS"

As a result of his youthful effort to overcome the disability of his malformed foot, Byron had become a strong swimmer. During his tour of Greece in 1810, he and a young English lieutenant took on the challenge of swimming the Hellespont (now known as the Dardanelles), the channel between Greece and Turkey. Despite rough currents, both swimmers succeeded.

In the poem Byron alludes to the story of the lover Leander, who was said to have swum the strait every night in order to visit his beloved Hero on the other side. Byron compares himself with the legendary Leander, mocking himself as a "degenerate modern wretch" who thinks he has "done a feat" to swim it once. Besides, he points out, instead of "Glory" the poet has brought on himself an "ague" (a fever).

"SHE WALKS IN BEAUTY"

This simple lyric is reminiscent of the Renaissance love lyric, in which the lady's physical beauty is seen as an indication of her inner beauty and purity of soul.

The poem was inspired by Byron's meeting his cousin when she was wearing a black mourning dress. With dark hair and fair face, the lady is a mingling of various lights and shades, comparable to the light and darkness of a night sky with stars.

In the final stanza, the mingled "tints" are signs of goodness, peace, and innocence. The calm, chaste tone of the poem is like the character of the lady.

"STANZAS FOR MUSIC"

This brief lyric shows Byron's facility for poetry. He imitates the rhythm of ocean waves as he develops images of the ocean under the calm influence of soft winds. He pictures the ocean at midnight as a gently moving surface that reflects the moon. These beautiful images are compared with the beauty of the person to whom the poet speaks. The quiet effect is partly a result of Byron's use of soft or "feminine" rhymes, which contain unaccented final syllables. For example, "gleaming" is rhymed with "dreaming" and "emotion" with "ocean." Each line seems to flow into the next.

"DARKNESS"

This blank verse is a dream-image of the end of the world, supposedly to be brought about by the death of the sun. It is the sort of horror we now associate with science fiction stories. Byron saw the civilized world as regressing through stages. At first people try to keep light by making huge fires. Then, as a famine spreads, people fight each other for food. Eventually, all life ends; the final image is of a silent, still, totally dead earth.

"WHEN A MAN HATH NO FREEDOM TO FIGHT FOR A HOME" AND "STANZAS WRITTEN ON THE ROAD BETWEEN FLORENCE AND PISA"

These two lyrics about glory and fame take a flippant tone. In each Byron uses the rolling rhythm of the anapestic foot, which has two unstressed syllables followed by one stressed syllable. Such a meter tends to seem forward-rushing and rapid. In "Stanzas Written on the Road" the meter is made more smooth by the addition of an extra unstressed syllable at the end of each line. Like the other romantic poets, Byron experimented with the melodic effects of various metrical patterns. He used the same galloping anapests in his battle poem "The Destruction of Sennacherib."

"When a Man Hath No Freedom . . ." This poem takes a cynical view of fighting, as if it were a sport or idle pastime. The reader is aware of the ironic contrast between the usual lofty language of heroic poetry and the low-level diction used here. For example, in Byron's poem to be injured in battle is called "to get knocked on the head."

"Stanzas Written on the Road . . ." Here Byron deflates fame and glory by treating them with a casual tone. The speaker asserts that the real point of winning "laurels" (honors) is to make the hero more desirable as a lover. The better glory, he says, is being loved.

CHILDE HAROLD'S PILGRIMAGE

Byron began writing this poetic travelogue about his first European tour just after leaving Cambridge University. He called it "a romaunt," suggesting that travel is like a romantic quest, the central idea of the Renaissance epic.

Style. *Childe Harold* is written in Spenserian stanzas, the form Spenser developed in the sixteenth century for his epic romance, The Faerie Queene. This nine-line stanza has two quatrains of interlocking rhyme (a b a b b c b c), plus one additional line with the "c" rhyme. All the lines are pentameter, except the final line, which has six feet. This form adapts well to a long, loose narrative poem; each stanza becomes a structured verse paragraph.

Byron's use of archaic diction was also in imitation of Spenser. His purpose was to let old-fashioned words such as *sooth* and *wight* in the second stanza of Canto I suggest the antiquity of the action. However, Byron does not maintain such diction beyond the opening stanzas.

Cantos I and II. The poem begins by presenting Childe Harold as a mock-hero who is motivated to travel not by a desire for glory or to carry out a quest but because he is bored and tired from indulging himself in drink and love. In stanza 5 Childe Harold suggests also that he has found a chaste lady to love but that she "could ne'er be his." So, "sick at heart," he decides to go away, to escape, in hopes that a change of scene will stimulate him.

Cantos I and II follow the course of Byron's travels around the various countries of the Mediterranean, from Portugal and Spain to Greece and Albania, and ends with a call for the liberation of Greece from Turkish rule.

The quality of the first two cantos is uneven. They do serve to introduce the Byronic hero, a character much like Byron himself, despite his denials that the poem was autobiographical. These two cantos, published in 1812, made Byron famous.

Cantos III and IV. These cantos were written between 1816 and 1818, after Byron had left England under a cloud of scandal. The cantos are set in the countryside and in the great cities of Belgium, France, and Italy. Byron arrived in Europe just after the defeat of Napoleon; some of the best passages of Canto III describe the events surrounding Napoleon's fall.

At the beginning of Canto III, Byron speaks in the first person. He addresses his infant daughter, Ada, whom he is forsaking as he leaves England. Byron depicts himself as an exile, driven away from England and without a destination, world-weary and turning to poetry as a refuge.

In the creation of the character of Harold, Byron suggests that he may have found a reason to go forward. In stanzas 8 through 16, the poet discusses the changes that have taken place in Childe Harold. He is no longer the bored playboy; he has suffered and been somewhat tamed by bitter experiences. He feels himself

. . . the most unfit / Of men to herd with man;
with whom he held / Little in common . . .

Harold goes forth in desperation and in proud isolation. Stanzas 17 through 35 discuss Waterloo, the scene of Napoleon's defeat. Byron alludes in stanza 21 to the ball held in Brussels on the evening before the battle of Quatre-Bras, two days before the decisive battle of Waterloo. He then recreates the rush to battle, the fall of heroes, and the battlefield strewn with corpses. The tone shifts from heroic to elegiac. Starting at stanza 36 the poet addresses Napoleon, whom he considers an ambiguous figure, both glorious and dreadful, almost godlike in power but tempted by fate to his own destruction. Byron then generalizes this concept: all who aspire to greatness find themselves hated and opposed by "those below."

Traveling on to the valley of the Rhine River in Germany, Harold views the ruins of old castles, once the settings of great deeds. Harold responds to the beauty of the present and contrasts it with the horrid images of war. However, nature's beauty restores some peace and joy to Harold; he remembers having been loved. The allusion here (stanza 55) is probably to Byron's love of his half-sister, Augusta. Harold travels on to the Alps, to the valley of the Rhone and to Lake Leman, commenting on the scenes and on the famous people, such as Voltaire and Rousseau, who are associated with various towns.

At the end of the third canto Byron speaks in the first person about the progress of his poem. In stanzas 113 and 114 he makes a defiant statement against the world that judges and condemns him:

I have not loved the world, nor the world me.

From stanza 115 to the end of Canto III Byron speaks to his little daughter. He expresses his regret that he will not see her grow up and his hopes that she will love him and sends her his blessings from across the sea.

The beginning of Canto IV finds Byron in Italy, in the "dying Glory" of Venice. Later, in Rome (stanzas 132–137), the poet looks on the city as the seat of Nemesis, the god of vengeance, and calls for revenge on all those who have caused his lonely suffering and wandering, all those who slandered and betrayed him. His revenge will be that he will forgive them, thus leaving them to the pangs of their own guilty feelings. In stanzas 135 and 136 he cries out against the many wrongs he has endured, but he points out also that he can bear them because he is made of better stuff than the "reptile crew" who slander him.

In the concluding stanzas of Canto IV, stanzas 175 to 186, Byron declares that he has accomplished the purpose of his pilgrimage. He has reached a state of spiritual reconciliation, enjoying the influence of nature. He feels ready to live among the elements with no companions except one "fair Spirit" whom he could love. In stanza 179 he speaks to the ocean, that part of nature most impervious to human influence. He sees it as a mirror of "the Almighty" and a fit object of his love. In the final two stanzas, Byron says farewell to his readers, leaving them to draw their own concluding moral.

MANFRED

This is a classic drama in the Gothic mode, set in an old castle in the Alps and among the surrounding mountaintops. The three-act drama is written in blank verse, with lyric passages in rhyme. The central character, Manfred, is a version of the Byronic hero. He is plagued by a sense of guilt for a nameless crime (there are hints that it is incest), yet he rejects the call for confession, feeling that he is not accountable to the moral code of ordinary mortals.

Act 1. In scene 1 of act 1, Manfred is alone in his castle. In an opening soliloquy he speaks of his sorrow and guilt, but he also claims to have special knowledge and power. He calls up a band of spirits of the universe, compelling them to appear by the strength of his own will. As each spirit enters, it sings a lyric describing its own nature. The seven spirits are those of earth, ocean, air, night, mountains, winds, and Manfred's star. These spirits can offer him power, strength, or long life. Manfred does not want these gifts; he wants only oblivion so that he can forget his guilt. Manfred tries to grasp at one spirit in the shape of a beautiful woman, but it vanishes and he falls into a trance. He hears an incantation from a bodiless spirit, who tells him that he is his own Hell and must undergo a trial, not of death but of life.

In scene 2, Manfred is on a cliff of Jungfrau Mountain, contemplating suicide. He is met by an old man, a chamois hunter, who speaks to him and prevents him from jumping to his death.

Act 2. In the beginning of act 2, Manfred is in the cottage of the chamois hunter. The hunter counsels Manfred to have patience, but he fears that Manfred is mad. Manfred claims that he can bear any torment without going mad.

In the second scene, Manfred meets the Witch of the Alps near an Alpine waterfall. He tells the witch his life history, leaving his crime vague, and he asks the witch's help. She demands his obedience, which he scorns to give to any being; he will suffer rather than submit. The witch vanishes. Manfred soliloquizes on the possibility that if he had never lived, the beloved whom he has wronged would be happy now instead of suffering.

In scene 3, on the summit of the Jungfrau, three Destinies discuss Manfred's fate. Nemesis, the god of vengeance or retribution, enters, and all the spirits fly away to the clouds. Scene 3 presents the Hall of Arimanes, a demon of chaos and destruction. Nemesis and the three Destinies enter and pay homage to Arimanes. Manfred follows, but he refuses to pay homage to the demon, causing a quarrel among the spirits. The first Destiny defends Manfred as one who, like themselves, has suffered greatly. Nemesis asks Manfred what he wants, and Manfred asks them to call up from the dead the spirit of Astarte, a goddess of love. Astarte appears, and Manfred speaks to her as to the beloved whom he has wronged. Astarte replies, "Tomorrow ends thine earthly ill." Then she disappears.

Act 3. Manfred is back in his castle, where he is visited by a priest, the abbot of St. Maurice. This holy man is alarmed because he has heard that Manfred has communicated with evil spirits. The abbot offers Manfred a Christian confession and penance, but Manfred replies that he is already in the Hell of his own remorse. Too proud for ordinary blessings, Manfred cannot "tame his nature down"; he leaves the old priest to lament his failure.

Scene 2 is a soliloquy by Manfred in which he says farewell to the setting sun. He will never see the sun again.

The last scene shows the death of Manfred in his castle tower. He rejects once more the good offices of the abbot and also scorns a spirit who has come to lead him to his death. The abbot and the demonic spirits battle for the soul of Manfred, but he spurns them all, saying that he has been his own tempter and his own destroyer. Finally alone with the abbot, Manfred says farewell and avers that "'tis not so difficult to die." After his death, the abbot "dreads to think" where his soul has gone.

The Character of Manfred. Manfred's rejection of the comforts and consolations of religion are not an attack upon the Church but an assertion of the grandeur of the character. He chooses to punish himself by enduring suffering; he is his own judge and never submits his will to any other power. He is therefore a monster of pride. Despite this qualitiy, readers are asked to admire Manfred for the courage of his own self-condemnation. In his extreme egotism, Manfred does not make excuses or cast blame. Thus, he has heroic stature; he is a man of great powers, corrupted by one terrible deed. However, the play's emphasis is not on his deed; the act is never made specific. Rather the play shows the aftermath of an evil action.

DON JUAN

This long, digressive satiric poem is a loose narrative held together only by the hero, Don Juan, and the narrator, Byron himself, who maintains a mocking, ironic relationship with the story. Byron claimed that he had no plot in mind as he wrote the poem, and he continued to add episodes as long as he lived, completing sixteen cantos before his death. He began the poem in 1818 in Italy during a period of wild self-indulgence and profligacy. The first two cantos were published in 1819. Like many satires, it was criticized by some as being immoral.

Style. The stanza form is ottava rima, an eight-line iambic pentameter stanza with the rhyme scheme a b a b a b c c. The final two lines of each stanza form a couplet which Byron frequently uses for a punch line or comic wind-up. Byron also creates comic effects with his use of forced rhymes ("new one" . . . "Juan") and rhymes of two or three syllables ("intellectual" . . . "henpecked you all"). The poem's light tone suggests that Byron does not take the characters and events seriously; the language is colloquial, conversational, and slangy.

The Don Juan Character. Certain incidents and characters are drawn from Byron's life, but he is not Don Juan. He names his hero after the most notorious lover and seducer of women in European literature. Originally a villain in a Spanish story, Don Juan had become the archetype of the heartless, remorseless seducer.

The Don Juan character represents a merely physical desire divorced from any spiritual or even humane feelings. Ironically, Byron gives the name of this cold and callous stock character to his own, more modest hero. Byron's young lover is, at first, simple and naive. Every woman who meets him finds him charming; thus he has no need for force, treachery, or the seductive arts. Byron projects his own, more worldly personality as the narrator.

Canto I. Canto I presents the birth, childhood, and education of Don Juan up through his first seduction and affair. Don Juan is the son of an aristocratic father and an intellectual mother. After the father's early death, little Juan is educated according to his mother's plan. She has him tutored in arts and sciences, but she forbids him to learn anything "that hints continuation of the species." Further, in his study of classical literature he cannot read any of the "looser" or suggestive poems; he must read only expurgated versions of these. In stanzas 52 and 53 the narrator protests such a distorted education.

The narration moves forward to Juan's sixteenth year, when his mother's friend, Donna Julia, begins to find him atractive. She is a pretty, young woman married to an elderly husband, and she deceives herself into believing that she can subdue her attraction to Juan. She vows not to see him but then goes the next day to visit his mother. Donna Julia imagines that she can maintain a platonic love for Juan, but all her resolve fails when she finds herself alone with him. Naive Juan, meanwhile, does not know the cause of his own discontent. He seeks answers in nature and in philosophy. Stanza 115 pictures Juan and Julia in a garden, half-embracing. The poet undercuts this romantic scene with a mocking tirade against Plato for spreading false ideas about love. In stanza 116 the temptation has become too great, and she "whispering 'I will ne'er consent'—consented." Byron shows the folly of self-deception that would deny the physical basis of love.

After a digression the poet returns to Julia and Juan six months later. Their affair has intensified, and Julia's husband, Don Alphonso, has become suspicious. He breaks into her bedroom one night with a posse of friends and servants, makes a comic search, but finds nothing. Sending the others away, he apologizes to his wife for his foolish jealousy. As he lingers by her bed, he sees Juan's shoes. Young and slim, Juan has been hiding in the bedclothes all the time. There is a confrontation between lover and husband, but luckily neither has a sword. Juan escapes, but scandal follows. Julia's husband sends her to a convent, and Juan's mother sends him away on a grand tour to, ironically, perfect his morals.

Canto I ends with an address by the poet to the reader in which he claims the story is true and gives as proof the many similar stories that appear in newspapers, plays, and operas.

Then Byron as narrator sets out some poetical commandments by which he claims his writing is governed. Generally, he follows the principles of classical and English poetry and rejects the taste of his romantic contemporaries. He claims also that his poem is moral and promises a very moral conclusion in the final canto.

Finally, he comments on his own situation. Finding himself used up and burnt out at the age of thirty, he says, "I have squandered my whole summer while 'twas May" (stanza 213). He laments the loss of freshness and creative power but believes he has gained in judgment. He resolves to live more tamely from now on. Finally, he dismisses fame as a delusion and as a false motive for writing poetry.

Subsequent Cantos. The next cantos of this poem describe young Juan's many and varied adventures. He loses his tutor when their ship becomes wrecked. The lovely and innocent Haidee discovers him washed ashore on a Greek island. Their ideal love is opposed by Haidee's father, the pirate Lambro. Juan loses a fight with Lambro and is put into chains. Haidee's heart is broken, and she fades away and dies. Meanwhile, Juan is sold as a slave to a sultana in Constantinople. She also loves him, but when she becomes jealous, Juan fears for his life. He escapes and joins the Russian army, eventually finding himself at the court of Catherine the Great, who, of course, also loves him. She sends him on a diplomatic mission to England.

The final cantos show Juan moving about in English society, providing an opportunity for Byron to satirize contemporary social behaviors of his compatriots. He attacks the hypocrisy of the English, their false morality, and their bad taste.

In *Don Juan* Byron found a form suited to his tastes and abilities. Unconfined by a set narrative line, he allows himself as narrator the freedom to comment ironically on the action and characters, to digress into personal allusion, and to instruct the reader about how to read and judge the poem. Having a seemingly endless supply of incidents and comments, Byron might have gone on forever. But the poem was cut short by Byron's heroic and fatal attempt to help liberate the Greeks.

PERCY BYSSHE SHELLEY (1792–1822)

Born into a wealthy aristocratic family in Sussex, Shelley rejected the conservative principles of his family to lead the life of a radical and a rebel. He was educated first at Eton, where, being of slight stature, he was an easy target of the bullies who were common at such elite schools. The result for Shelley was an intense hatred of tyrants and a sympathy for the oppressed.

Later, at Oxford, the idealistic Shelley collaborated with a friend, Thomas Hogg, on a pamphlet that took up the Enlightenment issue of the proof of God's existence. Taking the position that God's being is not provable on empirical grounds, they titled the pamphlet *The Necessity of Atheism*. University officials asked Shelley to withdraw the pamphlet and expelled him when he refused. Shelley was surprised and disappointed; his family was furious at him.

Shelley further alienated his father by marrying, despite his disbelief in the institution of marriage, a sixteen-year-old girl, Harriet Westbrook, the daughter of the proprietor of a local coffee house. Shelley was saving her, he thought, from her father's tyranny. The young couple moved from place to place, Shelley involving himself in various radical causes. They had two children, but the marriage was a dismal failure.

By 1814 Shelley had met and fallen in love with Mary Godwin, daughter of the radical philosopher William Godwin, whom Shelley admired, and of Mary Wollstonecraft. Abandoning Harriet, Shelley left for Europe with Mary and her stepsister, Claire Clairmont, daughter of Godwin's second wife. With an absolute lack of sensitivity for Harriet's feelings, Shelley wrote to invite her to join his household in France. Two years later, Harriet drowned herself. Shelley then married Mary, with whom he had returned to London. Finding themselves ostracized by London society, they moved to Italy in 1818.

Shelley, never robust, sought improved health in the warm Italian climate. Ironically and sadly, his two children by Mary both died within a year of their move, and Mary Shelley suffered a nervous breakdown.

Nevertheless, the Italian period was Shelley's most productive. Between 1819 and 1821 he wrote his most famous lyrics as well as *Prometheus Unbound* and his critical essay *A Defense of Poetry*. Learning of the death in Rome of the young poet John Keats, Shelley wrote the great elegy *Adonais*.

Finally settling in Pisa in 1820, Shelley surrounded himself with a sympathetic group of friends who are called his "Pisan Circle." He was sailing in a small boat with one of these friends when a storm came up. The boat sank and both men were drowned.

Shelley's Poetry "TO WORDSWORTH"

This early sonnet reflects both Shelley's idealism and his disillusionment. Shelley admired the early poetry of Wordsworth. In the poem he hails Wordsworth as the poet of nature and mentions one of his central ideas, the loss of youth. Shelley speaks in the past tense of Wordsworth as one who wrote poems "consecrated to truth and liberty." But Shelley also laments the decline of Wordsworth from his exalted poetic vision into the dull conservatism of middle age. (Wordsworth was forty-five at the time.) As far as Shelley is concerned, when Wordsworth stopped writing good poetry, he "ceased to be."

ALASTOR, OR THE SPIRIT OF SOLITUDE

The title of this poem has puzzled scholars. Shelley's friend Thomas Love Peacock suggested the title. He defined "Alastor" as "an evil genius." However, the central figure of the poem, the questing poet, is not evil, except perhaps in the sense that he is self-involved and self-destructive. His solitude is a state he has chosen for himself as he follows only the drive of his own desire, oblivious of society.

Style. In the preface Shelley calls the poem an allegory—that is, a symbolic story. The poet's quest for "intercourse with an intelligence similar to itself" is in vain, but he pursues this futile search to his death. Shelley has more sympathy for such a self-centered being than for the majority of "meaner spirits" who quest for nothing more than the security of aloofness and fail to love their "fellow beings." The poem is written in blank verse.

Stanzas. The poem's prologue is full of Wordsworthian echoes that praise the benevolence of nature as mother and beloved inspirer of poetry.

The narrative begins at line 49 with an image of the poet's grave as a mere heap of leaves; he has died unmourned. Starting at line 67 the poet's life history is told. His ideal childhood was shaped by the impulses of the natural world. He grew in knowledge, studying as a youth the learning of the past. He traveled to the scenes of the ancient world, where previous civilizations flourished and declined.

In lines 129 to 139 an Arab maiden loves him. He ignores her, indicating his single-minded pursuit of some higher form of love. In his sleep he has a vision of one he could love, a perfect maiden who fulfills his ideals in intellect, imagination, and sensuous responsiveness. Just as he embraces this maiden, the vision departs.

The remainder of the poem shows the poet's search for the visionary maiden who has been lost "in the wide pathless desert of dim sleep" (line 210). Her vision grasps him like a snake grasping an eagle. He wanders on, gradually wasting away and being transformed into an awesome figure who frightens anyone he encounters. Seeing a beautiful swan, the poet envies it because it has a mate as beautiful as itself. He yearns for death but continues his journey, sailing a little boat as it is driven on by a tempest. It carries him into a cavern and to the very brink of a whirlpool. Just as he is about to be capsized, a wind from the west catches the sail and drives the boat into a placid cove. The cove presents an image of Narcissism. The flowers around the cove droop over the water, gazing at their own reflected beauty (lines 405 to 408). The poet is tempted to indulge in this self-admiration, but he feels the need for solitude. Day and night the poet wanders on. He is tempted to find rest in the spirit of the beauty of the natural world, but it does not have "light," that is, intelligence (lines 470–492). He follows a running stream until he reaches a rocky dell where a single pine tree stretches across the running water. It represents constancy. Here the poet finally dies, resting in a nook where no human has ever been before. His last sight is that of the calm and majestic moon.

In the final passage, starting at line 672, the narrator of the poem wishes he had the power to bring the hero poet back to life. He eulogizes the dead poet as

> The brave, the gentle, and the beautiful /
>   the child of grace and genius.

But the narrator also says that the poet felt the despair of losing one so lovely is, using Wordsworth's phrase, "too deep for tears."

This richly descriptive visionary poem can be read as a representation of Shelley's early life. The poet leaves home and neglects the Arab maid (Harriet) to seek a higher, more ideal love (the veiled maid) who alienates him from ordinary and domestic affections. The poem describes the transformation of his self-awareness as well as his declining health and increasing isolation.

"MONT BLANC: LINES WRITTEN IN THE VALE OF CHAMOUNI"

In 1816 Shelley visited the Alps. He was moved to compose this blank-verse poem while visiting the Vale of Chamouni, where the river Arve flows down from Mont Blanc into France. Like Wordsworth's "Tintern Abbey," the poem describes the place and the poet's response to the scene. Here, though, instead of viewing a landscape spread out below as in Wordsworth's poem, the poet looks up.

The lofty peak of Mont Blanc is a central metaphor for the power of nature—inaccessible and regardless of human life. Nevertheless, the mountain is the source not only of destructive glaciers but also of life-giving water, which will provide "breath and blood" to distant lands (line 124). That is, the beneficial river and the cruel glacier are both outpourings from the supreme source of power, nature, as symbolized by the mountain. "Power dwells apart in its tranquility" (line 97).

The mind, and specifically the poet's mind, is affected by this power. It passively receives the influences of the powers of nature. They flow through the mind as a river through the valley. The poet calls up the shades or ghosts that inhabit his imagination, recreating the forms of nature. But the mountain itself is beyond human knowing, except insofar as the mind can imagine "silence and solitude."

"HYMN TO INTELLECTUAL BEAUTY"

Written in 1816, the same year as "Mont Blanc," this poem is in some ways a companion piece to it. Both poems deal with power. However, in this poem, power is not coldly remote but felt in the human mind.

Style. The poem is an ode made up of seven twelve-line stanzas with a rhyme scheme of a b b a a c c b d d e e. The beauty addressed in this poem is that of the mind rather than of natural objects, and the similes used to describe it are based on light, wind, and music.

Stanzas. In the first stanza Shelley asserts the existence of the power of intellectual beauty, which, though mysterious, can be known through the heart. In stanza 2 the speaker asks the spirit of beauty a series of questions— Where does it go when it leaves us? Why must it leave? Why must we suffer both hope and despondency? In stanza 3 Shelley offers no answers to these questions. Some, he says, have offered such inadequate answers as "the name of God and ghosts and Heaven." But what humans really experience, he says, is "doubt, chance, and mutability." The speaker asserts that the only delight in the dull and inconstant world is the light of beauty that sometimes comes to us like music from the eolian harp. If this were not so, he says in stanza 4, people would be immortal. They would be powerful if beauty were always in their hearts, but it comes and goes. Stanzas 5 and 6 refer to the poet's childhood, to his futile experiments with magic and his early vows to devote himself to the spirit of beauty. He contrasts two responses to beauty: In youth, when he was suddenly visited by the spirit of beauty, he "shrieked and clasped [his] hands in ecstasy"; in maturity he feels a calmness and serenity, "a harmony" like autumn. Finally, he calls upon the power of beauty to descend on him.

"OZYMANDIAS"

This is probably Shelley's best-known sonnet; it is an excellent choice for oral presentation.

In the first line the poet speaks, introducing the traveler, who speaks the rest of the poem. The traveler describes a huge ruined sculpture of a king, Ozymandias, that stands in the desert of "an antique land." The parts of the monumental sculpture are scattered on the sands. The face is partly buried, but one can still see its proud and sneering expression.

In the sestet of the poem, the traveler recites the inscription on the pedestal; it announces the king's name and boasts, "Look on my works, ye Mighty, and despair." Thus, when the monument was put up, the king intended to bully his rivals with the evidence of his power. Now all traces of his power have crumbled to dust. Thus any powerful person can see from these ruins what happens to power. Nothing will be left of it except dust and fragments.

"ODE TO THE WEST WIND"

Written in 1819 after Shelley's final move to Italy, this ode explores a central romantic metaphor: the wind as the poet's inspiration.

Style. The poem is written in terza rima. Shelley uses a three-line unit, a tercet, rhyming a b a; the "b" rhyme is carried into the next tercet—b c b. After four tercets of interlocking rhyme, a b a b c b c d c d e d, the stanza ends in a couplet using the "e" rhyme. Thus each stanza has fourteen lines, enough space for Shelley to develop the poem's sweeping movements of feeling.

Stanzas. In the opening stanza the poet addresses the wind. First he refers to the wind as the "breath of Autumn" that blows dead leaves and dormant seeds into cold winter beds and then as the breath of spring that will revive the earth with colors and sweet odors. He calls the wind Destroyer because it brings the death of plants and Preserver because it scatters seeds for rebirth in the spring. This first stanza, like the next two, ends with the invocation "O hear."

Images of the sky are developed in the second stanza. The clouds are broken up and scattered like leaves by the wind. Shelley compares them with the hair of a maenad, a female attendant to Dionysus, the ancient Greek god of vegetation. The clouds are blown about by winds of a coming storm. At night the dark dome of the sky is like the sepulcher of the "dying year."

Stanza 3 takes the reader back to summer, a sweet and sleepy time. Focusing on the ocean, it points out that water plants, "sea blooms and oozy woods," also respond to the change of seasons; when the winds of autumn make waves on the surface, plants below lose their foliage.

The descriptions in the first three stanzas are recapitulated in the fourth. The poet supposes that if he were a leaf, cloud, or ocean wave he would be moved by the power of the west wind. He recalls himself running freely in the wind as a boy. But now he feels no such freedom or power. He needs power and begs to be lifted by the wind of inspiration. He cries out in despair, "I fall upon the thorns of life! I bleed."

In the fifth and final stanza, the metaphor of wind as power and inspiration is shifted. The eolian lyre or wind harp is introduced. The poet asks to be made an instrument upon which the wind can play "mighty harmonies." He wants the windlike power to scatter and spread his ideas across the earth. "Be thou me," he asks the wind, that is, take "my words among mankind."

The final couplet suggests that hope is rising from the previous despair. It asks the rhetorical question "If Winter comes, can Spring be far behind?" If the natural cycle of life is from death to rebirth, then there is hope for the rebirth of the poet's ideas. The poem has used the classical elements of air (wind), earth, and water (ocean). In stanza 5, the fourth element, fire, is associated with the "sparks" of the poet's ideas, his prophecies of a new order.

"TO A SKYLARK"

In this light, swift, and melodious lyric, the poet addresses a skylark, a small singing bird that conveys the image of joy, freedom, and creativity.

Stanzas. In the first four stanzas the poet describes the bird as flying off toward the setting sun. Even though he can no longer see the bird, he still hears its song. The speaker calls the bird "an unbodied joy," a feeling not tied to any substance. Asking "What is most like thee?" (line 32) he creates a series of analogies: The bird is like a poet, a lovelorn maiden, a glowworm, and a rose, all of which send out their sound or light or fragrance from hidden retreats. The speaker wonders what the bird thinks of that gives it such rapture. He compares the bird's happy state with the human condition, which is never purely joyful but always tinged with some pain or longing (lines 86 through 90).

The final stanza is the poet's request that the bird teach him the secret of complete gladness. If the poet could sing "such harmonious madness," all the world would listen to his poem.

Like many romantic poets, Shelley associates creative power—the ability to make poetry—with spontaneous emotion, especially with the emotion of joy or bliss. They credit the child or the nonintellectual creature, such as a bird, with an emotional force that as poets they long to feel.

ADONAIS: AN ELEGY ON THE DEATH OF JOHN KEATS

As the subtitle makes clear, this pastoral elegy was written about the young poet John Keats, who died of tuberculosis in Rome where he had traveled in hopes of benefiting from the warmer climate. Although Keats was three years younger than Shelley, the older poet admired his poetry and despised the critics who had attacked Keats's early poem *Endymion*. Shelley imagined that Keats's death was partly caused by dejection over these attacks.

In his elegy Shelley gives Keats the poetic name Adonais, a version of Adonis, a beautiful youth in Greek myth who was beloved by Aphrodite, the goddess of love and beauty. In the myth, Adonis is wounded by a wild boar. He almost dies but is cured by the goddess Persephone on the condition that he spend half of each year in the underworld. Thus Adonis represents resurrection, springtime, or, in Shelley's poem, the return of beauty.

Style. *Adonais* is a pastoral elegy. It contains all the traditional parts of such an elegy, as if it had been written by an ancient Greek poet. It is pastoral in that its characters are shepherds, the dead shepherd representing the poet. It contains the following parts:

an invocation of the muse;

an expression of loss and grief;

a procession of mourners;

a questioning of death and a denunciation of false shepherds; and

a final turning from despair to consolation or renewed hopes.

Before this poem the most important pastoral elegy in English had been John Milton's "Lycidas." In his elegy, Shelley used Spenserian stanzas, the same form Byron had used in *Childe Harold*. This nine-line stanza has an extra foot in the final line, which Shelley uses to draw out the lament.

Stanzas. The opening is strong and abrupt: "I weep for Adonais—he is dead!" The muse is Urania, the mother of Adonais, who is called upon to weep again (stanzas 3 and 4) as she once wept for Milton, referred to as "the Sire" of the grand elegiac tradition of English poetry.

The poem is long (fifty-five stanzas), listing in lofty diction a long line of mourners, from the spirits of nature—Morning, Ocean, Echo, and Spring—to Urania herself, visiting the tomb of Keats, to Keats's fellow poets, Byron, Thomas Moore, Shelley himself, and Leigh Hunt.

From time to time the speaker alludes to the cruel reviewer, the critic whose malicious comments supposedly caused Keats's death. He calls the critic a dragon (line 238), a reptile (line 253), a worm (line 319), and a "noteless blot on a remembered name" (line 327). In stanza 38 the idea that Keats, being dead, is now safe from the wrongs of these "carrion Kites" begins to console the speaker. Keats's soul has escaped back into the fountain of light, which is Eternity.

In stanza 39 the turn of feeling from grief to consolation is clearly marked: "Peace, peace! He is not Dead." Keats is beyond the pain of life that we as mourners still suffer.

In stanza 41 Death itself is dead, and the earth is urged to return to its previous splendor and loveliness. Keats is transformed into a spirit residing in Vesper, the evening star. Finally the speaker visits the grave of Keats in Rome. He describes the city as a place of both decay and repose.

One of the most striking images of this long, rich poem is found in stanza 52. As a Platonist, Shelley conceives the material world as made up of the imperfect shadows of ideal, eternal forms. He compares earthly life with "a dome of many-colored glass." The colors in the glass are beautiful but less perfect than the "white radiance of Eternity." Death is the means of breaking the colored dome and entering that total light. In the last three stanzas the poet, speaking to himself, acknowledges the call of death, seeing the soul of Adonais as a beacon to Eternity.

There is a strain of self-involvement and even self-pity in the poetry of Shelley. Many of his poems evoke the struggling, suffering soul victimized by life. *Adonais* benefits from focusing on another poet, one whose efforts Shelley could imaginatively sympathize with. *Adonais*, then, is not only a tribute to Keats but also a mature and lofty poem wherein Shelley reaches beyond what Keats described as "the egotistical sublime."

Shelley's Prose Essay

A DEFENSE OF POETRY

Shelley was moved to write this essay by an ironic statement made by Thomas Love Peacock in his volume *The Four Ages of Poetry*. Peacock stated that poetry was no longer useful because of the progress of technology and science. Shelley began his defense of poetry by distinguishing between reason and imagination, asserting that reason is a lesser faculty, having to do only with the analysis of things. He argued that imagination sees values and relationships and therefore is a creative faculty. Poetry, Shelley stated, is the expression of the imagination.

Shelley traces the development of poetry from early "savage" times to mature civilizations. He believes that the function of poetry is to give order to the world and thereby to give pleasure. Thus, poets act as legislators, inventing the "art" of life, and also as prophets, because they focus on the eternal and infinite rather than just the local and temporary. By this broad definition even philosophers like Plato or Bacon were poets, and the great poets—Shakespeare, Dante, and Milton—were philosophers.

The effect of poetry is, first of all, pleasure. But more than that, poetry makes people better by softening their natures, by enlarging their sympathies, by encouraging love, and by not being narrowly moralistic. Shelley states that the best poets do not try to teach and that society needs poets. He argues that humans have more practical and technical knowledge than they can possibly use, but that without the values embodied in poetry such knowledge is used to exploit people and cause them misery.

Shelley further proposes that poetry does not come from the reason or the will but rather from the mind in moments of inspiration. He states that the imagination creates far more beautiful images than the composing poet can record. Thus a poet is a person of greater than ordinary sensibility. The poet is happy in the operations of his own mind because he "turns all things to loveliness."

Finally, Shelley proposes in a second part (never written) to discuss contemporary poetic practice. He felt that he was living in an era of great poetry, at a time when enormous social and political upheaval was inspiring poetry. What he called "the spirit of the age" gave power to each individual poet. Shelley concluded with the most famous phrase from the essay: "Poets are the unacknowledged legislators of the World."

A Defense of Poetry was not published until 1840, eighteen years after Shelley's death, but during the Victorian age it became a major critical statement of poetry's function.

*B*yron and Shelley turned the English romantic movement in the direction of protest. Each was capable of the rich and sensuous descriptive poetry that is thought of as essentially romantic, but each was also preoccupied by the need to protect himself against the social conditions prevailing in England.

Through his outrageous personal life and his denunciations of authority, each poet found himself forced to live abroad in the more permissive colonies of artists and intellectuals in Geneva and the major cities of Italy.

Byron created a character, the Byronic hero, who was based on his own feelings of discontent and disdain for convention. Shelley projected his great search for the ideal, for beauty, through figures such as Alastor and the dead Keats.

Byron and Shelley had such intense poetic sensibilities and drives that they could not rest in normal domestic settings. Both died young while in the act of taking risks.

Selected Readings

Blunden, Edmund. *Three Young Poets: Critical Sketches of Byron, Shelley, and Keats*. Tokyo: Kenkyusha, 1959.

Bold, Alan. *Byron*. Totowa, NJ: Barnes, 1983.

King-Hele, Desmond. *Shelley: His Thought and Work*. Teaneck, NJ: Fairleigh Dickinson University Press, 1971.

Krishna, Francine Ellison. *Studies in Shelley*. New Delhi: Associated Publishing House, 1973.

Reiman, Donald H. *Percy Bysshe Shelley*. New York: Twayne, 1969.

Trueblood, Paul G. *Lord Byron*. New York: Twayne, 1969.

5

Second-Generation Romantic Poet: Keats

1807 Byron, *Hours of Idleness*

1811 The Regency Act makes the Prince of Wales Prince Regent

1812 Byron, *Childe Harold* (cantos I and II)

1813 Byron, *Bride of Abydos*; Shelley, *Queen Mab*; Turner painting, *Frosty Morning*

1815 Battle of Waterloo; end of Napoleonic Wars

1816 Keats, "On First Looking into Chapman's Homer"; Byron, *Childe Harold* (Canto III); Shelley, *Alastor*; Schubert, *Tragic Symphony* (no. 4 in C Minor)

1817 Keats, *Poems*; West painting, *Death on a Pale Horse*

1818 Keats, *Endymion*; Byron, *Childe Harold* (Canto IV); Shelley, *Revolt of Islam*

1819 Keats writes "The Eve of St. Agnes" and publishes *Hyperion*; Byron, *Don Juan* (cantos I and II); Shelley, "Ode to the West Wind" and *The Cenci*

1820 Keats, *Lamia, Isabella, The Eve of St. Agnes and Other Poems*; Shelley, *Prometheus Unbound*

1821 Keats dies in Rome; Delacroix paints *Dante and Virgil in Hell*; Shelley, *Adonais*

*F*or many readers, the poetry of Keats sums up English romanticism. His exotic narrative poems, his polished sonnets, and especially the great odes contain some of the most sensuous and at the same time most carefully controlled imagery since Spencer and Shakespeare. Keats was able to get beyond the involvement with memory and biographical incidents that were so much a part of the poetry of the other romantic poets.

His work gives an impression of clear, impersonal loftiness and intensity. Keats thought about the problems inherent in romantic theory—too much concentration on self, too much feeling with too little mind behind what was being expressed. He opposed the "egotistical sublime" with his concept of "negative capability"—submerging self by entering imaginatively into a situation beyond oneself. In "Ode on a Grecian Urn," for example, the haunting question about truth and beauty seems to arise spontaneously from observation of a timeless work of art.

Many lovers of poetry have regretted the early death of Keats; they see in the work he did accomplish a promise of a magnificent productivity.

JOHN KEATS (1795–1821)

Keats's father, the keeper of a livery stable in London, died when the poet, eldest of four children, was only eight years old. His mother soon remarried, but she died within six years, so that when John was only fourteen he became the head of the little group of Keats children. Some money had been left to them, but the trustee of the estate, Richard Abbey, concealed and withheld from them the full extent of their inheritance, so that Keats and his younger brothers were constantly short of money.

Keats got a good education at a school run by John Clarke, whose son Charles Cowden Clarke became a teacher and mentor of Keats, introducing him to great poets and encouraging him in his early attempts to write poetry. When Keats was fifteen, Richard Abbey removed him from school and, as a practical plan for the boy's future, arranged for his apprenticeship to a surgeon and apothecary. Keats carried out this apprenticeship and became an intern at Guy's Hospital, but he never established a medical practice. He abandoned the medical profession in 1817. His early calling was to poetry, and later in the same year Keats published his first volume, *Poems.* Living precariously on limited funds, Keats entered into the literary circle of Leigh Hunt and others who encouraged him and printed some of his early poems.

Keats's life was not easy. Compounding the problem of his own relative poverty, his brother Tom developed tuberculosis, and his brother George emigrated to the United States, where he failed financially in his first attempts to establish a business. Both brothers depended on Keats for the help he could hardly afford to give.

His early work *Endymion* (1818) was strongly attacked by reviewers in conservative magazines. Keats found this a depressing setback, even though he himself recognized the weakness of the poem. In need of a change of scene, in the summer of 1818 Keats took a walking tour northward through the Lake District into Scotland with his friend Charles Brown. During this time Keats developed a sore throat that never fully cleared up. It led to tuberculosis the following year.

Despite his impecuniousness and illness, Keats was very productive. In 1819, his most productive year, he wrote "The Eve of St. Agnes," his five great odes, and the first part of "Lamia," as well as a number of shorter poems. During this time he fell in love with Fanny Brawne. Because his health was deteriorating, in 1820 Shelley invited him to join him and his family in Italy. Keats, however, had become wary of close poetic associations, fearing too much influence on his own work. Keats did finally manage a trip to Italy, but only when it was too late to improve his health. He arrived in Rome very ill and lingered in pitiable condition until his death in February 1821.

Keats was only twenty-five when he died, yet he had written a substantial body of poetry, including some of the best lyric and narrative works of the romantic movement.

The Poetry of John Keats

"ON FIRST LOOKING INTO CHAPMAN'S HOMER"

This is a very early sonnet by Keats, written for his former teacher, Clarke. They had been reading the Renaissance poet George Chapman's translation of Homer. Walking home afterward, Keats composed in his head this tribute to Homer and to Chapman's translation. Keats wrote down the sonnet the next morning and sent a copy to Clarke in the morning mail.

This is an Italian sonnet. In the first eight lines, the octave, Keats speaks metaphorically of his reading of great poets as traveling among "realms," "states," and "kingdoms." One realm the poet had not yet visited was that of Homer, since Keats read no Greek. Chapman's translations enabled him to visit this realm. In the sestet Keats expresses his feelings of awe and delight on finally reading Homer. He compares his feelings with those of an astronomer sighting a new planet or of an explorer discovering a new ocean.

"SLEEP AND POETRY"

This early poem is memorable because it contains a passage in which Keats, at the age of twenty-one, lays out for himself a program of poetic development. He proposes to start with the less demanding forms of the pastoral poems and go on to the most ambitious, the epic. Within the poem, Keats allows himself ten years for a poetic apprenticeship. Again, he uses the metaphor of traveling through "realms." The first realm of the pastoral is full of sensuous pleasure. The poet mingles with amorous nymphs among flowers and trees; he writes "a lovely tale of human life." But as he progresses from these pleasures, the poet becomes more serious; he visits more complex and difficult realms. For this journey Keats uses the metaphor of the charioteer, which represents the imagination that will carry him through "the agonies, the strife / Of human hearts." The charioteer is shown swiftly moving through a varied scene of winds, trees, and mountains, past "Shapes of delight, of mystery, and fear" that "murmur, laugh, and smile, and weep," that is, through the whole range of emotional experiences. Then the visionary chariot of the poetic imagination fades, and the "sense of real things" overwhelms the poet with doubt, against which he resolves to struggle.

"ON SEEING THE ELGIN MARBLES"

Many of Keats's early sonnets were written in response to some other work of art—for example, Chapman's translation of Homer or Shakespeare's *King Lear*. In this sonnet Keats responds to seeing the Elgin marbles at the British Museum. These are a group of marble sculptures that had been removed from the Parthenon in Athens by Lord Elgin and brought back to England. Keats does not describe the sculptures; he tries instead to re-create his emotional response to them.

Style. Using the Italian form of the sonnet, Keats begins by expressing his awareness of his own mortality. His limitations as a mere mortal result in a narrow realm compared with the immortal, "godlike" range of the figures represented in marble. He wishes to but cannot soar into the realm of immortality; he is "like a sick eagle looking at the sky." The conflict between the glories that the brain can conceive and the restraints of the human condition causes pain, just like the pain that results from the sight of these relics, once grand but now "wasted" by the effects of time.

ENDYMION

As part of his self-imposed poetic apprenticeship, Keats determined to write a long narrative poem. He chose as a topic his own situation as one who aspires to realize a visionary goal. Endymion is a young mythic lover of Cynthia, the moon goddess.

Preface. As Keats himself realized, the poem is uneven in quality. For that reason he added a preface in which he points out the poem's failure to achieve the poetic heights at which he had aimed. He cites the poem's "mawkishness," or tendency toward sickly sentimentality. However, certain passages of this poem are worth reading not only because they are good but also because they reveal some of Keats's ideas about poetry at this point in his career.

Book 1. In the opening passage of Book 1, Keats discusses beauty's effects on the soul: "A thing of beauty is a joy for ever." Thus beauty counteracts the depression caused by life's dark and gloomy aspects. Keats cites examples of beauty from the natural world—trees and flowers—and from art—legends and stories. These images and tales stay with us; they "haunt us till they become a cheering light / Unto our souls" (lines 30 and 31).

Late in Book 1 comes a passage that Keats referred to in a letter to a friend as "The Pleasure Thermometer," meaning that the passage sets out various degrees of happiness, from the simplest to the most lofty. In this passage, starting about line 770, Endymion is speaking to his sister, Peona, explaining why he pursues love rather than fame. He asks (line 777) what the source of happiness is and responds that it has three. First, happiness arises from sensual pleasure, from the direct experience of nature, as the wind makes music in an eolian harp. Secondly, happiness comes from the pleasures of art, especially of old heroic stories. But better still is the happiness of human "entanglements," of "love and friendship" that are "self-destroying"—that is, relationships that allow us to get beyond mere self and past the limits of a single existence. Friendship is a "steady splendor." Even more lofty is love, the "radiance" into which we blend and mingle and in which our souls become "interknit."

Therefore, Endymion explains, men who might have achieved heroic deeds have, instead, been content to be lovers. Love itself makes all the world seem sweet; it makes the soul feel its own immortality. This is worth far more than mere fame.

"WHEN I HAVE FEARS THAT I MAY CEASE TO BE"

In this sonnet Keats uses the Shakespearean sonnet form of three quatrains and a couplet. Each quatrain contains a "when" clause citing three different occasions when the speaker is struck with fear that he may die before he has had a chance to do all that he wants.

First, he uses the metaphor of harvesting grain to express his anxiety that he will not live to write all the poetry that his mind holds.

Second, he sees in the clouds the symbols of romantic tales that he could, if he lived long enough, compose.

Third, he is afraid that he will not live long enough to consummate his love. Keats is not known to have any particular woman in mind at the time he wrote this sonnet. The "unreflecting love" is a suggestion of his expectation, perhaps, rather than any actual feeling.

In the closing couplet the poet pictures himself overwhelmed by the thought of eternity as he stands alone and thinks beyond poetic fame or love.

THE EVE OF ST. AGNES

Keats's ambition to write a romance was best realized by this poem, a version of the Romeo-and-Juliet story about two young lovers whose families are enemies. Keats makes use of the legend of St. Agnes, the patron saint of virgins. On January 20, the night before the saint's day, a young girl was supposed to perform certain rituals before going to bed in order to have a dream of her future husband.

The poem is set in an old castle. The coldness of winter and the drafty castle are contrasted with the warmth of Madeline and her ardent lover, Porphyro. As in many romances, the hero and heroine promise a renewal of life in a setting of danger and decay.

Style. Keats used the Spenserian stanza, a form associated with adventure and romance.

Stanzas. The first character we meet is the beadsman, an old holy man praying in the cold chapel. As he leaves the chapel he hears the sounds of music coming from the main hall of the castle, where preparations are being made for a feast and a ball. The "golden tongue" of the music contrasts with the chill of the silent chapel.

In stanzas 4 and 5 the music blares in the hall, where guests in rich and glittering costumes burst in to start the festivities. Madeline is among the party, but she is absent-minded, thinking only of what she must do that night to have a dream of her future husband. She must eat no supper, she must go to bed without looking to either side or behind, and she must pray for the vision of St. Agnes. Thinking of these rules, Madeline barely notices the various guests and the young men who wish to dance with her. She is oblivious to the "looks of love, defiance, hate, and scorn" exchanged by the others.

Meanwhile, Porphyro approaches the castle. He is not an invited guest but an intruder, a member of a family at war with Madeline's kinfolk. He hopes to sneak in and find Madeline, to see and worship her, and perhaps to "speak, kneel, touch, kiss" (line 81). Entering a remote part of the castle, he happens to meet his only friend there, a feeble old dame named Angela. She is frightened for Porphyro and warns him, in stanza 12, that all his enemies are present at the feast. Undaunted, Porphyro asks about Madeline. When Angela relates Madeline's plan to pray to St. Agnes for a vision, he determines to enact the vision Madeline expects. Angela objects, calling Porphyro "cruel" and "impious" (line 140). But he protests and makes an ambiguous promise that he "will not harm her" (line 145). Then he threatens to make a noise and alert his enemies if Angela does not help him carry out his plan. Angela gives in and leads him to Madeline's bedchamber, saying, "Thou must needs the lady wed" (line 179). Porphyro hides in the closet while Angela hobbles off to get some fancy treats from the feast to bring to Madeline's room. These will enhance the idea that her vision is all a dream.

In stanza 23 Madeline enters her room. She is silent; the pale moonlight, shining into the dark room through a window of stained glass, casts colors on Madeline's breast as she kneels in silent prayer. Then, as Porphyro watches, Madeline takes off her jewels and her dress, and not looking behind, she lies down and falls asleep. Porphyro gazes at her and then sets to work creating a dream image in her room. He arranges a table full of the most exotic delicacies, a love-feast of fruits and spiced sweets. When all is ready he speaks to her, but she is lost in her dream. He takes up her lute and plays a love song.

In stanza 33 Madeline opens her eyes. She has just been dreaming of Porphyro, and when she sees him in reality he seems to her not so perfect as in her dream. In comparison the real Porphyro seems "pallid, chill, and drear" (line 311). She asks for her dream again. In response, Porphyro does what any lover would want to do; he "melted" into her dream, making it come true.

Outside, a cold windstorm has arisen. Calling her his "bride," Porphyro urges Madeline to escape with him from this hostile house and to come across the moors to where, he says, "I have a home for thee" (line 351). The two lovers glide down the great stairway and out of the main door while the partakers of last evening's feast lie about in drunken sleep.

The last stanza tells us that Madeline's father, the baron, had nightmares, as did many of his guests. And old Angela and the beadsman die before dawn. Thus Porphyro had done all that he planned—gaze, kneel, speak, touch, kiss—and more, carrying away a bride from the stronghold of hostility and death.

The poem works through a series of contrasts in imagery: light and dark, warm and cold, noise and silence, young beauty and aged deformity, to present contrasts between hate and love, dream and reality, passion and death.

"LA BELLE DAME SANS MERCI"

Style. This ballad is a literary imitation of a folk ballad, in which a story is unfolded by means of dialogue. Such poems were composed to be sung; the narrative elements are vague and cryptic.

Stanzas. The first speaker addresses a knight, asking him what ails him, since he does not seem to be doing anything in particular and looks pale and troubled. The lily and rose in stanza 3 are the conventional flowers or colors of courtly love. The setting is autumn; the knight seems to be withering away.

Starting in stanza 4 the knight responds. He tells of meeting a beautiful fairy who enchanted him, fed him strange foods, and took him to her "elfin got," or fairy cave. There they made love, after which the knight fell asleep. He dreamed of pale kings, princes, and warriors who warned him, "La belle dame sans merci hath thee in thrall" (the beautiful woman without pity has captured you). Awakening, the knight found that his dream of love was over. He is alone on a cold hillside. He had been seduced and abandoned and now is withering away.

The Character of "*La Belle Dame*." The image of the elfin lady is a conventional *femme fatale*, or fatal woman. She is a beautiful woman who destroys men by loving and then leaving them. Keats gives his version of the convention in haunting lines that are suggestive of the mysteries and horrors of love.

"ODE TO PSYCHE"

Psyche was a mortal beloved by Cupid, son of Venus. To conceal his identity Cupid visited her only at night, but Psyche brought a light to discover his identity. Venus punished Psyche by condemning her to wander for many years. Eventually Psyche became a deity. She is the personification of the soul. In this ode the poet observes that Psyche was the last of the Greek deities and therefore never had a temple. He volunteers to be her priest.

Style. This is the first in a series of the great odes that Keats wrote in 1819. Experimenting with stanza forms, Keats developed a flexible form of mostly pentameter lines with some shorter lines in stanzas of eleven to eighteen lines.

Stanza 1. The poet describes a dream of "two fair creatures" lying side by side among the flowers in a wood. These were Cupid and Psyche. Their pose suggests that they had just kissed as they fell asleep.

Stanza 2. In the second stanza the poet compares Psyche with Phoebe, the moon, and with Vesper, the evening star. Psyche is more fair, although she has neither temple nor ceremonies of worship.

Stanza 3. In stanza 3 the poet says that even today he can be inspired by Psyche and that he will act out the rituals in her honor.

Stanza 4. In the final stanza the poet promises to build a temple "in some untrodden region of my mind" and to decorate the altar with the flowers "of a working brain," that is, with the ornaments of his own fancy. The final image is of an "open casement" window to let Love in; this refers to Psyche's love, to Cupid, and to the emotion of love itself, which the poet would welcome.

Thus Keats refers in this ode both to his poetic intentions to celebrate the soul through the actions of his own mind in writing poetry and to his longing for love.

"ODE TO A NIGHTINGALE"

This ode traces through eight stanzas the poet's response to hearing the song of the nightingale, a bird that sings at night.

Stanza 1. The stanza begins with the poet's expression of a feeling of dullness. The poet feels as if drugged by the "full-throated ease" of the bird's song.

Stanza 2. In stanza 2 the poet calls for a drink of wine, creating images of the warm south of France, where wines are made. He gives a detailed description of how the wine looks as one drinks it. Wine, he says, might allow him to escape from the world into the dim forest realm of the nightingale.

Stanza 3. This stanza describes the world from which the poet longs to escape, a world full of sickness and sorrow. Keats alludes to the recent death of his brother: "youth grows pale, and spectra-thin, and dies."

Stanza 4. The fourth stanza begins with the cry "Away!" The poet rejects wine and prefers to travel by means of the imagination on the "wings of Poesy." He imagines that he is already with the nightingale in the dark sky.

Stanza 5. In stanza 5 the poet, "in embalmèd darkness," lets his imagination tell him what flowers surround him. He feels isolated from the griefs of the world.

Stanza 6. In the sixth stanza the feeling of being embalmed becomes a wish for death. The poet has longed for death before. This seems to be the perfect moment to die, while the nightingale is singing. But, having reached this point, the poet realizes that, once dead, he could no longer hear the bird's song. He would be merely "a sod," a clump of earth without feelings.

Stanza 7. The poet turns back to the idea of life. The nightingale seems to live eternally because its song is the same now as it was in ancient days. Perhaps the biblical Ruth, for example, heard the nightingale's song as she gathered grain in the fields. The last word of this stanza, *forlorn*, is repeated at the beginning of stanza 8.

Stanza 8. As the nightingale's song fades in the distance, the poet again becomes aware of his own situation. The imaginative escape is over; he evaluates what has happened, asking, "Was it a vision, or a waking dream?" But he has returned to reality or else he would not be asking these questions.

Thus the ode reenacts the emotional experience of a flight of imagination. The poet longed for escape, rejecting drugs and wine in favor of the combined effect of the nightingale's song and his own imagination. He reached a point of longing for oblivion and then turned back. He ends by pondering the nature of his own flight.

"ODE ON A GRECIAN URN"

This is one of the most discussed of Keats's odes because of the ambiguity of the closing lines. To determine their meaning, however, one must consider the whole poem.

The poet begins by addressing the urn, a large sculpted vessel that is unlike any real urn. Keats made up the figures on the urn from a variety of sources among ancient Greek works of art.

Stanza 1. The poet speaks of two qualities of the urn. As an "unravished bride" it is a perfect object, unmarked by the passage of time. As a "sylvan historian" it provides a record of a distant culture. The poet seems to ask the urn who or what are the figures carved on its sides. The questions suggest that the scene depicts maidens running from "men or gods" to the accompaniment of music. It is a Dionysian scene that represents the wild, uninhibited celebrations of the god of wine and fertility.

Stanza 2. In the second stanza the poet imagines what music is being played in the scene. He prefers to imagine it because music actually heard is never so perfect or ideal. Similarly, in the figure of a youth about to kiss a maiden, the anticipated kiss is better than either the reality or the maiden; as a work of art, the moment cannot grow old nor the maid unkissable. Art has the advantage over reality of being perfect and unchangeable.

Stanza 3. This stanza is an expression of pure joy on pondering the urn's scenes. The word *happy* is repeated six times. The happiness is then contrasted with "breathing human passion," which cannot be so satisfying or so lasting.

Stanza 4. Here the poet describes another scene, as if the urn has been turned to reveal a different surface. Here there is a procession; a priest is leading a cow to some ritual sacrifice. The poet imagines that the little town from whence the people in the procession came is empty because all the folk have joined the procession. Thus, the poet's imagination goes beyond what the work of art represents and sees what it merely suggests.

Stanza 5. In the final stanza the poet reviews the whole urn and recapitulates his perceptions. Looking at the urn, he has been "teased" out of thought. As when one tries to imagine eternity one gets to a point beyond which the mind seems unable to go. The poet calls the urn a friend, one who brings a message about truth and beauty and their sameness to the many generations since it was created. The urn will continue to bring that message to generations in the future. The truest thing, because it is perfect and unchanging, is a thing of beauty, a work of art like the urn. Truth is what does not decay, nor does it feel despair but only happiness.

"ODE ON MELANCHOLY"

This ode describes the sources of melancholy, which Keats feels is always a part of any experience of joy or pleasure.

Stanza 1. In the first stanza the poet dismisses the false and artificial sources of melancholy, such as drugs, poisons, and mourning. He rejects the conventional images associated with death.

Stanza 2. Rather, the poet says in stanza 2, when you feel melancholy, "glut thy sorrow" on a flower or a rainbow or some other beautiful sight, perhaps on the eyes of a mistress when she is angry.

Stanza 3. In the third stanza the poet begins by stating abstractly the idea that melancholy resides in beauty because beauty is always escaping from us or fading just at the moment of utmost pleasure; joy turns to pain at its height. The poet suggests an image of a temple of Delight within which there is a shrine to Melancholy, a mysterious goddess. Joy is like a grape that, to be enjoyed, must be burst against the palate and thereby destroyed. The soul of one who can experience joy can also experience sadness; that person's soul is like a trophy hung in Melancholy's shrine.

"ODE ON INDOLENCE"

To be indolent is to feel lazy, to avoid any exertion; it is the opposite of energetic. The poet describes himself as looking at three human figures carved on the side of an urn. As he turns the urn in his hands, they seem to pass by him, then to come back as he turns it again. The figures are Love, Ambition, and Poesy. To achieve any of these would require some effort on the poet's part. Having deciphered the three figures, in stanza 4 the poet rejects each one as inadequate because it is unlikely to last long or to be satisfying. He prefers to be indolent.

In the fifth stanza the three figures pass by again in his dream, driving out sweet and lazy visions of May flowers. He bids the figures farewell.

In the final stanza the poet claims that he does not want the fame that comes from effort; he calls it being a "pet-lamb" feeding on praise. He asks these figures to fade out of his sight, saying that he has other visions to occupy his soul.

The reader will notice that, in comparison with the other odes, this one seems static and uneventful. The turning around of the urn is an image of not going anywhere, of not really moving at all, like indolence.

"TO AUTUMN"

This poem is also an ode, although the title does not so name it. It is a tribute to the mood of autumn—a feeling of fullness, completion, and calm pleasure.

Stanza 1. The first stanza contains many images of ripe fruits. The poet observes that the bees have filled their hives.

Stanza 2. Stanza 2 presents the image of autumn as a female figure sitting on a barn floor where harvested grain is being winnowed; the tossed grain is the hair of autumn. She is drowsy and works slowly and quietly.

Stanza 3. This stanza begins by asking, "Where are the songs of spring?" But the question is put aside because autumn has her own different sort of music. The poem ends with the sadder, more soothing and calm sounds of autumn.

Keats's Letters

Keats had a talent for friendship and he maintained an active correspondence with many friends. These letters have a more than biographical interest because in them Keats showed his mind at work as he grappled with ideas about poetry, about the nature of the poet, and about the relationships between poetry, reality, philosophy, and feelings.

In his letters he strikes out some fascinating phrases and images. The ideas are not fully developed; one can see them taking shape as Keats gropes for the right words.

LETTERS TO GEORGE AND THOMAS KEATS

Certain phrases from Keats's letters have become well known and are much discussed by readers of his poetry.

Negative Capability. One of the most interesting phrases is "negative capability," from his letters to his brothers on December 21 and 27, 1817. In the second letter Keats tells how he was struck by the idea that anyone, such as Shakespeare, who is capable of great achievement in literature can set aside his own identity and can enter into the being of the character being presented. Thus, the great writer can be objective, showing what is, without demanding to understand why it is. "With a great poet," he writes, "the sense of Beauty overcomes every other consideration" so that the poet is not bothered by doubts about "fact and reason."

LETTERS ABOUT POETS

In other letters Keats criticizes the egotistical poetry of Wordsworth and others. Keats admired Wordsworth and learned from his poetry, but he also found there an undesirable egotism that he did not want to imitate.

Letter to John Hamilton Reynolds. Yet in comparing Wordsworth and Milton, in a letter to his friend Reynolds on May 3, 1818, Keats finds Wordsworth the greater of the two poets, citing Wordsworth's deeper explorations of "the burden of the Mystery" of human thought.

Letter to Richard Woodhouse of October 17, 1818. Keats discusses the poetical character, saying that a "poet is the most unpoetical of anything in existence; because he has no Identity." The poet is always sharing the identity of some other being or of the sun, the moon, or the sea. Keats contrasts this notion with what he calls "the Wordsworthian or egotistical sublime" that stands apart from other things.

LETTERS TO GEORGE AND GEORGIANA KEATS

In a long letter to his brother and his sister-in-law, who had emigrated to the United States, Keats explained his idea of the world as a "vale of soul making."

The soul begins as a "spark" of God that is acted upon during lifetime by intelligence, by the human heart, and by the world—that is, the place where the mind and heart act upon each other to form the soul. The pains and sufferings of the world give identity to the soul and teach it through experience to achieve salvation.

Keats puts forward these ideas with various images and many questions; the notions are tentative. He confides to his brother and sister-in-law whatever is in his mind, without fear of argument or of exposure to a broader public. But frequently the reader of Keats's poetry can see reflections of these ideas in the great odes of his most productive period, 1818 and 1819.

Building upon the breakthrough made by Wordsworth and Coleridge at the turn of the century, Keats took for granted his freedom from the restraints of classical literary theory. He did not, however, follow Wordsworth's lead in focusing on the situations and language of ordinary, simple folk.

Keats took his own way, making a conscious effort to avoid the undue influence of other poets.

The youngest of the three second-generation romanticists, Keats perfected the romantic ode. In his short career he freed himself of the powerful influences of his romantic predecessors and wrote poems of great beauty and fascinating insight into the contradictions of human experience.

Selected Readings

Bate, Walter Jackson. *John Keats*. Cambridge: Harvard University Press, 1963.

Dickstein, Morris. *Keats and His Poetry: A Study in Development*. Chicago: University of Chicago Press, 1971.

Goldberg, M. A. *The Poetics of Romanticism: Toward a Reading of John Keats*. Yellow Springs, OH: Antioch, 1969.

Sharp, Ronald A. *Keats, Skepticism, and the Religion of Beauty*. Athens: University of Georgia Press, 1979.

Sinha, V. N. *The Imagery and Language of Keats's Odes*. New Delhi: Bahri, 1978.

Wasserman, Earl. *The Finer Tone: Keats's Major Poems*. Baltimore: Johns Hopkins University Press, 1953.

6

Minor Romanticists

1817 Peacock, *Melincourt*; *Blackwood's Magazine* established; Coleridge, *Biographia Literaria*

1818 Peacock, *Nightmare Abbey*

1819 Lingard, *History of England*

1820–1830 Reign of George IV

1820 *London Magazine* established; Peacock, *Four Ages of Poetry*

1820–1825 Lamb, *Essays of Elia* appear in *London Magazine*

1821 De Quincey, *Confessions of an English Opium Eater*

1823 Hazlitt, *Liber Amoris*; Carlyle, *Life of Schiller*

1825 Hazlitt, *Spirit of the Age*; Macaulay, *Essay on Milton*

1828–1830 Hazlitt, *Life of Napoleon*; Taylor, *Historic Survey of German Poetry*

1830 Moore, *Life of Byron*

1831 Peacock, *Crotchet Castle*

*W*hile the major achievements of the writers of the Romantic Age centered around lyric poetry, the spirit of romanticism—the freedom, the sense of individuality, and the emphasis on feeling—was also expressed in prose. The essay, which previously had been mainly a vehicle for criticism, political ideas, and philosophical speculation, began to be used for more personal and idiosyncratic materials.

The romantic essayists tried to get close to their readers, to talk intimately about private life, observations, and memories. Here, Wordsworth's formula of "a man talking to men" was fulfilled. The personalities of the essayists were as important to the essays as the subjects; such essays are called "familiar essays," suggesting an intimacy between reader and writer as well as an informality of style.

Likewise, the minor poets of the romantic period often chose as subject matter the personal, the private, and the natural. Clare, Moore, and Beddoes, among many others, were greatly influenced by Wordsworth and Coleridge. They also re-created some of the lyric sweetness of the Elizabethan era. Joy and simplicity were again celebrated in song, and writers of minor talent occasionally turned out gems of lyric expression.

ROMANTIC-AGE ESSAYISTS

Essays flourished partly because there was a new market for them. In the early decades of the century several new reviews and magazines were established. These periodicals contained literary as well as political writings and provided a public for the essays of such writers as Lamb, Hazlitt, De Quincey, and Peacock, each of whom developed the essay form in his own way.

Charles Lamb (1775–1834)

The son of a law clerk, Lamb was born in the very heart of London, in the section called the Inner Temple, where the offices and lodgings of London lawyers were concentrated. Lamb's family was not prosperous; his father was a clerk and his mother worked as a seamstress. Lamb was sent to Christ's Hospital, a charity school, where he met Coleridge.

Like his father, Lamb became a clerk, but not in a law office. He worked for the East India Company, a huge trading enterprise. In 1796, when Lamb was twenty-two, his older sister, Mary, in "a fit of insanity," stabbed their mother to death. Lamb had himself suffered a brief psychotic episode, and he sympathized with his sister's condition while feeling horror at her act. Later, when Mary was released from a hospital for the insane, Lamb made a home with her; neither one ever married. When she suffered recurrent attacks, he took her back to the hospital. But most of their years were spent as compatible companions; their home became a social gathering place for literary friends.

Lamb was of the first generation of romantics. He was about the same age as Wordsworth and Coleridge, both of whom were his friends. But Lamb was an urban man and had no desire to live among the beauties of nature; indeed, he fully enjoyed the sights and social life of the city. Lamb liked to drink and to play practical jokes; he was also a man who inspired affection in others. He enjoyed the theater and tried to revive interest in plays of the Renaissance and Restoration periods. With his sister Mary he wrote *Tales from Shakespeare*, a retelling for children of the stories from Shakespeare's plays. Charles adapted the tragedies, while Mary retold the comedies. *Tales from Shakespeare* was his first successful literary venture. His own earlier writings, however, were not successful.

Lamb's best writings were the familiar essays in which he blended sentimental memory with adult wit and humor. The series called *Essays of Elia* was written for the *London Magazine* and later reprinted as a separate volume. These essays form the basis of his fame. (Elia was the name of one of his fellow clerks.)

Like Wordsworth, Lamb based his mature reflections on his memories of youthful experiences. These reflections create emotions of nostalgia, fondness, and sadness at the transitory nature of life.

"CHRIST'S HOSPITAL FIVE-AND-THIRTY YEARS AGO"

This essay is in the collection *Essays of Elia*. In 1813 Lamb published in a magazine a recollection of his old school. Now, in 1820, he writes as if Elia were also an "old boy" of the school, saying, "I remember Lamb," although Lamb later in the essay seems to forget to use the persona of Elia. Elia speaks of Lamb as a lucky student because, unlike most of them, Lamb lived near the school and attended as a day student. Thus Lamb's diet was not confined to the coarse bread, watery milk, boiled meat fat, and other wretched food the boys were fed.

Elia describes himself as a typical boy of this charity boarding school—lonely and hungry, fearing arbitrary punishments, and yearning for home. One poor student, despised as a "gag-eater" because he took the lumps of boiled beef fat that the other boy could not swallow, was found upon investigation to be taking the lumps of fat home for his poor parents, who were almost beggars.

School runaways were cruelly punished. A boy's first attempt to run away put him in fetters; his second attempt brought him solitary confinement in a small, dark cell; and his third attempt brought him, stripped of his blue school uniform, before an assembly of the entire school to be whipped with a lash. Ironically, Lamb calls these whippings "solemn pageantries" that did not "spoil the general mirth" of the other boys.

But Lamb also tells of good times. The master of the lower grammar school was a lax and erratic man who neither punished severely nor taught consistently, sometimes leaving the boys to their own idle pastimes for whole days and only occasionally hearing lessons. In contrast, the master of the upper grammar school inspired fear and loathing by his fury and tyranny. He turned out good scholars but at a heavy cost. Lamb then recollects some of his fellow students, especially Coleridge, whom he greatly admired, citing their later accomplishments or their early deaths. Although Lamb recounts the horrors of public school life, he conveys a sense of, if not acceptance, at least forgiveness, for the most part, for what was not uncommon rigor in schools at that time.

"TWO RACES OF MEN"

This is a comic essay on borrowing, written in the persona of Elia. He begins by classifying all men into two essential categories—borrowers and lenders. Then with mock praise he describes the borrowers as the "great race" of men—cheerful, trusting, and liberal, in contrast to the "lean and suspicious" race of lenders, who were born to serve them. The essay is rich in allusions to classical, biblical, and literary sources, which raise the ironic praise of borrowers to absurd heights. The borrower is made noble while his "victim," the lender, can only save his dignity by lending cheerfully, accepting his lesser status. Elia cites one arch-borrower, whom he names Ralph Bigod, who wasted his inherited estate to become a triumphant borrower. He borrows from multitudes, immediately getting rid of the borrowed money by drinking, giving, or throwing it away because he believes that "money kept longer than three days stinks," adapting the proverb about fish. Otherwise, says Elia, he could not have kept his purse empty and continue to borrow at such an heroic rate.

In the middle of the essay Elia turns to a specialized kind of borrower, the one who borrows books. He describes the gaps in the shelves of his library caused by the borrowings of the formidable book-borrower Comberbatch (an alias of Coleridge), who believes that a book properly belongs to the one best able to understand and appreciate it.

Elia describes each lent book with fond remembrance. On the other hand, sometimes Comberbatch leaves with Elia some books he has borrowed elsewhere, forming "a small under-collection" of orphan books Elia has adopted. Elia cites other, less widely predatory book-borrowers who have taken advantage of his collection. He ends by praising "S. T. C.," another allusion to Coleridge. In this personality, S. T. C. returns books after having added marginal notes, thus making the books much more valuable and interesting. On this positive note, Elia ends by recommending that the reader never close his library to a borrower like S. T. C.

"OLD CHINA"

One of the most popular essays by Elia, frequently republished in anthologies, is the delicate and charming "Old China." The essay opens with a description of the figures on china teacups. The sort of china Elia describes was commonly used in England, and he expects his readers to be familiar with it. Called willowware, the dishware was made in China for export to England beginning in the late eighteenth century. The blue or pink figures on a white background depict gentlemen and ladies in Chinese costume in a fragmentary landscape of willow trees, ponds, bridges, and tiny pavilions. There is no frame or Western-style perspective in the drawings; they form an almost abstract pattern. In the opening paragraphs of the essay Elia points out the fantasyland details of the figures in an impossible spatial arrangement, all of which give him pleasure. He is also pleased to be able to afford such a set of china. However, his satisfaction is contradicted somewhat by the second speaker in the essay, cousin Bridget, who is a representation of Lamb's sister, Mary. Her speech comprises most of the rest of the essay.

Bridget remembers earlier days, when they were not quite so prosperous, as days of great happiness. She remembers that when her cousin had to wear a threadbare suit so that they could afford to buy a rare old book, the new purchase was always a triumph. She recalls climbing up into the cheaper seats at the theater as a pleasure because it meant that they could enjoy the camaraderie of the rough and unlearned crowd with whom they sat. She recalls eating early strawberries or early peas, "cheap luxuries" that made life seem rich even though they were poor. Now, when most indulgences are within their means, the comfort is more but the excitement is less. Year-end accounts are no longer a trial, but they are also no longer a challenge. Elia replies to all these examples of the joys of the past by pointing out that while they were poorer then, they were also younger. They used to be able to put up with minor discomforts more easily. But, he says, if he could buy back youth, he would gladly give up all his wealth and more. In the last sentence, he turns Bridget's attention back to the figures on the china cup in his hand.

William Hazlitt (1778–1830)

Hazlitt came from a family with liberal political views. His father was a Unitarian minister who praised the revolution in France, and young Hazlitt remained true to his father's principles long after most disillusioned English liberals had drifted toward conservatism. Although he studied for the ministry he never followed that profession, becoming instead a painter and finally a journalist and a critic of art, literature, and drama.

Though his social manner was harsh and awkward, Hazlitt had close friends, Coleridge, Lamb, and Leigh Hunt among them. He suffered an unhappy marriage that ended in divorce, an unhappy attachment to a young woman who jilted him, and late in life a second unhappy marriage.

Nevertheless, Hazlitt was a successful writer. He was among the first in England to sustain a career based on criticism.

Hazlitt composed quickly in a plain, energetic style. His essays are not grounded in theory or philosophy but rather seek to recreate a strong impression of a poem, painting, play, or prizefight.

They are loosely structured and seem to run straight forward with zest or "gusto" as far as the topics will take them. They then abruptly end.

"ON GUSTO"

In this essay Hazlitt tries to define the quality of gusto, which he admires in art. The definition proceeds through multiple examples rather than logical analysis. Hazlitt rushes from one painting to the next, pointing out a figure, a face, a hand, or a tree that illustrates the quality of gusto.

Gusto is the power in the painting to make an impression on the senses. Rather than merely representing or imitating nature, it also makes the viewer feel. Hazlitt mentions not only specific paintings but also the most striking details of those paintings. The cumulative effect of all these examples is to make the quality of gusto clear to anyone familiar with even a few of the paintings.

In the final paragraph, after gusto has been defined in terms of the visual arts, Hazlitt applies the same word to literature. He finds that Shakespeare is not intense enough and too "discursive" to have gusto. He states that Milton has gusto, as do Pope, Dryden, Prior, and that popular ballad opera of John Gay's, *The Beggar's Opera*. And, one might say, Hazlitt's own zestful style illustrates gusto.

"MY FIRST ACQUAINTANCE WITH POETS"

In this essay, written in his middle age, Hazlitt presents an image of himself at twenty. He was a naive and intense young fellow, excited at the prospect of meeting Coleridge, the poet and preacher. This meeting took place in 1798, the year of the publication of *Lyrical Ballads*. Coleridge, a liberal Unitarian minister, like Hazlitt's father, had been assigned to a nearby parish. Just after his first sermon, Coleridge received the Wedgwood annuity which enabled him to quit the ministry. Young Hazlitt's disappointment at Coleridge's resignation was lessened, however, when Coleridge kindly invited him to come for a visit at Nether Stowey. This unexpected attention from the older poet inspired Hazlitt to try to write.

Hazlitt made his visit in the spring. He was cordially received by Coleridge and introduced to William and Dorothy Wordsworth. He heard Coleridge and Wordsworth read the poems they would publish in *Lyrical Ballads*, and he compared their styles. He was overcome by their originality and by the "new spirit in poetry" they had engendered. He came away from his visit full of enthusiasm.

Hazlitt's essay describing his visit not only shows a charming portrait of himself as an open-minded, intense, and joyful young man but also provides some interesting details about the two poets he visited.

Hazlitt contrasts the faces, voices, manners, and remarks of Wordsworth and Coleridge. He was able to see, through the sunshine of his own enthusiasm, that they were not perfect men. Details of the shape of Coleridge's nose ("small, feeble, nothing") and of the way Wordsworth devoured a Cheshire cheese mix the common with the sublime, humanizing the poets who had become, by the time Hazlitt wrote his essay, public idols.

Thomas De Quincey (1785–1859)

De Quincey was a hack writer, a paid contributor to various journals and magazines, whose writings occasionally rose to the height of memorable literature. A precocious, bright child of middle-class background, he was sent to several schools. But he was lonely at school and at sixteen ran away to London, where he endured homelessness and extreme poverty. The best account of this period in De Quincey's life can be found in his *Confessions of an English Opium Eater*. His vagrancy ended a year later when he went back to his guardians in Manchester. They sent him to Oxford, where he spent five years but did not finish his degree. It was at Oxford that De Quincey was first given opium for relief of pain. The dangers of addiction were not at that time understood.

De Quincey was a great admirer of Wordsworth and Coleridge. When he left Oxford, he moved to Grasmere in the Lake District to be near them. For a while he was able to support himself on a small inheritance, but his resources did not last long. De Quincey married a local woman after she had borne the first of their eight children.

De Quincey began to write translations, articles of criticism, and essays on a wide range of topics for various magazines and reviews. He supported his family on his earnings from writing, despite the weight of his addiction to opium.

In 1828 De Quincey moved from London to Edinburgh, Scotland, where the cost of living was cheaper. Nevertheless, his financial position was always shaky. For thirty years he turned out rapidly written pieces in a learned, ornate style, a poetic style of prose. He struggled with his addiction during all these years, and though he managed to reduce the amount of opium he consumed, he was never able to give it up completely. De Quincey did not fit the modern stereotype of a drug addict. He was a modest, conservative, and religious man of gentle manners who found himself caught in the web of addiction.

He wrote his most famous work, *Confessions of an English Opium Eater*, in order to reveal the terrors of addiction. By studying his own mental experiences, De Quincey became aware of the unconscious mind and of the significant role of dreams long before their systematic study by Freud and others.

CONFESSIONS OF AN ENGLISH OPIUM EATER

In this autobiographical treatise De Quincey described his life before, during, and after addiction. First published in 1821, it established De Quincey's literary fame. The enlarged edition, issued in 1856, is generally judged to be less dynamic in effect. The confession has three parts.

Part 1. In the first part, "Preliminary Confessions," De Quincey describes his youth, how he became an outstanding Greek student, how he was put into a school under an ignorant and coarse schoolmaster, and his determination to run away when his guardians refused to send him to a university. He hoped to exist on loans until he came into his inheritance at the age of twenty-one, but De Quincey found that he could not deal with moneylenders. At the same time, he was afraid to ask friends for help because they might notify his guardians and cause him to be sent back to school. Lonely and hungry, De Quincey survived in London by sleeping in an unoccupied building, keeping company with another neglected child, a ten-year-old girl. De Quincey was befriended by a young prostitute, Ann, one of many such women he met during his nightly wanderings. Ann's kindness to him in bringing him wine when he fell sick prompted De Quincey to act to help himself and Ann. He went on a trip to visit a friend to ask for financial help. On his return to London, De Quincey found that Ann had disappeared. He searched the streets for her but to his great regret he never found her. At this time, however, De Quincey was accidentally discovered by some friends and taken home. Each time he returned to London, De Quincey searched the Oxford Street area, where he had known Ann, in hopes of seeing her again and bringing her help. Later, she became a regular figure in his dreams.

Part 2. The second part, "The Pleasures of Opium," relates De Quincey's life after he had been to college and returned to London. Suffering from "excruciating rheumatic pains of the head," he took a college friend's advice to take opium for relief. He was able to buy it easily at a druggist's shop. He was immediately relieved of pain. The opium also had the effect of transporting him to ecstasies. Comparing the effects of wine and opium, De Quincey explains that opium's effects were much more lasting, more calming, and at the same time more elevating. "The opium eater feels that the diviner part of his nature is paramount." De Quincey contradicted the popular idea that opium causes a torpor or sluggish inactivity; on the contrary, it made him feel stimulated and free of care.

From 1804 to 1812 De Quincey took opium about once every three weeks to enhance the experience of going to the opera or mingling with the crowds in London markets.

Part 3. In the introduction to "The Pains of Opium," De Quincey reports being able in 1816 to reduce his dose from about 8,000 drops a day to 1,000 drops with good effect. He tells of offering a piece of opium to a poor Malay sailor who was trying to find his way to Bristol Harbour. The Malay took all the opium at one time, a huge dose. De Quincey was afraid it would be a fatal amount, but the sailor continued on his way with no known ill effects. This Malay also became a recurring figure in De Quincey's dreams.

Most of "The Pains of Opium" involves the terrible dreams suffered by De Quincey beginning in 1817 during a period of attempted withdrawal. Every attempt to reduce further his intake of opium caused intense agony, both physical and mental. De Quincey found himself unable to study, unable to complete a book he had written, and tortured by bizarre and terrible nightmares in which figures from his past, both individuals and crowds, haunted him.

The Malay came back as a "fearful enemy." Ann appeared, in tears, then faded into mountain mists. Weird landscapes merged into oceans of faces.

Feeling that he would die if he continued to take opium, De Quincey, with great pains, reduced his dose to twelve grains a day, feeling meanwhile all "the torments of a man passing out of one mode of existence to another." At the time of writing *Confessions*, he reports, "My dreams are not yet perfectly calm."

De Quincey wrote *Confessions* in order to correct many popular misunderstandings about opium. His experience was, he felt, an important contradiction to the false information disseminated by many, even doctors, who had not themselves experienced opium addiction. It was a general warning against opium.

"ON THE KNOCKING AT THE GATE IN MACBETH"

This is a good example of De Quincey's essay of literary criticism and shows his interest in the psychological effects of literary experiences. In this case, he discusses the intense "awfulness" of that moment in Shakespeare's *Macbeth* when Macbeth has just murdered good King Duncan and a loud knocking is heard at the gate of Macbeth's castle.

De Quincey argues that the effect on the audience comes not through their understanding but through their feelings. He shows how this moment of knocking throws the audience's sympathy not with the victim, Duncan, but with the murderers, Macbeth and Lady Macbeth. This sympathy does not take the form of pity. De Quincey suggests that the audience feels instead a reaction and that the terrible murder is felt more intensely when the ordinary course of human activities is resumed, as when the knocking begins at the gate.

The "pulses of life are beginning to beat again" in contrast to the "other world" of fiendish murders. De Quincey cites this scene as an example of the greatness of Shakespeare's art.

"THE LITERATURE OF KNOWLEDGE AND THE LITERATURE OF POWER"

This section of De Quincey's essay "Alexander Pope" is frequently reprinted as a separate essay. In it De Quincey distinguishes two types of literature—the literature of knowledge and the literature of power.

The Literature of Knowledge. De Quincey states that the literature of knowledge tries to teach us something. It is discursive and appeals to the intelligence.

The Literature of Power. The literature of power tries to move us, to evoke pleasure or sympathy; it does not tell us something new but presents eternal truths. Therefore, the literature of power, such as Milton's *Paradise Lost* and the plays of Shakespeare, never grows out of date. It is not superseded, as literature of knowledge may be, by later discoveries. De Quincey suggests that the literature of power is concerned with the highest moral capacities of the human being. It addresses the heart, a great "intuitive organ" that contains ideals of justice, truth, and hope, which need the support of illustrations from tragedies and romances, from tales and epics. The emotions that arise from reading great literature of power mold the moral being of the individual.

Thomas Love Peacock (1785–1866)

Peacock was a largely self-taught intellectual. He was a satirist who stood apart from the mainstream of romanticism and mocked it in satiric novels, essays, and poetic parodies. Peacock wrote poetry in his youth, publishing two volumes in 1812. He was a friend of Shelley's; both were political radicals. In 1819 Peacock married. The next year he took a job with the great East India Company, which managed British affairs in India. He was promoted to various executive positions while continuing to write novels, satires, and critical essays. He published his last novel in 1861 and died five years later at the age of eighty-one.

"FOUR AGES OF POETRY"

In this satirical essay Peacock develops an ironical history of poetry from ancient to modern times. His purpose was to prove that poetry was in a final decline and was soon to be superseded by more intellectually advanced studies such as the sciences, history, and political economy. Peacock's friend Shelley was so provoked by this essay that he composed his *Defense of Poetry* in 1821.

Peacock delineates the four ages of poetry as cycles of iron, gold, silver, and brass.

The Cycle of Iron. The first cycle included the age of barbarism, when bards celebrated the violence and glory of their chiefs. The social setting was crude and superstitious beliefs ruled people's lives.

The Cycle of Gold. The first golden age was the age of Homer, when poets looked back to earlier times and treated the past heroically. When civilization had advanced, poets created order out of the chaos of their ancestors. Poetry became an art and reached its highest perfection. But this condition did not last. Poets started to concern themselves with historical fact and rational speculation.

The Cycle of Silver. Poets of the silver age, such as Virgil, either recast and polished the poetic materials of the golden age or wrote original works of comedy and satire. Poetry became labored. Feelings were expressed in "ornamental and figurative language." Poetry was moving toward extinction.

The Cycle of Brass. The brass age rejected both the learning and the polish of its predecessors and sought novelty in a return to nature and to the crude ideas of the iron age. This was the dark age of poetry, after the decline of the Roman Empire.

Peacock then asserts that the cycle of poetry was repeated. The second iron age was medieval and the second golden age was the era of the Renaissance, epitomized by Shakespeare. Between the second gold and silver ages stood the greatest English poet, Milton, who had the energy of the Renaissance together with the elegance of the second silver age, the age of Dryden and Pope. This silver age saw the reign of authority and of intellect. But poetry declined because of the search for novelty. The new enthusiasm for nature was, in Peacock's judgment, a second age of brass, in which he was still living in 1820. He mocks and criticizes his contemporaries, the Lake poets Wordsworth, Coleridge, and Southey, as well as such popular figures as the novelist Scott and the young Byron.

Peacock suggests that poetry was left behind in the general progress of civilization. He calls poetry the "mental rattle" of the infant stage of culture; the modern bard is out of place, or out of his time, and will more and more, Peacock predicts, lose his readers.

As a satirist, Peacock may have taken an extreme position in order to emphasize the aspects of romantic poetry that annoyed him, but his scorn for individual poets was pointed. Shelley's response affirmed the power of poetry to make civilization better.

"THE WAR SONG OF DINAS VAWR"

This is a mock-heroic song, celebrating such crude and brutal deeds as might have been sung by a bard of the iron age of poetry.

Style. The song is made silly-sounding mainly by the use of trimeter—that is, a line with only three stressed syllables, which is usually associated with light or comic verse. In addition, each line ends with a feminine rhyme (on an unstressed syllable), thereby undercutting the impression of grandeur and brave deeds. Thus Peacock ridicules the pride of bloody victories and heroic emotions by describing them in a style usually associated with silly, flippant remarks.

In a short work of forty lines, he compresses a raid, a countermovement of troops, the destruction of a castle and its inhabitants, the beheading of a king, and the general slaughter of the defeated by the victors. The jolly tone of the bard reduces all this potentially horrible material to a mere occasion to sing "our chorus."

John Clare (1793–1864)

The romantic assumptions that poetry must be written in the language of ordinary people and must reflect a "spontaneous overflow" of feeling made it seem natural enough that a poet of the people should arise out of the peasant class. Such a poet was John Clare, the son of a farm laborer and himself a laborer. Clare was inspired by James Thomson's *The Seasons*, as well as by the poetry of Wordsworth and Coleridge.

In 1820 he published his *Poems Descriptive of Rural Life*, which was well received. On the basis of this success Clare married, but his subsequent volumes did not sell so well. Dejected by these failures and by the responsibility for a growing family, Clare fell into madness, suffering from delusions. He was placed in an asylum and spent most of the remainder of his life institutionalized. He continued to write poetry, much of which was not published until the middle of the twentieth century.

Clare's poetry spoke of nature directly observed rather than sentimentalized. He kept his Northampshire dialect and stayed close to the details of his experiences of nature and of his loves and losses. His poems of love are full of regret and longing.

"MOUSE'S NEST"

This poem vividly describes a striking experience. The speaker tells of an encounter with a female mouse and her litter of tiny offspring. Expecting to see a bird, the poet is startled and retreats, then stops and watches. The two abstract terms *odd* and *grotesque* stand in the middle line of the poem, indicating the speaker's feelings at the moment and also as he looks back.

The speaker's description of natural creatures is close and exact. His position is in contrast to that of the landscape poet, who sees a vista and philosophizes on it.

"CLOCK-A-CLAY"

This poem also renders a closeup of a natural creature. The clock-a-clay is a ladybug, the common red-and-black garden insect.

The poem is spoken from the point of view of the ladybug as it sits snug and protected in a flower. Its flower-home may shake under rain and wind, but the bug is secure as it counts the time, an allusion to its role in a child's game of telling time.

"I AM"

Unlike Clare's poems of nature observed, this lyric reveals his sense of loss, his loneliness, and his estrangement from those he loves. As "self-consumer" of his woes, he stresses his isolation from any sympathetic other person.

In the second stanza, he sees his life as a "shipwreck."

The final stanza suggests that the only comfort will be death, when he will abide with God and return to the peacefulness of sleep that he knew in childhood.

"AN INVITE TO ETERNITY"

With a sweet simplicity reminiscent of the Elizabethan song, this lyric invites the beloved to join the speaker/lover in a journey through death to eternity. Eternity is presented as a state of strange transformation, of being and not being simultaneously. The lover seems sure, however, that he and his beloved will know each other in eternity and be together there, unlike in this world, where those who should be most dear to us "know us not."

In the final stanza the idea of marriage is blended with this anticipation of eternity as a better state.

During the romantic period poets and prose writers tended to share the assumption that all literature was basically about feelings and that the role of the writer was to recreate and explore feelings. They felt that mutually sympathetic feelings made people more morally sensitive and at the same time gave pleasure.

Joy and the loss of joy were popular topics. As the reading public grew in number and in sophistication, a variety of journals, reviews, and magazines—different kinds of periodicals—created outlets for poets and essayists to develop and mold public taste. Carrying out Wordsworth's proposal in the preface to Lyrical Ballads, *they wrote familiarly, even intimately, of their own memories, dreams, and emotional histories.*

With the exception of Peacock, they found the self an inexhaustible source of material. Personal history and observation were assumed to be universally interesting, relevant, and full of meaning.

Selected Readings

Baker, Herschel. *William Hazlitt.* Cambridge: Harvard University Press, 1962.

Barnett, George L. *Charles Lamb.* New York: Twayne, 1976.

Dendurent, H. O. *John Clare, A Reference Guide.* Boston: Hall, 1978.

Ward, A. C. *The Frolic and the Gentle: A Centenary Study of Charles Lamb.* Port Washington, NY: Kennikat, 1970.

7

The Victorian Age (1837 to 1901)

1842   The Mines Act controls employment conditions of women and children in underground mines

1843   J. S. Mill's, *System of Logic* leads way to system of Free Trade

1843–1855   Macaulay's first collection of essays published

1843–1860   Ruskin's first great work of critical essays, *Modern Painters*

1845   Disraeli, *Sybil, or The Two Nations*

1846   Repeal of the Corn Laws

1846–1857   C. Brontë's novels written

1847   E. Brontë, *Wuthering Heights*; Chopin, *Minute Waltz*

1847   The Pre-Raphaelite Brotherhood founded; Marx and Engels, *Communist Manifesto*

1847–1859   William Makepeace Thackeray's important novels written

1847–1866   C. Rossetti's poems written

1847–1881   D. G. Rossetti's poems written

1849–1869   Arnold begins his writing career; *The Strayed Reveller and Other Poems* published

1850   Tennyson appointed poet laureate

1851   Great Exhibition held in the Crystal Palace; Verdi, *Rigoletto*

1853   Cheltenham Ladies College founded

1854–1856   Crimean War—Britain and France declare war against Russia; Florence Nightingale founds modern profession of nursing

1858–1876   G. Eliot's (M. Evans) novels written

1858–1891   Morris's poetry and prose written

1859   FitzGerald, *The Rubáiyát of Omar Khayyám*

Mill, *On Liberty*; Darwin, *Origin of Species*; Disraeli's Reform Bill

1860   Reade, *The Cloister and the Hearth*; Collins, *Woman in White*

1861   Imprisonment for debt abolished

1861–1865   Civil War in the United States

1863   Huxley, *Man's Place in the World*

1864–1876   Newman, *Apologia Pro Vita Sua* and poetry

1865   Carroll (C. Dodgson), *Alice's Adventures in Wonderland;* Lincoln assassinated

1865–1869   Tolstoy, *War and Peace*

1865–1904   Swinburne's poems written

1866 The Second Reform Bill extends voting rights; Dostoevsky, *Crime and Punishment*

1867 Dominion of Canada established; Marx, *Das Kapital*; Strauss, *The Blue Danube Waltz*

1868 Disraeli becomes British prime minister; Alcott, *Little Women*

1869 Suez Canal opens; Alger, *Luck and Pluck* series

1870 First Married Women's Property Act

1870–1871 Franco-Prussian War

1871 Darwin, *The Descent of Man*; religious tests for entry to Oxford and Cambridge abolished; Trade Unions legalized by Parliament

1871–1908 Hardy's novels and poetry written

1873 Pater, Studies in the History of the Renaissance; Judicature Act reforms the courts

1874 Factory Act limits the hours of labor of women and children in the textile industry

1876 The Education Act provides for committees to compel all children to attend school; Mark Twain (Samuel Clemens), *Tom Sawyer*

1877 Royal Titles Act makes Victoria Empress of India; H. James, *The American*

1878–1894 Stevenson's novels and poetry written

1879 Ibsen, *A Doll's House*

1880 Brahms, *Academic Festival Overture*

1880–1881 First Anglo-Boer War

1882 Second Married Women's Property Act

1884 Twain (S. Clemens), *Huckleberry Finn*

1885 Gordon and troops massacred at Khartoum, Sudan

1886–1910 Rudyard Kipling's novels and poetry written

1887 Queen Victoria's Golden Jubilee

1889–1939 Yeats's poems and plays written

1890 Tchaikovsky's *Sleeping Beauty* ballet

1891–1898 Wilde's dramas, novels, and poems written

1892 Doyle, *The Adventures of Sherlock Holmes*

1893–1923 Shaw's plays written

1895 Wells, *The Time Machine*

1897 Queen's Diamond Jubilee; Rostand, *Cyrano de Bergerac*

1898 French scientists Pierre and Marie Curie discover radioactive element radium; Spanish-American War

1901 Queen Victoria dies

In the age of Queen Victoria the British people's long struggle for personal liberty was accomplished and democratic government became fully entrenched. The monarchy, which had been established in the late medieval period, was now headed by a symbol of the unity of the empire rather than an active ruler. The aristocracy became a mere remnant of a faded social hierarchy. The House of Commons was now the center of political power in Great Britain. Parliament passed a series of electoral reform bills, entitling the men of the nation to choose their leaders and representatives for themselves.

THE AGE OF FREEDOM

The Victorian Age is remarkable not only for the growth of democracy after the first Reform Bill of 1832; it also saw rapid developments in the arts and education, important mechanical inventions, and immense advancements in scientific knowledge.

The Victorian Age was a period of comparative peace. The British Empire reached around the world, and colonial holdings enriched the mother country. Ambitious sons of the middle-class went to India and brought home fortunes. The dominance of middle-class values meant that the English people desired domestic peace and stability rather than the glory of conquest. Also, the public began to realize that it was the common people who endured the sacrifices of war while the privileged classes reaped the financial rewards.

The spread of democracy also promoted more education for the working class, more tolerance of religious differences, and a general awareness of the need for social reform. Novelists whose works portrayed life among the poor helped develop the social conscience of their middle-class readers. Roman Catholics had been given full political rights in 1829. Four years later the slave trade was made illegal. Also in the 1830s, the public awoke to the fact that multitudes of men, women, and children who worked in mines and factories were victims of a terrible form of industrial slavery. The labor movement and unionism slowly began to develop in response to economic exploitation. In 1882 the Second Married Women's Property Act gave women a measure of economic independence from their husbands. At the same time rapid progress in science and technology began to make labor less burdensome. In mechanical looms and railroads, in gas-lights and electrical goods, power was being put to work for human convenience.

VICTORIAN LITERATURE

In literature, the excitement of the romantic revolution in poetry began to dissipate. By the 1830s Wordsworth had written all his best work. Blake, Burns, Coleridge, Byron, Shelley, and Keats were all dead, and they began to be replaced by their poetic disciples—Alfred, Lord Tennyson; Elizabeth Barrett; and Robert Browning. A new era of vigorous prose writers rose in response to the growing middle-class readership. Dickens, Thackeray, Carlyle, and Ruskin helped shape the tastes and ideas of that class, even as Arnold dismissed its members as "Philistines" who were oblivious to "the best." Periodicals were abundant, representing every variety of intellectual and political position, and many literary figures began their careers as contributors to journalistic and literary reviews. More people read more kinds of publications than ever before.

Paradoxically, in this age of liberation and expansion, social and political reforms existed alongside growing disillusionment with the power of religion to guide and console the individual. New scientific advances seemed to undermine faith. Geologists found that the earth was much older and had undergone more drastic changes than biblical history would indicate. Darwin caused religious turmoil by explaining the origins of humankind in a non-Christian context. One theme that pervades Victorian poetry is the loss of faith and the struggle with spiritual doubt. At Oxford some students reacted by forming a conservative religious movement that took them into Anglo-Catholicism and greater reliance on church authority. Other students lost faith entirely and left the universities. Arnold saw great literature as a substitute for the truth of religion. It was an uncomfortable age for the religious intellectual.

Victorian Novelists

While the romantic period was dominated by lyricists, both in poetry and prose, the novel, which had developed in the mid-eighteenth century, became the dominant literary form of the Victorian Age. In these extended prose fictions, the Victorian writer was able to explore the complex and dynamic relationship between the individual, growing from childhood to find his or her place in the adult world, and society, full of social and economic inequities, snobbery, and oppression caused by an exploitative economy.

In the social novel of this era, Thackeray, Dickens, Eliot, and the Brontë sisters satirized the hypocrisies they saw in British social life and evoked pathos, if not tragedy, in the lives of their central characters, the men and women overwhelmed by false and cruel social institutions. Great Britain had grown to be the world's premier power in trade and commerce, but things were not well at home. The novelists pointed out, directly and indirectly, the folly and the suffering of the people. Even though the standard novel concluded with "the obligatory happy ending," the novelists did not find solutions to the social ills that they observed. To the reader of today, such happy endings, while satisfying in a formal way, often seem forced or artificial. But the Victorian reading public tended to get what it wanted from its novelists. Until the gloomy novels of Thomas Hardy broke this mold, Victorian novels affirmed the possibility of private virtue and pleasure in a cold and corrupt world. The marvelous comic characters of this era are perhaps why the great Victorian novels are still read with relish today.

The Victorian Novel Form

The Victorian novel described everyday life. The majority of its readers, and a significant proportion of its writers, were women. Middle-class women had the leisure time for reading and they could afford books, or, if they could not, the local circulating library made books available at a modest fee. Because authors understood that many of their readers were women, they tended to impose a self-censorship in the area of sexual relationships. The general prudery of Victorian society did not allow for frank discussion of sexual desires or behavior, even though courtships and domestic situations were at the center of most stories.

MULTIVOLUMES AND SERIALIZATION

Novels were long in the Victorian Age. Intended to occupy hours of leisure, they were most often published in multiple volumes.

Multivolumes. The most frequently used multivolume format was the "three-decker"—that is, three separate volumes of about 200 pages each.

Serialization. In the 1840s serial publication became popular. Novels were published in monthly installments, either as separate slim volumes or as serial periodicals containing other materials. There were usually eighteen installments. This meant that the novelist could still be writing the last chapters of a novel while the public was already reading earlier chapters. The writer could adjust his or her emphasis or could even alter the plot to respond to public reaction to the earlier chapters. Even such a gifted novelist as Charles Dickens was known to change a novel's ending to meet readers' expectations.

Major Novelists

The major novelists of the early Victorian Age were Thackeray, Charlotte and Emily Brontë, and the young Dickens. Dickens was still writing in the mid-Victorian era, along with George Eliot. The last decade of the nineteenth century was dominated by Hardy and, to a lesser extent, George Meredith. What distinguishes these great novelists from their contemporaries is the psychological depth of their central characters. Although social conditions have changed and restrictions are fewer, the characters' struggles to realize their identities and to maintain integrity in a hostile and repressive world make them real and appealing to modern readers.

WILLIAM MAKEPEACE THACKERAY (1811–1863)

Thackeray's father was one of the many middle-class English civil servants who went to India to administer the Indian Empire under the control of the East India Company. Thackeray, who had been born in Calcutta, returned to England after the death of his father. When his mother remarried, Thackeray was sent to Charterhouse School and later to Cambridge University, which he left without taking a degree. He traveled to France and Germany, where he studied art. Thackeray's father had left him an adequate inheritance, but when he came of age and took possession of the small fortune, he gambled some of it away and lost the remainder in a bank failure. In order to earn his living, Thackeray turned to illustrating and writing for journals, and later to writing novels.

Vanity Fair. Thackeray's first major novel was his greatest. *Vanity Fair* (1847–1848), written in monthly installments, is a panoramic survey of the state of English society during the era of the Napoleonic Wars. This was the period just after Thackeray's birth, and thus the book was an "historical" novel of recent but not contemporary events. In this wide-ranging book Thackeray presents scenes of the battlefield, high society, the English countryside, and the capitals of Europe.

His other major novels were *Pendennis* (1848–1850), *The History of Henry Esmond* (1852), and *The Newcomes* (1853–1855). Thackeray also continued to write for magazines, especially the humor magazine *Punch*. He also gave lectures on literature and history.

CHARLES DICKENS (1812–1870)

The imprisonment for debt of Charles Dickens's father and his own child labor gave him both a driving ambition to rise out of poverty and a sympathetic understanding of the lives of the poor. As a child he helped support his family by pasting labels on bottles, working from dawn to dark for a few pennies. A small legacy enabled his father to leave prison and Dickens to attend Wellington House Academy. When only fifteen, Dickens left the school and again went to work, this time as an office boy. He later became a parliamentary reporter and then a writer of light "sketches" of contemporary life for magazines.

Early Novels. His early success with the comic *Pickwick Papers* (1836) established Dickens as a popular humorist. The following year he published *Oliver Twist*, the most autobiographical of his novels. Dickens published continuously from his mid-twenties until his death at fifty-eight. His many novels were released in monthly installments. He also edited several periodicals, finally founding his own weekly, *Household Words*.

Besides *Oliver Twist*, Dickens's early novels include *Nicholas Nickleby* (1838–1839), *The Old Curiosity Shop* (1840–1841), and *Barnaby Rudge* (1841), stories of great humor that feature neglected or orphaned children. His classic Christmas book, *A Christmas Carol* (1843), was the first of an annual series of Christmas books.

Mature Novels. The more mature novels of Dickens include *David Copperfield* (1849–1850), *Bleak House* (1852–1853), *Hard Times* (1854), *A Tale of Two Cities* (1859), and *Great Expectations* (1860–1861). In these complex and somber tales Dickens exposed the cruelty and hypocrisy of public institutions and economic arrangements that indulged the rich and exploited the poor. But Dickens also created subtle and haunting central characters, young men whose search for identity had universal relevance. Dickens is generally considered less successful in developing convincing female characters; these tend to be either too good or too dreadful to be true.

In middle age Dickens undertook tours in England and the United States, where he read aloud passages from his novels. He also involved himself in amateur theatrical performances, an interest that led to his acquaintance with the young actress Ellen Ternan, with whom he had a long affair. (His marriage had deteriorated.) Dickens became exhausted after his second American tour. He died in 1870, leaving one novel, *Edwin Drood*, unfinished.

CHARLOTTE BRONTË (1816–1855)

Daughter of a rural clergyman, Brontë grew up in a household of creative, imaginative siblings who created fictional worlds and wrote poetry as part of their childhood games. Using the pen names Currer, Ellis, and Acton Bell, three of the sisters, Charlotte, Emily, and Anne Brontë, published a volume of their poems in 1846.

Charlotte attended a school for clergymen's daughters and later traveled to Brussels to study French. She worked as a governess and as a teacher. Her first novel, *The Professor*, was based on her stay in Brussels; it was not published during her lifetime.

Jane Eyre. *Jane Eyre* (1847), Brontë's second novel, reflected some of her hardships at school. It was her greatest popular success, although it was criticized for "coarseness."

Its heroine is a small and plain girl who fights to maintain her integrity against the pressures and temptations of suitors who offer her unacceptable marriages. *Jane Eyre* violates the conventions of the courtship plot as well as the more restrictive moralism of Victorian fiction.

In 1849 Brontë completed and published *Shirley*, a novel dealing with the effects of industrialization and wartime economic policy on the lives of two young women, one independent and one more traditional. Brontë's final novel, *Villette*, was a new treatment of her Brussels experience. Its plot is based on the frustrations of a love opposed by barriers of nationality, religion, and family prejudices.

By this time Brontë's sisters, Emily and Anne, had died. At the age of thirty-eight she married her father's curate. She died within a year, having suffered poor health since her school days.

Charlotte Brontë's novels are intensely studied by modern feminist critics. The Victorian poet Matthew Arnold's comment that Brontë's mind contained "nothing but hunger, rebellion, and rage" was considered negative then, but is now seen by some as an acknowledgment of her strength.

EMILY BRONTË (1818–1848)

A younger sister of Charlotte, Emily Brontë was educated mostly at home. Her personality was less aggressive than Charlotte's, and she was more attached to the local scenery of the Yorkshire moors. Like Charlotte, Emily worked as a governess and studied French in Brussels.

Wuthering Heights. Emily Brontë's one great novel, *Wuthering Heights*, was published in 1847. Its first readers were baffled by the strange, near-Gothic setting and the gloomy, violent psychology of the major characters. But during the early twentieth century the novel began to be praised for its insightful treatment of passion and obsession. Emily Brontë did not live to write another novel. Her sister Charlotte republished *Wuthering Heights* with an explanatory preface in 1855.

GEORGE ELIOT (1819–1880)

Mary Ann Evans is still referred to by her pen name, George Eliot. Eliot, who did not begin to write until she was nearly forty years of age, became the most important living English novelist of the decade between 1870 and 1880.

The daughter of an estate agent in Warwickshire, Eliot was an avid student from her youth. She is often called the most intellectual of the English novelists. During her lifetime Eliot underwent distinct shifts in her religious outlook, ranging from evangelical dissent to later agnosticism. However, worthy clergymen and the benign influence of faith in ordinary lives are found frequently in her fiction.

Eliot's early work as a translator led her to the study of German religious works of questioning. Through these translations she became an assistant editor of the important *Westminster Review* and enjoyed the friendship of leading intellectuals. Among these was George Henry Lewes. Although Lewes was separated from his wife, he was not able to divorce. In spite of this, Eliot chose to live with him as his wife, which was entirely against the social rules of Victorian society. Lewes was a catalyst to Eliot's career; he encouraged her to write fiction. She started with short sketches for a magazine. The sketches were then republished in a collection called *Scenes of Clerical Life*. Eliot's first full-length novel was *Adam Bede* (1859). It was a great success. The next year she wrote her most autobiographical novel, *The Mill on the Floss*.

Middlemarch. Eliot's major work is *Middlemarch*, a comprehensive study of an English village in the 1830s. Conventional society does not allow the book's heroine, Dorothea, to undertake some great beneficial work.

Eliot produced four other substantial novels. She combined a humorous and affectionate treatment of rural and small-town characters with a deep analysis of major characters who aspire to more than the mediocre roles that society offers.

In 1878 Lewes died and Eliot's career declined. In 1880, at the age of sixty, she married an old friend, John W. Cross. She died later that same year.

THOMAS HARDY (1840–1928)

The last of the great Victorian novelists, Hardy lived well into the twentieth century. Most of his major works of fiction were written in the 1880s and 1890s.

Hardy was born in Dorset, in southwest England. The area, Wessex, and the city of Dorchester became the setting for his novels. Hardy's father, a stonemason, apprenticed the boy to an architect and later sent him to London for further study. Hardy returned to Dorset to follow a career in architecture. He soon fell in love, first with a cousin and later with the young relative of one of his clients. About this time he began to write fiction. His fourth novel, *Far from the Madding Crowd* (1874), was successful enough to allow Hardy to marry and to give up architecture. His unhappy marriage did not prevent him from being a prolific writer. He turned out more than a dozen novels in the next twenty years, as well as poetry and collections of short stories.

Major Novels. The most widely read of Hardy's novels are *The Return of the Native* (1878), *The Mayor of Casterbridge* (1886), *Tess of the D'Urbervilles* (1891), and *Jude the Obscure* (1896). Critics complained of the immorality of the last two (each one contains men and women living together out of wedlock). Disgusted by the restraints of Victorian conventions, Hardy decided to write no more novels. Subsequently he wrote poetry instead.

However, Hardy's reputation as a novelist grew during the last decades of his life, and his poetry was relatively neglected. It is mostly as a novelist that Hardy is read today. His novels share a pessimistic view of the human condition. Nature is indifferent to a person's desires and efforts; perverse luck is as important as individual character in determining one's fate. The bitter ironies of fruitless efforts and lost affections give an ironic and tragic tone to Hardy's novels, making them unlike mainstream Victorian novels with their hopeful conclusions.

While many novelists emerged during Victoria's long reign, most of them do not fit into easily defined categories. Many of them were immensely popular in their day but have since been entirely forgotten.

The age of Victoria was the great age of the British middle class. Having consolidated their political power at home through voting reform, they financed new industrial growth and power by the development of new enterprises at home and the expansion of the British Empire abroad. The literary form most responsive to the tastes of the middle class, the social novel, had its greatest period of popularity. Women were avid readers and, increasingly, writers of fiction and poetry. Among poets, the heritage of the creative power generated by the romantic movement continued to influence and inspire, but a new moral seriousness, an earnestness about social and philosophical issues, gave Victorian poetry a different flavor, less spontaneous and less intimate. Social questions and the great debates raised by Darwin's new theories of man made history and the essay an important part of the literary output of this period, and toward the end of the century, some of these issues began to emerge in the new drama of social problems.

Selected Readings

Bowyer, John Wilson, and John Lee Brooks, eds. *The Victorian Age: Prose, Poetry, and Drama.* New York: Crofts, 1938.

Leavis, F. R., and Q. D. Leavis. *Dickens: The Novelist.* New York: Pantheon, 1979.

Mitchell, Sally, ed. *Victorian Britain: An Encyclopedia.* New York: Garland, 1988.

Pierce, Gilbert A. *The Dickens Dictionary: A Key to the Characters and Principal Incidents in the Tales of Charles Dickens.* London: Chapman, 1878.

Schneewind, J. B. *Backgrounds of English Victorian Literature.* New York: Random House, 1970.

Seaman, L. C. B. *Victorian England: Aspects of English and Imperial History, 1837–1901.* London: Methuen, 1973.

Thompson, F. M. L. *The Rise of Respectable Society: A Social History of Victorian Britain, 1830–1900.* Cambridge: Harvard University Press, 1988.

Young, G. M. *Victorian England: Portrait of an Age.* London: Oxford University Press, 1977.

8

Early Victorian Essayists

1837–1901 Queen Victoria reigns

1839 Carlyle, *Chartism*

1841 Carlyle, *On Heroes and Hero-Worship*, and *The Heroic in History* published; Newman, *Tract 90*

1843 Carlyle, pamphlets, *Past and Present*; Mill, *System of Logic*

1843–1855 Macaulay, *Critical and Historical Essays*

1845 Carlyle, *The Letters and Speeches of Oliver Cromwell*; Newman becomes Roman Catholic; Irish potato famine initiates massive emigration to the United States; Kierkegaard, *Fear and Trembling*

1848 The Pre-Raphaelite Brotherhood founded

1849 Macaulay, *History of England from the Ascension of James the Second*, vols. I and II; Thoreau, American essayist, *On Civil Disobedience*

1850 Carlyle, *Latter-Day Pamphlets*

1851 Spencer, *Treatise on Education*

1852 Newman, *The Idea of a University*; Stowe, *Uncle Tom's Cabin*

1853–1861 De Quincey, *Collected Essays*

1854 Newman appointed rector, Catholic University, Dublin, Ireland

1854–1856 Crimean War

1855 Lewes, *Life of Goethe*; *Daily Telegraph* newspaper founded

1857 Divorce courts established

1858–1865 Carlyle, *The History of Friedrich II of Prussia, Called Frederick the Great*

1859 Mill, *On Liberty*; Darwin, *Origin of Species*

1863 Huxley, *Man's Place in Nature*

1864–1876 Newman, *Apologia Pro Vita Sua* and poetry

1865 Carlyle, Lord Rector of Edinburgh University; Mill elected to Parliament, aligned with radicals he urged extension of suffrage to women

1867 Second Reform Act passed; Dominion of Canada established

1869 Mill, *On the Subjection of Women*

1870 First Married Women's Property Act

1871 Darwin, *The Descent of Man*; religious tests for university teachers ended

1873 Mill, *Autobiography* published posthumously

1880–1881 First Anglo-Boer War

During the Victorian Age every educated man or woman felt the pressures of social change that led to a reexamination of customs and institutions, of power and authority, and of the nature of the individual. Talented prose writers defined and discussed these issues in essays, lectures, tracts, and treatises. But writers went beyond intellectual analysis; they revealed their own passions and fears. Each writer had a highly individual—perhaps even eccentric—style of discourse. Writers' personalities colored their prose. They wrote autobiographically, exploring their own feelings and their own crises of belief.

VICTORIAN PROSE WRITERS

Rich and intense expository prose is best exemplified by Thomas Carlyle, Cardinal Newman, and John Stuart Mill. These men felt an urgent need to help England solve its problems and relieve the distresses of its people.

Thomas Carlyle (1795–1881)

Carlyle rose from a modest background to become one of the most influential thinkers of the Victorian period. His father, a stonemason, was a believer in the Scottish-Calvinist ethic of hard work. A staunch member of the Presbyterian church, he sent his son Thomas to school to become a minister. But while at the University of Edinburgh, Carlyle's religious faith was shaken by his study of the great rational philosophers of the eighteenth century. He abandoned the ministry for teaching, tutoring, the study of law, and then writing. He did not write like other rationalists, however. Carlyle believed that English society was in chaos partly because of an excessively analytical, "mechanical" treatment of its social problems. In place of his former traditional Christian beliefs, Carlyle developed a faith in the vital force of human energy.

He sought a new spiritual approach to improving the human condition. Eventually he came to feel that only the leadership of great men, "heroes," could effectively revitalize society. This reliance on the leadership of a strong individual makes Carlyle's social commentary antidemocratic and, in the view of some critics, fascistic.

But Carlyle was a great favorite with the young people of the mid-Victorian years. He was a popular lecturer and a spellbinding conversationalist. He was called "the sage of Chelsea," not because he expounded any coherent philosophical system but because he seemed to perceive the faults of England with great insight and penetration. He was a major influence in bringing the ideas of the German romantics, the transcendentalists, to England. He helped forge an idea of progress and a spirit of hope that was heartening and energizing.

CHARACTERISTICS

Given new books of philosophy to evaluate for the *Edinburgh Review*, Carlyle used the occasion to write about society's ills. In this early essay Carlyle tries some ideas that he will more fully develop in *Sartor Resartus*.

Carlyle's Insights. Pointing out that a healthy society does not question itself but merely works, Carlyle sees the current tendency to analyze social ills as a sign of spiritual sickness. In a self-conscious society, religion is mechanical rather than vital, literature descends into mere reviewing, and philosophy spreads doubt like a disease. Young people do not feel called to action by high ideals. Those who believe that life should be based on more than mere satisfaction of appetites can either try to live by the worn-out symbols of the past or they can say no to the past and seek out a new idea of the divine.

Carlyle names many of his contemporaries who are unable to look past old ways into the new. He sees the necessity of passing through an era of doubt and skepticism to accomplish radical change, but he feels that humankind is advancing. Carlyle believes in progress even though he cannot predict what the new condition of society will be. He offers hope for the future and rallies the spirits of his readers to move forward in "heroic joy."

SARTOR RESARTUS: THE LIFE AND OPINIONS OF HERR TEUFELSDRÖCKH

This book is central to Carlyle's career. Its title means "The Tailor Retailored," alluding to the metaphor of clothes that is used throughout the book. *Sartor Resartus* is at once a satire and an autobiography.

Part 1. In the first part the philosopher Teufelsdröckh, whose German name translates as "devil's dung," expounds the idea that all the outward forms and institutions of human life are merely clothes (appearances), and as clothes they become worn and threadbare. They must therefore be changed from time to time. This Clothes Philosophy distinguishes between the *reality* that is the permanent spiritual vitality of nature and human beings and the *appearances* that conceal or disguise this reality, causing error and doubt. Here Carlyle is clearly influenced by such German thinkers as Kant and Goethe.

Part 2. In the second part Teufelsdröckh is referred to as The Wanderer. This part alludes to Carlyle's loss of faith, his suffering and doubt, and his final spiritual affirmation.

The section titled "The Everlasting No" is the most crucial one in part 2. Here the sick and depressed Wanderer overcomes his chronic fear and becomes defiant. One day while walking in the street he asks himself, "What art thou afraid of?" His reply is that he will defy Death and the Devil; he will stand up and declare himself free. From that moment he feels a "Spiritual New-birth."

In "Center of Indifference" the Wanderer considers the nature of heroes, great men who put ideas into practice. He realizes that the invention of guns makes all men equally "tall" and concludes that mere physical power is not decisive: "savage Animalism is nothing; inventive Spiritualism is all." Thus he begins to free himself from a sense of limitation.

In "The Everlasting Yea," Teufelsdröckh, having withstood the temptations of the devil, awakens to "a new heaven and a new earth." He realizes that nature is not a machine but is the clothes, the appearance, of God. He now can love his fellow man as a brother. He solves the problem of the origin of evil by rejecting the idea that people deserve to be happy. Saying "close thy Byron; open thy Goethe," Teufelsdröckh reaches a higher plane than happiness; it is the love not of pleasure but of God. "This is the Everlasting Yea," an assent to act as one embodiment of the spirit of the Universe. These three sections narrate, insofar as a spiritual conversion and revelation can be narrated, the history of Carlyle's own religious experience.

Part 3. In a final section, "Natural Supernaturalism," Carlyle develops the idea that miracles are not violations of the "Laws of Nature." We see only very shallowly into nature's laws. Time and space are appearances that veil nature from our perception. Every act we can perform is in this sense a miracle, since we do not fully understand how we do it. Each one of us at birth takes on an appearance to cover the spirit. At death we lay aside that appearance. But where the spirit comes from and where it goes is God's mystery.

Carlyle's Style. The style of *Sartor Resartus* is dense and even confusing. The fictional "Editor" is sorting through a bag of papers left by the philosopher Teufelsdröckh, also called the Wanderer. Thus there are two speakers, one relatively objective and analytical; and the other, whose words are enclosed in quotation marks, passionate either in scorn or exaltation.

In keeping with the Germanic personality of the philosopher, the text is full of made-up compound words, such a "Profit-and-loss Philosophy" and "Celestial Bed." Carlyle invents terms such as *Ideopraxist*, a word analogous to *ideologist*.

Allusions to philosophical thought abound; Carlyle expects his readers to be familiar with contemporary schools of philosophy. But the wit and eccentric imagery of Carlyle make his writing stimulating even to those who are not able to grasp every allusion.

THE FRENCH REVOLUTION

In this three-volume work, Carlyle has written an unusual history of France from the death of Louis XV to the rise of Napoleon. Carlyle did prodigious research among the documents of that revolution, but he did not write in the conventional style of a history. Using the present tense, he creates a contemporary character, a revolutionary or Patriot, to be the speaker, and thus dramatizes the events. We seem to be reading a first-person, eyewitness account.

Carlyle's facts are not always precise, but he creates exciting and horrible descriptions of the violence and agony of mob actions, of hysterical trials and capricious judgments, of great bloodshed, of tender farewells among the doomed royal family.

Carlyle sees the circumstances that set the revolution in motion as the ultimate result of centuries of tyranny, yet he shows sympathy and compassion for the aristocrats who were caught at the crucial historical moment and perished by the thousands. This history established Carlyle's reputation as a colorful, spellbinding writer and it provided some of the background for Dickens's great novel of the French Revolution, *A Tale of Two Cities*.

PAST AND PRESENT

In response to the severe economic conditions of 1843, with widespread unemployment, hunger, and social disorder, Carlyle wrote this energetic analysis of the causes and possible remedies. He saw workers alienated from their work in the isolation of individual freedom, the "cold universal lais-sez-faire" in which the poor worker and his family became as exploitative and inhuman to each other as the society was to them. He cited the example of parents killing their own children for the burial money.

Looking into the past, Carlyle saw that in the medieval, feudal world, the rulers, the aristocracies, had functioned to create a sense of order and belonging wherein each man, high or low, had a feeling of his place and his purpose. But now the aristocracy had become useless; with no battles to fight, they were preoccupied with the trivia of protecting their prerogatives and their hunting rights. The new aristocracy, which would arise from among the industrialists, were the "Captains of Industry." Such men as could set aside mere monetary accumulation could become the leaders which the poor workers needed. The new "captains" would find a way to organize the world of work, giving the laborer once again a sense of belonging.

Carlyle calls upon these men to take a larger vision of their role, to go beyond concerns of individual wealth to create a new social order based on the organization of industrial labor in a more humane and less alienated way. If this leadership is not undertaken, Carlyle predicts a second "French Revolution"—that is, a crisis of wild and poorly led rebellion leading to chaos. Carlyle believed in the need for strong individuals, "heroes," to take hold of dynamic historical developments and to mold them into well-functioning social institutions. Governments cannot lead; they only reflect the mood of the people. Superior men must lead, as they had done in the past. Only when such men emerge will the future take shape.

John Henry Cardinal Newman (1801–1890)

Newman, the son of a London banker, spent his life in various academic and church positions.

Newman was a leader of the Oxford Movement, a group of young men centered at Oxford University who reacted against the liberalism of most Church of England thinkers. The Oxford Movement saw supernatural dogma and religious ritual as the antidotes to excessive rationalism and the conventional moralism of the established church. These men were Anglo-Catholics, believing that the authentic Catholic church was not the one centered in Rome but was the Anglican church or Church of England in its original medieval form. Although these conservatives shared with the romanticists a distrust of reason as the way to truth, unlike them they stressed authority rather than individual free expression.

Newman and his group were also called "tractarians" after *Tracts for the Times,* which they published from time to time during the 1830s. (Tracts are extended essays in pamphlet form put forth to argue or persuade readers to a position.)

As an Anglican clergyman at St. Mary's, Oxford, Newman was a powerful spokesman for the Oxford Movement, but his position was so extreme as to provoke opposition from the church authorities. In 1843 he resigned, and two years later he surprised his followers by joining the Roman Catholic church. He traveled to Rome and was ordained as a priest. In 1854 Newman was appointed rector of the Catholic University in Dublin, Ireland, where he wrote and lectured on education. He wrote his book *The Idea of a University* (1852) after his retirement. Newman was provoked to write a spiritual autobiography titled *Apologia Pro Vita Sua* by an attack on his integrity by Charles Kingsley.

Newman's later years were spent as a priest in Birmingham, England. In 1879 he was made a cardinal of the Roman Catholic church. Newman was a prolific writer, publishing not only tracts, sermons, and lectures, but also poetry, two novels, and a wide range of miscellaneous prose.

THE IDEA OF A UNIVERSITY

This book is a compilation of the lectures or discourses Newman prepared as rector of the Catholic University at Dublin, a newly founded school. It is a defense of liberal education against demands that education be practical or focused on professional training. With compelling logic, Newman defended liberal knowledge as a desirable end in itself, saying that "cultivation of the mind is surely worth seeking for its own sake." Newman's thought is lofty and abstract: "Knowledge is power."

In Discourse Seven, Newman claims that the general training of the mind disciplines it, enabling it to distinguish truth from falsehood. Therefore, the liberally educated mind can apply its abilities to practical tasks as well. It becomes a useful tool, an "instrument of good," and like other good things, it will spread its good influence around. Newman makes the analogy of bodily health and a cultured mind. Just as we do not ask what use it is to be healthy, because the benefit of good health is obvious, so we should not ask what use it is to be liberally educated, because the benefits of such mental training are good in themselves. The man of cultivated mind becomes a good citizen, a useful member of society. He may not be a great genius but he will help raise the general level of his society. He will "see things as they are" and be able to mingle with and understand others from various social levels. This gift of mind that makes him a useful member of society is also a private satisfaction and pleasure.

APOLOGIA PRO VITA SUA

A spiritual leader who changes his position, abandoning his followers for a new loyalty, is apt to be criticized for lack of sincerity. Newman defended his decision to become a Roman Catholic by explaining the history of his beliefs in this autobiographical work.

In the third chapter Newman cites the controversy provoked by his Tract 90 in 1841. At that time Newman was sure of the correctness of his Anglo-Catholic position. But having reached the height of his logical arguments, Newman saw that the same arguments could justify a belief in the Roman church.

In describing his position, Newman starts with the premise of God's existence. He sees that the world is out of step with God and that outside the Catholic church all are tending toward atheism. He sees the establishment of the Roman church as God's way of countering the "suicidal excess" of people's rationalism. The infallibility of the Roman Catholic church is a necessary restraint to the freedom of thought that leads to skepticism. Only such a church could adequately counteract the intense evil that has possessed humankind.

Newman's Appeal. What was attractive about Newman's *Apologia*, even for those who could not agree, was the intense passion of his arguments, his clever and insightful statements, and his profound sincerity. These qualities gained sympathy for his spiritual struggle, if not for his beliefs.

John Stuart Mill (1806–1873)

Mill's father, James, and the philosopher Jeremy Bentham were the founders of utilitarianism, a belief in the arrangement of social and economic institutions to benefit the greatest number of people.

As a boy John Stuart Mill was rigorously educated at home under his father's guidance. He was a prodigy in languages, mathematics, and economics, but the more humanistic side of his education was neglected. While still a young man, Mill had an emotional crisis, a breakdown, from which he recovered by turning to the poetry of Wordsworth, among others.

Mill saw that his education had neglected the necessary cultivation of the emotions.

In 1831 he met Harriet Taylor, a married woman, with whom he fell in love. He discussed his ideas with her and felt that she inspired him. Twenty years later, when she became a widow, they married. Meanwhile, Mill worked for the East India Company and wrote many works on history and political and economic theory.

John Stuart Mill was an influential spokesman not only because of the forceful, plain style of his arguments, but also because of the breadth of his sympathies. He defended the individual against the tyranny of the political system. One of the most liberal thinkers of his day, he defended free speech and was an advocate of full political rights for women.

Late in life Mill became rector of St. Andrews University. His *Autobiography* (1873) was an account of his intellectual development and his moral positions throughout a long life of active participation in the growth of the social philosophy of his era.

"WHAT IS POETRY?"

In this early essay Mill attempts to define poetry, which he admits is undefinable. He rejects the superficial definition based on metrical form; his concept of poetry is broader, encompassing some kinds of art and music as well as some prose writings. Mill defines the essential quality that makes a work of art poetic by contrasting poetry and eloquence. Both are expressions of feeling, but eloquence addresses itself to an audience, a public, while poetry seems to be the private meditations of the past, confessing to itself and overheard by the reader. Therefore, "all poetry is of the nature of soliloquy." When the poet turns from introspection to address the world, his poetry becomes eloquence. Mill then uses the criteria of poetry and eloquence to evaluate certain great works of music and painting. He finds Mozart more poetic and Rossini more eloquent. Similarly, among painters, Rubens is merely eloquent while Raphael is poetic. Even epic poetry is not consistently poetic. As mere narrative, it is not poetry at all, but it may contain passages of poetry.

ON LIBERTY

In 1859 Mill published *On Liberty*, in which he argues that the individual should have as much personal freedom of thought and action as is consistent with the liberty of other individuals. The state has no right to interfere with the liberty of an individual except to protect other individuals or society as a whole. Mill saw that in a democratic society the majority would tend to enforce conformity by tyrannizing the minority.

In the third chapter Mill points out the values of individuality. While no one can be free of the influences of society, and while everyone should be taught to benefit from the experiences of others, the individual reaches full potential only by evaluating customs and the teachings of experience in relationship to his or her own needs and feelings. The individual expresses human faculties by making choices. He or she should exercise not only intellect but also feelings, impulses, or desires. Only then does he or she have "character." Mill saw his own age as a time of too much restriction and conformity. He felt that obedience and duty were valued more than self-assertion and self-development. He called for the development of individ-uality because society can learn only from the person who does not conform. The general tendency of a mature society is toward mediocrity; therefore, the mature society should be alert to the energy and noble ideas that exceptional individuals can provide. In Western society Mill saw business as the only outlet for creative energy. He contrasted it to Eastern culture, where, he said, custom had become so despotic as to make the culture stagnant. He pointed to China as an example of the kind of tyranny of conformity that Europe should avoid.

"THE SUBJECTION OF WOMEN"

Mill's attitudes about the position of women in European society were shaped by his long friendship and finally his marriage with Harriet Taylor, who shared many of his interests. Mill did not write this essay until 1861, three years after Harriet's death, but he had developed many of its ideas in collaboration with her. The document became important to the American women's rights movement. Consistent with his belief in the greatest practical freedom for every individual, Mill decided that the "legal subordination of one sex to the other . . . is wrong in itself, and . . . one of the chief hindrances to human improvement." He argues on logical grounds that there is no inherent justification for this subordination, and he attacks the idea that it is "natural" for women to be subject to men. What is merely customary always seems natural to those who enjoy its benefits. Making analogies to slavery in ancient Greece and in the southern United States, Mill shows how the universal subjection of women deprives us of any other experience against which to judge the inherent qualities or abilities of women. Had there been a society in which men and women were legally and socially equal, then one could determine by experience the "natural" tendencies of women. But this experience is not available for analysis. Mill points out that women do complain and protest; in the Victorian Age, more women were writing than in any previous time and place. Most women, however, have been educated to accept, or to act as if they accept, their subordinate roles. Men have little access to what women really think and feel. A man usually knows well only one woman, his wife, but since he has authority over her, he cannot expect that she will show him all her thoughts.

Mill dismisses the idea that if women were liberated they would neglect their natural duties as wives and mothers, arguing that if these roles are "natural," women will continue to fulfill them. He thinks that men are afraid to give women freedom of choice because marriage may not be an attractive choice if other options are available. But gradually, as women read more and express themselves more openly, Mill foresees that they will become increasingly free if social institutions do not prohibit them from expressing their true sentiments.

AUTOBIOGRAPHY OF JOHN STUART MILL

The main interest of Mill's autobiography lies in his description of his early education based on utilitarian principles, which ignored the emotions and the imagination in favor of the intellect. Mill tells of his emotional crisis at the age of twenty-one, when, apparently successful, he lost his sense of purpose and experienced a transformation of character. As a dedicated social reformer, Mill had felt happiness in the anticipation of good effects from his efforts. But there came a time when he found that he did not really expect any "great joy and happiness" if his goals should be achieved. He fell into a depression and had no one to whom he could confide his hopelessness. In analyzing his own condition, Mill realized that the very habits of analysis in which he was so well trained had tended to weaken his feelings, to undermine his capacity for pleasure. But understanding this did not relieve his melancholy. He felt he could not go on living. Then one day, while reading the *Memoirs* of Marmontel, Mill was moved to tears by a pathetic passage. He was relieved to discover that he was not without feeling. He subsequently came to believe that the well-being of the individual requires not only intellectual cultivation but also "cultivation of the feelings." That is, he generalized from his own condition and assumed that similar periods of depression must be experienced by many others. About two years after Mill's first bout of depression, he discovered in some of the poetry of Wordsworth a pleasure that was "medicine for [his] state of mind." First, he enjoyed Wordsworth's treatment of natural scenery and simple objects of rural life. But more important, Mill felt the joy caused by beauty that Wordsworth describes. Mill especially responded to "Ode: Intimations of Immortality," in which Wordsworth describes his youthful joy and other compensating pleasure as an adult. Mill saw Wordsworth's experience as similar to his own. He remarks that Wordsworth is not one of the great poets but that he is a good poet for "unpoetical natures" like himself.

The essayists of the early Victorian period were men caught up in a time of change. Although they interpreted this change as progress, they nevertheless had doubts and fears about where the changes would lead. They tried to influence public opinion, to raise fundamental questions about the role of the state and the freedom of the individual. They were serious, rigorous thinkers, energetic in their application of logic. Each man also had a strong personal bent that showed itself in an idiosyncratic style. Even readers who could not share the values of Carlyle, Newman, or Mill were still impressed by these writers' sincerity. For all their logic, they also revealed themselves intimately; they took their readers into the mental arenas where they grappled with difficult and painful ideas. Thus they raised discourse on public issues to the level of art. Unlike novelists, who speak their emotionally charged words through characters, the essayists spoke directly to the reader in passionate tones.

Selected Readings

Campbell, Ian. *Thomas Carlyle*. New York: Scribner's, 1974.

Ellery, John B. *John Stuart Mill*. New York: Twayne, 1964.

Fielding, K. J., and Rodger L. Tarr, eds. *Carlyle Past and Present: A Collection of New Essays*. New York: Barnes, 1976.

Harrold, Charles Frederick. *John Henry Newman: An Expository and Critical Study of His Mind, Thought, and Art*. London: Longmans, 1945.

Ralli, Augustus. *Guide to Carlyle*. London: Allen, 1920.

Ryan, Edwin. *A College Handbook to Newman*. Washington, DC: The Catholic Education Press, 1930.

Schneewind, J. B., ed. *Mill: A Collection of Critical Essays*. Notre Dame, IN: University of Notre Dame Press, 1969.

9

Major Victorian Poets

1827 Alfred and Charles Tennyson, *Poems by Two Brothers*

1830 Tennyson, *Poems Chiefly Lyrical*; Tennyson wins Cambridge University's Chancellor's Medal for his poem "Timbuctoo"

1832 Tennyson, *Poems*; *Penny Magazine* founded, first inexpensive mass-circulation weekly

1833 Browning, *Pauline* published anonymously; Tennyson begins writing *In Memoriam*

1835 Browning, *Paracelsus*

1837 Browning's play *Strafford* has short run

1837–1901 Queen Victoria reigns

1840 Browning, *Sordello*; Queen Victoria marries Albert, who later becomes the Prince Consort

1841 Browning, *Bells and Pomegranates*; *Punch* magazine founded

1842 Tennyson, *Poems* (vols. I and II); Browning, *Dramatic Lyrics*

1843 Wordsworth appointed poet laureate

1844 E. Barrett, *Poems* (vols. I and II) includes poem "Cry of the Children"; Dumas, *The Three Musketeers*

1845 Browning, *Dramatic Romances and Lyrics*

1846 Charlotte, Emily, and Anne Brontë, *Poems*

1847 Tennyson, *The Princess*; Longfellow, *Evangeline*

1849 Arnold, *The Strayed Reveller and Other Poems*

1850 Barrett Browning, *Sonnets from the Portuguese*; Tennyson, *In Memoriam*; Tennyson appointed poet laureate; Hawthorne, *The Scarlet Letter*

1851 Barrett Browning, *Casa Guidi Windows*; Arnold marries and becomes an inspector of schools

1852 Arnold, *Empedocles on Etna and Other Poems*; Browning, "Childe Roland"

1853 Arnold, *Poems*; Tennyson moves to the Isle of Wight

1855 Tennyson, *Maud*; Browning, *Men and Women*; Whitman, *Leaves of Grass*

1856 Barrett Browning, *Aurora Leigh*

1857 Arnold becomes professor of poetry at Oxford, where his famous lectures *On Translating Homer* are given

1859–1886 Tennyson, *Idylls of the King*

1860 Barrett Browning, *Poems Before Congress*

1861 Barrett Browning's *Last Poems* published posthumously; Prince Consort Albert dies, Queen Victoria goes into mourning

1864 Browning, *Dramatis Personae*

1865–1888 Arnold, *Essays in Criticism*

1866 Arnold, *Thyrsis*; Swinburne, *Poems and Ballads*; Dostoevsky, *Crime and Punishment*

1868 Browning, *The Ring and the Book*

1869 Arnold, *Culture and Anarchy*; Suez Canal opens

1871 Arnold, *Friendship's Garland*; Verdi, *Aïda*

1873 Arnold, *Literature and Dogma*

1881 Browning Society established in London

1884 Tennyson accepts peerage and becomes Lord Tennyson

1885 Arnold, *Discourses in America*; Degas, *Woman Bathing*

1888 Arnold dies

1889 Browning, *Asolando*; Tennyson, "Crossing the Bar"; Browning dies

1892 Tennyson dies

The major poets of the Victorian Age were aware of the abundant outpouring of poetry during the first decades of their century. As post-romantics they found the legacy of the romantic poets both stimulating and staggering. Wordsworth had broken new ground, but it was Keats, with his experiments in meter and sound patterns, who provided the greatest challenge. Turning away from the intense self-absorption of the early romantics, Victorian poets spoke with a new energy and earnestness about the conditions of their times, even as they used settings and characters from the past. Their sense of progress was moderated by a feeling of loss, a melancholy longing for simpler times when faith seemed less complicated and duty was clearer. For Tennyson and Browning, the dramatic monologue made possible a more objective, more analytic approach to problems of religion, society, and love. But these poets also produced beautiful lyrics.

Readers found much of Browning's work "difficult" and obscure. The popular voice was that of Tennyson, who succeeded Wordsworth as poet laureate in 1850. In Tennyson's poetry readers found beautiful sounds and images as well as wisdom. Tennyson spoke to their concerns in a calming, enchanting voice.

At the same time, Matthew Arnold was urging his audience to be better. In tones earnest and stimulating yet urbane and tasteful, he assured them of the continuity of their culture and of its importance, even as he called for progress and revitalization.

ALFRED, LORD TENNYSON (1809–1892)

Alfred Tennyson was made a baron solely for his poetry. He was the only English poet to be so honored. He was immensely popular for his ability to capture and articulate the central attitudes and concerns of Victorian society.

His life did not begin auspiciously. Tennyson was one of twelve children of an angry and frequently drunken Anglican clergyman in an obscure village in Lincolnshire. Lacking money for schools, Reverend George Tennyson educated his sons at home, in a household that was dominated by quarrels and resentments. One of Alfred's brothers became insane and another became an opium addict. Alfred Tennyson was sent to Cambridge University, where he found a new, freer existence. Although shy and rustic in manner, at Cambridge he was invited to become one of the "Apostles," a group of young men interested in intellectual conversations. Within the group he found friendship and encouragement. In particular, he formed a firm friendship with Arthur Hallam, who became engaged to one of Tennyson's sisters. In 1831 Tennyson was called home from Cambridge by the death of his father. The next year he and his friend Hallam took a European tour together. In 1833 Hallam died in Vienna, a momentous loss to Tennyson and the occasion for his beginning to write the long and complex elegy *In Memoriam*, which he did not complete until 1850. Meanwhile, his lyric and narrative poetry began to establish his reputation.

In 1836 he became engaged to Emily Sellwood but did not marry her until 1850, by which time he had become comfortably prosperous from his writings. Tennyson's poetry continued to be well received, and he became a kind of British institution.

Tennyson had a huge and powerful build and was somewhat hairy and craggy in appearance. He read his poetry in a deep, melodious voice. Like Wordsworth, Tennyson is generally judged to have written his best poetry early in his career. His technical perfection did not falter, but the ideas and images of later narrative poems tended to be more commonplace and less poetically intense. His poetic output was vast, however, so it is not surprising that it is not all of a uniformly high quality.

"Mariana"

This lyric is based on a character and situation from Shakespeare's *Measure for Measure*. Mariana's lover, Angelo, has deserted her for another woman. Mariana is taking part in a scheme by which Angelo will go to a remote farmhouse, or grange, expecting to meet the other woman but instead will find Mariana.

STYLE

This poem explores Mariana's longing and frustration as she awaits Angelo. It provides a good example of Tennyson's descriptive power. Here the details create an emotional atmosphere that is then made explicit in Mariana's speech at the close of each stanza.

The grange is isolated on a plain, with only a single poplar tree breaking the monotony of the landscape. It is surrounded by a moat. The dreary silence is broken only by the distant sounds of a cock crowing and of oxen lowing and, closer, the buzz of a fly, the chirp of a sparrow, and the shriek of a mouse. The gloom and isolation seem overwhelming. Mariana's wish that she were dead is a recurring cry of frustration and despair. Although nothing happens in this poem, its theme develops by intensification of the single emotion.

The Lady of Shalott

This poem can be read in comparison with "Mariana." In each poem the central figure is a woman who is isolated and frustrated in her wait for something or someone—a lover, in Mariana's case; possibly also in the Lady's.

STYLE

Tennyson carefully builds the scene with details that suggest symbolic meanings.

Part 1. The beginning establishes the Lady's isolation. She dwells in the tower of a castle on an island in a river. Camelot, the city of King Arthur, is downstream; on either side of the river lie fields of grain.

Part 2. This part describes the Lady as she sits alone at a loom. In the mirror hanging opposite her loom the Lady sees who and what passes along the road outside her window. She never looks directly on life but merely on reflected images. She weaves images of these reflections into her tapestry— her "magic web." While ordinary folk come and go, she must stay at her loom, always observing life but never participating. All this is because of a mysterious curse; she must keep on weaving, and she must not look directly on Camelot. At the end of part 2 the Lady utters a complaint after watching the reflections of two lovers: she is "half sick of shadows"—that is, of being confined to a world of reflected "shadow" images.

Part 3. In part 3 Lancelot, one of the heroic knights of King Arthur's court, appears. Starlike and gorgeous, Lancelot parades by the Lady's tower in shining splendor. The Lady, seeing his image in her mirror, is compelled to leave her loom and look down to Camelot, thus activating the curse.

Part 4. We see in part 4 that it is a curse of death. The Lady descends from her tower and finds a boat, on the prow of which she writes her own name. She boards the boat and at the close of day unties it and drifts downstream toward Camelot. She floats along singing, and by the time the boat arrives in Camelot, she is dead. Everyone in the town comes to the river to see the Lady lying dead in the little boat. The knights bless themselves in fear, except for Lancelot, who says that "she has a lovely face" and prays for God's mercy on her.

This poem, like an old folk ballad, narrates the bare events of a story, giving no interpretation and offering no moral. How the Lady came to be cursed is not suggested. Tennyson teases the reader with many suggestive details, but the Lady and her death are essentially mysterious. She is a maiden imprisoned by enchantment for whom reality is fatal.

The Lotos-Eaters

Tennyson based this poem on an incident from the *Odyssey* of Homer. When Odysseus and his men arrive at the island of the Lotos-Eaters they are given the fruit of the lotos tree, which makes men forget their homes or remember them only vaguely and wish no longer to travel or toil. They become like people who have taken a narcotic.

STYLE

The first five stanzas are narrative. They are in the Spenserian stanza form, which is associated with tales of adventure and action.

Stanza 1. The opening word of Odysseus to his men is *courage*, an ironic command because the rest of the poem shows their courage ebbing away. Arriving on the shore of this beautiful and dreamy land, the mariners disembark amid a crowd of the inhabitants, who offer them the fruits of the lotos tree. As soon as they taste the fruit the men feel weary. No longer eager to return home to Ithaca, they are content to rest where they are.

The last stanzas. The rest of the poem, from line 46, is the song sung by the mariners. In it they express the beauty of lotos-land and their own heavy and melancholy sense of fatigue.

In the fourth stanza of the song the repeated phrase "Let us alone" captures their feelings. The lines of the song are irregular in length but repetitious in phrasing, giving a lazy, undisciplined feeling. The stanzas gradually become longer toward the end of the poem.

The last stanza has twenty-eight lines. In it the mariners suggest that they will lie about like the gods on Olympus, who casually and carelessly disrupt the lives of people on earth for their own idle amusement. Since the gods can so easily spoil people's lives and thwart their efforts, why should the mariners aspire to anything but rest and relaxation? They conclude, "We will not wander more."

"Ulysses"

This blank-verse poem reflects the character of Ulysses (Odysseus), who at the end of Homer's epic returns home after his years of adventures. Tennyson imagines that domestic life must have seemed too tame for Ulysses after a while and that he must have grown restless and bored.

This poem is a dramatic monologue spoken by Ulysses in his old age. It reveals his restlessness and his determination to set out for new adventures, to end life heroically rather than in peaceful dullness.

Ulysses begins by describing his current life, using such terms as "idle" and "barren." In line 10 he announces his decision not to rest. He then thinks back over the heroic life he has lived already. Reflecting on his hardships, triumphs, and fame makes him want more. To stop now, it seems to him, is "dull." He speaks abstractly of his adventures as "experience" and of his goal as "knowledge."

Turning his attention to what he will leave behind, Ulysses mentions his son Telemachus, a decent and prudent ruler, fit to stay at home and govern. He is in contrast to his father, the roving adventurer.

In the concluding section Ulysses approaches the port, where his ship awaits. He calls upon his old mariners to push off for a new voyage, perhaps to end their lives at sea. They will sail westward, into the sunset, a conventional metaphor for death. But perhaps they will reach the "Happy Isles," that paradise of heroes, where they might find the dead Achilles. The end of the poem is a rousing cry to action: "To strive, to seek, to find, and not to yield."

"Tithonus"

Another dramatic monologue in blank verse, "Tithonus" alludes to the mythic situation of a mortal being loved by an immortal. The prince Tithonus was loved by the goddess of the dawn, called Eos or Aurora. Zeus had granted her the favor that Tithonus would live forever, but she forgot to ask also for his perpetual youth. Therefore, while she remains young and beautiful, he has grown old, wrinkled, and white-haired.

In this poem Tennyson speaks of how all living things eventually die. Tithonus longs to die well; he regrets ever having asked for immortality. As in many fairy tales and myths, the one who gets his wish is now sorry. Tithonus sees Eos weeping because she knows that he must live on in endless old age. In the passage starting at line 50, Tithonus recalls the days of his youth when they were first lovers. He describes how lovely she was and how he adored her kisses. But that time of sensuous pleasure is gone.

At the end of the poem the word *cold* is repeated, indicating the change from youthful love to aged regret. Tithonus now sees death as a happy state, a release from love and life.

In Memoriam A. H. H.

This is the longest elegy in the English language. When Tennyson's college friend Arthur Hallam died suddenly and unexpectedly in Vienna in 1833, Tennyson was profoundly shaken. His grief for his friend was complicated and deepened by his melancholy doubt about the purpose and meaning of life. His questioning of fate, which is a conventional part of the elegy, became overwhelming.

Tennyson began writing these memorial verses soon after Hallam's death. He continued to expand and revise the elegy for seventeen years, until its publication in 1850. The sheer length of the poem makes it a reenactment of the process of grieving; the shifting moods of denial, questioning, doubt, despair, consolation, and hope are all fully explored.

The changing of the seasons and the return each year of the Christmas holidays serve to mark the passage of time, against which the various stages of grief are played out.

STYLE

The slow-moving poem is made up of numbered units, like the sonnet cycles of the Renaissance. Each section is a separate lyric, with its own central concept and image. Each lyric is made more poignant by the context of the whole. Tennyson used a quatrain or four-line stanza with the rhyme scheme a b b a, a structure well suited to the slow movement of the elegy. The quatrain provides a steady framework for the varieties of emotion portrayed. The lines are short (tetrameter, or four-foot lines), but the suspension of the a-rhyme to the last syllable makes each stanza a long, sustained statement. Tennyson adapted and developed this stanza form so well that it is now called the In Memoriam stanza.

DESCRIPTION

Tennyson's images come not only from nature—the tree, the flower, the bird, the river—but also from human life—the Christmas party, the worship service in church, the city street at night. The scenes of Tennyson's and

Hallam's friendship are painfully familiar, while the imagined scenes of the return of Hallam's corpse by sea have the strangeness of death.

Tennyson compares his sense of loss with that of others: the parents' loss of a child, the wife's loss of a husband, and the girl's loss of her lover (Hallam had been engaged to Tennyson's sister).

In Tennyson's mind, however, masculine friendship was a rich and exalted relationship allowing the free, heartfelt interchange of ideas and feelings. Tennyson almost revered Hallam, and his death was a blow to his faith.

In Memoriam also contains some consolations. Two of its most quoted lines are found in section 27:

'Tis better to have loved and lost

Than never to have loved at all.

Tennyson mourns Hallam's death in the context of doubt, of loss of faith in the benevolent Christian God and in the salvation of the soul. Recent scientific discoveries, particularly in geology, indicated that the earth was much older than had been assumed and that entire species of creatures had dropped out of existence. Nature seemed cruel. If "a thousand types are gone," as nature says in section 56, can it be that human beings also will sink into oblivion? Nature is "red in tooth and claw," the poet observes. Will even those who loved God also become mere dust?

The alternation of hope and fear, of trust and doubt, makes up the major emotional structure of the poem. The Christmas holidays and the anniversaries of Hallam's death are painful ceremonies because of the contrast between past joy and present suffering. Gradually, however, the pain of loss is softened by consoling images.

For example, in section 106 the new year is celebrated by the ringing of church bells. Tennyson perceives the bells as ringing *out* falseness, grief, and strife, and ringing *in* positive influences such as truth, love of good, and peace.

In the last line of this section, "Ring in the Christ that is to be," Tennyson suggests that the second coming of Christ is approaching. He goes on to imply that Hallam was a type of new man, a man of the future born too soon and thus fated to an early death.

By the end of *In Memoriam*, the spirit of Hallam has become a companion spirit, and faith has been restored. The poet looks to a better future. The epilogue is a celebration of a wedding, the standard feature of the conclusion of a comedy. Here, rather than comic, the tone is hopeful and cheerful. Tennyson's sister Cecilia (it was Emily who had been engaged to Hallam) is marrying; her sons will be men of a better and higher form of life. All life is moving toward some "far-off divine event."

Locksley Hall

In this long and bitter poem the speaker is a young man whose beloved, the daughter of his kinsman who lives in Locksley Hall, has forsaken him in order to marry a wealthier suitor chosen by her parents. As he stands looking across the moors to the Hall, he speaks first to his friends, asking to be left alone, and then to the beloved, who of course is not present.

The form is couplets of seven-foot lines, an unusual stanza made even more unusual by the use of mostly trochaic feet, which have the stress on the first syllable.

The emotional effect is of anger and complaint. The speaker first recalls the sweet days of his springtime courtship, including the famous line, "In the spring a young man's fancy lightly turns to thoughts of love" (line 20). Then he scornfully describes the "clown" of a husband she has chosen and curses the social situation that makes wealth the overriding consideration in marriage. He conjures up dreary images of what the marriage will be like; after the first novelty of passion wears off, the dull husband will ignore a wife whom he is too coarse to appreciate. She will grow worse under his influence and become an "old and formal" woman, teaching her own daughter to marry prudently.

The forsaken lover thinks of his own future. He has a vision of the future as moving toward peace worldwide and a world federation based on "the common sense of most" (line 129). He imagines that scientific progress will be slowly spreading.

At this point, the speaker hears his comrades calling to him. He intends to leave his home and go out adventuring in remote parts of the world. Perhaps he will marry a "savage woman," but he is convinced of the lower natures of the "gray barbarian" (line 174). Turning from that image of beastly satisfaction, he rouses himself to go, saying farewell to Locksley Hall. He confronts the storm of life, going seaward to new experiences.

Idylls of the King

Tennyson wrote a series of narrative poems drawn from the matter of Arthur, the medieval stories of King Arthur and the Knights of the Round Table, based mainly on the *Le Morte d'Arthur* of Sir Thomas Malory.

The first and most widely praised of these poems was "The Passing of Arthur," which Tennyson wrote in 1833, shortly after the death of his friend Hallam. Tennyson produced eleven other books or poems concerning the various knights and their deeds, republishing the whole collection in chronological sequence in 1891. Thus Tennyson worked on this project for his whole career, more than fifty years.

The poems, written in blank verse, begin with the union of Arthur and Guinevere and end with Arthur's death. As a whole they show the degeneration of a culture based on ideals of honor and chivalry to one based on deception and betrayal. The central act of betrayal is the adulterous relationship between Guinevere and Sir Lancelot, but at his death, Arthur is under attack by his own nephew, Sir Mordred. The movement of the poems seem to suggest the inevitable fall of a civilization as its ideals are undermined by desire and dissention.

"The Passing of Arthur." The tale "The Passing of Arthur" was originally published with a narrative framework called "The Epic" that describes the occasion when the poet read it to a group of his friends. This framework was omitted when "The Passing of Arthur" was incorporated into the *Idylls of the King* as the final book.

The book tells how Arthur lost his last battle, which was fought in a foggy mist by the edge of the sea. His enemies were some of his own people, led in revolt by the traitor Mordred, Arthur's younger kinsman. The mist hides most of the battle from any one warrior, until finally silence falls. The white-haired old king has been wounded by Mordred, but he has killed Mordred with a blow of his magic sword, Excalibur.

Arthur then tells his one remaining supporter, Sir Bedevere, to take the sword and throw it into the lake. Bedevere, however, is dazzled by the richly jeweled hilt of the sword, so he hides it instead. Bedevere's disobedience is an indication of the decline of Arthur's power and of the disorder of his kingdom. When he returns to Arthur, the king asks him what happened to the sword, and Bedevere lies to him. Arthur again commands Bedevere to throw the sword into the lake. Only at the third request does Bedevere finally carry out Arthur's request.

Immediately an arm rises out of the lake to take Excalibur—the same arm that had given the sword to Arthur years before. Bedevere then lifts his wounded king onto his shoulders and carries him to the lake, where a mysterious black barge is waiting with three queens dressed in black. They take Arthur onto the barge.

Bedevere laments and asks, "Where shall I go?" Arthur answers, "The old order changeth, yielding place to new." Arthur will go to Avalon, the paradise of warriors, but Bedevere, watching the barge move into the distance, predicts that Arthur may return to be king in a new and better age.

Thus Arthur's departure is a "passing." Rather than a death, it is a removal to some other state of being. The mournful conclusion of the poem also contains a grain of hope for the future.

"Crossing the Bar"

In this late lyric Tennyson considers his own death. He uses the metaphor of putting out to sea, the sea representing the vastness of eternity to which the individual soul returns at death. He wishes for a quiet death, one without mourning because, as he states in the last stanza, he expects after death to see the face of God. The "bar" of the title is a sandbar that forms at the mouth of a river, marking the boundary between land and sea, or, here, between this life and eternity.

ROBERT BROWNING (1812–1889)

Browning's father, a clerk at the Bank of England, was a learned man with an immense personal library. This library formed the basis of his son Robert's education. Robert was educated mostly at home with the assistance of tutors. Later, he briefly attended the University of London. His mother was a deeply religious woman whose intense faith affected her son, but as a young man Browning became, for a while at least, an atheist. His mature religious beliefs are only indirectly discernible in his poetry.

Browning's Poetry

Browning's early poetry was not well received. His "Pauline," published in 1833, was negatively reviewed as being too preoccupied with the self. In reaction Browning began to turn away from the typical romantic focus on introspection and personal memory. He wrote for the theater, but again was unsuccessful. However, theatrical writing led him in the direction of his most productive poetic form, the *dramatic monologue*. His volume *Dramatic Lyrics* (1842) broke new ground in the use of this form, and his *Men and Women* (1855) established him as the master of the dramatic monologue.

Setting his poems in distant times and places, Browning presents a series of portraits of strange and sometimes even grotesque characters who are revealed through their own speech or thought. A third important collection of dramatic monologues was *Dramatis Personae* (1864).

Browning's Character

Browning's life has been a subject of story and drama. As a young poet he admired the poems of Elizabeth Barrett, a semi-invalid who seldom left her house. He wrote to her and then visited her and found her very attractive. Her father was a tyrant who forbade his daughter to marry. But in 1846 Barrett eloped with Browning and escaped with him to Italy, where the couple lived for the next fifteen years. She regained full health, and the couple had a son.

After her death in Florence in 1861 Browning returned to London, where his reputation as a poet began to grow. He became a celebrity and a popular dinner guest at the homes of intellectuals.

Browning concealed his disposition behind a bluff, hearty, and rather unpoetical social presence. He would not discuss nor decipher any of his difficult and perplexing poems, insisting that they stand on their own. Once, when a reader asked Browning what a particular poem meant, he is reported to have said, "When I wrote it, only God and I knew; now only God knows."

Browning's development of the dramatic monologue was an important influence on modern poets such as Ezra Pound and T. S. Eliot. It stands in contrast to the emotional and personal writing of the great romanticists and marks the beginning of the modern voice in poetry.

"Porphyria's Lover"

This dramatic monologue is a good example of Browning's use of the form. It has a rhyme pattern—a b a b b—but the informal phrasing does not emphasize the rhyme, so that we seem to be hearing the spontaneous thoughts of the speaker. A few details provide the setting: a stormy night, a cottage with a fireplace. But the speaker, since he is thinking, does not give background information, so that the reader must piece together various details to grasp the situation as a whole.

More than most poems, the dramatic monologue requires several readings before it becomes clear. Here, the lover describes how he waited, lonely, for Porphyria to visit him. She came in, having left a "gay feast" to be with him, tended his fire, and sat next to him with sweet affection. As they sat together by the fire, the lover was overwhelmed with pride and pleasure that she loved him. He wanted the moment never to end.

In sudden madness, he decided to kill Porphyria and thus to keep her his forever. He strangled her with her own long, blond hair, assuring himself that she wanted to die at that moment and that he did not really hurt her.

As the poem ends the reader realizes with a shock that the lover is still sitting with the head of the dead Porphyria propped on his shoulder, waiting to see what God will do to him now.

"Soliloquy of the Spanish Cloister"

The speaker of this dramatic monologue is one of Browning's grotesque characters. He is a bitter and spiteful friar who focuses his anger and frustration on the bland and innocent Brother Lawrence. We see what may happen when a man unsuited to a confined and celibate life becomes a monk.

The object of the speaker's hatred is the gardener of the monastery. The setting is the garden. While Lawrence moves about tending his plants, the speaker watches in secret. At first the speaker remarks on the gardening activities of Lawrence, but then his mind wanders to other events, such as conversations at mealtimes and the cleaning and putting away of plates at meal's end.

In stanza 4 the speaker thinks of the beauty of two local girls who come to wash their hair at a fountain outside the cloister wall. He projects the lust he feels onto Lawrence in order to make him seem guilty.

In stanzas 7 and 8 the speaker contemplates a scheme to bring about the damnation of Lawrence. He will tempt Lawrence to impure or unholy thoughts by leaving sinful books in his way or by asking him difficult questions about biblical interpretation.

In the last stanza the speaker thinks of the ultimate means to damn Lawrence: he will sell his own soul to the devil as part of a bargain for Lawrence's damnation, only being careful to make the bargain in such a way as to leave an escape clause for himself. But the speaker is suddenly called back to reality by the sound of the vesper bell. He ends his monologue with a growl.

"My Last Duchess"

This is probably Browning's most famous dramatic monologue. It is often used as a prime example of the form.

In this poem the speaker, the duke of Ferrara, is addressing a second character, an agent of an unnamed count whose daughter the duke plans to marry. The situation is taken from the life of an actual sixteenth-century Italian duke, but Browning has imagined the specific incident.

The duke is showing the count's agent a portrait of his first wife. She was a beautiful woman, but to the duke's mind she had too little pride. He was frequently offended by her courtesy to others of lower rank, and he found her too easily pleased by a compliment or by a small favor from a servant or some other "unimportant" person. The duke felt that she should derive pleasure essentially only from himself. She should glory in the high social rank into which she had married. The duke could not lower himself ("stoop") to tell her what she did that annoyed him. Instead, he took action, or "gave commands." The exact nature of the commands is not made explicit, but whatever they were, the duchess is gone, most likely dead. Now the duke is negotiating the terms of a new marriage agreement.

He tells the count's agent about his displeasure with his first wife in order to make clear to the second woman what sort of conduct he will expect from her, but of course he does not stoop to stating his demands explicitly. As the poem ends, the two men turn away from the portrait and go downstairs to join the rest of the company at the duke's palace. As they go, the duke casually points out one of his other works of art, a bronze statue of Neptune.

"The Laboratory"

The setting for this dramatic monologue is given as the "Ancien Régime," meaning France before the revolution. During the reign of Louis XIV courtiers often got rid of rivals and other enemies by poisoning them.

Browning imagines an aristocratic lady who has come to the laboratory of an old man who deals in poisons. She knows that her husband or lover is with another woman; jealousy drives her to get poison to kill her rival. As she sits in the laboratory watching the old man prepare the poison, she is fascinated by the beautifully colored powders, gums, and liquids. She imagines herself carrying these poisons in various parts of her clothing—her fan, her earring—to do away with various women she dislikes.

In stanzas 7 and 8 she receives the specific poison for her immediate purpose, but she finds it too dull in color and she is afraid it will not be potent enough. Her rival is not a delicate woman; the night before she had focused a killing stare at her rival, but to no effect. Still, she doesn't want the death to be too quick; it should be painful. Finally, she offers the old man all her jewels as payment. She also offers him a kiss, an example of the kind of shocking detail that Browning tends to use near the end of a dramatic monologue. It shows the perverse mingling of lust and vengeance in the lady who speaks the monologue.

"The Lost Leader"

This poem is about Wordsworth. Many of the later romanticists and the early Victorians had been inspired by Wordsworth, who in his youth had been both a liberal and a sympathizer with the French Revolution. When in 1842–1843 Wordsworth accepted a government pension and the post of poet laureate, some of his followers felt that this showed his growing conservatism and self-indulgence. It seemed to them that they could no longer look to him for leadership or inspiration but instead would have to fall back on the examples of Shakespeare, Milton, Burns, and Shelley, poets who had remained firmly liberal.

The emotion Browning expresses is strong. Wordsworth is called a lost soul, and his defection is seen as a "devil's-triumph." The speaker rejects the idea that Wordsworth could ever regain leadership because the younger poets have all lost confidence in him. His only hope is that perhaps Wordsworth will be pardoned after death and that they will all meet in heaven.

STYLE

The poem is written in dactylic, an unusual meter, in which a stressed syllable is followed by two unstressed syllables. Dactylic makes for a strong, emphatic line, adapted here to express anger and disgust.

The second stanza starts "We shall march," suggesting the militancy of the speakers, the "we" who represent a body of young, aspiring liberal poets who will not be deterred, although they are distressed by the loss of Wordsworth's leadership.

The Bishop Orders His Tomb at Saint Praxed's Church

Browning once more goes back to the Italian Renaissance, to sixteenth-century Rome, for the setting of this dramatic monologue. The fictional speaker is a dying Roman Catholic bishop whose directions about his burial and the construction of his tomb reveal his worldliness, his love of luxury, and his jealousy of rivals in the church hierarchy. He is speaking to a group of attendants and his "nephews" as he reflects on his past life, the present moment of death, and visions of the magnificent tomb he will enjoy, he thinks, in the future.

The nephews are actually his illegitimate sons. The priestly requirement of celibacy did not prevent some from having mistresses, and the bishop remembers that he defeated his rival Gandolf in obtaining the favors of the particularly beautiful mistress who was the mother of these sons. Now they gather about his deathbed to hear his final words.

STYLE

The poem is in blank verse, a form more suited than rhymed verse to the rambling discourse of the dying bishop.

The bishop speaks first as a holy man, quoting the Bible in the opening line. His thoughts then focus on his dead mistress, the mother of these sons. Her death reminds him of his own. At line 15 the tone shifts; the bishop gets down to the business of ordering the elaborate and costly tomb that will hold his remains. Although his tomb will not occupy the best location in the church, he decides that his niche will be good enough. The tomb is to be made of the richest stone—peach marble columns around a dark basalt slab. He reveals to his sons the location of a piece of the semiprecious stone lapis lazuli, which the bishop had stolen years before when his earlier church had burned. He hid it then, saving it to adorn his own tomb. He describes the size of the stone in grotesque terms: "Big as a Jew's head cut off at the nape," emphasizing his greed and inhumanity as well as his love of luxury.

But the bishop is afraid, not for the salvation of his soul, but that his own sons will, like himself, be greedy and keep the lapis lazuli for themselves. Perhaps they will not want to spend money on a magnificent tomb, even though he is leaving them his wealth and his country villas. This fear is mingled with the bishop's gloating pleasure to think that his tomb will be so much more impressive than that of his old rival, Gandolf.

The bishop elaborates on his orders. Instead of basalt, the slab should be black marble. He describes a bas-relief frieze that he wants placed around the base. It will show a gaudy and bizarre combination of pagan figures—nymphs and Pan—and Christian figures—Christ and Moses. Even as he suspects that his sons will substitute a common marble, travertine, he changes his mind and orders green jasper, an even more costly stone, instead of black marble. He bribes his sons with the promise that he will get Saint Praxed to provide them with luxuries such as horses, fine manuscripts, and beautiful mistresses. In return, they must make his inscription in the best classical Latin.

The bishop supposes that after his death he will see church services, hear the mass, smell incense, and be conscious of the splendor of church rites. The bishop practices for death by assuming the position he will have in the tomb. At about line 94 his thoughts become more confused, drifting from the church to Christ to his mistress to rich marble and pure Latin. The fear of his sons' ingratitude returns in line 114, and he finally dismisses them.

His last thought is the satisfaction of having beaten old Gandolf, both in the rivalry for his mistress and in the richness of his tomb. The bishop's worldliness, love of luxury, and shallow faith reflect Browning's assessment of the condition of the church in the sixteenth century.

Fra Lippo Lippi

This dramatic monologue recreates the character of an actual fifteenth-century Italian painter as Browning knew him from Vasari's *Lives of the Painters* and from Lippi's paintings in Florence.

The opening shows Lippi's reaction when a band of watchmen stop him in the street at night. Lippi identifies himself first as a "poor brother." The question of his identity is one of the recurrent ideas in this poem.

Written in blank verse, the poem consists of Lippi's conversation with the chief of the watchmen, the rest of the men having been sent into a nearby tavern to buy drinks with the money that Lippi has given them.

Lippi explains that he has been working and staying at the house of Cosimo de' Medici, the most powerful man in Florence. Bored and restless, Lippi was tempted to sneak down a rope of bedclothes to join a group of jovial passersby. After partying with this group for awhile he is now going back to the Medici palace.

He has been asked the question "Who am I?" in line 14, and after dismissing the watchmen to drink, he tells their chief in line 39, "Yes, I'm the painter," since the patronage of the Medicis is sure to gain respect. Having confessed to joining the revelers he asks in line 80 for indulgence: "Come, what am I a beast for?" He then gives a brief autobiographical sketch: He was an orphan living on the streets when an old woman rescued him by taking him to a Carmelite monastery, where he was fed and enrolled as a monk. He was a poor student, but he loved to draw, so the monks set him to painting on the walls of a new church. Lippi, having learned to be a close observer of faces while living on the streets, covered the church walls with a rich variety of realistically painted faces. But the prior disapproved, preferring a more spiritual style of painting, such as that of the late-medieval painter Giotto.

At this point, Lippi begins to defend his own style of painting and explains to the chief watchman a more Renaissance theory of art. Lippi rejects the concept of "painting the soul" as artificial. If the painter captures the body, the posture, and the facial expression of each subject, the soul will show through.

Lippi's ideal is to create beauty—not mere prettiness but the various beauties of the real world as God created it. He points out that although we can look directly at nature, we do not see it acutely until the painter recreates it. The painter helps our perception by showing us what he or she sees.

Here Browning is also explaining his theory of his own verbal portraits, the dramatic monologues that is, art does not have to teach a moral. Lippi declares (lines 217–218):

> If you get simple beauty and naught else,
> You get about the best thing God invents

But Lippi can paint to please both the old-fashioned tastes of the prior and the more modern tastes of the Medici. He has become famous and sought after. He has a pupil, the young Masaccio, who also advanced the Renaissance style of painting. Lippi cites a painting he had recently done in the town of Prato. It depicts Saint Laurence being burned to death. The faces of

Laurence's torturers have been scratched out by zealous members of the church, who were roused to fury by the scene of martyrdom. Lippi is disgusted by such a reaction to his work. He describes one painting he is planning to do for the nuns at the convent of Saint Ambrogio. He will please them by making a sweet madonna figure surrounded by "bowery flowery" angels and other conventional pious decorations, but he will put in one corner a portrait of himself as if he were stepping up into heaven and is stunned and shy at discovering himself in such company.

The final answer to the question "Who am I?" will be "I'm the man" (line 364)—that is, the one who created the painting with all its beautiful figures. While not beautiful himself, Lippi is able to create beauty because he sees God's world as beautiful.

At the conclusion of the poem Lippi invites the chief watchman to go to the convent and view the painting in six months. Then he bids him good-night just as dawn is breaking.

In Lippi, Browning has created an image of the artist as exuberant and joyful. He celebrates creation in all its rich variety for its own sake. Browning's theory of art was developed in the late Victorian period by the pre-Raphaelite artists and poets.

MATTHEW ARNOLD (1822–1888)

Matthew Arnold's father was a well-known liberal churchman who became the headmaster of Rugby School, where he instituted educational reforms. Matthew, his oldest son, attended that school and then went on to Oxford University, where he did not take his studies seriously. As a youth, Arnold rebelled against the restraint and self-discipline demanded during the Victorian Age. He became a self-indulgent, silly, irreverent, and foppish individual. After Oxford he was employed as a private secretary by Lord Lansdowne.

In 1851 Arnold married and entered the civil service as an inspector of schools. He took this position seriously and stayed in it for thirty-five years. He traveled throughout England, visiting schools in various towns and becoming acquainted with many middle-class people. Arnold found the lives of these people dull and joyless. He came to refer to them as "Philistines," after the biblical enemies of the Israelites. Philistinism meant, for Arnold, a life dominated by convention and devoid of ideas or culture. Such people are preoccupied with respectability and material comfort; they lack ideals or imagination.

Arnold believed that the improvement of mass education would rejuvenate English society. He wanted the youth of the middle class to become acquainted with the great ideas of the past and with the best the Western cultural tradition had to offer. He studied the educational systems of France and Germany and wrote essays promoting his ideas on education.

Arnold's Career

Arnold wrote his best poetry during the 1850s, early in his career. He expressed the widespread Victorian sense of loss and of the failure of religion to help people cope with the problems of modern life. In his later works, which were mostly prose, he dealt with these issues as social problems that could be solved by the cultural elevation of the public. He became a literary critic, stressing the role of literature in inspiring an earnest and energetic approach to life.

"TO A FRIEND"

This early poem is a sonnet in the Italian form. Like Keats, Arnold is responding to classic literature, where he finds wisdom, intellectual stimulation, and consolation. He mentions first "clearest-souled" Homer, then the Greek philosopher Epictetus, and finally the playwright Sophocles, who, with his "even-balanced soul," is an example of the best way to live.

One of Arnold's most famous phrases is used here to praise Sophocles:

"Who saw life steadily, and saw it whole."

This attribute is central to Arnold's idea of what the modern reader can gain from a thorough knowledge of classical literature.

THE FORSAKEN MERMAN

This poem is based on a Danish tale of a human maiden who weds a merman, the king of the sea, and lives with him in a cavern under the sea. They have several children and live happily until one day the wife hears the tolling of church bells from her town on the land. The bells call her back; she is afraid she will lose her soul if she stays any longer in the beautiful, exotic world under the water.

The poem is told from the point of view of her husband. After his wife leaves he tells his children to call to their mother. He also calls to her by her name, Margaret, but she does not respond. They seek her in the cold town and find her in the gray church. Still she fails to answer or even to look at them. They go back to their home under the sea, feeling forsaken. Margaret has given up her life of richness and beauty for the narrow, pious life of ordinary mortals. The merman imagines how she sits spinning at her wheel, singing songs. But sometimes she must stop her work and think of them, sadly remembering her former life of love.

The poem is remarkable for the spellbinding lyrical beauty of the merman's song, expressive of love and longing. It contrasts the magical undersea world of color and feeling with the constrained, walled-in, and colorless life of the human town.

"ISOLATION TO MARGUERITE" and "TO MARGUERITE—CONTINUED"

These two lyrics are related by their titles and by their expression of loneliness. Both are written in a six-line stanza with a rhyme scheme a b a b c c. They seem to be responses to a disappointing love affair Arnold experienced before his marriage, but the woman in question has never been absolutely identified.

In each poem the speaker is a lover who has been faithful to one who has not been faithful to him. The lonely heart feels its separateness, its isolation, as an inevitable part of the human condition. This is what life is like—to be alone like an island, to feel "a longing like despair."

The tone and images of these early poems are also found in Arnold's great lyric "Dover Beach," which he may have begun writing at this time but did not complete until several years later, after his marriage.

"MEMORIAL VERSES: APRIL 1850"

This elegy, a tribute to Wordsworth, was written shortly after the great poet's death. Unlike some of the younger romantic poets, Arnold was not disillusioned by Wordsworth's declining powers in old age. He compares Wordsworth with two other great and influential figures of nineteenth-century literature, Byron and the German poet Goethe. Byron was a poet of force and energy; he engaged in "Titanic strife." Goethe was the wise man of European poetry; he was a "physician" who diagnosed the illnesses of the modern age. But Wordsworth's strength was of a different kind. He taught people how to feel, to put aside the doubts and controversies of the age in favor of direct emotional contact with nature. Arnold calls Wordsworth the great "voice" of nature and honors him the most.

THE SCHOLAR GYPSY

As in "The Forsaken Merman," Arnold here adapts a traditional story for modern purposes. A tale about a poor Oxford student who left the university to join a band of Gypsies was written by Joseph Glanvill in the seventeenth century. Arnold reprinted Glanvill's story as a note to his own poem and refers to Glanvill in the poem.

Arnold had himself been an Oxford student, and he recalled good times there and while ambling among the neighboring hills. The poem's descriptions of the countryside re-create those happy memories.

Style. The poem is written in ten-line stanzas of mostly pentameter lines, but the sixth line has only four feet (tetrameter). The first six lines of each stanza have the rhyme pattern a b c b c a. The last four lines start a new rhyme: d e e d. Such a long stanza is well suited to a slow narrative with rich, descriptive detail. Each stanza can act as a paragraph, developing a single image or incident.

Content. At the opening of the poem, the poet speaks to a shepherd boy who is helping him find the Scholar Gypsy. The first stanza ends with the word *quest*, which signifies the theme of the poem. The speaker tells the shepherd boy that he will wait for him until evening, when they will pursue their quest. Sitting down with Glanvill's book, the speaker briefly recapitulates the story of how the scholar forsook Oxford to travel with Gypsies and study Gypsy lore, especially how to "rule . . . the working of men's brains" (lines 45 and 46). Other students had seen the Scholar Gypsy roaming about the countryside near Oxford. At about line 62 the poet begins to speak to the Scholar Gypsy directly, using the pronoun *thou*. In the next six stanzas the speaker imagines a series of scenes, from May through summer and from harvest time into winter, wherein the local farm folk encounter the Scholar Gypsy in various places. But, in line 131, the speaker suddenly realizes that 200 years have passed since the Scholar left Oxford; he could not still be wandering in the area. In the next stanza the speaker denies his previous thought, declaring that the Scholar Gypsy still lives because, not having had to endure the wearing and exhausting life of an ordinary mortal, he is timeless and "exempt from age" (line 158).

Unlike the modern man, who is full of doubt and scatters his energies to no purpose, the Scholar Gypsy lives in hope, waiting for "the spark from heaven" (line 171).

In the next four stanzas the speaker describes the modern era as a time when even the best and the wisest are baffled by grief and a sense of loss. Life now is a "strange disease" (line 203) that the Scholar Gypsy should avoid. Unless he keeps himself isolated from "the infection of our mental strife" (line 222), he will fade and die.

The final two stanzas develop an analogy between the Scholar Gypsy and modern man with the poet displaying the fear of contaminating him with the sickness of modern life. On the other hand, the Scholar Gypsy's quest for the heavenly spark, for the revelation of mysteries, can continue, or at least the poet can be comforted by the idea that it continues, hidden in the landscape around Oxford.

"DOVER BEACH"

This is Arnold's best-known poem. It recreates a quiet conversation that touches on the central feeling of mid-Victorian poetry, the sense of loss of faith and the longing for something to believe in.

It is a dramatic monologue in which the speaker seems to be a man addressing the woman he loves, sharing with her his sadness and his hope of finding some solace in her love.

Form. The lines of the poem are irregular. There is no rhyme, but the rhythm recreates the sound of waves lapping the beach, in keeping with the scene.

Content. The beach at Dover in southeastern England overlooks the English Channel. France is visible about twenty miles away. The speaker is in a room with his beloved, looking out the window and across the water. He describes the scene and invites her to join him at the window to look at and listen to the sea. The thought occurs to him that in ancient times the Greek playwright Sophocles must also have listened to the sea and must have been influenced by its sad sound as he wrote his great tragedies.

The sea is similar all over the world and in all times. The speaker then carries his idea one step further: He makes an analogy between the sea and the Sea of Faith—that is, the widespread and long-lasting belief in religion. But the Sea of Faith is now ebbing, drawing back and leaving people stranded in doubt and confusion.

In the last stanza the poet imagines modern civilization not as a sea but as a plain, a land where pointless conflicts are acted out by people who don't know what they are fighting for. The speaker therefore asks the woman for love as a refuge, as something to believe in, and he offers her the same: "let us be true/to one another!" he cries, because everything else is uncertain.

THYRSIS

This is an elegy written for Arnold's old college friend Arthur Hugh Clough, also a poet, but of minor rank. Arnold uses the convention of the pastoral elegy, the same form used by Milton in "Lycidas" and by Shelley in "Adonais," poems that honored the deaths of poet friends.

Form. In the classical form of the pastoral elegy the speaker takes the role of a shepherd grieving over the death of a fellow shepherd-poet, calling on a muse to help him. He cites a procession of mourning figures and questions the justice of fate in causing his friend's death. He finally accepts the inevitability of death and finds some consolation in the remaining influence of the dead shepherd's spirit. In pastoral elegies it is also usual to describe the details of the landscape, especially the flowers that can be strewn upon the grave.

Arnold calls his poem a monody, meaning that it is the mourning of a single voice. He departs somewhat from the usual tone of a pastoral elegy. He is more conversational, more modern, in his diction. For example, in contrast to Shelley's cry "O weep for Adonais, he is dead," Arnold says simply, speaking of the past, "We still had Thyrsis then." Arnold neglects to invoke a muse but instead begins by describing a quiet visit to the village where he and Clough had walked together as youths. They had walked up a path to see a single elm tree at the summit of a hill; the tree that had provided a destination in those youthful walks became the symbol of the goal of a quest. Arnold calls it the "signal-elm," suggesting that it has more meaning than can easily be expressed. As he, whom he calls Corydon in the poem, walks about in the early twilight on his visit to the village after the death of Thyrsis, he cannot find the elm; perhaps he has lost the way. He remembers that the elm and the image of the Scholar Gypsy had been shared symbols for Thyrsis and himself. But now Thyrsis is dead and he is wandering around half-lost.

In the fifth stanza the speaker remembers that Thyrsis left Oxford early, impatient because of his awareness of more troubled, less idyllic lives elsewhere. The speaker compares his leaving with the flight of the cuckoo bird. But the cuckoo will return next spring; Thyrsis will not. After some allusions to classical elegies and some more reminiscences of their earlier ramblings on the hills, Arnold/Corydon pauses to consider his own approaching old age and death, saying, "Round me too the night/In ever-nearing circle weaves her shade" (lines 131–132). In the midst of these musings, he suddenly sees the tree, the signal-elm, and calls it a "happy omen" (line 166). It makes him feel that the spirit of Thyrsis is still with him, that he need not despair. He mentions the quest of the Scholar Gypsy and feels that each person's quest for "the light" will not be in vain.

The last two stanzas contain the consolation. Even though his life was short, Thyrsis was true to his quest for light. His voice is now a comforting whisper that visits his living friend "to chase fatigue and fear."

The final four lines of the poem are a hopeful message from Thyrsis, encouraging Corydon to continue the quest. In the manner of the pastoral elegy, the ending is a determination to move on, to make something of the life that remains.

Arnold's Prose

In his later years Arnold virtually gave up poetry to write essays on social and literary topics.

THE FUNCTION OF CRITICISM AT THE PRESENT TIME

This 1865 essay lays out some of Arnold's essential ideas about the role of ideas in the history of civilization.

Style. Arnold's prose style is straightforward, with none of the highly personal quirks of essayists such as Lamb and Carlyle. Arnold's tone is urgent and serious, as if the issues he discusses were of the greatest importance to setting the correct course for life in the second half of the nineteenth century.

Content. Arnold begins by admitting that the creative faculty of humans, the ability to make great literature and art, is higher than the critical faculty, which deals in ideas. But creativity is only possible when and where a ferment of ideas provides it with a nurturing environment. The role of the critic is to initiate and sustain such a "free play of ideas."

Arnold believes that the lack of a play of ideas was a weakness of Wordsworth and his contemporaries, men whose ideas were not mature, who did not read enough books. The critic should deal with ideas for their own sake, not as a service to some faction or political ideology. Criticism, says Arnold, "obeys an instinct . . . to know the best that is known and thought in the world, irrespective of practice." The critic must be *disinterested*—that is, not concerned with immediate, practical considerations.

This detached intellectual free play is a satisfaction in itself. It also provides, in the long run, ideas that enable the progress or enlightenment of the mass of humankind who are never much concerned with ideas. Such people Arnold calls "Philistines," after the biblical enemies of the Israelites. The Philistine is impatient with ideas and is concerned only with what works in the short run. But without ideas, there can be no change for the better in society. Thus the critic plays a vital cultural role.

CULTURE AND ANARCHY

This book is a central statement of Arnold's ideas about culture and the narrowness of English middle-class life. Published in 1869, it is a collection of essays about the difficulty of finding what is best in culture and making it a part of modern culture.

Content. In this book Arnold used several terms and phrases that have become widely used by later critics. For example, the first essay is called "Sweetness and Light." Alluding to Swift's spider-and-bee images in "Battle of the Books," Arnold associates the bee with the open-minded sampling of all the sweet flowers of classical and modern literature. The spiderlike Puritan, on the other hand, prides himself on the narrow virtue of self-restraint and does not seek enlightened understanding. The bee, producing both wax for candles and honey for food, gives the world "sweetness and light."

Hebraism and Hellenism. Such writers as Virgil and Shakespeare epitomize the best of human nature. Their writings contrast with the petty disputes and jealousies of modern Puritan discourse. Later in the book Arnold identifies sweetness and light with an attitude he calls Hellenism in Greek culture, which seeks in art and science to "see things as they really are" and to find the best in nature.

Arnold contrasts this attitude with Hebraism, which is based on Christian morality and the work ethic. The strength of Hebraism is strict moral conscience, but it tends toward fanaticism. Arnold urges the English people to moderate their tendency toward Hebraism by giving more attention to the advantages and virtues of Hellenism, the cultivation of intelligence and openness to new ideas. He believes his compatriots should not act as partisans of some faction or class interest but rather should promote what is best for the whole society. Arnold deplores excessive materialism, vulgar displays of wealth, and the false definition of freedom as merely doing whatever one wants. He is always against the pettiness of self-interest and the anarchy of self-promotion.

Arnold tries to make the English see themselves as a nation capable of improvement. Although England is a good nation, it could be great. Arnold's vigorous voice tries to persuade the English in the direction of greatness.

Tennyson, Browning, and Arnold are the most characteristic voices of the Victorian Age in England. The dreamy sensuousness of Tennyson's descriptions of nature provides a setting for his expressions of doubt, longing, and the melancholy of loneliness. Browning, putting a distance between himself and the characters of his poems, also explores situations of frustration and longing that sometimes even approach violence. His grotesque characters implicate the degenerate society that produced them. Arnold, also feeling doubt and isolation, turns toward the future, trying to establish the hope for an intelligent and open culture.

All three writers combine the feeling of regret for former times, when the human condition was simpler, with the earnest desire for improvement and new ideas. Ultimately, each writer retains some hope for the future.

Tennyson, Browning, and Arnold were conscious of living in changing times. They saw themselves, as poets, as interpreters of the meanings and best uses of new knowledge. But each also reflected the influence of his romantic predecessors. They delighted in rich and specific descriptions of landscapes, trees, and flowers, which held for them special meanings as signs of the spirit of the natural world.

Selected Readings	Bloom, Harold, and Adrienne Munich, eds. *Robert Browning: A Collection of Critical Essays.* Englewood Cliffs, NJ: Prentice-Hall, 1979.

Bloom, Harold, and Adrienne Munich, eds. *Robert Browning: A Collection of Critical Essays.* Englewood Cliffs, NJ: Prentice-Hall, 1979.

DeLaura, David J., ed. *Matthew Arnold: A Collection of Critical Essays.* Englewood Cliffs, NJ: Prentice-Hall, 1973.

Jack, Ian. *Browning's Major Poetry.* Oxford: Clarendon, 1973.

Nicolson, Marjorie H. *Selected Poems of Alfred, Lord Tennyson, Edited for College Students.* Boston: Houghton, 1924.

Ross, Robert H. *In Memoriam: An Authoritative Text, Backgrounds and Sources, Criticism.* New York: Norton, 1973.

Tinker, C. B., and H. F. Lowry. *The Poetry of Matthew Arnold: A Commentary.* London: Oxford University Press, 1940.

10

Minor Victorian Poets

1837–1901 Queen Victoria reigns

1838 Barrett, *The Seraphim and Other Poems*

1842 Browning, *Dramatic Lyrics*; Mundie's Circulating Library founded

1844 Barrett, *Poems* (vols. 1 and 2), which includes "Cry of the Children"; establishment by Parliament of The Factory Act, which regulates employment of women and children in factories

1846 Barrett and R. Browning elope and live in Italy

1847 C. Brontë, *Jane Eyre*; E. Brontë, *Wuthering Heights*

1848 Clough, *The Bothie of Tober-na-Vuolich*

1850 Barrett Browning, *Sonnets from the Portuguese*; Tennyson appointed poet laureate; Clough, *Dipsychus*

1851 Barrett Browning, *Casa Guidi Windows*; Meredith, *Poems*; Melville, *Moby-Dick*

1853–1856 Crimean War

1856 Barrett Browning, *Aurora Leigh*

1857 Matrimonial Causes Act establishes divorce courts

1859 Meredith, *The Ordeal of Richard Feverel*; translation by FitzGerald of *Rubáiyát of Omar Khayyám*

1859–1886 Tennyson, *Idylls of the King*

1860 Barrett Browning, *Poems Before Congress*; *Cornhill Magazine* founded

1861 Barrett Browning dies in Florence, Italy; her volume *Last Poems* published posthumously; Meredith, *Evan Harrington*; Clough dies

1862 Meredith, *Poems and Ballads*; Clough, *Poems* published posthumously

1864 Browning, *Dramatis Personae*

1866 Arnold, *Thyrsis*, an elegy to Clough; Hopkins converts to Roman Catholicism

1868 Browning, *The Ring and the Book*; Alcott, *Little Women*

1868–1883 Hopkins enters Society of Jesus, works in parishes

1875 Hopkins, *Wreck of the Deutschland*

1877 Hopkins ordained as Jesuit priest

1879 Meredith, *The Egoist*

1880 Browning, *Dramatic Idyls* (second series); women admitted for degrees at the University of London

1883 Burton, translation of the "Arabian Nights"

1884 Hopkins appointed classics professor, University College, Dublin, Ireland

1887 Golden Jubilee of Queen Victoria

1889 Hopkins dies of typhoid; Browning, *Asolando*; Tennyson, "Crossing the Bar"

1918 Hopkins's *Poems* published posthumously, edited by poet laureate Robert Bridges

*T*he reading public during the second half of the nineteenth century read poetry extensively. Although the novel was the most popular form of literature, many readers found, or at least sought, a sense of direction or spiritual comfort in poetry. The great romantic poets had put poetry at the center of the life of feeling. Then, as the force and relevance of religion seemed to decline, as new scientific ideas became more influential, readers looked to the poets for answers. Shelley had called poets "legislators" and Carlyle had called them "prophets." Arnold predicted that poetry would replace most religions and philosophies.

In response, the Victorian poets considered essential issues of value and of how to live. They experimented with a wide variety of styles and techniques, adapting unfamiliar modes and irregular metrical forms. From the traditional love lyrics of Elizabeth Barrett Browning to the witty iconoclasm of Clough and the world-weary Orientalism of FitzGerald, these poets looked back fondly on more settled times or forward to the disruptions of a broken tradition. Brontë and Meredith were mainly novelists, but they expressed in poetry a greater intensity, a more personal anguish than the novel form allowed them. As a group these Victorian poets wrote as if they *had awakened in a strange world and, for the most part, were not comfortable in it.*

ELIZABETH BARRETT BROWNING (1806–1861)

The childhood and education of Elizabeth Barrett were dominated by her father, a domestic tyrant who held all of his twelve children under rigid control. Elizabeth's confinement was reinforced by an illness that kept her in a semi-invalid condition during her late twenties and into her thirties. But she had been a very precocious child. Educated at home, she had read extensively and studied Latin and Greek. Some of her early works were translations of Greek poetry.

In the 1840s Barrett became a popular and respected poet. Her poetry attracted, among other admirers, Robert Browning, who first wrote to her and later visited her at her father's house on Wimpole Street, London. Their relationship became romantic, but because of her father's refusal to let her marry, in 1846 she and Browning eloped and immediately left for Italy. They settled in Florence, where she regained her health. They had a son and remained in Italy until her death fifteen years later.

During Mrs. Browning's lifetime her poetic reputation was greater than her husband's. When Wordsworth died in 1850, some in England proposed that she be appointed the next poet laureate. However, the relative fame of husband and wife reversed after her death. Many readers of the next generation found her work too melodramatic. In recent years feminist critics have initiated a reevaluation of Barrett Browning's poetry, reading beyond her familiar love sonnets into her works of social and political issues and especially into her verse novel, *Aurora Leigh*, which presents the life of a woman poet as she survives in a hostile social world.

Sonnets from the Portuguese

Browning sometimes called his wife his Portuguese, alluding to a character in one of her poems. She published these poems as if they were translations, but actually they are a very personal record of the development of her love for Robert Browning.

BARRETT BROWNING'S STYLE

In the cycle of forty-four sonnets published in 1850, the poet traces the stages of her and Browning's love affair from her early doubt and hesitation to her later acceptance and full, intense involvement. She uses the Italian sonnet form of octave and sestet, adapting it to express the contrasts of her doubt and confidence.

Sonnet 22. In sonnet 22, for example, the octave contains an image of the two lovers meeting in heaven, but the sestet gives an image of love on earth as the preferred state. The contrasting, unloving moods of ordinary people create an isolated space for the lovers to dwell in.

Sonnet 32. In sonnet 32 the poet develops the conceit of herself as a musical instrument in poor condition and her husband as the master musician who can play the instrument well, that is, love well, despite the instrument's imperfections.

Sonnet 43. The most frequently quoted of these sonnets is the forty-third, which begins with the question "How do I love thee?" and answers with a list of ways ranging from the lofty to the everyday and from the naive to the passionate. This catalog of ways of loving concludes with the poet's hopes that love will endure after death.

Aurora Leigh

This novel in blank verse tells the life story of a fictional woman poet. Born in Italy of an Italian mother and an English father, Aurora, whose name means "the dawn," is an orphan by the age of thirteen. She goes to England to be cared for and educated by her father's sister. This aunt is a narrow, convention-bound woman who imposes on Aurora an education intended to prepare her to be an ordinary middle-class wife. The girl studies religion, languages, a little math and science, and some music and art. Feeling like a caged bird, Aurora keeps her inner life free while outwardly conforming to this training to be a humble wife, a "cushion." She decides to become a poet. Her aunt's cousin, Romney Leigh, proposes marriage to her. He is dedicated to social service and wishes Aurora to help him in his political career, but she rejects him in favor of her own vocation as a poet. Romney then decides to marry a lower-class woman, Marian Erle, but she is discouraged from the marriage by an aristocratic lady, a rival for Romney's love. Sent away to France, Marian is trapped and raped, as a result of which she becomes pregnant. She and her child are later rescued by Aurora. The three set up a home together in Italy, where Romney later appears. He has been blinded by an accident and has become somewhat softened by experience. Meanwhile, Aurora has learned the value of love from living with Marian and her child. She marries Romney in a new spirit of modest self-effacement. While not giving up poetry, she will write in service to the ideas of her husband.

Thus Barrett Browning closes with a compromise between the artist's drive for self-expression and the Victorian wife's role of submissive service.

"Mother and Poet"

During her residence in Italy after 1846, Barrett Browning and her husband became involved in the struggle for Italian liberation and unity.

The speaker of this dramatic monologue is Laura Savio, an actual poet and patriot of Turin, Italy, whose two sons were killed in military actions. The mother expresses her bitter grief. She tells her compatriots to expect from her no songs celebrating victory. Without her sons, the future of Italy is pointless to her. She describes the progress of her sons, their first happy letters home from the war, her shock at the death of one son, the consoling letter from the other, and then the news of his death coming impersonally by telegraph. Now the joyful victory bells seem to mock her grief. The Italy she loved lies buried in the graves of her two boys, and she has no song of freedom to offer.

EDWARD FITZGERALD (1809–1883)

FitzGerald came from an affluent family. Educated at Cambridge University, his sole occupation was to study, compose, and translate poetry. He lived on his family's country estate in Suffolk, near the eastern coast of England, where he enjoyed sailing. He made many trips to London, where he became friendly with Thackeray, Tennyson, and Carlyle. He published his first translations when he was forty years old.

Most of his translations attracted little interest, and even his *Rubáiyát* was ignored until the book was praised by the poet Dante Gabriel Rossetti. It then became very popular, and its popularity has continued up to the present time.

Rubáiyát of Omar Khayyám

Omar Khayyám is the only great mathematician who was also a poet. A Persian of the twelfth century, he wrote rubais, or quatrains, expressing a disdain of worldly ambition, a preference for a life of pleasure, and the enjoyment of beauty. His tone is often mocking, ironic, and skeptical of human goals and of divine benevolence.

FITZGERALD'S STYLE

FitzGerald translated Khayyám's poems rather freely, making a series of revisions for successive editions. The languid and self-indulgent tone contrasted markedly with the prevailing Victorian tone of earnest and energetic seriousness.

Form. First published in 1859, these lyrics are written in the quiet voice of a poet-philosopher who is both melancholy and ironic about life. The 101 quatrains of pentameter lines have a rhyme scheme a a b b, or two couplets. This form adapts well to a single statement or to a question and response. Sometimes the first two lines make a statement that is repeated using a different metaphor in the second two.

For example, in verse 13 the "Glories of this World" are compared with the "Paradise to come." Then, in the third line of the verse the language changes: "take the Cash [the World] and let the Credit [Paradise] go." The abstract concepts of the future are reduced to financial terms. Most of the poem's images are universal—kings and prophets, flowers and ashes, gates and thrones.

The most famous quatrain is the twelfth. Here the poet prefers a "Book of Verses" along with bread, wine, and "Thou/Beside me" to any other paradise that might be attained by greater efforts. Time is passing; the carpe diem theme recurs.

In the seventy-first quatrain, the inevitability of time's passage is expressed as "The Moving Finger," which, having written our personal destinies, can never be called back to change any part of them. Faced with the indifference of time, the individual's only course must be to enjoy the pleasures of the moment.

Quatrains 82 to 90 contain a conversation among some pots standing in the shop of their creator, the Potter. They question the Potter's skill and motives, as people might question God's, but they can reach no sure conclusion. However, they can forget their doubts by being filled with wine, the universal solution to life's troubles.

EMILY BRONTË (1818–1848)

The sister of Charlotte and Anne Brontë, Emily was the most reclusive and the most attached to the rather vacant moorland landscape near their parsonage home in rural Yorkshire. Except for brief stays at school and in Brussels as a governess, Emily lived only in her father's house.

In 1845 her sister Charlotte discovered a bundle of poems written by Emily. Convinced of their quality, Charlotte persuaded Emily to publish them in a combined volume with other poems by Charlotte and Anne, writing under the names Ellis, Currer, and Acton Bell. About this time, Emily was working on the only novel she completed, the famous *Wuthering Heights*. Always in poor health, Emily died of tuberculosis at the age of thirty.

Many of Emily Brontë's poems were written as part of the saga of Gondal, an imaginary world created by Anne and herself. Gondal, an island in the Pacific, was a realm of violence and intrigue. It was suggested by the family's reading but also reflected the solitary and perhaps morbid sensibility of Emily herself. Both the Gondal poems and the more autobiographical poems of personal feeling are somber in tone.

"The Night-Wind"

This dreamy lyric is a dialogue between the poet and the night wind. The poet, sitting by her open window at midnight, is visited by the seductive voice of the wind. Like a lover it tempts her to come out of her parlor and into the dark woods. She resists, expressing her will to remain in the realm of "human feelings."

In the last two stanzas the wind tries again to persuade her to come out, warning her that human life will end soon enough and she will be alone in her grave. The poem's trimeter quatrains have the rhyme scheme a b a b, but the "a" rhymes fall on unstressed syllables (feminine rhyme), giving a soft and whispering effect.

In the last two stanzas the voice of the wind is more assertive. Here the rhymes are all stressed monosyllables. Alternate lines are longer, having four feet instead of three.

"Stars"

Like "The Night-Wind," this lyric is written in quatrains in a b a b rhyme. The poet speaks to the stars, complaining that they have left the sky at dawn, depriving her of the sweet thoughts and dreams that the stars influence. She prefers the "cool radiance" of stars to the sun's "fierce beams." Like the fly buzzing in her room during the day, she feels imprisoned by too much sunlight; she wishes to sleep through the day and awake again to starlight.

"Remembrance"

This lyric was one of the poems about the imaginary land of Gondal. It is the heroine's lament for her beloved, who has been dead for fifteen years. She still mourns for him, thinking about his cold grave whenever she is alone. But her life has gone on and, although she is still faithful to his memory, she must participate in life and experience "other desires and other hopes." Though she has known no happiness since his death, she has learned to resist despair. She has fought off the desire for her own early death.

The poem has a sad, unusual rhythm because of a preponderance of dactylic feet (a stressed syllable followed by two unstressed). Dactyls are used in the first half of each line, creating a soft, rocking sound pattern well suited to the patient lament.

"The Prisoner. A Fragment"

This poem is also from the Gondal saga, although it is a fragment rather than continuous with other parts of the narrative. A young man is visiting the dungeons of his father's castle. He speaks first to the guard, then to one of the prisoners, a sweet captive maiden. The guard mocks her, telling her that she will never be released. She answers him mildly that she does not wish for release. Because her kinsmen have been killed she only longs to die herself. Now she feels calm, being assured that her imprisonment will soon cause her own death, her ultimate release. Her "inward essence" feels it is approaching freedom from the "outward sense." When she falls silent, the young man and the guard are also silent. They are struck dumb by their awareness of the injustice of keeping such a person captive.

ARTHUR HUGH CLOUGH (1819–1861)

Most readers of Victorian poetry first encounter the name of Clough (rhymes with *enough*) in connection with "Thrysis," Matthew Arnold's elegy on Clough's death. But Clough is interesting in his own right as a poet of the Victorian religious skepticism that others shared but stated less boldly.

Clough left Oxford University when he found that he could not sustain his belief in the authority of the Church of England, or even in the basic doctrines of Christian faith. Clough, like Arnold, worked in education; he became an examiner for the Education Office in London. He also traveled widely in Europe and even visited America.

During his lifetime Clough published several verse narratives in which the young male protagonists are students seeking the best way of life. He thought that poetry should deal with "general wants and ordinary feelings." Clough's poetry does not have the descriptive richness or natural imagery of most of the poetry of his time. His verse is rather rough and discordant. Its strengths are irony and wit. Clough dares to disappoint expectation and defy conventional beliefs. Most of his best poetry was not published until after his death.

"The Latest Decalogue"

The Decalogue, the biblical Ten Commandments, is a basic statement of Christian morality. In updating the commandments Clough creates a cynical parody, implying that the commandments receive only lip service in the modern world. Each commandment is accepted on a superficial level, but its essential meaning is distorted so that the self-interest of the supposed worshiper is evident.

The poem is made up of couplets, one couplet for each commandment. Sin is made out to be inconvenient or unnecessary rather than wrong. Those who break the rules are merely inefficient in getting what they want. Lines 21 to 24 form a sort of epilogue based on the golden rule, which puts self-love at the head of all expedient policies.

"Say Not the Struggle Nought Availeth"

In this lyric Clough addresses the questions that must occur to one who has lost religious faith: What is the point of living? What good is life? Clough's answer suggests that conditions on earth can be improved by human efforts, even though the struggle for improvement seems long and difficult.

In the second stanza, the struggle is presented in terms of a battle, the outcome of which is hidden in smoke. In the next stanza Clough compares the slow pace of progress with the gradual washing away of the shoreline by the sea, barely perceptible until the sea suddenly breaks through. The final stanza uses the image of daybreak to represent progress. The poem's earnest tone here becomes joyful.

"I Dreamt a Dream"

This is a song from Clough's dramatic poem "Dipsychus." Here he uses the sound of bells to represent the hero's oppressed state of mind. In a dream, Dipsychus, whose name means "two minds," hears the ringing of bells as a chorus that is responding to his own thoughts. Church bells, ordinarily associated with a call to worship, here are used ironically to intensify the feeling that God does not exist. In the dream the absence of God seems to mean that all values are undermined. Successive stanzas deny the worth of pleasure, work, love, conquest, and all the usual goals that people pursue. The repeated "dong, dong" of the bells beats the reader into a sort of submission to this loss of faith, until the dreamer awakes with the angel of light at his head and realizes that it was only a dream. But the question remains; does the poet mean that God is dead or that the death of God is merely a bad dream from which we will awaken?

This poem is a good example of the use of onomatopoeia, the verbal imitation of nonverbal sounds. The heavy sound of "dong, dong" not only recreates the tolling of a large bell but also suggests the heavy emotions of dread and depression that accompany a conviction that "there is no God."

"'There Is No God,' the Wicked Saith"

Also from the dramatic poem "Dipsychus," this cynical lyric describes a series of types of people who deny or try to ignore the existence of God and the duty to obey His commandments. The youngster seeking pleasure, the tradesman seeking wealth, and the self-confident rich man assure themselves that God is not relevant and need not be served. Others don't bother to think about God at all unless they are sick or in need. Only the naive and the old-fashioned maintain an active faith.

The poem contrasts worldly self-indulgence with the shallow faith that grows out of guilt or old age. From a Christian point of view, one is as bad as the other. Belief and disbelief seem to depend on a person's circumstance at the moment rather than on any commitment of faith.

GEORGE MEREDITH (1828–1909)

Meredith came from a lower-class family in Portsmouth. His father, a tailor, sent Meredith to several schools, including one in Germany. Meredith was much influenced by German and French ideas. He started to study law but switched to a literary career, working first as a journalist and then as a publisher's reader.

Meredith thought of himself as a poet. Though his writing career begins and ends with poetry, his fame rests primarily on his many novels, of which the most famous are *The Ordeal of Richard Feverel* (1859), a novel about education; *The Egoist* (1879), about the battle of a young woman to free herself from an engagement; and *Diana of the Crossways* (1885), a feminist novel and one of his most popular.

Meredith the novelist was a humorist. His *Essay on Comedy* is a standard source in the theory of comedy. But his style is often intricate and obscure; the multiple ironies and oblique jokes make him difficult to read.

Modern Love

This sequence of fifty sonnets describes the failure of a marriage. In 1849 Meredith had married a young widow who was the daughter of Thomas Love Peacock. The couple did not get along, and she left him in 1858 to elope to Europe with a painter.

SONNET FORM

Meredith's unhappy experiences are reflected in his poems, sonnets of sixteen rather than fourteen lines, or, one could say, of four quatrains, each rhyming a b b a. Each sonnet explores a moment in the sequence of events that leads to the end of the marriage.

The story is told from the husband's point of view as he becomes disillusioned, anguished, and disgusted by his wife's alienation and infidelity. He hates her even as he perceives that she is beautiful. He is jealous of the rival who has won her love. Together they play the social/hypocritical role of a happily married couple while hiding their real feelings. Yet an attempt at frank speech in sonnet 48 ends in more distress. Ultimately, no one is to blame; "wrong is mixed" in the tragedy of love. Set in bedroom, parlor, and beside the ocean, the scenes present a growing intensity of emotion, leading up to a crisis of revulsion and a final retreat to pity.

"Lucifer in Starlight"

This poem is a regular sonnet of the Italian form. It pictures Satan, the archdemon, who one night in a fit of restlessness leaves hell to survey the earth. Satan leans across the sky and remembers his revolt against God in heaven. What he sees now is the orderly and unalterable pattern of the "law" of the universe, which he can do nothing to disrupt. He is the eternal outsider.

GERARD MANLEY HOPKINS (1844–1889)

Because of his influence on modern poetry Hopkins is the most important of the minor Victorian poets.

Hopkins came from a middle-class family of varied cultural interests and deep religious convictions. A talented student, he went to Oxford University, where he absorbed the ideas of Newman and the Oxford Movement, eventually converting to Catholicism in 1866. When he left Oxford and became a Jesuit priest, he burned the poetry he had written so far, although Hopkins's friend from Oxford days, the poet Robert Bridges, kept some copies. Hopkins began to write poetry again in 1875 on the occasion of the wreck of the ship *Deutschland*, which was carrying five nuns. Though the poem's obscurity prevented its publication, Hopkins continued to write, frequently feeling a conflict between his priestly duties and his poetic activity.

In 1884 Hopkins was made a professor of Greek and Latin at University College in Dublin. Teaching and administrative responsibilities were too heavy for him and he became depressed. During this time he wrote the sonnets of doubt and frustration that are usually called his "terrible sonnets." However, his last poem, "Thou Art Indeed Just, Lord," shows reconciliation with his faith. He died of typhoid in 1889.

Hopkins's Style

The modernism of Hopkins has made his work seem difficult to many readers. Unlike many other post-romantic poets, he did not demand harmonious beauty in his poetry.

INSCAPE

Hopkins developed the concept of "inscape." Named by analogy to landscape, inscape refers to the essential, inner individual form or nature of each created thing. This is what Hopkins's poems seek to express. Inscape is a characteristic pattern that informs the actions of a creature. This pattern of action Hopkins calls "instress," the dynamic design of the individual. In order to find poetic means to express inscape, Hopkins violates conventional diction and meter.

To find an adequate vocabulary, Hopkins coins new terms, often by analogy to terms already in use. For example, the term *leafmeal* describes how leaves fall one by one, an analogy to the term *piecemeal*. *Quickgold* is made by analogy to *quicksilver*. Hopkins invents compound terms: *dapple-dawn-drawn* and *wind-walks*.

The energy of his verse breaks out of regular metrical patterns. While the lines of a sonnet by Hopkins have a fairly constant number of stressed syllables, the number and arrangement of unstressed syllables are variable.

Hopkins calls this "sprung rhythm." He also adds emphasis by alliteration, much like Anglo-Saxon poetry. He concentrates energy by leaving out minor words. Many of Hopkins's poems create an impression of rushing energy; so much is being said that the reader cannot grasp it all, but the main emotional statement is clear and strong.

"God's Grandeur"

Like most of Hopkins's sonnets, this one uses the Italian form, octave and sestet. The first four lines depict the grandeur of God in images of flashing light and cohesive richness. In contrast, the next four lines express human existence in dull and heavy terms such as "trod," "smeared," and "smudge." Humankind is out of touch with grandeur and isolated from nature. But, in the sestet, nature still retains her beauty and freshness. Although night comes to hide that beauty, it always reemerges at dawn because God cares for it. The final image of God as the hovering Holy Spirit is a complement to the opening image of God as glory.

"Spring"

This sonnet opens with a simple proselike statement: "Nothing is so beautiful as spring," but the poem has a tripping rhythm from the multiple unstressed syllables. Images of spring's beauty, both for eye and ear, fill the rest of the octave. The sestet begins with a question about the meaning of all this beauty. The answer is that spring's beauty is a fragment or "strain" of what paradise was like before the fall. The poet calls urgently for Christ to come and save the world in this springtime state, lest it "cloud" and "sour" from sin. In its full beauty the earth is worthy of being saved by Christ.

"The Windhover"

A windhover is a kind of falcon. This poem celebrates the gliding movement of the bird as analogous to the beauty of Christ. The sweeping, rushing movement of the first six and a half lines imitates the falcon's flight. Admiration stirs the speaker as he observes the falcon. In the sestet, the swooping falcon suddenly changes its movement. The verb "buckle" suggests that it falls or dives. The light reflecting from its feathers inspires awe.

The last three lines attempt to explain the beauty of the falcon by comparing it with other unexpected flashes of beauty in apparently dull settings: the shine of soil newly turned up by a plow and the intense color of embers when the ashes fall from them. In other words, surprising inner light and beauty inhabit many natural things that would seem to be ordinary or drab.

"Spring and Fall"

Not a sonnet, this poem in couplets has short lines with three stresses in each, as if adapted for speaking to a child. The poet asks Margaret why she is crying and answers his own question: She is sad because the leaves are falling from trees in Goldengrove. He predicts that as she grows up, falling leaves will not cause her to cry anymore, but she will have other reasons to cry. Whatever she cries about as an adult, ultimately hers will be part of the same general grief, the sorrow of the spirit that all humans must suffer. As an adult the poet knows that human beings, like leaves, were born for "blight." Margaret will come to feel the same way and will weep because of it.

"Carrion Comfort"

Written in 1885 at a time of spiritual frustration for Hopkins, this is one of the so-called terrible sonnets. The speaker is struggling with despair, which is a sin. Feeding the heart on despair is like eating carrion, dead and decaying flesh. Despair is a comfort only because giving up, abandoning all effort, is more comfortable than continuing to try. But the poet still says "I can," although what he "can" do is left vague and uncertain.

The tortured, distorted sentence structure of the second quatrain supports the image of God punishing the poet while he wants to run away. The sestet deals with reasons why God causes human beings to suffer. First, it is to test and purify human beings, as winnowing grain separates the good grain from the useless chaff. But more important, the struggle with God is an intimate encounter, like a wrestling match. In the last line the poet is stunned to realize with whom he has been battling—God Himself. Despair turns into awed submission. The angry tone of the opening has been converted into a worshipful realization that the struggle has been useful.

"Thou Art Indeed Just, Lord"

This sonnet, written a few months before his death, expresses Hopkins's response to the question "Why do the ways of the wicked prosper?," found in Jeremiah 12:1. That is, why do apparent sinners find success in life while godly people seem to fail in their efforts to do good? The poem opens with a restatement of the biblical question. The second quatrain contrasts the defeat of the speaker with the thriving state of men who are sots (drunken fools) or given over to lust. The pleading poet addresses God as "Sir," as if politely pleading before a judge. In the sestet, he points out how easily nature thrives; plants and birds seem to grow and build with little effort. But the poet's striving yields nothing; no matter how long and hard he strains, time brings forth no results. The final line is a prayer for God's help.

Hopkins's desperate questioning of God in his "terrible sonnets" comprises one of many attempts by Victorian poets to come to terms with the challenges of their times. Religious doubt and the questioning of social institutions cause them emotional distress that is expressed either directly, as by Hopkins and Brontë; ironically, as by Clough and FitzGerald; or through situations and characters, as by Barrett Browning and Meredith. No poet seems at ease in the world. The beauties of nature become a bitter contrast to inner anguish. The lyric impulse continues, but the quiet joys of romantic poetry seem too simple now and do not render a complete picture of the condition of modern humanity. If God seems to be retreating from human beings, social relation-

ships such as marriage are also going sour. The appeal of FitzGerald's Rubáiyát is its urging that one just forget it all and escape into the pleasures of the moment. For Brontë and Hopkins, however, the present moment holds not pleasure but pain. These poets describe the mental stress experienced by many of their readers.

Selected Readings

Bergonzi, Bernard. *Gerard Manley Hopkins*. New York: Macmillan, 1977.

Craik, W. A. *The Brontë Novels*. London: Methuen, 1968.

Harris, Wendell V. *Arthur Hugh Clough*. New York: Twayne, 1970.

Jewett, Iran B. Hassani. *Edward FitzGerald*. New York: Twayne, 1977.

McCullen, Maurice, and Lewis Sawin. *A Dictionary of the Characters in George Meredith's Fiction*. New York: Garland, 1977.

Moffatt, James. *George Meredith: A Primer to the Novels*. London: Hodder, 1909.

Peters, W. A. M. *Gerard Manley Hopkins: A Critical Essay Towards the Understanding of His Poetry*. Oxford: Blackwell, 1970.

Radley, Virginia L. *Elizabeth Barrett Browning*. New York: Twayne, 1972.

Smith, Anne, ed. *The Art of Emily Brontë*. New York: Barnes, 1976.

11

Mid-Victorian Essayists

1860 Ruskin, *Unto this Last* published in *Cornhill* magazine; Spencer, *Programme of a System of Synthetic Philosophy*

1862 Ruskin, "Munera Pulveris" published in *Fraser's Magazine*; Mill, *Utilitarianism*

1863 Thomas Huxley, *Man's Place in Nature*

1865 Ruskin, *Sesame and Lilies* and *Ethics of the Dust*; Arnold, *Essays in Criticism* (second series); *Fortnightly Review* founded

1866 Ruskin, *The Crown of Wild Olives*; first permanently established transatlantic cable

1867 Marx, *Das Kapital,* vol. 1, written in London

1868 Disraeli becomes prime minister

1870 Huxley, *Lay Sermons, Addresses and Reviews*; competitive examinations for civil service begin; French scientist Pasteur devises process for killing bacteria in milk

1870–1879 Ruskin as Slade Professor of Art at Oxford

1871 Darwin, *The Descent of Man*; trade unions legalized; Stanley finds Dr. Livingston in African jungle

1871–1884 Ruskin, *Fors Clavigera*

1873 Mill, *Autobiography* published posthumously

1875 Public Health Act consolidates sanitary legislation; first performance of Bizet's *Carmen*

1878 James McNeil Whistler sues Ruskin for libel and wins a farthing in damages; Gilbert and Sullivan produce comic opera *H.M.S. Pinafore*

1880 Elementary education made compulsory

1880–1881 First Anglo-Boer War

1882 Married Women's Property Act; Darwin dies

1884 Ruskin, *The Storm-Clouds of the Nineteenth Century*

1885–1889 Ruskin, *Praeterita*

1886 Huxley, *Science and Morals*; the Statue of Liberty dedicated

1892 Huxley, *Essays on Some Controverted Questions*; Tchaikovsky, *The Nutcracker*

1899 Huxley, *Science and Education* published posthumously

By the mid-Victorian Age, the 1850s to the 1870s, England had a wide array of outlets for literary productions and public discourse. Each faction or cause had its journals; prose fiction took up social conditions for critical examination; and the public lecture, later printed, became an effective forum for influencing public opinion. Book reviewers took up new ideas, explaining and evaluating them. Freedom of discussion counterbalanced the conservative social tendencies of the Victorian middle-class. Some of the best thinkers and writers addressed themselves to the general reading public. Huxley taught the nonspecialist how scientists think and work. Darwin drew together various implications from geology and biology to make a unified and comprehensible theory of humankind's origin. Eliot introduced clear thinking and moderation into the discussion of women's role in society. Ruskin put art criticism into the context of history and economics. Ordinary working people were addressed by the best-trained minds and invited to think broadly about their roles in social change. These lecturers and essayists were engaged in redefining English society in the hope of making it better and of freeing it from old mistakes.

JOHN RUSKIN (1819–1900)

Like Carlyle before him, John Ruskin made a reputation as an essayist who went against the mainstream of English progress. He came from an affluent middle-class family. His mother taught him extensively from the Bible and his father took him on tours of Europe. Ruskin was educated mostly at home but also went to Oxford University. His family's wealth enabled him to spend his life as a writer and lecturer, developing his tastes and interests in art and his ideas about the relationship of art to modern industrialized society. He was also a painter and a patron of other artists.

He had an unhappy marriage that lasted only six years. Late in life he had an attraction, equally unhappy, to a young Irish woman who refused to marry him on grounds of religious incompatibility. In the last decades of his life Ruskin suffered periods of mental illness marked by delirium. But he was a popular lecturer and was briefly a professor of art at Oxford. Although many of his contemporaries found Ruskin's ideas eccentric, he had a profound effect on the school of painters and poets who called themselves Pre-Raphaelites.

Modern Painters

This was Ruskin's first important work. It began in 1843 with Ruskin's defense of the innovative landscape painter J. M. Turner. Ruskin went on to develop, in five volumes, a study and appreciation of modern painting in Europe. In the course of these discussions he defined certain concepts that became common currency in nineteenth-century art criticism. To Ruskin a work's greatness depended on its ability to generate great ideas in the mind of the spectator. Thus the artist's ability to imitate nature, which had been the central criterion in classical theories of art, became less important than the work's effect on the moral nature of the individual.

RUSKIN'S STYLE

Ruskin's prose is full of vigorous and detailed descriptions of scenes and natural objects. However, he does not deal with the human figure in painting. Ruskin also criticized "the pathetic fallacy"—that is, the attribution of human feelings, motives, or actions to natural objects. Thus, Ruskin believed, the poet falsely ascribes his or her own feelings to the "cruel" ocean or the "happy" flower. The best poets, says Ruskin, will avoid such descriptions. Ruskin, however, does not always manage to avoid them himself, since they are so much a part of literary conventions in describing nature.

The Stones of Venice

This treatise is a major study of Venetian architecture. Ruskin believed that all architecture has moral qualities that reflect the power and virtues of the culture that built it and form a part of its cultural memory.

In this book Ruskin studies the architecture of Venice, Italy, an old commercial city built in a lagoon and laced with canals. He shows how the moral and social conditions that prevailed in the city influenced the forms and the technical details of its structures. The city's history is recorded in the stones of its buildings and plazas.

THE GOTHIC IDEAL

One famous passage in the second volume of this work deals with Gothic architecture, which radically contrasts with Venetian architecture. Ruskin finds that the rough and irregular medieval Gothic architecture of northern Europe is beautiful despite its imperfections. Churches and castles in Gothic style lack the polish, the fine finish, of the classical buildings of southern Europe but reflect the individual skills and imagination of the workmen who built them. In order to achieve perfection, the worker must be absolutely submissive, a slave, to the overall plan. But the free worker on Gothic buildings could develop details according to his own ideas. Thus Gothic buildings reflect a freer, more open, and more humane culture and are thus more beautiful.

Ruskin's praise of the Gothic departs from a long critical tradition of dismissing the Gothic as crude and ugly in its roughness. Ruskin saw that the dignity of work requires that the worker's ideas and tastes be engaged in his or her labor. Modern industrial systems made workers subservient to machines; they became mere slaves. Therefore, Ruskin argued, the products of such systems of manufacture would be sterile and degrading, like the products of slave labor. He urged the English public not to demand perfection in their furniture, for example, but to look for evidence of the worker's imagination. Thus Ruskin links social criticism to art criticism, showing the interplay of the economic condition and the cultural products of a nation.

The Storm-Clouds of the Nineteenth Century

This book is a series of lectures from late in Ruskin's career, when considerations of the social context of art had led him to become a social critic.

In the first lecture, for example, Ruskin gives one of the early warnings that industrial development causes air pollution and can change the local climate. Ruskin's evidence was based not on scientific testing but on his own recorded observations of the visible quality of light and air. As a painter and writer, Ruskin had been recording these observations in sketches and notebooks since his youth. He is thus able to fill his lecture with quotations from descriptive passages dating from after the air became polluted, thus documenting the loss of clarity and brightness. Ruskin dates the coming of the "plague-wind" at about the year 1871. He points out that while scientific instruments are not precise enough to accurately record the changes he describes, to the eye the difference is evident.

At the end of the lecture, Ruskin does not call for government regulation, a more modern approach. Instead, he asks his listeners to improve their own lives, to return to "paths of rectitude and piety" in the hope of achieving God's blessing. Ruskin was ahead of his times in perceiving the problem of air pollution, but he keeps his discussion in a prescientific religious context. Industrialization is a plague from God, he suggests, and the only medicine for it is faith.

THOMAS HENRY HUXLEY (1825–1895)

Huxley was a scientist and a popularizer of scientific ideas. His importance to English literature lies in his role in the great Victorian debates about culture, education, and the progress of society.

The son of a schoolmaster, Huxley was attracted to logic and to scientific theory and especially to the newly developing field of geology. He took a degree in medicine and signed on the ship Rattlesnake as a surgeon, taking advantage of ocean travel to make scientific observations on marine zoology.

Back in England, Huxley published research papers on his scientific studies. He also became involved in defending scientific education and explaining new scientific ideas to the general reading public. When Darwin's *The Origin of Species* was published in 1859, the influential *Times* of London asked Huxley to review the book. This began Huxley's involvement in the controversies generated by the theory of evolution, Huxley always defending Darwin's ideas against the theological establishment. But Huxley was interested in more than the issue of evolution alone. He aimed at raising the level of public understanding about many scientific findings and at introducing into general education a more practical and scientific training, not to the exclusion of literary education but in order to equip the new generation to think rationally about scientific knowledge and its uses. His ideas provoked a response by Matthew Arnold, who defended the traditional humanist education. Huxley was also an advocate of education for women.

Part of Huxley's influence can be attributed to his direct and simple prose style, which lacks the personal quirks that characterize Carlyle, for instance. His public speeches were organized clearly and with compelling logic, but his tone was good-natured and moderate. While unable to accept orthodox Christianity, he did not attack those who sincerely believed. His quarrel was with rigid theologians who refused to admit that science had any validity. He called himself an agnostic.

Science and Culture

The essays in this volume reflect Huxley's eagerness to show how vital the understanding of science and its methods is to modern culture.

His speech "The Values of Education in the Sciences" was given at the opening of the Scientific College in the industrial city of Birmingham. He praises the founder of the college, Sir Josiah Mason, a self-made man who provided funds for the school and established a practical program of study. Huxley focuses on Mason's dictum that the college "make no provision for 'mere literary instruction.'" Higher education in England had in the past been almost wholly concerned with literature and language. Huxley explains why this was so. In medieval times, theology was considered the essential source of truth, and the Latin language gave students access to theology's major texts. In the Renaissance humanists promoted the study of Greek as necessary to understand the literature of antiquity and Greek studies in physical science. But these eras have passed; modern empirical studies of nature have revealed new truths that contradict ideas that were accepted in medieval and Renaissance times. Latin and Greek have little to offer students of modern science; they are better off studying German, French, and English. These languages are offered in the new college. Besides, the student can study the "criticism of life" through readings in three essential sources: the Bible, Shakespeare, and Milton. This seems an excellent plan to Huxley.

"Agnosticism and Christianity"

Huxley's experience taught him that the scientific method of investigation was compatible with the way the human mind works and that the truths of religion were incompatible with science. He coined the term *agnosticism* to describe his inability to believe what seemed to him illogical statements. The term was poorly understood, in his opinion, so he undertook a definition to clarify his position. He says that agnosticism is not a creed. It has only one essential principle: One should not say that he believes in the truth of any proposition "unless he can produce evidence which logically justifies that certainty." Without such evidence one is bound to suspend judgment, to admit that he does not know. Huxley points out that the 2,500-year history of philosophy shows one set of doctrines being supplanted by another set, with no real progress. He sees the contemporary conflict as being between agnosticism and ecclesiasticism, which requires one to declare belief in foregone conclusions. But an agnostic would feel he was lying if he stated a belief in a doctrine that seemed incredible. It cannot be moral to require people to lie, even to preserve public harmony. The ecclesiast would require people to believe in what they think is impossible; the agnostic is ready to believe if given "good grounds for belief." Thus Huxley puts the agnostic position on a high moral plane, diminishing the apparent honesty of militant opponents.

GEORGE ELIOT (1819–1880)

Although best known as a novelist, Eliot had an earlier career as an essayist and reviewer for important intellectual and literary journals in London, including *The Westminster Review*, of which she became an editor. Her range of subjects was broad. She was well read in philosophy and theology, but she also took a special interest in reviewing publications by and about women. Not a militant feminist, Eliot believed that the cultivation of women's minds through solid, useful education was the key to raising their status and making them happy beings.

"Margaret Fuller and Mary Wollstonecraft"   In a review article Eliot compares and contrasts two important contributions by women to the question of women's rights and women's proper role in society. She finds that Wollstonecraft's *Rights of Woman* and Fuller's *Women in the Nineteenth Century* have many similarities. Both point out that weak-minded or poorly educated women frequently have considerable power because of their attractiveness and that such power is usually misused for petty or foolish purposes. Many uncultured women are unmanageable, not being open to reason.

Further, Wollstonecraft and Fuller agree that women cannot be summed up as a single type; their natures and capacities are varied. Some may be able to take on professions usually carried out by men, but the majority would probably be more interested in domestic responsibilities, even if they had other choices.

Eliot responds by advocating a gradual improvement in women's social position as women gradually improve themselves. Eliot agrees with Wollstonecraft and Fuller that, as they now exist, women are not morally excellent, but that given wider education and opportunity, their moral sensitivity would improve. While citing minor imperfection of style in these author's books, Eliot praises them as correctly setting out the essential outlines of the question of women's role in society. Eliot uses her review as an occasion to restate these basic points and to add the weight of her judgment in favor of Wollstonecraft and Fuller.

"Silly Novels by Lady Novelists"

In this article, written for *The Westminster Review*, Eliot mocks the trite, sentimental novels some women writers produced for popular consumption during the mid-nineteenth century. With cutting wit she ridicules the absurdly perfect characters, the overblown situations, the artificial diction, and the banal sentiments found in such novels. They show no real sense of how people live or of how they speak and act in situations of crisis.

Eliot classifies the novels into four categories:

> the "mind-and-millinery" novels, whose exaggerated heroines are as deeply learned as they are well dressed;
>
> the "oracular" novels, which set before the reader "a complete theory of life and manual of divinity" in falsely elevated style;
>
> the "white neck-cloth" novels, with insipid young curates involved in evangelical romances; and
>
> the "antique species" of novel, which pretends to recreate the past but displays no imaginative grasp of history.

Eliot cites examples of each type of novel and quotes illustrative passages. She expresses surprise and disappointment that such novels are usually favorably reviewed, as if women writers could not be expected to do any better. Most women, she argues, have more intelligence than is evident in these specimens of feminine literature. But because prose fiction is a relatively open field with few requirements for education, ill-prepared women have rushed into novel writing, with the resulting silliness in novels.

The great social, religious, and cultural questions of the mid-nineteenth century drew widespread attention to journals, lectures, and essays that aimed to sort out the issues and show society the right direction. Such problems as the dislocating effects of industrial development, the role of women in a changing political climate, and the challenge of scientific theories to traditional religious belief challenged writers to help shape public opinion. They developed a precise and convincing prose of public discourse, often witty but basically earnest and well reasoned. The best of these writers—such as Ruskin, Huxley, and Eliot—achieved literary quality in their essays. With rich and invigorating description, with clear and compelling arguments, and with wit and inventive language they made social commentary an art.

Selected Readings

Creeger, George R., ed. *George Eliot: A Collection of Critical Essays.* Englewood Cliffs, NJ: Prentice-Hall, 1970.

Landow, George P. *The Aesthetic and Critical Theories of John Ruskin*. Princeton: Princeton University Press, 1971.

Liddell, Robert. *The Novels of George Eliot*. New York: St. Martin's, 1977.

Paradis, James G. *T. H. Huxley: Man's Place in Nature*. Lincoln: University of Nebraska Press, 1978.

12

The Pre-Raphaelites and Aestheticism

1837–1901	Queen Victoria reigns
1843–1860	Ruskin, *Modern Painters*
1848	The Pre-Raphaelite Brotherhood founded by D. G. Rossetti; Rossetti becomes pupil of artist Ford Madox Brown
1849	Ruskin, *The Seven Lamps of Architecture*; Dickens, *David Copperfield*
1850	D. G. Rossetti, "The Blessed Damozel"; magazine *Germ* founded; Tennyson appointed poet laureate
1851–1853	Ruskin, *Stones of Venice*
1854	Ruskin assists founding of the London Working Men's College
1856	Poems by Rossetti and Morris published in *Oxford and Cambridge* magazine
1857	The Indian Mutiny
1858	Morris, *The Defense of Guenevere and Other Poems*
1859	Meredith, *The Ordeal of Richard Feverel*; FitzGerald, *Rubáiyát of Omar Khayyám*
1859–1886	Tennyson, *Idylls of the King*
1860	D. G. Rossetti marries E. Siddal; Eliot, *The Mill on the Floss* and *Silas Marner*; Reade, *The Cloister and the Hearth*
1861	Morris opens interior decorating and crafts business; imprisonment for debt abolished

1862   C. Rossetti, *The Goblin Market and Other Poems*; D. G. Rossetti gives up writing after the death of his wife

1865   Swinburne, *Atalanta in Calydon*; Ruskin, *Sesame and Lilies*

1866   C. Rossetti, *The Prince's Progress and Other Poems*; Swinburne, *Poems and Ballads*

1867   Morris, *The Life and Death of Jason*

1867–c.1886   In France the "impressionist" movement of painting, featuring paintings by Monet, Pissarro, Renoir, and others

1868–1870   Morris, *The Earthly Paradise*

1870   Rossetti, *Poems*

1871   Swinburne, *Songs Before Sunrise*; Buchanan attacks Swinburne and Rossetti in "The Fleshly School of Poetry"

1872   C. Rossetti, *Singsong*

1873   Pater, *Studies in the History of the Renaissance*; Arnold, *Literature and Dogma*

1875   Artisans' Dwelling Act, the first public-housing legislation

1876   Morris, *Sigurd the Volsung*; Bell invents telephone

1880   Gladstone elected prime minister

1881   D. G. Rossetti, *Ballads and Sonnets*, "House of Life," and "The White Ship"; C. Rossetti, *A Pageant and Other Poems*

1882   D. G. Rossetti dies

1885   Pater, *Marius the Epicurean*

1889   Morris founds Kelmscott Press at Hammersmith; Pater, *Appreciations*

1891   Morris, "News from Nowhere" published in *Commonweal*

1896   Kelmscott Chaucer printed by Morris; Morris dies

Influenced by the art criticism of Ruskin and inspired by the example of Keats, a group of young painters and poets in mid-century England formed a movement to counteract the dull, didactic, and morally earnest culture they saw around them in favor of an art that exalted beauty and the spirit. Founded in 1848 by Dante Gabriel Rossetti, the movement called itself the Pre-Raphaelite Brotherhood. Who was Raphael and what was his influence? Raphael was an Italian painter of the high Renaissance (the beginning of the sixteenth century), a younger contemporary of Michelangelo's. To this group of Victorian painters and poets, Raphael's polished style epitomized mere technical skill, a cool perfection that they found lacking in spirit and devoid of feeling. By contrast, painters working in the late Middle Ages, before Raphael, were less skillful but had achieved a romantic intensity of feeling that the members of the Brotherhood sought in their own work. They worked for simplicity and purity; they opposed the prevailing academic style of painting as too formal.

The chief painters of the group were Rossetti himself, John Millais, and William Holman Hunt. The main poets were Rossetti; his sister, Christina Rossetti; and William Morris. Walter Pater and his disciple, Algernon Swinburne, later broadened the aims of the movement to include a more extreme aestheticism or "art for art's sake." The group advocated a complete separation of art from all contemporary social issues and aimed for a pure and intense experience of beauty. The poet Coventry Patmore, who had contributed to the Pre-Raphaelites' periodical, Germ, *was also a member of this group, as was Oscar Wilde at the start of his career. Although as a movement these painters and poets agreed in their rejection of the moralism and dullness of middle-class society, at the same time they developed their own particular styles. The Brotherhood was therefore short-lived, its members tending to separate as each artist pursued his or her own vision of beauty.*

DANTE GABRIEL ROSSETTI (1828–1882)

Rossetti's father was an Italian political activist living in exile in England. His home was a center of political activity and of the discussion of ideas, both political and artistic. Dante went to Kings' College School in London and also studied painting. At twenty he joined with some fellow painters, including William Holman Hunt and John Everett Millais, to form the Pre-Raphaelite Brotherhood, dedicated to opposing technical skill without imaginative inspiration. He was a poet as well as a painter, and some of his poems were published in *Germ,* founded in 1850, the official literary organ of the movement. *Germ* was edited by Dante's brother, William Michael Rossetti, another member of the Brotherhood.

In 1854 the group was encouraged by the favorable notice of the influential art critic John Ruskin. In 1856 Dante Rossetti married his model, Elizabeth Siddal, who was also a painter and poet. Seldom in good health, she took laudanum and died from an overdose in 1862. Distraught, Rossetti gave up writing and buried with her a manuscript containing many of his poems. However, Rossetti began to write again because of the benign influence of Jane Morris, another model and the wife of his friend, the painter and poet William Morris. By 1869 Rossetti changed his mind about the buried poems and had them dug up. Rossetti and the

Morrises established a joint household in 1871, where Rossetti continued to write and to paint.

In his famous essay "The Fleshly School of Poetry," Robert Buchanan savagely attacked Rossetti and his friends as immoral and obscene. Rossetti wrote a vigorous response. Eventually his health began to fail. In the last years of his life he became addicted to chloral, a drug used to induce sleep. During this time Rossetti enjoyed the status of leader of young aestheticists such as Walter Pater and Oscar Wilde. In 1881, the year before he died, Rossetti republished a selection of his earlier work in a volume called *Poems*.

"The Blessed Damozel"

This poem contains good examples of the painterly images of Pre-Raphaelite poetry. Written when Rossetti was only eighteen, it develops the image of a beautiful woman, now dead and in heaven, who longs for her lover still alive on earth. (The lover's point of view is given in stanzas and lines that appear inside parentheses.) At the beginning of the poem she is pictured with long golden hair and a white, flowing robe, leaning over the ramparts of heaven with a spray of lilies over her arm. She prays to be joined by her lover; she has been in heaven ten years, awaiting his arrival. As she speaks she describes what will happen when her lover comes to heaven—how they will meet, how they will sing and pray together, how she will present him to Mary to be blessed.

The poem blends the sensuous imagery of reunited lovers with images of religious worship. The damozel's ultimate prayer, given in lines 129 and 130, will be "to live as once on earth/With Love." In the final stanza the damozel weeps into her hands, and the lover on earth hears her.

"My Sister's Sleep"

This poem narrates an imagined incident. Set around midnight on Christmas Eve, it presents three figures in a bedchamber: a dying young woman, Margaret; her watchful and attentive mother; and the narrator. As Margaret falls asleep the mother leaves her bedside to sit and sew at a worktable. The church bells strike midnight, the beginning of Christmas Day. The mother, echoing the Angel's announcement of Christ's birth, says, "Glory unto the Newly Born!" (line 34). The silence is broken again by the sound of people moving in the room above. Fearing that Margaret might be wakened, the mother returns to the bedside and bends over her. She realizes after a moment that the girl is dead. The narrator, watching the mother's face, also realizes that death has come. They kneel and together ask "Christ's blessing on the newly born!" in this case meaning Margaret, who, having just died, is newly born in heaven.

The poem is memorable for combining ordinary domestic detail of light and sound with a sense of spiritual experience during a moment of crisis.

"The Woodspurge"

A woodspurge is a small wildflower. In this short lyric the speaker pictures himself walking across some hills on a windy day when he is feeling the full impact of grief, a "perfect" or absolute grief, the cause of which is not explained. As the wind dies down he sits with his head between his knees, looking down at the plants between his feet. He focuses upon one plant, the woodspurge, noticing that it has a triple flower. Now, some time later, the feeling of grief has faded but the clear image of the flower remains, having been strongly impressed on him in that moment of intense feeling. The poem suggests a mental quirk, that our minds retain seemingly minor and arbitrary details experienced during moments of crisis.

The House of Life

ROSSETTI'S STYLE

Rossetti worked on this sonnet sequence for several decades. Considered his masterpiece, it represents his mature work. It idealizes the love of a man and woman, presenting love both spiritual, as in the platonic concept of the Renaissance, and physical.

"Lovesight." Sonnet 4 depicts spiritual love. It begins with the lover asking, "When do I see thee most . . . ?" Such diction is usually reserved for the sacred; her face is the altar at which he worships. At dusk, when vision is less acute, "my soul only sees thy soul." This is the best kind of seeing. In the sestet, not to see the beloved is the equivalent of loss of hope, of death itself.

"Nuptial Sleep." By contrast, the sonnet "Nuptial Sleep" suggests sexual pleasure. This is the sonnet Buchanan most objected to in his criticism of Rossetti's "immorality." The sonnet re-creates the moment after lovemaking as the married lovers lie apart and sink into sleep. The images suggest their union and separation at the same time. In the sestet the lover dreams, then emerges from his dream to become aware, once again, of his wife at his side.

"Willowwood." The forty-ninth through the fifty-second sonnets are titled "Willowwood" and renumbered 1 through 4 to indicate their status as a minor sequence within the larger whole. In these sonnets the lover is sitting beside an open well among some willow trees, which are conventionally associated with weeping for lost loved ones. On the opposite side of the well sits a cupidlike figure called Love. As they both gaze into the well the lover imagines that the reflected face of Love is the face of the woman he loves. He bends forward to kiss the face in the water. Love sings a song while the lover imagines that the surrounding trees are the forms of himself and his beloved in former days. In the third sonnet Love sings a mournful song of longing and loss. When the song is over the face in the water fades away, and the lover, leaning into the well again, feels the face of Love upon his neck in a gesture of pity.

"A Superscription." One of the best known of the whole sonnet sequence is 97, "A Superscription." The speaker, a personification of regret, in the opening lines identifies himself by such names as "Might-have-been" and "Too-late." The speaker torments the lover by holding up to his eyes a mirror showing the forms of Life and Love as they once were but are no more. In the sestet regret promises, or threatens, that if the lover should ever know a moment's peace, regret will be sure to "ambush" his heart once more and deprive him of sleep. Generally, these sonnets present images of love as melancholy and painful. The moments of pleasure are far outnumbered by moments of grief and loneliness.

CHRISTINA ROSSETTI (1830–1894)

Younger sister of Dante, Christina Rossetti enjoyed the same domestic atmosphere of political and poetic discourse. She was educated only at home. When family fortunes sank she tried to work as a governess but was prevented from doing so by her frail health. She was a member of the Pre-Raphaelite Brotherhood and published some early poems in its periodical, *Germ*. The dominant influence of her life was the Anglican church, especially the Anglo-Catholic movement, a high-church movement influenced by Newman. Rossetti broke off an engagement with James Collinson, another member of the Pre-Raphaelites, when he reverted to Roman Catholicism. She lived a celibate life, devoted to poetry and to charitable work. Her health was never good.

Rossetti's Poetic Form

Christina Rossetti's poetry fulfills the ideals of the Pre-Raphaelite movement in that it is both simple and intense. It is so simple in diction and form that it sometimes suggests nursery rhymes. *The Goblin Market*, her most famous poem, was first seen as a story for children. It is intense in feeling, especially in expressions of devotion and renunciation.

Often compared with the American poet Emily Dickinson, Rossetti uses wit and eccentric, concentrated images to provoke surprising feelings. The poetry of her later years was increasingly religious in subject and tone.

"Song"

This early lyric shows Rossetti's unconventional wit as she mocks the convention common in love songs of devotion to the memory of one's dead beloved. The speaker is the corpse. In the first stanza she refuses the usual tributes, accepting a simple covering of grass for her grave. Remembering and forgetting will be indifferent to her. In the second stanza the term "haply" suggests that it will be a matter of chance whether she remembers her lover, and either way, a happy chance.

"A Birthday"

This lyric uses rich imagery to celebrate the coming of love. The first stanza presents a series of similes that compare the awakening heart with a bird, a tree, and a seashell. While each is in a state of gladness, the heart is more glad.

In the second stanza the speaker calls for a dais, a platform, on which to act out the birthday celebration. The dais is bedecked in silk, precious metals, fruit, and exotic birds. It is a fit place for the reception of love. The poem suggests the queenly, luxurious feeling of being loved.

"In an Artist's Studio"

This sonnet stands out because it seems to provide a glimpse into Rossetti's brother Dante's studio and into his relationship with Elizabeth Siddal, his model and later his wife.

In the sonnet a visitor to the studio remarks that the same face looks out of all the paintings in the studio. The pose of each painting differs, but the woman's face is always kind and fair, full of joy and hope. This is the model's face as it was before sorrow came. (What caused the sorrow is not mentioned.) The artist continues to paint her face as he dreams of it, not as it really is. The woman is an image, an object of the painter's fancy; her real life is not reflected in the paintings.

"Winter: My Secret"

This teasing poem is similar to a dramatic monologue. It represents the speech of one who does not wish to reveal herself.

The speaker addresses someone who asks the secret. She refuses to tell, giving the unconvincing reason that, being winter, it is too cold to open up, in any sense. She even wears a "mask" for warmth and protection. Perhaps there is no secret at all. She distrusts the good will of the questioner. However, she plays with the idea that she might tell the secret sometime later. In the spring? Probably not, because some coldness might still linger, or might return.

The final stanza begins "Perhaps." In summertime the secret might be told, or perhaps guessed. The imagery of cold and warm reinforces ideas of isolation and emotional caution on one side, contrasting with warm feelings and ease.

The Goblin Market

ROSSETTI'S STYLE

This poetic tale also displays the rich piling-on of descriptive details characteristic of Christina Rossetti. It is a deceptively simple story of two sisters, Laura and Lizzie, who respond differently to temptation. Strange goblin-men pass their dwelling, offering a variety of beautiful fruits. The first thirty lines of the poem list the many fruits in overwhelming profusion and describe the seductive song of the goblins.

Both sisters feel the danger of the seduction, but only Laura yields, first looking out at what the goblins offer, then going out to meet them. They are grotesque, each one resembling some animal. One, for example, has a cat's face, and another moves like a rat. But Laura overcomes her revulsion in order to buy their fruit. Penniless, she offers in exchange a lock of her golden hair. She then gorges herself on the sweet fruits, sucking juices to the point of drunkenness. She takes home the seed, the "kernel stone," of one unknown specimen of fruit. At the gate she is met by Lizzie, who disapproves and warns Laura against the goblins. But Laura merely boasts of the rare and delicious feast of fruit, promising to bring some for Lizzie the next day.

However, the goblin-men avoid Laura from then on. Having once made her yield to their temptation they are no longer interested in her. Only Lizzie can hear their seductive songs, their "fruit-call." Laura grieves and yearns; she grows thin and gray-haired. She plants the kernel-stone, but nothing grows. Lizzie, sympathetic and anxious for her "dwindling" sister, decides to get some of the restorative fruit for Laura, even if by doing so she puts herself at risk. She takes a silver coin to the goblins, who rejoice with grotesque gestures and try to overwhelm Lizzie's reserve. She will not eat the fruit herself, even though they press it on her. She offers only her coin, and they react with rude pushing and plucking at her, mashing the fruits at her face. Still she resists, not opening her lips. Eventually they give up, flinging her silver coin back and departing in disgust. Lizzie runs home and offers to Laura the fruit pulp and juices that have clung to her face, saying, "Come and kiss me."

Laura reacts with surprise and gratitude that Lizzie would run such a risk for her. She kisses Lizzie, tasting the fruit again, and she is restored. The fruit is no longer delicious to her ("She loathed the feast," line 494), yet Laura feels suddenly freed from her illness and melancholy. She passes from a deathly anguish to a new life, waking as if from a dream into renewed innocence. Her hair becomes golden once again. Thus Laura has been tempted and fallen and then passed from despair to self-forgetfulness to redemption.

Long afterward, the tale concludes, the sisters both marry and have families. Laura warns her children of the wicked goblin-men and tells them "there is no friend like a sister."

The poem presents its moral as a simple story of sisterly fidelity with a happy ending. But the poem's dense, exotic, and sensuous imagery and its emphasis on physical contact—on tasting, kissing, feeling, clawing, and pushing—creates a highly charged sexual atmosphere, suggesting an imagination fueled by suppressed desire. Driving appetite and loss of innocence are the central actions of the poem, and they lend themselves to a wider range of interpretations than the closing nursery-moral encompasses.

Critics have compared this poem with Coleridge's "The Rime of the Ancient Mariner" as a moral fable charged with mystery.

ALGERNON CHARLES SWINBURNE (1837–1909)

Swinburne, who came from an old aristocratic family in Northumberland, went to school at Eton and then at Oxford University. In London he met the poets and painters of the Pre-Raphaelite Brotherhood. He lived a bo-hemian life and was given to self-indulgent drinking and unconventional sexual practices, but he also read extensively in modern and classical literature and was continuously productive in a wide range of literary forms.

Swinburne wrote poetry, drama, novels, and criticism. He was influenced by Greek and Elizabethan poetry and drama, by the American poet Edgar Allan Poe, and by the French poet Charles Baudelaire.

By 1878, while he was in his early forties, Swinburne's health had deteriorated to the point of collapse. He put himself in the care of his friend, Theodore Watts-Dunton. The two took up residence outside London in the town of Putney, where Swinburne brought his drinking under control. His health improved and he continued to write, but his earlier work is considered to be his best.

During his lifetime Swinburne was notorious for the "immorality" of some of his writings. He was a disciple of the Marquis de Sade and openly rejected the Christian religion. He liked to shock, and he pushed at the limits of public tolerance. Yet Swinburne's poetic style was often beautiful, rich, and gorgeous.

"When the Hounds of Spring"

This luscious lyric is from Swinburne's early play, *Atalanta in Calydon*, which is based on Greek models. The lyric is a chorus celebrating the goddess Diana, the "mother of months," who, as goddess of the moon, rules the seasons. The end of winter and coming of spring is a time of rushing motion, and Diana is depicted as running into the new season, followed by her devotees, as "blossom by blossom the spring begins" (line 32).

In the last two stanzas the imagery shifts from weather and vegetation to the dances of a Dionysian festival, dances of gods and humans celebrating spring and involving sexual pursuit.

SWINBURNE'S STYLE

The eight-line stanzas are akin to ottava rima, but the couplet occurs not at the end of the stanza but in lines five and six. The rhyme scheme is thus a b a b c c a b. The forward-rushing meter is created by liberal use of anapestic feet, wherein two unstressed syllables lead into one stressed. The lyric contains feminine rhymes, such as "rivers," "quivers," "shivers" in the second stanza and "sing to her," "cling to her" in the third. But the sound patterns are many and varied. Simple alliteration is used in the second line: "The mother of months in meadow or plain"; but two lines later we read of "the brown bright nightingale," which combines alliteration with assonance. Sometimes the meaning of a line or phrase is vague, but it is linked to a voluptuous sound pattern so that it *seems* to mean what the poet intends.

The pleasure of the poem is sensual. The reader is treated to a banquet of images and sounds offered promiscuously but not for analysis.

"Hymn to Proserpine"

This poem is presented as the speech of a Roman poet of the fourth century, at the time when Christianity was displacing the old pagan religion. Thus the poem works as a dramatic monologue, the utterance of a character from a distant time and place.

The speaker is old and facing death. He addresses the goddess Proserpine or Proserpina, who is both the daughter of Demeter, the earth goddess, and the queen of the underworld, where she must spend half of each year. The myth of Proserpine accounts for the seasons, because the earth does not flourish when Demeter is without her daughter. The speaker prays to Proserpine as a goddess of death; he foresees no resurrection. He does not desire rebirth or even longer life, because the world has changed and he is no longer comfortable in it. The coming of Christianity has made his world "gray"—that is, to him the old pagan world was more beautiful, its gods and goddesses more lovely and splendid. The mercy and compassion of the new God, Christ, seems dull to the speaker; he is repelled by the idea of a god and saints who have been crucified and tortured. Therefore, he says, "I kneel not" (line 46). To him, all time seems like an ocean that eventually washes away everything, even gods. He predicts that in due time the new God will also die. He compares Mary with the Greek goddess Aphrodite. Mary as a pale maiden does not appeal to him; he prefers the splendor of Aphrodite. But finally he calls on Proserpine to befriend him by letting him die. He does not expect or wish for any rebirth, believing that even gods die.

"Ave Atque Vale: In Memory of Charles Baudelaire"

This Latin title means "hail and farewell," a greeting taken from the poet Catullus. Swinburne adopts it as the title of his elegy to the French poet Charles Baudelaire, who died in 1867. Baudelaire was a poet of isolation and melancholy; in beautiful language he explored images of evil and degradation.

In this elegy Swinburne addresses the dead poet as a brother. In the opening stanza he asks what flowers are fitting for the poet's grave. He attributes to Baudelaire a secret knowledge of the hidden sorrows, sins, and pleasures of men. Now Swinburne imagines him to be in the keeping of some "dim gods of death," where the body and soul will separate. Swinburne wonders what death is like. What gods or goddesses are to be met there? What sorts of fruits and flowers? But by stanza 8 he stops asking these questions, realizing that Baudelaire is beyond the reach of words. Swinburne puts his hand upon a scroll, Baudelaire's poetry, in order to feel communion with the dead poet. Alluding to the deaths of figures in Greek mythology, Swinburne imagines that Baudelaire is mourned by the spirits of Apollo and Venus. The elegiac consolation begins in stanza 16; no songs will reach the dead poet or bring him back. He sleeps, either sweetly or bitterly, as all must eventually sleep.

In the final stanza Swinburne says, "take . . . this garland" (the poem itself) and bids the poet be at peace, having reached a state beyond conflict. The elegy is full of images of vegetation—leaf, flower, bud, and seed. The flower and tree are emblems of the spiritual state of being, ranging from dewy fruition to dried dustiness. The dead are said to dwell in a "mystic and mournful garden" (line 180), surrounded by sick and poisonous plants.

These images play upon the title of Baudelaire's major work, *Les Fleurs du Mal* (Flowers of Evil). They also link death with the vegetation cycle and reflect the symbolic plants of mourning, the flowers that strew the grave.

WALTER PATER (1839–1894)

A critic and essayist, Pater was the prose theoretician of aesthetic movements, a friend of Dante Rossetti's, and an influence on Oscar Wilde and other young writers of the late Victorian Age.

Pater was a shy and bookish man. He attended Oxford University, remaining there as a fellow after taking his degree. He later lived in London with his sisters. His first book was *Studies in the History of the Renaissance* (1873), a collection of essays on Renaissance art. This book made him famous.

He later wrote a fictionalized autobiography and other biographies and historical romances. Pater is known primarily for promoting the idea of "art for art's sake," meaning that art need not have social or political usefulness or teach a moral truth. Art exists for the sake of the pleasure it offers.

Pater was sometimes criticized as having a morbid fascination with violence in art. He was enjoyed, nonetheless, as a great prose stylist.

Studies in the History of the Renaissance

In this collection of essays Pater describes his impressions of some of the greatest poetry and artworks of the period from the late Middle Ages through the fifteenth century and up to the "comely decadence" of the early Enlightenment. Pater finds fifteenth-century Italy especially interesting because, he says, it was one of the few eras when many great personalities came together to form one "general culture" with a common spirit that gave unity to all their various productions.

In his preface Pater takes up the problem of the definition of beauty. He says the definition lies in the individual experience, in the kind and degree of pleasure that the song or picture causes. The aesthetic critic looks at all art objects as having more or less power to influence, to produce "pleasurable sensations." The critic's job is to analyze these impressions of beauty, separating the beautiful from what accompanies it and distinguishing the special nature of its power. The true critical temperament realizes that beauty exists in many forms and is not centered in any one type or school or period of art. Using the example of Wordsworth, Pater points out that passages of great beauty may occur in poems that are otherwise ordinary and forgettable. The critic separates the "fine crystal here or there" that exists in the range of Wordsworth's works.

In the conclusion to his book Pater discusses the nature of the aesthetic experience. Out of the flood of objects that one perceives, on reflection some objects make impressions of color, odor, or texture. These isolated experiences of the individual mind are transitory. Time changes these impressions at the moment we are trying to grasp them. But the aesthetic experience, however fleeting, is the purpose or reason for living. Experience is not a means to some other end; it is life itself, felt as energy. Intensity of experience is the goal of life. "To burn always with this hard, gemlike flame, to maintain this ecstasy, is success in life," Pater concludes. The greatest wisdom is the love of art for its own sake. The amoral implications of such a philosophy were shocking to some of Pater's audience, but he in turn was shocked to realize that his criticism was being read as mere self-indulgent hedonism.

The Child in the House

In this fictionalized autobiography Pater explores the process by which a young child develops mentally. The boy Florian, who corresponds to Pater himself as a child, is affected by the beauty of his physical surroundings, by the charm and neatness of the first house of his childhood. This early experience of beauty causes him to become sensitive to beauty in ways that last into adulthood. Pater believes that children naturally discover and delight in light, color, form, and detail in the objects that make up their environment.

In later life similar aspects of things work on the imagination, and the child finds pleasure in whatever reminds him or her of those early sensory experiences. Thus we store up a range of "attractions and associations," which become our "sanctuary of sentiment" and cause a mental sense of home. In this "process of brain-building" the sense of beauty develops out of discrete and memorable aesthetic impressions such as, for Florian, the overwhelming beauty of the red hawthorne tree in full bloom, rich in perfume and color. Such an impression remains always, causing a longing for things of beauty, "a kind of tyranny of the senses" over the feelings of the individual.

In Florian, Pater explains, this longing for beauty became associated with a fear of death. He found comfort in religious sentiment—not in the teachings of religion but in the sensual impressions of sacred ritual and objects. He developed a "mystical appetite for sacred things" and began "to love, for their own sakes, church lights, holy days," and all the order and objects of religious ceremony. That is, like Pater, the boy Florian is depicted as creating a religion of aesthetics based on the beautiful sensations of the church.

Although the term "Victorian" usually carries connotations of propriety, correctness, and restraint of feelings, there was during the Victorian Age a vigorous counterculture of pleasure-seekers and pursuers of beauty for its own sake. Closely allied to painting and the decorative arts, the poetry and essays of this other culture were characterized by richness of descriptive detail. Poets sought to recreate the look, feel, and sounds of experience, of love and melancholy. They tried to create impressions of scenes beyond experience, of heaven or of dream worlds. The beauty of women was one of their favorite subjects. There existed a reciprocal relationship between the arts, such as verbal descriptions of paintings or points based on poetic subjects. The poets and painters were friends and reinforced each other in their various projects and ideas. But the absence of any clear moral framework made the works of these artists suspect to most of the Victorian public. Their work was seen as tending toward decadence, a charge that became even more pronounced in the final decade of the nineteenth century.

Selected Readings

Boos, Florence Saunders. *The Poetry of Dante G. Rossetti: A Critical Reading and Source Study*. The Hague: Mouton, 1976.

Dobbs, Brian, and Judy Dobbs. *Dante Gabriel Rossetti: An Alien Victorian*. London: MacDonald, 1977.

Levey, Michael. *The Case of Walter Pater*. London: Thames, 1978.

Thomas, Donald. *Swinburne: The Poet in His World*. New York: Oxford University Press, 1979.

Welby, T. Earle. *A Study of Swinburne*. New York: Doran, 1926.

Zaturenska, Marya. *Christina Rossetti: A Portrait with Background*. New York: Macmillan, 1949.

13

Victorian Humanists and Satirists

1893   Wilde, *A Woman of No Importance*

1894   Wilde's play *Salome* published in English, translated by Lord Alfred Douglas, and illustrated by Aubrey Beardsley

1895   Wilde, *The Importance of Being Earnest* and *An Ideal Husband*; Wilde brings action for libel; Wilde loses, is arrested, tried, and sentenced to prison

1896   *Salome* produced in Paris by Sarah Bernhardt

1897   Wilde released from Reading prison; Queen Victoria's Diamond Jubilee; Ellis, *Studies in the Psychology of Sex*

1898   Wilde, *Ballad of Reading Gaol*

1900   Wilde dies; Freud, *Interpretation of Dreams*

1901–1910   Reign of Edward VII

1905   Wilde, *De Profundis* published posthumously

1949   Suppressed part of *De Profundis* published in Holland

When a society reaches that state of maturity in which its institutions are well established and its social conventions tend to be rigid, the field is open to writers who see the absurdities of that society and want to have some fun at its expense. The fun is serious to the extent that it exposes and debunks those received ideas that have lasted beyond their usefulness. Satire is the product of a world in decline, where the public consensus about proper and good behavior is belied by actual behavior, where appearances are kept up but the substance is rotting away. The Victorian Age had its social critics, men like Arnold and Ruskin who tried to define social problems and point to solutions. But other writers, such as Lewis Carroll and Oscar Wilde, created mocking images of society, pointing out through irony and parody the absurdities of Victorian social conventions. The nonsense verses of Carroll and Edward Lear take satiric aim at the self-important seriousness and the solemn earnestness of major Victorian writers. The late Victorian Age was one of the richest for satire and nonsense poetry.

EDWARD LEAR (1812–1888)

Lear is famous as the popularizer of the limerick, a set form of comic verse. By profession a landscape painter and an illustrator of books, Lear traveled extensively around the Mediterranean and as far east as India.

Lear's poetry was mainly written for children, in particular for the grandchildren of his patron, the earl of Derby. In 1871 he finally settled in the Italian city of San Remo, living there until his death. His major collections of verse are *A Book of Nonsense* (1846) and *Nonsense Songs, Stories and Botany* (1870). He illustrated these volumes with cartoon drawings. Modern critics of Lear's verse have tended to approach it psychoanalytically, finding signs of repression and melancholy.

Limericks

LEAR'S STYLE

As a set form, the limerick has five lines rhyming a a b b a; the a-lines have three feet and the b-lines have two feet, these feet being mostly anapests. Part of the comic effect of a typical limerick comes from the absurd, fractured phrasing that results from fitting the sentences into such a rigid form. Here is one of Lear's typical limericks:

There was an Old Man of Coblenz
The length of whose legs was immense;
He went with one prance,
From Turkey to France
That surprising Old Man of Coblenz.

In a limerick the person is identified in the first line by his or her location and is then described as doing something odd or silly in lines two through four. The last line gives an adjective, "surprising" in this case, and usually repeats the identifying phrase from line one. There are minor variations, but this is the most common form of limerick used by Lear. There is a county in Ireland called Limerick, but no one has shown what connection these verses have, if any, with that location.

"The Owl and the Pussy-Cat"

This is the first poem from the collection *Nonsense Songs, Stories and Botany*. It is a mock love story about two very improbable lovers, an owl and a pussycat. The poem admits only one impediment to this preposterous marriage—the lack of a wedding ring. After a year's voyage the two find a pig with a ring in his nose, purchase the ring, and promptly marry. Lear was no particular advocate of marriage, having observed that most marriages he knew of were miserable. But the tone of this little song is sweet and the ending happy, as the ill-matched lovers dance in celebration of their marriage.

"How Pleasant to Know Mr. Lear"

In this unflattering self-portrait the poet adopts the voice of an observer, pretending to give a fair and balanced portrait of an old, eccentric English gentleman who, though of round shape and "hideous" face, is "pleasant enough" to know. The comedy arises in part from the awkward combination of disparate details, such as the man's "fastidious" mind and his big nose.

In the fifth stanza, one line tells us that he had "many friends, laymen and clerical" and the next the name of his cat, as if this were one of his many friends. The poem is written in the jogging rhythm of a nursery rhyme.

"The Jumblies"

Who or what Jumblies are cannot be known for sure, but they seem to be small creatures of a childlike perversity who try to do the impossible and succeed. Everyone warns them that they can't use a sieve for a sailboat, but they do it anyway. "Their heads are green and their hands are blue," and they think of themselves as very wise, while everyone else sees them as foolish. After a twenty-year-long voyage, during which they buy many strange and useless items, they come back to tell of their adventures. Everyone who warned them not to go now wants to make the same trip. The poem suggests a happy childhood fantasy of doing something adventurous against the advice of adults and getting away with it. It has the rollicking rhythm of a little boat on choppy waves.

LEWIS CARROLL (1832–1898)

Lewis Carroll was the pen name of Charles Lutwidge Dodgson, a strange and versatile intellectual who had a special fondness for little girls. Dodgson was a lecturer in mathematics at Oxford University. He enjoyed verbal and mathematical games and puzzles and was also an amateur photographer. He took many fine portrait photographs of young girls, the daughters of his friends. One such girl was Alice Liddell, one of three daughters of H. G. Liddell, an educator and a dean at Oxford. Dodgson wrote his two most famous books for Alice—*Alice's Adventures in Wonderland* (1865) and *Through the Looking Glass* (1871). These books avoid the usual moralizing tone of Victorian children's literature and are infused with the spirit of games and nonsense. Some of the songs in the book are parodies of popular songs of the day. Alice brings with her into the strange world she visits the good manners and correct behavior that she has learned at home. She deals with monsters and bizarre creatures as if they were so many unruly children at a nursery party. Alice is a heroine with good sense and polite behavior, holding her own in realms of unpredictable and arbitrary events.

"Jabberwocky"

This nonsense poem from *Through the Looking Glass* parodies romantic adventure literature. It describes the adventure of the hero, who goes out, sword in hand, to slay a monster, the jabberwock. He kills it and returns home to the joyous congratulations of his old father. But the description of this simple event is embedded in dense descriptive details about other beasts that take no part in the central action. These beasts are described with many newly coined terms and portmanteau words. As Humpty Dumpty explains to Alice, a portmanteau word is one made up of parts of two familiar words. For example, the word *brunch* is a portmanteau word made by combining parts of *breakfast* and *lunch*. In this poem, *slithy* combines *lithe* and *slimy*. But some words in the poem are invented on other principles. A *Bandersnatch*, for example, is a beast that, perhaps, threatens to snatch a bystander. The whole poem resembles a child's perception of a complex story that he can only partly grasp.

"The White Knight's Song"

In this poem Carroll mocks the highly respected "Resolution and Independence" by William Wordsworth. Wordsworth's poem praises a decrepit old man for his brave perseverance despite poverty and physical weakness. In this poem the white knight sings of meeting an intrepid old man who ekes out a living, not by gathering leeches but by engaging in several other absurd occupations involving gathering. Meanwhile, the knight as narrator is paying almost no attention to the old man's story, being involved in his own hare-brained schemes. The poem takes a very Wordsworthian turn in the final stanza. Here the knight explains that he recollects the old man, not in moments of tranquility but at times when he, the knight, has gotten himself into some silly trouble. The parody deflates the high-minded self-criticism of the original poem.

"The Walrus and the Carpenter"

Also found in *Through the Looking Glass*, this absurd narrative poem is written in the familiar form of the nursery rhyme, with alternating lines of four and three feet. In Carroll's poem, however, each stanza is extended from the usual four to six lines. Like many nursery rhymes, Carroll's story is not sweet. The Walrus and Carpenter are two bland bullies who deceive and then devour the silly and innocent oysters. Dignified and self-important, the Walrus and Carpenter seem to unbend a bit when they invite the little oysters for a walk along the beach. But after some distracting conversation about nonsense (about "shoes—and ships—and sealing wax—Of cabbages—and kings") the Walrus and the Carpenter suddenly and calmly begin to eat their guests. The Walrus makes small talk about the fine view while the Carpenter makes petty complaints about the bread. The Walrus offers the remaining oysters false sympathy, while the Carpenter ironically invites them to take the return walk home. By the final stanzas the helpless oysters have all been eaten. It is a fable of exploitation, showing how the callous nature of the exploiter is hidden under a facade of courtesy and concern.

OSCAR WILDE (1856–1900)

His full name was Oscar Fingall O'Flahertie Wills Wilde. He was Irish, born in Dublin, and attended both Trinity College in Dublin and Oxford University. While at Oxford he was influenced by the aesthetic ideas of Ruskin and Pater, especially the "art-for-art's-sake" movement, which became the foundation not only of Wilde's literary productions but also of his flamboyant and hedonistic life-style. Witty and self-indulgent, Wilde cultivated an image of effeteness with his velvet knee-pants and large carnation in his buttonhole. He was master of the shocking and paradoxical utterance; for example, "I can resist anything except temptation." He wrote in several genres. After the publication of his *Poems* in 1881 he made a lecture tour of the United States. His one novel was a Gothic tale, *The Picture of Dorian Gray* (1891), in the preface to which Wilde set out his artistic credo that "There is no such thing as a moral or an immoral book. Books are well written or badly written. That is all." Wilde also wrote fairy tales for children and other kinds of stories. His greatest success came in the 1890s with a series of satiric comedies for the stage: *Lady Windermere's Fan* (1892), *A Woman of No Importance* (1893), *An Ideal Husband* (1895), and his masterpiece, *The Importance of Being Earnest* (1895). This last play was particularly successful. In the same year disaster struck. Wilde, who was married and had two sons, had developed a relationship with a young aristocrat, Lord Alfred Douglas. Lord Alfred's father, the marquis of Queensbury, disapproved of the relationship and accused Wilde of homosexuality. Wilde sued him for libel but lost. Wilde was subsequently arrested and jailed under the British laws prohibiting homosexual acts. He emerged from jail two years later, divorced and bankrupt. He went into exile in France, dying three years later in a Paris hotel. Among his last works was *De Profundis* (From the Depths), a defense and confession of his life.

The Importance of Being Earnest

Earnestness—that is, a high-minded and serious devotion to duty and virtue—was a quality advocated by such central Victorian figures as Arnold and Tennyson, but it was mocked as a trait of the rigidly moralistic middle class by those other Victorians who found middle-class values self-serving and middle-class tastes dull.

WILDE'S STYLE

In this satire, being earnest is made as superficial a trait as possible; it means simply having the name Earnest. The characters are motivated and controlled by a hollow and artificial set of social standards that have little substance but are used to maintain social distinctions and social class privileges. Against this rigid system of controls the young lovers pursue their dreams of romance. The play is structured as a series of verbal fencing matches in which showing the right form is as important as making one's point. The plot is nonsensical, a mere excuse for causing the lovers some temporary setbacks before the inevitable comic happy ending. The tone is brightly serious; none of the characters have any inkling that they are speaking absurdities. Even the self-indulgent Algernon is earnest in his self-indulgence.

Act 1. The opening act takes place at tea time in Algernon's fashionable London apartment. Algernon immediately establishes his role as an aesthetic by the "artistic" style of his room and by the sentimental style of his piano playing. He contrasts with his guest, Jack, who claims to be seeking pleasure but who is actually rather serious and plans to propose marriage to Algernon's cousin Gwendolen, who also comes to tea, along with her mother and Algernon's aunt, Lady Bracknell. Before the ladies arrive Algernon requires Jack to explain who Cecily is. She is Jack's ward, the granddaughter of his adoptive father, and she lives in Jack's country estate while he comes up to town on supposed visits to his nonexistent brother, Earnest. Thus he is called Jack in the country by Cecily and is known as Earnest in town by Algernon and Gwendolen. This confession leads Algernon to reveal that he has an imaginary friend, Burbury, whose recurrent illnesses provide excuses for Algernon to leave town whenever he wants to get away from his relatives, particularly from his aunt. At this point Lady Bracknell and Gwendolen arrive. After some chitchat about the newly widowed Lady Hanbury, whose "hair has turned quite gold from grief," Algernon gets Lady Bracknell to leave the room so that Jack/Earnest can propose to Gwendolen. This he does in proper form, on his knees, and she accepts. They are interrupted by the return of Lady Bracknell, who disapproves of the marriage on the grounds that Jack/Earnest has no proper family, having been left as an infant in a handbag at a railway station. Admonishing Jack to obtain some proper parents, she hurries Gwendolen away. But Gwendolen sneaks back for a moment to pledge eternal love to Jack/Earnest and to get his country address. Algernon overhears and makes note of the address, having developed some curiosity to meet Jack/Earnest's hidden ward, Cecily.

Act 2. The second act takes place in the garden of Jack/Earnest's country house. At the opening, his ward Cecily is resisting the lessons of her governess, Miss Prism. Cecily keeps a diary of her fantasy life, and Miss Prism admits that she once wrote a novel, though it was lost and never published. The local clergyman, Dr. Chasuble, enters, and it becomes obvious that Miss Prism aspires to marry him. When these two have moved off to take a walk Cecily is surprised by the unexpected arrival of Algernon, who pretends to be Jack's younger brother, the ne'er-do-well Earnest. He finds her charming and she sees him as the fulfillment of her romantic dreams. Miss Prism and Dr. Chasuble return from their walk. Jack enters in mourning dress and announces the death of his (invented) brother Earnest. In the midst of expressions of sympathy Cecily comes out of the house to announce that the supposedly dead Earnest is in the dining room. Algernon, still pretending to be Earnest, emerges from the house and dares Jack, through meaningful looks, to reveal the truth that there is no Earnest. Jack orders a cart to take Algernon/Earnest back to the train station for his return to town, but he refuses to go, saying that he has fallen in love with Cecily. She returns to the scene and they cancel the order for the cart. In the subsequent love scene Cecily reveals that she has been conducting an imaginary courtship with Earnest in her diary ever since learning of his existence from Jack. She declares that she could marry only a man who was named Earnest. Algernon rushes off to arrange to be newly christened with that name. In his absence Gwendolen Fairfax arrives, intending to visit her fiance, Earnest (really Jack). In a scene of high comic tension, both Gwendolen and Cecily claim to be engaged to Earnest. As they have tea together and make icily candid remarks, Jack returns, followed closely by Algernon. The truth comes out that neither of these men is named Earnest. The two deceived young women, now that they realize that their fiances are two different men, join together in sympathy and outrage at the deception. They retreat into the house, leaving Jack to blame Algernon for the debacle while Algernon consoles himself by eating muffins.

Act 3. The final act follows without any time lapse. The two young women are inside, looking out at their rejected suitors and hoping they will come in to be reconciled, although the women vow to each other that they will be cold. When Jack and Algernon do enter, there are mutual recriminations, but the final point of conflict is that neither man is really named Earnest, a name both women insist on as the only acceptable name for a husband. Jack and Algernon both volunteer to be christened with that name, causing an outburst of admiration from Gwendolen and Cecily. Just as the lovers have been reconciled, Lady Bracknell arrives, having followed her daughter Gwendolen to prevent mischief. Cecily is introduced to her as Algernon's betrothed, but Lady Bracknell rejects the engagement until she hears that Cecily is heiress to a substantial fortune. Lady Bracknell persists, however, in objecting to Jack as a son-in-law on the ground that he lacks family status. Jack makes a countermove, denying permission for his ward Cecily to marry Algernon. During this impasse Miss Prism comes in. By the wildest of coincidences, Miss Prism turns out to be the absent-minded nurse who had misplaced Jack as an infant, putting the manuscript for her novel in the baby carriage and the baby into her handbag, which she left in a railway station. As it turns out, Jack is the nephew of Lady Bracknell and Algernon's brother. Therefore, he *is* of good family and can marry his cousin Gwendolen. And his original name was Earnest. The play ends with multiple embraces: Earnest and Gwendolen, Algernon and Cecily, and even Dr. Chasuble and Miss Prism. Earnest's final line is the title of the play.

Any outline of this comedy's silly plot misses its essence—the witty word play that reveals the disparity between the artificial social customs of English aristocratic society and this group's mercenary values and shallow family relationships. Everything is evaluated according to its style, its conformity to high fashion.

The reaction against the high-minded, serious preoccupations of the middle class in Victorian England took many forms. The aesthetics retreated into a search for beauty. Some writers, like Lear and Carroll, found fun in nonsense and in mocking the idols and the attitudes of the middle class. Oscar Wilde's satiric weapons were aimed against the aristocracy, a class on the brink of ruin, clinging absurdly to its artificial forms and standards. None of these writers tried to probe the economic and political problems that underlaid the social rigidities that they mocked. Irony does not advocate a program of change; it merely shows up what is wrong. But both the satirists and the aesthetics were preparing the way for new directions in literature at the turn of the century.

Selected Readings

Carroll, Lewis. *The Annotated Alice: Alice's Adventures in Wonderland and Through the Looking Glass*. Illustrated by John Tenniel, with an Introduction and Notes by Martin Gardner. New York: New American Library, 1960.

Fisher, John. *The Magic of Lewis Carroll*. New York: Simon & Schuster, 1973.

Hardwick, Michael. *The Drake Guide to Oscar Wilde*. New York: Drake, 1973.

Jackson, Holbrook. *The Complete Nonsense of Edward Lear*. New York: Dover, 1951.

Williams, Sidney Herbert, and Falconer Madan. *The Lewis Carroll Handbook*. Hamden, CT: Archon, 1979.

14

The Twentieth Century (1897 to Present)

1890   Wilde, *The Picture of Dorian Gray*; American philosopher and psychologist William James, *Principles of Psychology*

1891   Doyle, *Adventures of Sherlock Holmes*; beginning of the "little theatre" movement

1892   First American automobile

1892–1933   Yeats's poetry written

1893   Art Nouveau in vogue

1893–1932   Shaw's dramas and criticism

1895   Hardy, *Jude the Obscure*; Crane, *The Red Badge of Courage*

1895–1923   Conrad's novels written

1896   Beerbohm, *Works of Max Beerbohm*; Austin made poet laureate

1896–1922   Housman's poetry written

1897   Queen Victoria's Diamond Jubilee

1898   Wilde, *Ballad of Reading Gaol*; Wells, *War of the Worlds*

1898–1928   Hardy's poetry written

1899   Irish Literary Theatre founded in Dublin; Boer War

1900   Freud, *Interpretation of Dreams*; Planck sets forth quantum theory

1901   Kipling, *Kim*

1901–1910   Reign of Edward VII

1902   Boer War ends with British takeover of the Transvaal and the Orange Free State

1902–1937 Masefield's poetry written

1903   Wright brothers make first airplane flight

1904   Barrie, *Peter Pan*; Japan defeats Russia

1905   Wilde, *De Profundis* published posthumously; Wharton, *The House of Mirth*; Einstein proposes theory of relativity

1905–1953 Forster's novels, essays, and libretto written

1906–1921 Galsworthy, *The Forsyte Saga*

1907   Beerbohm, *A Book of Caricatures*; Synge, *Playboy of the Western World*

1909   Galsworthy, *Plays*; in the United States, the National Association for the Advancement of Colored People (NAACP) is established

1910–1936 Reign of George V

1911–1915 Brooke's poetry written

1911–1922 Mansfield's short stories written

1912   Bridges, *Poetical Works*; Matisse and Derain found movement known as fauvism

1913   Bridges named poet laureate; Cather, *O Pioneers!*; Stravinsky, *The Rites of Spring*

1913–1928 Lawrence's novels and poetry written

1914–1918 Archduke Ferdinand assassinated, World War I ensues

1915   Kafka, *The Metamorphosis*; German submarine sinks the *Lusitania*; trench warfare begins in France

1915–1941 Woolf's novels, essays, and criticism written

1915–1944 Maugham's novels and short stories written

1915–1959 Eliot's poetry, drama, and criticism written

1916   Joyce, *Portrait of the Artist as a Young Man*; Shaw, *Androcles and the Lion* and *Pygmalion*; Lenin, *Imperialism: The Last Stage of Capitalism*

1916–1939 Joyce's novels and poetry written

1916–1962 E. Sitwell's poetry and prose written

1917   Gurney, *Severn and Somme*; United States enters World War I on Allied side; Bolsheviks take power in Russian Revolution; British government issues Balfour Declaration supporting creation of Jewish state in Palestine

1918 Brooke, *Collected Poems* published posthumously; Bridges publishes Gerard Manley Hopkins's *Poems*; Germany agrees to armistice, World War I ends

1918–1931 Strachey's biographies written

1919 Gurney, *War's Emblems*; Mussolini establishes Fascist movement in Italy; in United States, Volstead Act implements Eighteenth Amendment, bringing about Prohibition

1919–1956 Sassoon's poetry written

1920 Owen, *Poems* published posthumously; Gorki, *Recollections*; decade of "The Roaring Twenties"

1921 Kipling, *Verse*; Irish Free State established; O'Neill, *The Emperor Jones*

1923 Germany experiences extreme inflation

1924 Mann, *The Magic Mountain*; Union of Soviet Socialist Republics (USSR) established, Stalin introduces socialism

1925 Huxley, *Selected Poems*; Gide, *The Counterfeiters*; in the United States, *The New Yorker* magazine founded

1926 O'Casey, *The Plough and the Stars*; Milne, *Winnie-the-Pooh*; coal miners' strike leads to first general strike in Britain; Hemingway, *The Sun Also Rises*

1927 Chesterton, *Collected Poems*; Jeffers, *The Women at Point Sur*; Millay, *The King's Henchman*

1929 Priestly, *The Good Companions*; Faulkner, *The Sound and the Fury*; Wolf, *Look Homeward, Angel*; in the United States, the stock market crashes and "The Great Depression" begins

1929–1957 Lewis's poetry written

1929–1961 MacNeice's poetry written

1929–1977 Grave's poetry, novels, and translations written

1930 Coward, *Private Lives*; Waugh, *Vile Bodies*; Masefield named poet laureate; Crane, *The Bridge*

1930–1970 Auden's poetry written

1931 Binyon, *Collected Poems*; Japan invades Manchuria

1932 Huxley, *Brave New World*; Caldwell, *Tobacco Road*

1932–1955 Spender's poetry written

1933 Hitler becomes chancellor of Germany; Stein, *Autobiography of Alice B. Toklas*

1933–1949 Sitwell's poetry and prose written

1933–1949   Orwell's novels and essays written

1934   Lewis, *A Hope for Poetry*; in the United States, "Harlem Renaissance" establishes poets Langston Hughes and Countee Cullen

1934–1954   Thomas's poetry, prose, and drama written

1936   Accession of Edward VIII followed by his abdication and the succession of his brother to the throne; Spanish Civil War begins; in the United States, *Life* magazine established

1936–1952   George VI reigns

1936–1966   Smith's poetry written

1938   Prime Minister Chamberlain meets with Hitler at Munich and sacrifices Czechoslovakia rather than risk war; Cummings, *Collected Poems*; Rawlings, *The Yearling*

1938–1989   Beckett's dramas written

1939   Isherwood, *Goodbye to Berlin*; Yeats dies; Hitler destroys Czechoslovakia; Germany overruns Poland; Great Britain and France declare war on Germany

1940   Greene, *The Power and the Glory*; German *Luftwaffe* begins Battle of Britain; Wright, *Native Son*

1941   Koestler, *Darkness at Noon*; Woolf commits suicide; Joyce dies; Japan attacks Pearl Harbor; United States enters war against Germany, Italy, and Japan

1942   Lewis, *The Screwtape Letters*

1943   Saint-Exupéry, *The Little Prince*; Germans defeated in the Battle of Stalingrad

1943–1944   Douglas's poetry written

1944   Cary, *The Horse's Mouth*; Western Allies launch D-day invasion of Normandy; Copland, *Appalachian Spring*

1945   Orwell, *Animal Farm*; Waugh, *Brideshead Revisited*; Germany surrenders; United States drops atomic bombs on Japan; Japan surrenders, World War II ends; United Nations established; Labour party wins majority of seats in House of Commons for first time

1945–1973   Larkin's poetry written

1946   Winston Churchill, former prime minister, delivers "Iron Curtain" speech in United States

1949   The North Atlantic Treaty Organization (NATO) established

1950–   Lessing's novels written

1952–   Reign of Queen Elizabeth II

1954–	Gunn's poetry written
1956	The Suez Crisis
1957–	Hughes's poetry written
1957	Pinter's dramas written
1962–	Stoppard's dramas written
1963–	Hill's novels, short stories, and dramas written
1973	After de Gaulle, Great Britain enters Common Market
1979	Margaret Thatcher becomes Britain's first woman prime minister
1985	Ted Hughes named poet laureate

Queen Victoria lived until 1901, past the end of the nineteenth century, but the Victorian Age was already breaking up in the 1890s. The dominance of middle-class ideas and values was being challenged in the arts and in intellectual circles. The doctrines of the Pre-Raphaelite and aestheticist movements had unsettled previously held ideas about the purposes and function of art. It was now not so universally assumed that art's role was to teach and to elevate the soul. It was becoming accepted that art exists for its own sake, that art is its own kind of truth.

The time was ripe for experimenting in literary forms and for broadening the subject matter of literature. In France the symbolist movement had reacted against realism and objectivity, favoring instead the suggestive power of direct description, the power to evoke feelings and moods. The symbolists, such writers as Mallarmé, Verlaine, and Rimbaud, refined the sound patterns of poetry, seeking subtle musical effects.

As a group, writers felt more free to explore ways of presenting impressions of the inner life, the experiences of mind and feeling.

The most revolutionary development of the early twentieth century was the "stream of consciousness" technique in fiction. It had counterparts in poetry and drama as well, where chronological sequence and expository coherence were sacrificed to impressions acquired by the mind's random or obsessive movement over the field of memory. The psychological life, with its symbols and fantasies, was depicted, rather than the life of the individual finding his or her niche in society, which had been the overriding concern of nineteenth-century fiction and drama.

THE EDWARDIAN AND GEORGIAN PERIODS

The early years of the twentieth century are sometimes called the Edwardian Era. This period extends from the death of Queen Victoria in 1901 until the outbreak of the World War in 1914, even though the reign of Edward VII lasted only from 1901 until 1910.

Edwardian Era

During the Edwardian era it seemed on the surface that the comfortable and stable life of prosperous England continued. The great country houses were still staffed by numerous efficient servants, and the railroads made travel between London and the country easy. England seemed the confident and competent ruler of the world.

However, a new spirit of liberalism and freedom of expression was felt after the death of Victoria. Sexual matters were mentioned more freely. Criticism of social injustice and of the impoverishment of the working class was more freely asserted. During this time, ideas of socialism were put forth and the Labour party gained followers. The excessive materialism of the upper classes was blamed for the stagnation of society.

Critics such as George Bernard Shaw and H. G. Wells wrote provocatively of the inequality of the economic and social stratifications in England. Relative peace and success abroad allowed the British to look more critically at conditions at home. Underneath the glittering surface they began to see the unsolved problems of the masses.

The Georgian Era

George V was king from 1910 until 1936. The term "Georgian" is used in a very limited way to name a group of lyric poets who flourished during that time. They were later overshadowed by the more challenging and influential poetry of William Butler Yeats and T. S. Eliot.

WORLD WAR I AND THE POSTWAR ERA

World War I caused a great disillusionment throughout Europe, including the British Isles. The poets of World War I—Wilfred Owen and Siegfried Sassoon—helped finish off the concept of war as heroic and glorious. After the war the public turned to peacetime pleasures and self-indulgence.

"The Roaring Twenties"

During the decade of the Roaring Twenties (1920–1930s) popular culture emerged as forceful and liberating. This was the jazz age, the era of fast cars and of women who dared to smoke in public. It was also a decade of increasingly wild financial speculation, climaxed by the failure of the stock market system at the end of the twenties and general worldwide economic depression in the thirties.

The Wasteland Era

Widespread unemployment and the loss of great fortunes made it seem that capitalism was a bankrupt system. Rival economic and social theories were put forward. Socialism and communism gained many sympathetic followers.

In literature, the era of the wasteland seemed to have arrived, and social protest was a pervasive theme. However, the experiments of the Edwardian period were also yielding interesting fruit. James Joyce, Virginia Woolf, and D. H. Lawrence broke new ground in the novel. In poetry, the mature work of W. B. Yeats and the new voice of T. S. Eliot reflected the power of the imagist movement.

The role of the writer had changed. No longer the spokesperson of the moral sentiments of the majority, the artist now began to be seen as an alienated figure who sought isolation or was pushed into exile because he or she would not conform. The values of the artist were offended by the cultural mainstream. The artist looked at society from a distance and found it false or shallow. Such writers as James Joyce and D. H. Lawrence exposed the stultifying prudery of the middle class. The war poets debunked traditional notions of patriotism and the glory of war. Instead of responding to popular culture, the writers of the Bloomsbury group made their own social and intellectual world, going so far as to set up, as Leonard and Virginia Woolf did, their own printing press. The playwright George Bernard Shaw deliberately shocked his audiences, challenging them to rethink their assumptions about society, and the novelist George Orwell, repelled by the horrors of totalitarian states, predicted a dire future of mindless conformity.

THE LATER TWENTIETH CENTURY

After a decade of economic depression, the British people were aroused to new energy by the spread of German fascism in Europe. Their wartime suffering and resistance restored a sense of national unity and purpose.

World War II Poets and Beyond

If World War I had caused disillusionment in British writers and the reading public, World War II created the expectation of renewal and social change. Although Winston Churchill, the great conservative prime minister, had led the British to victory, his leadership was found inadequate for the new economic and social climate of the postwar period. Fearing a return to prewar economic depression, the Labour party initiated a new era in social welfare. The government took responsibility for housing, employment, and health care. The educational system was revised to make it more democratic, and the power of unions was solidified. Meanwhile, the far-flung Empire, which had been a major source of national wealth, began to break up as one by one the former possessions became free nations. England began to lose a sense of itself as a dominant world power, and the English learned to settle for less glory in exchange for greater security and a more modest level of expectation.

In poetry the furious energy of the war years, as reflected in the poems of W. H. Auden and Dylan Thomas, began to be replaced by a more dry, sardonic tone. Emotions were flattened down; the speaker became a neutral observer of a declining, antiromantic, material world. Writers of The Movement, such as Philip Larkin, adopted a more rational, empirical attitude toward the world.

The growth of modernism in the twentieth century was not a coherent movement with stated purposes. Rather, it was a gradual and increasing liberalization, beginning as a reaction against the restraints and sentimentality of the previous era, the Victorian Age, and gaining energy by exploring the new ideas put forth by Freud and Marx. Writers were rebels, rejecting conventions both in their works and in their lives. The alienated writer, exiled from his or her homeland or at least rejecting the control of the majority culture, became the leader, opening new grounds and experimenting with new techniques. The direction of modernism is away from the easy, the obvious, and the expected. The modern novelist, poet, or playwright is willing to risk being obscure or offensive in order to challenge the audience, to shock the reader into a new awareness.

Selected Readings

Bergonzi, Bernard. *The Myth of Modernism and Twentieth-Century Literature.* New York: St. Martin's Press, 1986.

Corrigan, Robert W., ed. *Laurel British Drama: The Twentieth Century.* New York: Dell, 1965.

Cunliffe, J. W. *English Literature in the Twentieth Century.* New York: Macmillan, 1933.

Gillie, Christopher. *Movements in English Literature: 1900–1940.* London: Cambridge University Press, 1975.

Temple, Ruth Z., ed. *Twentieth-Century British Literature: A Reference Guide and Bibliography.* New York: Ungar, 1968.

15

Transition to the New Century

1901–1910 Reign of Edward VII

1902 Conrad, *Heart of Darkness* and *Typhoon*; Boer War ends

1903 Emmeline Pankhurst founds Women's Social and Political Union

1904 Conrad, *Nostromo*

1904–1908 Hardy, *The Dynasts*

1905 Shaw, *Major Barbara*; Einstein, *Special Theory of Relativity*

1906 Conrad, *The Secret Agent*

1910 Conrad, *Under Western Eyes*

1910–1936 Reign of George V

1912 Conrad, *The Secret Sharer*; Shaw, *Pygmalion*

1914 Archduke Ferdinand assassinated, World War I begins

1915 Conrad, *Victory*; German submarine sinks the *Lusitania*; trench warfare begins in France

1916 Joyce, *Portrait of the Artist as a Young Man*; Shaw, *Androcles and the Lion*; Lenin, *Imperialism: The Last Stage of Capitalism*

1917 Conrad, *The Shadow Line*; United States enters World War I on Allied side; Bolsheviks take power in Russian revolution

1917–1920 Shaw, *Back to Methuselah*

1918 Hopkins's *Poems*; Germany agrees to armistice, World War I ends

1919 Hardy, *Collected Poems*; Gurney, *War's Emblems*; in United States, Volstead Act implements Eighteenth Amendment, bringing about Prohibition

1920 The League of Nations formed

1922 Housman, *Last Poems*

1923 Conrad, *The Rover*

1924 Shaw, *St. Joan*; Stalin introduces socialism to USSR

1925 Shaw receives Nobel Prize for literature, which he had previously declined

1928 Shaw, *The Intelligent Woman's Guide to Socialism and Capitalism*

1930 Hardy, *Collected Poems*; Masefield named poet laureate

1932 Shaw prose, *The Black Girl in Search of God*; Huxley, *Brave New World*

1933 Housman, *The Name and Nature of Poetry*; Hitler becomes chancellor of Germany

1934 Lewis, *A Hope for Poetry*; in the United States, "Harlem Renaissance" establishes poets Langston Hughes and Countee Cullen

1936–1952 George VI reigns

Several of the British writers who were successful in the first years of the twentieth century had already established themselves during the 1890s. Thomas Hardy had written his major novels and was soon to turn to poetry. George Bernard Shaw had launched his career as a playwright with his early social comedies and dramatic criticism, although his major plays were yet to be written. Likewise, Conrad's early novels date from the late 1890s, but his best work was done after the turn of the century. The era represented by these writers had a new spirit of skepticism about Victorian society's comfortable social arrangement and a new, daring directness.

Shaw impudently called some of his plays "unpleasant," indicating that he was more interested in disturbing the self-satisfaction of his audience than in entertaining them. Hardy and Conrad wrote poetry and fiction that probed the sore spots of the mind and that confronted the conscience of the reader with ambiguous and mysterious problems. Housman's lyrics have an undercurrent of pessimism. To writers of this generation, both the earnest optimism of mid-Victorian poets and the self-indulgent dreaminess of the aesthetics seemed too simple. The writers grappled with social and psychological complexities much more perplexing than their predecessors had imagined.

THOMAS HARDY (1840–1928)

Hardy was born near the city of Dorchester in the county of Dorset in southwestern England, a rustic and backward area from which he later drew his characters and his symbolic landscape settings. He was apprenticed to a local architect and then sent to London for further architectural training. He was a bookish young man and self-educated in literature.

After the success of his first novels in the 1870s, especially *Far from the Madding Crowd* (1874), Hardy gave up architecture and married. His marriage did not turn out to be a happy one. Hardy wanted above all to be a poet, but his need to earn a living kept him working as a novelist for the next two decades. He was famous and greatly admired, but in 1895 the negative reception of his novel *Jude the Obscure* made Hardy give up fiction in disgust and turn to poetry. Beginning with his first volume, *Wessex Poems* (1898), he published a book of poems about every four or five years, completing eight volumes in all. He also wrote short stories, which were published in several collections.

The area around Dorchester where Hardy grew up and where he returned to live in middle age was called Wessex in his novels and poems. In this rustic area, the old customs and folkways persisted while the rest of England was becoming industrialized. People still lived by farming and depended on the weather for their prosperity. In this setting, Hardy showed a tragic sense of human existence, an awareness that the best efforts of human beings are frequently thwarted in the apparently meaningless coming-together of chance and the indifferent forces of nature. The fate of the individual is determined by ironic, seemingly antagonistic circumstances, yet each one contributes to his own fate through the pursuit of his own desires. Having the moral toughness to recognize the ironies of fate, and to endure them, is about the best one can hope for.

Hardy was often called a pessimist, but he rejected that label, claiming to be a "meliorist"—that is, one who does not expect to achieve an ideal state but who bends his efforts in the direction of betterment. In his lyric poetry, however, the tone is frequently gloomy, not suggesting much hope of relief.

"Hap"

This poem is typical of Hardy in its tough confrontation between the speaker's sense of injustice and the cold indifference of the powers of the universe. The title means chance, or luck; it implies that things happen arbitrarily, without reason or fairness. The speaker states that if his suffering could be explained, even if the cause of it was not justified, he could perhaps accept the suffering and die as a martyr. But he is afraid that his suffering, like all human grief, is without meaning. There are no gods causing it; it merely happens, and it is as meaningless as the throw of dice. It would have been just as easy for him to have received joy as pain, and just as meaningless. Hardy cannot see any system of rewards and punishments operating on earth.

"Neutral Tones"

The "tones" of the title are, first, the dull colors of the setting. The speaker and a woman he has loved have met on a cold and bleak winter day near a pond, beneath a leafless tree. Both sky and land are white or grayish-white. The tones are also their voices as they discuss the death of their love, blaming each other for the loss. The woman's smile is also a dead, colorless thing. The speaker remembers that day as one on which the bleak and ashen landscape was a perfect reflection of the emotions they both felt. The gray leaves have become mental images associated with dead love.

"A Broken Appointment"

This lyric is spoken by a man who feels that love has died. He has waited for his former love to meet him, as she had agreed, but she does not appear. He feels especially grieved that she did not retain enough of her former good will to spend an hour with him to sooth his loneliness, even if she had no love to offer. That is, he is less disappointed that she did not come than he is that she is so unkind, that her character is less compassionate than he had expected.

"The Darkling Thrush"

This poem, written on December 31, 1899, takes place on a bleak winter evening. The speaker leans upon a gate, listening to the wind, when suddenly the gray and empty air is full of the song of a thrush hidden somewhere in the shadowy branches overhead. The bird's song is joyous, breaking the gloomy mood. In the final stanza, the speaker wonders why the bird sang so richly in such uncongenial surroundings. Perhaps the bird felt some intuition of hope, "some blessed Hope," of which the speaker was not aware. This ending, suggesting hope and joy in nature, is more romantic in tone than most of Hardy's lyrics.

"The Ruined Maid"

In the form of a dialogue, Hardy presents two young women who chance to meet in a marketplace. The first works hard at manual labor on a nearby farm. The second, Amelia (called "Melia"), used to do such work also, when the two were friends. Now Amelia is dressed up in fancy, expensive clothes. The farm girl marvels at these clothes and asks how Amelia got them. The ironic reply is Melia's casual "O didn't you know I'd been ruined?" Ruined, in this context, means that she has become the mistress of a rich man who takes care of her and dresses her well in exchange for her sexual services.

Hardy stresses the disparity between the notion of respectability that would condemn such a girl as Amelia for immorality and the outward signs of prosperity and well-being that are her reward.

The farm girl recollects, in stanza 2, Amelia's tattered clothes when she was an honest working girl, contrasting them to her new dress and ornaments. In the following stanzas, the farm girl describes Amelia's former rustic, unpolished speech, how rough the skin of her hands and face used to be, and the headaches and bad dreams from which she used to suffer. These are all the normal conditions of a poor farm laborer, and they are probably the conditions of the speaker herself. Honesty and hard work offer meager rewards. The incentives to become "ruined" are very great.

This is shown in the final stanza when the farm girl expresses her envy and her wish that she too could enjoy fine clothes and leisure. But Amelia cuts in with the cold remark that her former friend should not expect such pleasures, because she isn't "ruined." Her speech shows an inversion of values, an irony based on the contrast between accepted moral standards and the actual rewards and punishments that life offers. The girl who does not submit to the rules of conduct laid out by society is the one whom society actually treats the best.

"A Trampwoman's Tragedy"

This simple narrative of peasant life and death is based on the theme that unanticipated and undeserved tragedy can befall anyone. The speaker is a young woman, energetic and flirtatious but essentially honest and loyal to her lover.

At the opening of the poem she and her lover and two friends, Mother Lee and "jeering John," are walking across the open countryside of Wessex, traveling from inn to inn. The purpose of their journey is not specified; the jogging rhythm of the verse seems to suggest that walking, or tramping, is an end in itself. Though the scenes they pass are "fine sights," the walk is tedious. The speaker begins to tease her lover, pretending to be fond of "leering John."

One evening when they have reached a remote inn, the speaker sits down on the settle, a high-backed bench opposite the fireplace. She sits not with her lover but with John. But the lover does not accept this teasing game. Suddenly, he demands to know whose is the child that the speaker is carrying. She, annoyed that he will not play along, lies and indicates that the child is John's. At that, her lover springs up and knifes John, killing him.

In stanza 10, there has been a leap forward in time, as in a folk ballad, and the lover is pictured hanging for the murder at Iver-Chester jail. After that, tragedy engulfs the remaining companions. Mother Lee dies and the child is born dead; only the speaker is left, alone in the world. Visited by her lover's ghost, she confesses to him that she was always faithful to him, that the teasing was all false. Nevertheless, she is bereft of lover, child, and friends as a result of a moment's careless teasing and the destructive power of jealous passion. It is the kind of melancholy story that might be repeated around the fireside of a country inn for generations.

"Channel Firing"

Just before the outbreak of World War I in 1914, the English began, as part of their preparations for war, artillery practice over the English Channel, the water that separates England from the European continent. This poem depicts the reactions of people buried in a church near the Channel. They have been awakened from their long sleep by gunfire, and one of them describes their feelings of bewilderment and disgust.

This first speaker tells how they were awakened by the shaking of their coffins and the cracking of panes of glass in the church windows. Dogs bark; the church mouse and worm shrink back. They all assume that God is awakening them because it is Judgment Day. But the voice of God explains that it is only gunnery practice, not the final judgment. Foolish men are still making war and neglecting religion. God goes on to remark that it is lucky for the gunners that Judgment Day has not come because they would surely be damned. God laughs sarcastically, comparing His capacity to make things "warm" with the guns used by men. Then the dead settle down in their coffins again, discussing the hopelessness of mankind, who never seem to learn or improve. One, the ghost of a clergyman, says that he might as well never have preached for all the difference it made. The final stanza reports that the sound of the guns can be heard as far away as Stonehenge and Camelot, both of which are associated with the distant history of England.

Again, the implication is that although the weapons are modern, the tendency to fight is ancient.

"Ah, Are You Digging on My Grave?"

This is one of Hardy's best-known poems. Its irony is recognized by anyone who has felt unloved or unappreciated.

In the first part of each stanza a woman who has died speaks. She senses some disturbance at her grave and asks repeatedly who is digging there. In each stanza she makes a different guess as to who the digger might be: her lover, her kinsmen, or her enemy. None of these guesses is correct. Finally, her little dog admits that he has been digging at her grave. She is pleased that the dog, at least, is still faithful to her memory. He responds that actually he had forgotten that this was her grave; he was only trying to bury a bone.

The poem leaves a completely bleak impression of human affections as shallow and soon forgotten. Even the sentimental idea of a dog's fidelity is debunked.

"He Never Expected Much"

Written two years before Hardy's death, this poem sums up his fatalistic views while adding a note of resignation or acceptance. Again, Hardy uses dialogue to dramatize the moment of realization.

The poet speaks first, telling the World that it has "kept faith" in that the poet's life has turned out pretty much as he had expected. Even in childhood, he had not counted on much joy or pleasure or excitement.

The World responds in the middle of the second stanza. It agrees that it has not promised much to anyone, whether that person has loved the World or showed contempt for worldly things.

At the conclusion, the poet calls the World's words a "wise warning" and says that because he took this warning to heart, he has been able to endure each year's "strain and ache." The events of a life, the poem claims, are mostly "neutral-tinted"—that is, minor and bland. One who accepts this truth can get by all right. Hardy puts forth an unromantic image of life.

GEORGE BERNARD SHAW (1856–1950)

Shaw is another figure who made the transition from late-Victorian to modern times. Like Hardy, he had a long career and lived most of a century. Shaw was born in Ireland, although his family had originally been English. His family was not affluent; Shaw left school at fourteen to work. He was largely self-educated through reading. His mother, a musician and music teacher, educated Shaw in music. He was especially influenced by the works of Mozart and Wagner.

In 1876, when his mother moved to London to further her teaching career, Shaw followed her. He launched himself as a writer, beginning with several unsuccessful novels. He then found employment writing music reviews and, later, reviews of plays.

Shaw was attracted to socialist ideas and in 1884 became one of the founding members of the Fabian Society. The Fabians advocated the spread of socialism, not through revolution, as the Marxists did, but by gradual reform of the inadequate and unjust social and economic institutions and laws of England. Shaw was a reformer in many ways. He criticized the triviality of contemporary drama, sought to promote social reform, and promoted his belief in the "Life Force," the vitality and power of the individual genius who can, by force of will, change society. A few such supermen are born in each generation. If society responds to their ideas and energy, it will be reinvigorated and improved.

In pursuance of vitality in his own life, Shaw became a vegetarian and drank nothing containing caffeine or alcohol. He also promoted schemes to simplify English spelling by use of a phonetic alphabet.

Shaw's career as a playwright began in the 1890s. He was favorably impressed by the social-problem plays of the Norwegian playwright Henrik Ibsen. Shaw saw that the theater could be used to shake up the English middle class and make them reexamine their assumptions about right and wrong. Plays could contain intelligent discussion in which the characters reflect on the false ideas of the majority. But Shaw also understood stage conventions and had benefited from his years as a drama critic. He used clever plotting and theatrical surprises to keep the audience's attention as well as to emphasize his ideas. He was a master of paradox, taking a familiar assumption and seeming to stand it on its head so that the apparent good was seen as bad and the bad as, if not good, at least less bad than it at first appeared. His vital characters, those who embodied the Life Force, dazzled the audience with wit and sometimes shocked them by taking up radical positions.

Among Shaw's early plays were *Widowers' Houses* (1892), about slum landlords, and *Mrs. Warren's Profession* (1893), about the economic basis of prostitution. This play was not permitted to be produced because of the bold treatment of its theme. These plays and several others were published in 1898 in *Plays Pleasant and Unpleasant*. Realizing that he could reach a wider audience through the publication of plays than he could through their performance only, Shaw later published plays and included lengthy prefaces in which he further discussed the characters, their social backgrounds, and the issues in which they were involved.

Shaw's dramatic output was greatest in the first two decades of the twentieth century. Among his best-known plays, still frequently staged, are *Arms and the Man* (1894), an antiwar statement; *Man and Superman* (1904), a depiction of his ideas on the Life Force; *Major Barbara* (1907), an attack on charity as a social good; and *Pygmalion* (1912), a treatment of language and social-class barriers. This last play was made into a musical comedy, *My Fair Lady.* Shaw also wrote a serious treatment of Joan of Arc called *Saint Joan* (1923).

Shaw continued writing plays, but less frequently, into the 1940s. He also wrote the important prose works *The Quintessence of Ibsenism,* which he revised in 1913, and *The Intelligent Woman's Guide to Socialism and Capitalism* (1928). His influence as a playwright served to bring his ideas about society to public attention and also to contradict the idea that the playwright's only purpose is to amuse and entertain. He made audiences expect to hear ideas discussed onstage and opened the way for other, less conventional forms of drama.

Mrs. Warren's Profession

In this play Shaw examines the economic and social forces that shape the lives of women. He shows how men exploit women economically and at the same time expect them to adhere to a higher standard of morality, have greater sexual restraint, and be submissive.

SHAW'S CHARACTERS

The character Vivie (full of life) is Shaw's image of the new woman. She is intelligent, independent, and energetic, taking control of her own destiny. From the start, Vivie is outside convention.

Act 1. This act introduces the main characters and hints at their past relationships. Vivie is the center of attention. She is found in her cottage retreat, studying law books and preparing to launch herself on a law career. She is visited by Mr. Praed, an old friend of her mother's. Then Mrs. Warren arrives, accompanied by Mr. Crofts. Mrs. Warren, Vivie's mother, is hearty and vulgar, but she hopes to make a lady of her daughter. Crofts is a gentleman on the surface, strong and assertive. He has known Mrs. Warren since the time of Vivie's birth. He discusses with Praed who Vivie's father might be. Perhaps one of them? But Praed claims his relationship with Mrs. Warren never went beyond friendship. Finally we meet Frank Gardner, the ne'er-do-well son of the local clergyman. He is attracted to Vivie. Finally, Frank's father, Reverend Samuel Gardner, comes in, warning Frank against any involvement with a woman. The reverend cites his own youthful entanglement with an unsuitable woman. At the end of Act 1 Mrs. Warren emerges from the cottage, where she has been taking tea. She recognizes Reverend Samuel as a former lover; she is the very woman whom he was just citing to his son as a potentially costly youthful mistake.

Act 2. That evening the whole party gathers at the cottage for supper. The question arises of who will marry Vivie. Frank puts in his claim to Mrs. Warren, calling her daughter "my Vivie" and declaring that he can't give

Vivie up, even as he flirts with Mrs. Warren. But Frank makes no pretense that he plans to do any useful work; on the basis of style alone he feels superior to such men as Crofts. Crofts asks Mrs. Warren for Vivie's hand on the grounds of his wealth and social status. He will make both Vivie and her mother comfortable, but such a low-level, dull existence is rejected by Mrs. Warren, who has more ambition for her daughter.

The main action of Act 2 is the confrontation between Vivie and Mrs. Warren. Vivie rejects the authority of Mrs. Warren because she does not really understand her mother. In response, Mrs. Warren lets the truth come out. She confesses that when she was a poor but attractive young woman she decided not to waste away in a life of drudgery, like her stepsisters, but instead to use her good looks to make money by pleasing men. In short, she and her sister Liz worked as prostitutes until they could save enough money to establish their own fancy brothel in Brussels. She defends this choice as the only reasonable one, given the starvation wages of most women's work. Mrs. Warren compares her and Liz's profession with the prudent marriages of middle-class girls, who find men who can support them and keep them from want. Neither decision is good, but each is better than "the gutter." Mrs. Warren is not ashamed, despising the hypocrisy of society and the pretenses made by other women.

After this long explanation and defense, Vivie accepts and loves her mother. As a young woman of intelligence and independent mind, Vivie sees the justification for her mother's way of life. They embrace as the act ends.

Act 3. The next morning at the rectory Reverend Samuel is showing the ill effects of having sat up drinking with Crofts on the previous night. Frank tells his father that Mrs. Gardner and her daughter Bessie have gone up to London for the day in order to avoid a social call from the unacceptable Mrs. Warren. When Vivie and Mrs. Warren arrive the embarrassed Reverend Samuel takes Mrs. Warren and Crofts with Praed for a tour of the old church, leaving Frank and Vivie together. Frank mocks Vivie for her sentimental attachment to her mother, but Vivie explains that her attitude toward her mother has changed from priggish rejection to understanding. Frank's position is that Mrs. Warren is "a bad lot" and that Vivie must not live with her mother or she will become disgusted by Mrs. Warren's vulgarity. They are interrupted by Crofts, who dismisses Frank as a man of no profession, no property, and no money.

Crofts has sought out Vivie to make his proposal of marriage, a very businesslike proposition in which he bargains for her affections with his title, wealth, and secure social position. He reveals that he has been Mrs. Warren's business partner, investing in the "private hotels" that Mrs. Warren operates. He also shocks Vivie by stating that this business, which she knows is really prostitution, still goes on. He points out that Vivie's own lifestyle and education have been paid for by it. He sees no reason why he, like other members of his class, should not profit from investments that exploit poor women, either factory girls or prostitutes. He assures Vivie that, as Lady Crofts, she will never be confronted with embarrassing questions about the sources of her income. Instead of being persuaded to marry him, Vivie is revolted, and she rings a bell to summon Frank, who appears from the rectory carrying his gun.

The confrontation between Frank and Crofts borders on violence. Spitefully, Crofts tells Frank and Vivie that they are half-brother and half-sister, since they were both fathered by the Reverend Samuel. Repelled by the whole situation, Vivie declares that she will follow her original plan and go to London to work and study law.

Act 4. Some few days later Vivie has begun to work in a London law office, filling in for a female friend who is on vacation. Frank has come to visit her, still pressing his marriage proposal. He tells her that the story of their being half-brother and sister is a lie. Praed also stops to see Vivie; he is taking a trip to Italy and would have liked her to accompany him. Vivie firmly rejects both "love's young dream" as offered by Frank and the "romance and beauty of life" as offered by Praed. She reluctantly and indirectly reveals to both men that her mother is the madam of several houses of prostitution. Overcome by emotion, Vivie goes into an inner office to regain her composure. Frank tells Praed that he can no longer propose marriage to Vivie, explaining that while he still loves her he will not live on Vivie's income if it ultimately comes from prostitution. He knows Vivie will understand his scruples. At this point Mrs. Warren arrives, seeking a reconciliation with Vivie. Both Frank and Praed advise Mrs. Warren to leave, but she persists. Vivie reenters, says farewell to Praed and Frank, and then announces to her mother that she, Vivie, will be self-supporting from now on. She had sympathized when her mother had explained how her career of prostitution had come about, but she cannot accept that it is still going on, since poverty is no longer a threat. But Mrs. Warren tries to tempt Vivie with images of the great wealth she could enjoy and to convince her that the world really cares only for money, not for how it was earned.

Mrs. Warren declares that "fashionable morality is all a pretense" and that Vivie is a fool to think otherwise. But as she continues to talk, she reveals more and more of her own vulgarity and selfishness. She claims her right to Vivie and accuses her of being a "pious, canting, hard, selfish woman." But Vivie holds out against all these arguments. Even as she admits that, in poor circumstances, she might have done as her mother did, she is still determined to do honest work and to cut herself off from her mother and her mother's money.

Finally, Mrs. Warren sees that Vivie is only doing what is best for herself. She goes out, angrily slamming the door. Vivie immediately feels relieved and sets about working at the papers on her desk. She is Shaw's new woman, active and free, made independent through work.

EARLY PERFORMANCE

This play, written in 1893, was forbidden to be performed by the lord chancellor's office, the government bureau for stage censorship. The character of Mrs. Warren and the frank discussion of prostitution were considered too sensational. It was privately produced in London and publicly produced in New York in 1905, but after one performance the play was closed by the New York City police.

However, while the play could not be performed, it could be published. It appeared in the volume *Plays Pleasant and Unpleasant* in 1898. Only in the second decade of the twentieth century was it legally presented onstage in England.

Mrs. Warren's Profession is a comedy because of its witty dialogue and its surprising turns of plot, but it does not have the conventional comic ending—the marriage of the principal lovers and the reconciliation between the old and new generations. Its "happy" ending is more modern; Vivie finds joy in *not* being obliged to marry and in being free of the duties of a daughter.

JOSEPH CONRAD (1857–1924)

Conrad, whose original name was Teodor Josef Konrad Korzeniowski, was of Polish origin. His father was a nationalist patriot at a time when Poland was under Russian domination. By the time Conrad was twelve, both his parents had died and he was under the guardianship of an uncle. At fifteen, Conrad gained permission to go to sea, fulfilling a boyhood dream. He began as a seaman based in Marseille, France, later becoming a British subject and a master seaman. In 1894, having sailed all over the world for twenty years, Conrad decided to retire in England. He married the next year and published his first novel, *Almayer's Folly*. Although he did not begin to learn English until he was twenty, now at thirty-eight he wrote entirely in English. Most of his novels and short stories use the sea, the ship, and the harbors of the Orient as their settings.

Conrad's Fiction

Conrad's fiction explores the moral ambiguities and dilemmas of experience. He frequently uses a framework narrator or multiple narrators in order to present a problematic action from more than one point of view. He avoids being didactic and aims instead at recreating the sense of things, the mysterious complexities of events that make it impossible to find clear and satisfactory explanations.

In his famous preface to the novel *The Nigger of the Narcissus*, Conrad tries to explain his sense of the artist's task. Making an analogy between fiction and music or painting, Conrad says that all art appeals essentially to the senses. The artist does not try to teach, amuse, or console his reader. But by a "perfect blending of form and substances," the writer of fiction tries to make the reader feel, hear, and see a moment in a person's life with such clarity that the truth of it reaches into the reader's heart and makes him or her feel a solidarity with the rest of humanity. Thus Conrad tried to distinguish his purpose from the contemporary movements of realism, naturalism, and the ever-present sentimentalism. He hoped to make his readers pause from their busy personal pursuits to attain "a moment of vision."

Heart of Darkness

Well into the twentieth century the modern African nation of Zaire was called the Congo. It was controlled by the Belgians, who exploited its mineral wealth through mining. The native inhabitants of the Congo were forced to work in these mines by brutal and callous methods. During a visit to an outpost on the Congo River in 1890, Conrad was shocked and repelled by what he saw.

This short novel, or novella, is based on Conrad's brief encounter with the agent of a European company that had pushed into the jungle, setting up outposts for the ivory trade.

The narrator of the story is Marlow, an experienced and thoughtful captain who serves as the storyteller in several of Conrad's novels, including *Youth* and *Lord Jim*. Marlow's narration creates a framework. As he tells his story to a quiet group of fellow seamen or, as in this case, a group of shipping company men, he seems to direct his observations to them as a perceptive audience. Sometimes he pauses for their reactions and responds with further attempts to explain what is, finally, unexplainable.

In *Heart of Darkness*, the four listeners sit on board a ship in the Thames below London, waiting for the tide to shift so that they can move downstream. As the evening turns to night, Marlow slowly begins his tale, starting with some general observations about how wild, dark, and savage the Thames must have seemed to the early Roman explorers who ventured along its banks. The listeners know, however, that they are about to hear one of Marlow's "inconclusive experiences."

Having felt from boyhood that he would like to explore the heart of Africa, Marlow, with the help of an admiring aunt, obtains a job on the Congo River as captain of a steamboat, a boat that was to move cargo and personnel between various outposts. In Brussels he visits the company headquarters, where he meets two strange women who sit like the fates in an outer office. He signs a contract with the company director, a "great man" of five feet, six inches who controls immense and far-flung enterprises that bring in great wealth. Marlow has a brief medical examination, during which the doctor asks to measure his head for scientific purposes. The doctor hints that few men return from the Congo and asks Marlow if there is madness in his family. Finally, Marlow says farewell to his aunt, who believes that voyages like Marlow's bring the light of European culture to the unfortunate savages. Marlow remarks how women are "out of touch with truth," a comment that helps explain his behavior in the final scene of the novel.

Having traveled to Africa on a French steamer, Marlow then gets passage upriver on a smaller steamboat. Arriving at the company station, he witnesses scenes of chaos and pointless cruelty. He sees gangs of chained black men hauling dirt to build a railroad. He is appalled by the sight of a group of sick, broken, and starving men left to die in a dark grove of trees. Stepping out of this horrible grove, he encounters the company's chief accountant, a man neatly, and even elegantly, dressed in white, all starched and brushed and apparently oblivious of the confusion and suffering around him.

The accountant tells Marlow that the steamboat he has come to command is unfortunately wrecked some 200 miles upstream. Marlow makes the journey overland on foot. When he arrives at the trading station, the manager is not happy to see him. He says it should take about three months to repair the boat. The manager also speaks of their agent, Kurtz, a man of great skill and effectiveness who works at an ivory station farther up the river. More than any of the other European agents attached to this station, men Marlow calls "pilgrims," Kurtz clearly arouses admiration and envy. Realizing that this journey to the interior is being delayed on purpose, Marlow becomes curious to meet this phenomenon, who seems to be both a great idealist and a great profit-maker. Everyone is jealous of Kurtz but afraid to criticize him. Meanwhile, Marlow has to use a combination of bullying and persuasion to get a supply of rivets to fix the boat. While he waits, a series of five new white men, with accompanying bearers and donkeys, arrives to "tear treasure out of the bowels of the earth." Marlow ironically calls them the Eldorado Exploring Expedition. One of these new men is an uncle of the manager. Marlow overhears the uncle and nephew speaking of Kurtz with anger and jealousy. Marlow is now all the more eager to see and speak with Kurtz.

The rivets finally arrive, the boat is repaired, and Marlow, along with the manager and "three or four pilgrims," starts up-river toward Kurtz's station. The boat crew is made up of several members of a local cannibal tribe. The trip is slow and difficult; wood must be cut every night to feed the fires of the steamboat the next day. They pass many hostile villages. They stop at an abandoned hut that once belonged to some unknown European, where they find a supply of firewood, a book on seamanship, and a strange note warning them to approach Kurtz's station cautiously. As they near the station, the river divides into two channels, forcing them to steer close to the bank. They become surrounded by fog and have to stop the boat. Suddenly, battle cries, arrows, and spears are hurled at them from the shore. The "pilgrims" fire back ineffectually into the foliage. The cannibals in the crew are eager to catch and eat some of the attackers.

In the midst of this chaos, the helmsman is killed by a spear. Finally, it occurs to Marlow to blow the steam whistle. The sudden noise shocks the attackers and they fade into the forest. The white men speculate that perhaps Kurtz is dead, but Marlow hopes not. He realizes that he very much looks forward to talking to Kurtz, as if Kurtz alone might be able to explain the strange darkness of the inner continent.

Marlow interrupts his story to light a pipe. He admits the absurdity of his feelings. He moves ahead of himself in the narrative, mentioning Kurtz's fiancée, whom he refers to as Kurtz's "intended." Returning to the main story line, Marlow tells of loading the steamboat with ivory. He discovers that Kurtz is alive but sick. He has been attended by a young Russian sailor, the fellow at whose hut they had found the book and the message of warning.

Talking to the Russian, Marlow comes to understand that Kurtz has been able to ship so much ivory because he has subdued the natives of the surrounding tribes, making himself their god. Marlow sees the ghastly evidence of Kurtz's rule in a line of shrunken heads on the fence posts surrounding Kurtz's house. The attack on the steamboat was launched because the people do not want Kurtz to go away; they worship him. After overcoming them with the power of his guns Kurtz had established elaborate rituals of obedience, so that even the chiefs crawl in his presence. Finally, Kurtz has lost his own sense of civilization, and at times even believes in his own divinity. Kurtz is carried into the boat, but he escapes at night and attempts to rejoin his followers. Marlow finds him on the path at night and carries him back to the boat. His people come to the riverbank, but Marlow once again scares them off with the steam whistle. Some of the whites fire at the attackers and at a magnificent dark woman, who is the only one not frightened away.

As the boat starts downstream, Marlow finally gets to hear Kurtz talk. Kurtz trusts Marlow with his private papers and with a tract he has written called "The Suppression of Savage Customs." Marlow comes to understand the spellbinding power of Kurtz's voice, even as Kurtz begins to fall into incoherence. His final words are "The horror, the horror!"

Marlow leaves Kurtz to go to the mess room. Shortly thereafter the servant of the manager comes in to say, sarcastically, "Mistah Kurtz—he dead." The manager and the other white men, the "pilgrims," are glad to be rid of him. They bury him hurriedly on the river bank.

Marlow, however, feels a strange and perverse loyalty to Kurtz. He feels that he understands Kurtz's final comment, "The horror! the horror!" Marlow conceals his knowledge of Kurtz's madness, thus protecting his reputation. He takes the papers back to Brussels, giving some to relatives and some to the press. He takes the personal letters to Kurtz's "intended," a loyal and idealistic woman who mourns the death of Kurtz and worships his memory. She is sure he was a genius. Marlow, embarrassed by her expectation that he also admires Kurtz's genius, nevertheless does not disillusion her. He lies, telling her that Kurtz's last word was her name. To tell her the truth would have been "too dark."

At the end of his story, Marlow falls silent and his listeners also remain in meditative silence. Finally the director notices that they have lost the ebb tide that was to carry them downriver. They look out into the overcast morning sky.

In telling the story about Kurtz, Conrad focuses on the conflicts and moral ambiguities of European exploration and of Europe's exploitation of its colonial empires. While claiming and perhaps intending to bring the light of European culture and civilization to the "dark continent," the traders and their agents in fact introduced a new level of savage brutality, aided by the superior technology that made Western culture so "advanced." The hungry cannibals in Marlow's boat crew seem benign compared with the callous, destructive manager and accountant.

Shortly after the publication of *Heart of Darkness*, international panels of inquiry investigated the outrageous treatment of Africans in the Belgian Congo.

A. E. HOUSMAN (1859–1936)

Housman's career provides an early example of a link that becomes more and more common during the twentieth century: that between academia and poetry writing. In the absence of other kinds of patronage, universities have become the support of writers whose excellent work does not have great popularity. However, academic life was not always kind to Housman. After being an outstanding student of classics at Oxford University, Housman suddenly lost control of his major subject and failed his final examinations. His failure seems to have been connected to repressed attraction for one of his fellow students. After leaving the university, Housman took a minor civil service position in the London patent office. He continued his classical studies on his own, eventually becoming a well-recognized and respected authority on Latin texts. At the same time Housman began to write poetry in a series of notebooks. These show the many painstaking revisions that lie behind his seemingly simple and spontaneous lyrics.

In 1892, after ten years at the patent office, Housman was recognized for his scholarly work by being appointed Latin professor at University College in London. In 1911 he gained the more prestigious professorship of Latin at Cambridge University.

Housman's poetic output was not of great quantity. His fame rests on two small volumes, one published before the turn of the century and the other some twenty years later. In 1933, a few years before his death, Housman gave an influential lecture on the nature of the creative process in poetry, "The Name and Nature of Poetry," in which he expressed his idea that poetry has a direct, physical effect on the reader, an effect that cannot be analyzed.

A Shropshire Lad

This volume of poems, privately printed in 1896, gained recognition very slowly, becoming most popular during the era of World War I, when the pessimistic tone of the poems found the greatest public acceptance.

The poems, as expected, were heavily influenced by Housman's Latin studies. They especially reflect the stoical tone and polished compression of classical lyrics. But the forms of Housman's lyrics are based on English ballads and songs.

Shropshire is a rural area near the area where Housman grew up. The "lad" of the title is a "persona," an adopted character through whom the poet speaks. The apparent simplicity and lightness of the lyrics disguise the cynicism and bitter disappointments that lie at their heart. Unlike the easy carpe diem message of earlier classicists such as the seventeenth-century cavalier poets, Housman's lyrics have a more modern sense of irony:

> Life is a test; there are no rules.
>
> The only guide is one's own manly sense of perseverance.
>
> Nature is beautiful but indifferent;
>
> It can be enjoyed but it has no benevolent intentions toward mankind.

"TO AN ATHLETE DYING YOUNG"

Probably the best-known of the poems in *A Shropshire Lad*, this lyric is spoken by one of the athlete's townsmen.

In the first two stanzas, the speaker compares two occasions when the athlete's young friends carried him on their shoulders. The first was when he won a race and was carried home a champion, and the second was when he died and was carried through the town in his coffin. The cause of the athlete's death is not indicated. The speaker addresses the dead athlete, telling him that early death is best. It is preferable to die while one is still famous rather than years later when one's fame has been forgotten and one's records have long since been surpassed. At the end, the speaker imagines the young athlete being received among the dead, his laurels of victory still fresh.

"WHEN I WAS ONE AND TWENTY"

The two stanzas of this poem present a before-and-after image of a young lad who has learned about the sorrows of love.

In the first stanza, the speaker is only twenty-one. He hears a wise man's warning not to fall in love, but he ignores it.

In the second stanza, a year later, the speaker hears the same warning, but by now he has had an unhappy experience of love. He recognizes the truth of the wise man's warning. In each case, the wise man depicts love as giving away something vital, some part of oneself, and getting only sorrow in return.

"TERENCE, THIS IS STUPID STUFF"

This poem is a dialogue, written in the conversational tone of two friends having a minor argument. The first speaker complains to Terence that the poetry he writes is "stupid" because it is too gloomy and too full of death. He asks Terence to write more cheerful poems, poems "to dance to" while they are enjoying their beer.

Terence responds that his friends might as well just drink beer for pleasure and forget about poetry. Beer is a much more reliable source of temporary joy and forgetfulness of the sorrows of the world. "Malt" is more effective than the poetry of, for example, Milton in making the world seem a good place.

Housman paraphrases Milton's famous statement of purpose in writing the great moral epic *Paradise Lost*: "To justify the ways of God to man." Then the poet points out that he himself has been drunk and has had the experience of being satisfied with the world while lying in "lovely muck." But the next morning always brings the return of sober realization. Therefore, he will keep on writing the poetry of pessimism, to keep in training for the bad luck that is sure to catch up with him. If his poetry is "sour" it will be more useful to his friend when life turns "dark and cloudy."

Finally, the poet tells a story, an analogy drawn from the ancient myth of King Mithridates. This king, fearing that he would be poisoned, prepared himself by ingesting small doses of poison, thus building up a tolerance to poison. Though all his enemies killed each other off with arsenic and strychnine, Mithridates, Terence tells his friend, "he died old." The moral of the poem is that life's bitterness is best acknowledged and endured rather than ignored until it is too late.

"WITH RUE MY HEART IS LADEN"

In this short lyric of two quatrains Housman captures a feeling of rue; that is, pity and regret. His heart is weighted down (laden) with rue when he thinks of the companions of his youth, fresh and pretty girls and agile "lightfoot" boys who now exist no more. The speaker is perhaps an old man looking back on the friends of childhood.

In the second stanza these friends have all died. The boys no longer leap across brooks but lie buried beside them. The girls have faded and sleep in their graves. This is one of Housman's best-known lyrics, easily memorized and expressing a familiar, poignant feeling.

"COULD MAN BE DRUNK FOREVER"

This is another short lyric in which Housman expresses the essence of an impulse. Here, the two quatrains present two contrasting states of being. In the first, drunkenness is pictured as a desirable condition, full of drinking, loving, and fighting. One is occupied with the here-and-now. This is the state the speaker claims to prefer. (*"Lief"* is an archaic word meaning willingness or desire.) But in the second quatrain the speaker realizes that moments of sobriety must come and when they do, sober thoughts bring pangs of doubt or fear caught in the final image of putting one's hand upon one's own heart.

The transitional authors writing in the last decade of the nineteenth century and the early decades of the twentieth use remarkably different forms, but they are united by their sense that God has abandoned the world. They have no faith in ultimate moral order or justice. Faced with a world that provides no grounds for hope, they stake out positions of tough endurance and ironic distance from sentiment and naive hope. Irony pervades their work. The irony of the modernist suggests that the faith that sustained people of previous generations was a bitter cheat. It is better to live without illusions and without false, futile attachment to the pious truths of romantic idealism or Victorian earnestness. As poets, Hardy and Housman recreate moments when this illusion is stripped away, leaving a bitter aftertaste. They dip into the lives of rural and small-town folk, not to celebrate their simple goodness but to show the universality of disappointment and despair. Conrad uses a larger canvas to penetrate the essence of corruption of false idealism. Only Shaw seems hopeful, but even he demands an honest acceptance of all that is unlovely and hypocritical in established social life. For Shaw, the Life Force of the individual may be able to break through the barriers of old authority and social restraint, but the struggle will not be easy and many cherished notions about what is good will have to be abandoned along the way. Only a few strong personalities will be capable of making a breakthrough; when they succeed, their success will be uncomfortable and precarious.

Selected Readings

Gregor, Ian. *The Great Web: The Form of Hardy's Major Fiction*. Totowa, NJ: Rowman, 1974.

Guerard, Albert, ed. *Hardy: A Collection of Critical Essays*. Englewood Cliffs, NJ: Prentice-Hall, 1963.

Hardwick, Michael and Mollie Hardwick. *The Bernard Shaw Companion*. London: Murray, 1973.

Karl, Frederick R., ed. *Joseph Conrad: A Collection of Criticism*. New York: McGraw-Hill, 1975.

Kaufmann, R. J., ed. *G. B. Shaw: A Collection of Critical Essays*. Englewood Cliffs, NJ: Prentice-Hall, 1965.

Price, Arthur J. *An Appreciation of Joseph Conrad*. Folcroft, PA: Folcroft, 1973.

Ricks, Christopher, ed. *A. E. Housman: A Collection of Critical Essays*. Englewood Cliffs, NJ: Prentice-Hall, 1968.

16

Poetry of World War I

1910–1936 Reign of George V

1911 Brooke, *Poems*

1912 Bridges, *Poetical Works*; *Titanic* sinks

1913 Bridges named poet laureate; Proust, *Remembrance of Things Past*

1914 Archduke Ferdinand assassinated, World War I begins

1915 Ford, *The Good Soldier*; Maugham, *Of Human Bondage*; second battle of Ypres; Brooke dies; English and French troops land at Gallipoli; German submarine sinks the *Lusitania*; trench warfare begins in France

1916 The Battle of Verdun

1917 Gurney, *Severn and Somme*; United States enters World War I on Allied side

1918 Brooke, *Collected Poems* published posthumously; second battle of the Somme and of the Marne; Germany agrees to armistice, World War I ends

1919 Sassoon, *The War Poems;* Gurney, *War's Emblems*; in United States, Volstead Act implements Eighteenth Amendment, bringing about Prohibition

1920 Owen, *Poems* published posthumously; decade of "The Roaring Twenties"

1926 Sassoon, *Satirical Poems*

1928 Sassoon, *Memoirs of a Fox-Hunting Man*

1930 Sassoon, *Memoirs of an Infantry Officer*

One kind of idealism that was swept away by the tide of modernism was the glorification of war, the celebration of men performing brave deeds in combat for the sake of their homeland. This association of combat and glory went back to the epic literature of Greece and Rome. At the beginning of the nineteenth century, Napoleon was idolized by many on the Continent and in England. Napoleon's great adversaries, Lord Nelson and the duke of Wellington, had been celebrated as military heroes.

With the development of more deadly firepower, the scale of slaughter increased and the illusion of glory in combat began to fade. World War I was the culmination of that tendency. Subsequent images of the battlefield tended to show the deadly folly and senseless waste of life caused by war. Military commanders began to be seen as incompetent or maniacal.

Most of the British poets who fought in World War I were educated young men who went to war expecting to prove their own bravery. Some died in the mass slaughter; most survived to bring home images of the horror of modern warfare.

The setting of many postwar poems is the trench. For most of its duration, World War I was a stalemate between German forces in western France and the forces of the Allies—mostly French and British. Dug into position in long lines facing each other, the soldiers practically lived in trenches. Cold, dirty, and diseased, they struggled for survival in the mud. From time to time the order came to advance. The area between German and Allied trenches, called "no man's land," was rutted and barren from heavy artillery fire. It was crisscrossed by lines of barbed wire. Soldiers could rake the area with machine-gun fire at the first sign of enemy troop movement. Charging forward under those conditions was almost suicidal, and hundreds of thousands lost their lives with no significant change in battle position. The poetry reflects the bitterness and agony of the soldier caught in such dire conditions.

RUPERT BROOKE (1887–1915)

Brooke was a naval officer who died early in the war, before the grinding slaughter had become entrenched. Thus he remained a spokesman for the earlier attitude that war was glorious, though his poems provide a hint of the change that was to take place before the war's end. Influenced by the Elizabethan sonneteers, Brooke wrote in the traditional lyric form of the sonnet.

"The Soldier" The most famous of Brooke's five war sonnets written in 1914, "The Soldier" caused a sensation because it seemed to express the whole nation's determination and patriotic idealism at the outset of the war.

In this sonnet, the soldier is speaking of his own death. He expects to die and accepts his own death as an expression of England's glory. He sees himself as a part of that idealized England of "flowers" and "gentleness." If he dies in war, the place of his burial will be transformed into a more English,—that is, a better,—place. Meanwhile his heart, being purified by its Englishness, will become part of the eternal mind. He will bring to his existence with God all of the excellent gifts of his English nature.

The poem at once glorifies the soldier in his brave and quiet acceptance of death and glorifies England for having produced such grand soldiers. It expresses a pious faith in the fitness and ultimate goodness of a death by self-sacrifice.

SIEGFRIED SASSOON (1886–1967)

Son of a wealthy Jewish family, Sassoon seemed to have been cut out for the life of a country gentleman who dabbled in poetry. But the shock of his experiences as an officer in the trenches roused him to protest the war. Sassoon was an authentic war hero, having been wounded and receiving the Military Cross for bravery. But when he began to make public statements against the war, protesting it as unnecessary and needlessly prolonged, his superiors charged that he was suffering from "shell shock," the condition of many soldiers who broke down mentally under the stress of trench warfare. Sassoon was sent to a military hospital for recuperation and to keep him out of the public eye. There he met the young poet Wilfred Owen, whom Sassoon encouraged. After the war, Sassoon returned to his country estate and lived a quiet life. His later poetry was religious, reflecting the increasing piety of his life. Sassoon's war poems frequently contrast the naive attitudes of people who are not part of the fight—the bishops, the generals, the women at home—with the horrible suffering and dying on the front line. Like Hardy, Sassoon uses contrasting voices in dialogue.

"They" In the first stanza of this two-stanza poem, a bishop speaks in heroic terms of the "boys" who have gone off to fight. He declares that they will be transformed by the "last attack on anti-Christ," thus establishing the war as a great moral struggle, a final battle of good and evil. Having fought, they will be welcomed home by the bishop to "breed an honorable race." They will be heroes, ready to father a new generation of heroes.

In stanza 2, the "boys" point out that they have suffered a different kind of transformation. Rather than splendid heroes, they have come back maimed, blinded, or dying of diseases or unhealed wounds. Thus instead of enhancing their manhood, the war has destroyed it. Baffled, the bishop can only reply weakly that "The ways of God are strange."

"The Rear-Guard"

This poem is set in an underground tunnel at the Hindenburg Line, an infamous entrenchment in northern France. The tunnel is one of many that connected trenches and places of retreat. The poem describes a soldier coming through the tunnel toward the front lines. Groping his way by the dim light of a flashlight ("torch"), he sees the litter from broken and discarded objects. He trips over something on the floor of the tunnel. Looking down, he sees the form of a soldier lying under a blanket ("rig"). Angry at the soldier's laziness, he pulls at and then kicks him. His pity has been smothered by his fatigue. Finally, aiming his light downward, he sees that he has stumbled on a corpse. The face and body reflect a death agony. Stunned, the soldier continues his search for headquarters, passing dark shapes of soldiers huddled in the tunnel as the noise of bombardment is faintly heard overhead. Finally, he finds a shaft leading to the surface. He ascends as if climbing out of hell.

"Glory of Women"

This is a sonnet, a form associated traditionally with lovers speaking to women. But the context here is different. The poet recounts the many ways that women on the home front glorify and celebrate their soldiers who come home on leave. Ignorant of the horrors of the war, the women want to be thrilled by heroic war stories. They want to hear about brave adventures. They don't want to be told about the ugly and disgraceful actions of war, of the retreats when men trample over the corpses of their fellow comrades. It is the same on the other side. The final image shows a loving German mother knitting socks for her soldier son who is already dead and trampled into the mud of the battlefield. There is nothing glorious about any of it.

IVOR GURNEY (1890–1937)

The son of a tailor in Gloucester, Gurney's musical talent won him a scholarship to the Royal College of Music. He composed many songs. His poetic career began during the war. He volunteered at the beginning of the war and served as a private on the western front, where he was wounded. He later returned to the front and was overcome by poison gas.

His first collection of poems, *Severn and Somme*, was published in 1917, while the war was still going on. It is named for two rivers, one in his native Gloucester and one in France, at the front. After the war, Gurney continued to suffer from the effects of the gas and from the entire horrible experience of war. He resumed his musical studies, but his sanity remained fragile. He was committed to a mental hospital in 1922 and never again lived outside of an institution, although he continued to write and compose.

"To His Love"

This short lyric is spoken to a woman whose beloved has gone to war and been killed. It contrasts the beautiful and strong young man that he was with the mangled body that is left for burial. He no longer has the form that she loved. The speaker urges her to "cover him soon" with flowers, to "hide that wet red thing" that his body has become. That form of him must be forgotten.

"Towards Lillers"

In this poem Gurney recreates a moment during the war and a group of soldiers who marched toward the front. The weather is good and the soldiers enjoy the march, even though they see that the landscape has been spoiled by war. Only a few bare chimneys and tree trunks stand in the smoky air. Reaching a town, the soldiers hope to quench their thirst at a tavern, but they soon realize that all such comfortable places have been ruined. "This is war," they tell themselves, and imagine that they know what sort of fight they are in for. It will be a good fight, a test of strength. But what they actually find is not men standing in confrontation but "two ditches of heart-sick men" divided by barbed wire. Overhead, airplanes circle. This is modern "scientific" warfare.

In the second half of the poem, the focus shifts to the planes. Tiny as flying insects, they seem lovely and wonderful. But then a fight breaks out among the planes. After some "bitter smoke puffs and spiteful flames" the planes are gone. The soldiers realize that they do not know who the fighters were; the pilots are lost in distance and anonymity. They are as far away as the ancient Greek heroes of the battle of Marathon. Death caused by war is impersonal.

"The Silent One"

This poem also recreates a moment on the battlefield. The trenches on each side are bordered by barbed-wire fences. In order to charge forward, the soldier has to make or find a gap in the wire or else climb the wire and hope that the weight of his body will crush the fence.

At the opening of the poem, the speaker, a soldier, observes another soldier who was shot and killed while climbing a fence. His body is still hanging from the wires. The speaker thinks of the dead soldier as a "noble fool" for stepping over the wires and getting killed. He, the speaker, will lie low and wait for a line of soldiers to advance with. But as he lies there, an officer's voice comes to him through the darkness. In an upper-class, polite voice the officer asks him to crawl forward through a hole in the wires. The speaker as politely declines, saying there is no hole. He will not be another noble fool; he will preserve himself. He retreats under fire, then turns back and faces the wire again. The soldier is seen negotiating between the folly of hopeless advance and the shameful cowardice of retreat. He survives by following his own instincts rather than the foolish notions of the officer. He keeps his wits about him by praying and thinking of music. Unlike the silent one, he still has a voice and it says "no" to noble folly.

WILFRED OWEN (1893–1918)

Like Rupert Brooke, Owen did not survive the war. He was born and grew up in Shropshire and began to write poetry at an early age. He worked briefly as an assistant to a clergyman but became disillusioned with the established church. In 1913 he went to France as an English teacher. When the war broke out, he came back to England and enlisted in the army.

Owen fought in the trenches and suffered the inevitable consequences— disease, wounds, and eventually the mental breakdown called shell shock. He was sent to recuperate at an Edinburgh hospital, where he met Siegfried Sassoon. Sassoon encouraged Owen in his poetry writing and helped him find a tougher, more modern style. Owen returned to the front and was killed in battle just a week before the end of the war.

Most of Owen's poetry was written during the last year of his life; very little of it had been published at the time of his death.

"Apologia Pro Poemate Meo"

This Latin title translates as "apology for my poem," but the word *apology* here does not mean regret; it means instead a justification or defense of something that seems out of the ordinary. This is a poem about God, joy, love, and beauty—the usual themes of poems. But in this case, the themes are distorted because the setting is the "hell" of war. The speaker of the poem claims to have experienced all these fine feelings despite the horrible suffering of his comrades. They have all, as a group, passed into a state beyond fear. Now they feel only the absurdity of war. The total hopelessness of their situation seems to liberate them from any concern other than for the moment and for the fellowship of men doomed to die. This is a closed community, not comprehensible to outsiders. The "mirth" of such men can be experienced only by these sufferers of hell. The poet, expressing the horror of their state, also sees beauty in the way they meet it.

"Dulce et Decorum Est"

This Latin phrase is part of a well-known line from the poet Horace. The full line, quoted at the end of Owen's poem, states that it is good (sweet) and fitting to die for one's country. The quotation is ironic; the poem shows how ugly and pointless death during war can be.

Owen describes a small party of men, worn out and wounded, marching away from the battlefront for a period of rest. As they march, suddenly they become aware of a cloud of poison gas, the painful and often fatal mustard gas used by the Germans in that war. The weary men are jolted into quick action; they put on their gas masks. One soldier is not quick enough. He is overcome. The others watch from inside the dull glass panes of their masks but can do nothing to help the unlucky soldier who writhes and chokes as he drowns in the gas. His death is painful, ugly, and sickening to witness. It still haunts the dreams of the speaker.

At the end of the poem, the poet addresses his friend, one who teaches children, saying that the glory of patriotic death is an "old lie" that no one should teach anymore.

"Strange Meeting"

One of the standard situations of ancient heroic literature is the hero's descent into Hades, the underworld, where he encounters the spirit of some dead comrade who tells him strange truths.

In this poem, the situation is transposed to a modern war, and the underworld is a tunnel dug beneath the battlefield. The speaker is moving through the tunnel, where he sees the forms of sleeping or stupefied men. Suddenly, one of the men jumps up and confronts the speaker. This "other" has a dead smile; he is a speaking corpse. What the "other" says is that he was a poet who sought beauty and could have told truths. But he has died, leaving many truths untold. The world will go on in its old destructive way, ignorant of these truths.

Finally, the "other" identifies himself as one of the enemy, the victim of the speaker, who has stabbed him to death. The "other" suddenly breaks off, saying, "Let us sleep now." *Us* could refer to the dead, or it could include the first speaker, who will also die soon.

"Disabled"

This poem develops an image of a wounded World War I veteran who has lost the lower half of each leg and part of one arm. He sits helpless in a public park, listening to the voices of boys at play. He remembers the old days when he was whole. He used to like to dance and to feel the slim waists and warm hands of the girls he danced with. He also remembers himself as strong and handsome; only a year ago he was sought after by an artist as a model. He was a champion athlete who had been carried on the shoulders of his teammates, enjoying victory despite a bloody knee. In the enthusiasm of that victory, he decided to join the army. He did not think much about the danger but only anticipated the smartness of military dress and the fun he would have with comrades on leave. He was too young and thoughtless to care about the issues at stake in the war.

When he came home wounded, he was met by fewer cheers. Now he is ignored by pretty young women. He feels tired and impatient when he is taken in from the cold park to be put to bed. His suffering and loss of limbs is not glorious; it is a pointless waste.

The young men who wrote poetry about World War I initiated a change in the public's perception of war and of what it means to be a soldier. Rupert Brooke, who died early in the war, was still able to express the traditional notions that battle is a glorious test of manly courage and that even those who die in battle have lived fully because such a death makes them heroes. But other young poets who fought in the trenches on the western front developed quite different images. They depicted ugly deaths and pointless suffering. They identified the battlefield with hell, not with glory. They saw modern warfare as futile mass slaughter. Even the survivors came home damaged, both mentally and physically. They contributed to a widespread disillusionment in the postwar era that was to be expressed in images of waste and barrenness.

Selected Readings

Corrigan, Felicitas. *Siegfried Sassoon: Poet's Pilgrimage*. London: Gollancz, 1973.

Keynes, Geoffrey, ed. *The Poetical Works of Rupert Brooke*. London: Faber, 1946.

Lane, Arthur E. *An Adequate Response: The War Poetry of Wilfred Owen and Siegfried Sassoon*. Detroit: Wayne State University Press, 1972.

White, Gertrude M. *Wilfred Owen*. New York: Twayne, 1969.

17

William Butler Yeats

1880 Irish insurrection; the Irish National Land League begins policy of "boycotting" rents as protest of evictions; Parnell, M. P. for the Irish Nationalist party, imprisoned

1881 Land Law Act for Ireland legalizes the three "f's": fair rent, free sale, and fixity of tenure

1882 Arnold, *Irish Essays*; Manet, *Bar at the Folies Bergère*

1885 Yeats's early poems published in *Dublin University Review*

1886 Gladstone introduces Home Rule for Ireland Bill; defeated, the bill brings defeat to Liberal party

1889 Yeats, "The Wanderings of Oisin"

1890 Parnell resigns as Irish Nationalist leader

1891 Yeats, Dowson, and others form the Rhymers' Club; Irish Literary Society

1892 Yeats, *The Countess Cathleen*

1893 Yeats, *The Celtic Twilight*; Yeats publishes edition of Blake

1893–1932 Shaw's dramas and criticism written

1894 Yeats, *The Land of Heart's Desire*

1895 Yeats, *Poems*

1896 Yeats meets Lady Gregory, Irish writer, and stays for first time at Coole Park, Galway; Austin named poet laureate

1897 Yeats, "The Secret Rose"

1899   Yeats, *The Wind Among the Reeds*; Irish Literary Theatre founded in Dublin; Boer War

1901–1910   Reign of Edward VII

1902   Yeats, *Cathleen ni Houlihan*

1903   Yeats, *In the Seven Woods*

1904   Yeats, *The King's Threshold* and *Stories of Red Hanrahan*; opening of Abbey Theatre, Dublin

1905   Sinn Fein ("Ourselves") formed by Arthur Griffith to unite competing Irish nationalist bodies

1906   Yeats, *Poetical Works*, vols. I and II

1907   Synge, *The Playboy of the Western World*; Yeats, *Deirdre*

1910   Yeats, *The Green Helmet and Other Poems*

1910–1936   Reign of George V

1912   Liberal party proposes limited form of self-government for Ireland

1913   Ulster Volunteer Force, a paramilitary group, formed by Protestants of Ulster who oppose home rule; arms smuggled to U.V.F. from Germany

1914   Yeats, *Responsibilities*; Conservatives and the Unionist opposition to Irish home rule bring United Kingdom to verge of civil war; World War I begins; Joyce, *Dubliners*

1916   Easter Rebellion, armed nationalist insurrection in Dublin

1917   Yeats, "The Wild Swans at Coole"; Yeats marries, moves to "Thoor Ballylee," the Norman tower on Lady Gregory's land

1918   Germany agrees to armistice, World War I ends

1919–1921   Anglo-Irish war; Irish Republican Army (I.R.A.), British government forces, and Royal Irish Constabulary ("Black and Tans") exchange sporadic attacks, which escalate into guerrilla warfare

1920   Yeats, *Michael Robartes and the Dancer*; The Government of Ireland Act

1921   Anglo-Irish Treaty results in Irish Free State becoming a self-governing dominion within British Empire; six northeastern counties opt out

1922   Yeats, *Later Poems*

1922–1923   Irish civil war sees open hostilities between new Irish government and anti-treaty I.R.A. forces ("Irregulars"); assassinations and reprisals result in deep and long-lasting divisions in Irish society

1922–1928   Yeats serves as senator of the Irish Free State

1923   Yeats wins the Nobel Prize in literature

1925   Yeats, *A Vision*

William Butler Yeats wrote many literary works over several decades—from the late 1880s to the 1930s. Many critics believe that he is the most important twentieth-century poet who wrote in English.

His powerful style developed through several stages, from the dreamy fantasies of his early Pre-Raphaelite beginnings through an increasingly elaborate and occult symbolism in his mature poetry. Yeats produced eighteen volumes of poetry in addition to many prose works—essays, stories, autobiographical sketches, and poetic dramas.

WILLIAM BUTLER YEATS (1865–1939)

Yeats was born in Dublin of a formerly affluent and powerful Anglo-Irish family. His father was a painter. The family moved to London for several years during Yeats's childhood and adolescence, and Yeats had also spent part of his childhood with his mother's family at Sligo, a largely undeveloped area of northwest Ireland.

These three areas—Dublin, London, and Sligo—are each associated with distinct sources and influences in Yeats's poetry. In Dublin, Yeats was reluctantly involved in the politics of the Irish movement for independence from England. In London he had been associated with the younger poets of the Pre-Raphaelite movement and with the world of publishing. In Sligo, Yeats had found a rich tradition of Celtic folklore that stretched back to the great heroic era of Ireland's past. These influences, along with Yeats's reading and his lifelong study of mysticism, provided him with a rich and complex body of symbols and images.

Yeats's Career

Scholars divide Yeats's career into four main periods, but the reader must keep in mind that Yeats himself did not acknowledge this division. He tended to revise early poems for later republication, changing them according to his later tastes and insights.

THE EARLY PHASE: 1889–1899

During his twenties and early thirties, Yeats lived and wrote in London as a member of a movement that developed from the Pre-Raphaelite Brotherhood and their literary purpose to create beauty in art for its own sake. Yeats was a founding member of the Rhymers' Club, a loosely organized but congenial group of young poets who were disciples of Walter Pater. During this time Yeats was also studying the history and mythology of Ireland, which he wove into his early poems.

THE SECOND PHASE: 1899–1909

Yeats was recruited by the Lady Gregory to help establish the Irish National Theatre. He both managed and wrote for the theater, which produced original plays based on Irish characters and Irish history.

The theater group, which later became established in the Abbey Theatre in Dublin, was a part of a cultural revival that accompanied the increasing pressure for national independence. During this decade, Yeats wrote fewer poems but he produced a number of poetic dramas for the theater. Among the actors in his dramas was the beautiful and politically active Maud Gonne, with whom Yeats fell in love but who refused to marry him. Her image appears in many poems of this and later phases.

THE MIDDLE PHASE: 1910–1918

During his late forties and early fifties, Yeats's poetry began to change. He had left his managerial position with the Abbey Theatre and refocused his attention on poetic technique.

Yeats was influenced by the contemporary poets Ezra Pound and T. S. Eliot to write a less romantic, less sensuous poetry. Eliot and Pound advocated a tougher and more intellectual approach, as exemplified by the seventeenth-century metaphysical poet John Donne. Yeats's style grew more colloquial, reproducing the patterns of ordinary speech.

In 1917 Yeats married Georgie Hyde-Lees, a woman sympathetic to his poetic ambitions. She immediately began to help him by means of automatic writing. Sitting with pen in hand, she wrote whatever came to her mind without any conscious effort to shape the words into a composition. From these writings as well as other sources in occult literature, Yeats began to formulate a great historical, mythical, and psychological system that was to provide the set of symbols that dominate his mature poetry.

THE MATURE PHASE: 1919–1939

During these years Yeats found a set of interlocking symbols—the spiral, the tower, the cycles of the moon—that he integrated into a quasi-historical framework for his poetic ideas. This period, most critics agree, produced his finest poetry. He received the Nobel Prize for literature in 1923.

In 1925 Yeats published a prose treatise called *A Vision*, which provides a key to his symbolic system. In it he presents the history of civilization as two interlocking conical spirals or gyres that point in opposite directions. The point of each spiral represents some historical moment, such as the birth of Christ, when a new source of energy focuses historical forces and sets them going in a new direction. These forces expand but lose intensity for the next twenty centuries. To Yeats, then, the current century was approaching the end of an historical era, and he anticipated tremendous change.

Personally, after having served as a senator in the Irish Parliament from 1922 to 1928, Yeats retreated from public life and lived in a refurbished tower on Lady Gregory's estate. He could not reconcile himself to the physical decline of old age and in 1934 submitted to an experimental operation aimed at restoring his sexual potency. His late poems are full of protest against becoming "an aged man."

"The Madness of King Goll"

This poem is a dramatic monologue in which King Goll, the legendary king of the Celts, describes his descent into madness.

In the opening stanza King Goll pictures himself in kingly power, ruling over a prosperous and peaceful land. But the refrain in the last two lines of the stanza suggests that even then the king was troubled by a restlessness of spirit that is echoed by the fluttering leaves of the beech trees.

In the second stanza, trouble begins. A herdsman comes to ask the king for help; he needs protection from pirates who make inland raids to steal pigs, taking them on board their ships as provisions. The king rallies his men and swoops down on the pirates as they lie on shore. The king and his warriors slay the pirates and capture their gold. But in the midst of battle the king feels a strange disturbance. He laughs to himself and leaves the field of victory, rushing off alone into the wild countryside.

The king becomes a creature of the wood. He is at home among the wolves, deer, and hares as he wanders about seeking peace of mind. But he is always pursued by the disturbing flutter of the beech leaves.

In stanza 5, the king, passing through a remote village at night, finds a tympan, an ancient Celtic lute played by plucking the strings or, as the king calls them, wires. Taking the tympan into the woods, the king consoles his restless spirit by singing to its accompaniment. But now he laments that he has ruined the instrument by his playing, and he still wanders distracted among the woods and hills.

The refrain of the fluttering beech leaves echoes throughout the poem, showing how at every stage of Goll's kingship and mad wandering the same madness haunts him. This poem is a very early example of Yeats's imaginative retelling of tales from Celtic folklore.

"The Rose of the World"

The rose is a traditional symbol of beauty. In Platonic idealism, beauty is an absolute perfection, unchanging and never to be realized completely on earth. In this poem Yeats deals with the effects of beauty.

In the first stanza he shows the drastic results of men's love for beautiful women. Troy was destroyed as a result of Paris's love for the beautiful Helen, and in Celtic folklore the three sons of Usna died because one of them had abducted the beautiful Deirdre.

Then Yeats explains that human beings are subject to change and they pass away; beauty itself is constant. According to the last stanza, beauty existed before people, even before angels. God first created the world as a place for beauty to exist. Thus this poem combines ideas of beauty from ancient Greek, Platonic, ancient Celtic, and Christian sources. The one constant in all these realms is the search for beauty, a primary motive.

"The Lake Isle of Innisfree"

In this early poem, one of his best known, Yeats combines the lovely sensuous appeal of aestheticism with a quiet and well-controlled tone.

It is a poem of retreat. The poet recalls the island in Lake Innisfree. He longs to go there, to experience again the quiet beauty and peaceful simplicity of the place. The only sounds are natural ones: the hum of bees, the chirp of crickets, the lapping of waves. He will build a small cabin there and plant a garden and enjoy the peace and quiet as he watches the changing lights of day and evening. The poet longs for the peace of Innisfree so strongly that he hears the sound of waves lapping the shore even while he is standing far away on a busy city street.

The recollection draws him back to the island; each stanza begins with his intention to go back.

"The Folly of Being Comforted"

This poem reflects Yeats's unfulfilled love for Maud Gonne, a beautiful woman and a passionate nationalist deeply involved with the resistance to British rule. Yeats associates her with images of female beauty during most of his poetic career.

"The Folly of Being Comforted" is an irregular sonnet, being written in couplets rather than a conventional sonnet rhyme pattern. But it is like earlier sonnets in its expression of love-longing. It creates a dialogue between the poet's friend, "one that is ever kind," and his protesting heart, which cannot accept the friend's comforting words. This friend intends to lessen the poet/lover's intense love by remarking that his beloved is beginning to show signs of age, that she is becoming less beautiful with the passage of time.

But the lover absolutely rejects any such notion. To him the beauty of his beloved is not based on physical beauty but on the nobility of her soul, the "fire that burns about her." Actually, he finds her more beautiful now than in earlier days, when she was, perhaps, prettier but less noble. He knows that if she were to turn toward him, he would be fully captivated by her beauty. He thus feels as strongly as ever the pain of her rejection.

"Adam's Curse"

When Adam and Eve disobeyed God and were cast out of the Garden of Eden, Adam and his descendants were cursed with the need to work to make a living.

In this poem Yeats presents a conversation about the need to work between the poet and the woman he loves as they sit quietly with a friend on a summer evening.

The poet is the first to speak. He talks about how difficult it is to write poetry. It is easier to scrub floors or break stone, yet most people consider the poet to be a lazy "idler."

The woman he loves responds, saying in her sweet low voice that the essential labor of women is to be beautiful. The poet answers that everything "fine" or worthwhile requires much labor. In the old days, even lovers worked at being lovers by studying in learned books the correct and courteous ways of behaving toward their beloved. Now, their efforts seem to have been wasted. Once love has been brought into the conversation, no one speaks. Sitting quietly together, they see the moon rise; it is a mere shell of a moon, almost at the new phase when it will be totally dark. It suggests the passage of time, and the poet thinks it looks worn and hollow. But he says nothing; he only thinks about how he labored to be a proper lover and how all his efforts failed. Despite their initial happiness, he and his beloved have become "weary-hearted" from the effort of loving.

"No Second Troy"

This poem speaks more explicitly of Maud Gonne. Ancient Troy was thrown into war by the abduction of the beautiful Helen. Yeats sees the beautiful Maud Gonne, like Helen, as an instigator of revolt, this time among "ignorant men," those Irish nationalists who wish to rebel against British rule but do not have enough courage. Yeats sees that Gonne must become a revolutionary because of her intense and noble nature. She is too heroic for the age she lives in. But lacking great heroes of Trojan proportions, she must try to inspire heroism in the lesser men of her own time and place.

This poem was written in 1908, six and one-half years before any actual rebellion took place. Yeats did not expect the Irish to achieve any great victories or to be able to throw off British rule in the foreseeable future. A later poem, "Easter 1916," shows how he changed his opinion of the Irish patriots.

"The Fascination of What's Difficult"

This is an irregular sonnet, having only thirteen lines. It reflects Yeats's frustration with the practical details of management when he was the director of the Irish National Theatre. He complains that the job has taken away his creative energy, his "spontaneous joy." Tying a poet to the day-to-day problems of managing a theater, he says, is like harnessing Pegasus, the mythical winged horse, to a heavy cart to perform dull labor. Continuing the analogy with Pegasus, in the last two lines he swears to escape from the "stable" of dull work.

"The Wild Swans at Coole"

Yeats's friend and associate in the founding of the Irish National Theatre was Lady Augusta Gregory, a cultivated aristocrat of great benevolence. Her country estate was called Coole Park. Yeats visited Coole Park often and eventually, after his marriage, retired there to live in an old tower, which he renovated. At the time of this poem Yeats had been visiting Coole Park and watching the swans there for nineteen years.

The lovely autumn scene described in the opening stanza includes an impressive flock of fifty-nine swans that live on a stream in Coole Park. In stanza 2 the swans suddenly take off and scatter across the sky. Watching them, Yeats ponders how much he and his situation have changed in the nineteen years since he first saw these swans. The swans, by contrast, seem completely unchanged. They are still faithful to each other and seem to have overcome the effects of time.

The poet wonders where these beautiful creatures will go when he finally loses sight of them. He implies that when he can no longer see them, it will be because he has changed, not they. Their beauty and mysterious nature cannot be wholly comprehended by his limited sight.

"Easter 1916"

In this poem Yeats expresses his reaction to the Easter uprising by the Irish nationalists. During this unsuccessful uprising the people Yeats had previously discounted as weak and foolish became transformed in his eyes into heroes. A "terrible beauty" was born from their self-sacrifice and daring. Now Ireland has genuine martyrs, and Yeats is awestruck by their deeds.

In the first stanza, he describes his superficial acquaintance with some of those who later rebelled and how, thinking them insubstantial and "motley," he sometimes made jokes at their expense.

In the second stanza, Yeats recalls specific members of the rebellion, women and men with varying strengths and weaknesses who gave up their own interests and future prospects for the cause of independence. Their joint actions have become like a stone, a permanent marker in the ongoing stream of life. Others will come and go, but the deeds of these martyrs will remain "to trouble the living stream." That is, the stream of life will be different because of their enduring heroism.

In the final stanza, after raising the question of how England will respond to the Irish nationalist movement, the poet then plays his role as recorder of the deeds of heroes. He repeats the names of those who were executed for treason because of their patriotic fervor and who therefore have become "beautiful in martyrdom."

"The Second Coming"

Christians who believe that Christ will return to redeem mankind speak of this anticipated event as the Second Coming. As a believer in the cyclical nature of history, Yeats held that every twenty centuries some cataclysmic event changes the direction of civilization. The birth of Christ was such an event. Now, nineteen centuries after the birth of Christ, the world is falling into chaos. Some dire event, radically unlike Christ's birth, must be about to happen. The gyre or spiral of history has spread out so far that a new center point must come to reorganize history.

This poem presents an image of that new force as a "rough beast," merciless and un-Christlike.

The first part of the poem describes the chaotic state of the world, comparing it with a falcon that has flown too far from its keeper, the falconer. The world is full of anarchy and war. People of good will "lack all conviction" while "the worst are full of passionate intensity."

In the second part, the speaker interprets these conditions as a sign of the Second Coming, of some new revelation. He glimpses an image of a creature who has a human head or intellect on a lion's body. The face is "pitiless"; this is not Christ but His antithesis. The vision fades, but the speaker realizes that it means that we have reached the next turning point.

The poem ends in a question—who or what is it that is coming? The question suggests terror rather than comfort or hope.

"Sailing to Byzantium"

Byzantium is the ancient name for the city of Istanbul, which stands at the crossroads between Europe and Asia. Yeats was fascinated by what he read of this city. To him it represented an ideal place where life was transformed by art and the whole culture was unified and purified by the creation of a beautiful, enduring city. It came to symbolize for Yeats a state beyond life, an escape from the effects of time and the cycles of history, where the individual soul escapes nature and joins in the "artifice" of timeless being.

The first stanza describes the state of nature, including humankind. We are all caught up in the cycle of birth, growth, reproduction, and death. This is a sensual rather than an intellectual existence, and it is controlled by time.

In the second stanza, Yeats pictures himself as an old man, "a tattered coat upon a stick" but striving to reach some state of detachment from the ravages of time. To achieve that state, he has come to Byzantium, his "holy city."

In stanza 3 the speaker sees figures of wise men in the mosaics on the walls of Byzantium. He calls upon them to show him how to escape from the body, the "dying animal," and escape into eternity, leaving the cycles of birth and death.

In stanza 4 he chooses an artificial shape to replace his body. He will become a bird, a singer of songs, made of gold and jewels. But of course his shape is modeled on that of a living creature, and the song he will sing is about time, about "what is past, or passing, or to come." So the escape from nature into eternity is a transposition from one state to a higher state that nevertheless repeats the forms of nature.

"Among School Children"

As a member of the government of the new Irish Free State, Yeats paid occasional visits to public schools.

In this poem he presents a flight of imagination that came about during one of these visits. He first pictures himself in the schoolroom, questioning the old nun who is in charge as the little children gaze at him. He sees himself in their eyes as merely a kindly old man. But suddenly he remembers a story his old love, Maud Gonne, told him one night as they sat by a dying fire. She related some unhappy event that happened at school during her childhood. He had felt an impulse of sympathy, almost a union, as if Plato's idea of the original oneness of man and woman were actually true.

In stanza 3 he returns to the present. He looks at the little girls in the classroom, wondering how she, his beloved, must have looked as a child. Though beautiful now, she might have been very plain, like the ugly duckling that became a beautiful swan in the children's story. Suddenly, he feels overwhelmed by the image of her that he has conjured up.

In the fourth stanza, he sees her as she is now, a woman of surpassing beauty, such as those painted by the artists of the Italian Renaissance. He recalls that he, too, though never extremely handsome, was once better-looking than he is now. Now, he realizes, he is just an old man, a "comfortable kind of old scarecrow" in the eyes of the children. Once more he has shaken off images of the past to return to present reality in the schoolroom.

The second half of the poem, stanzas 5 through 8, are a meditation on images and the changes time causes. The poet wonders if a mother of an infant would feel that her labor of giving birth was worthwhile if she could see her baby as he would be at sixty.

In the sixth stanza, Yeats recapitulates ideas about images and reality as described in the philosophies of Plato, Aristotle, and Pythagoras. Yeats dismisses their ideas as mere notions, "old clothes upon old sticks." The scarecrow image is applied to abstruse philosophical concepts that provide no satisfactory explanations.

Then Yeats turns to women again, to mothers and to nuns. While the mothers "worship" their images of their infants as grown sons, the nuns worship the unchanging image of Christ as depicted in marble and bronze statues. These statues, though made by men, mock the changing lives of men who will die, leaving behind the monuments of their labor as objects of worship.

The final stanza considers labor as a "blossoming or dancing"—that is, creative but transitory. The image of the chestnut tree is the essence of nature, constantly changing from leaf to blossom to seed. Human beings are like dancers and their lives like dances. The final question probes the ambiguity of life. How can we perceive life without living it? The poem begins and ends with questioning, as if that were the only constant.

"Byzantium"

This poem is a further elaboration on the ideas presented in "Sailing to Byzantium." To Yeats, this holy city is a place of purification and escape from nature and from change. Byzantium is presented in a series of images, each one suggestive but none explicit. Many of the images are echoes of phrases and images in other poems by Yeats, and the cumulative effect is of a cleansing of the soul from the "mire or blood" of worldly existence. This ritual purification is like the unwinding of a mummy from its bands of cloth, the creation of a miraculous golden bird, and dancing in a purifying fire. Finally, the souls ride on dolphins into the sea, the symbol of eternity.

"The Circus Animals' Desertion"

In this late poem, Yeats looks back over his long poetic career and revisits the major themes and images of his work. These have been his "circus animals"; he has made them perform in his poetry and plays. He begins as an old man looking for a poetic idea, but none will come. He then recalls his early poems about Irish legendary heroes, "stilted boys" in their artificiality and immaturity. Listing his "old themes," the poet comes next to the wandering poet/hero Oisin, driven by the love of Maud Gonne. He remembers the play he wrote celebrating the selfless but fanatic efforts of Maud Gonne, the "counter-truth" about her. Yeats recalls other plays he wrote and his involvement in managing the theater, the "players and painted stage."

In the last stanza, the poet says that he made those grand images of his early poetry and plays out of the ordinary stuff of common life, the "old iron, old bones, old rags" and such refuse of his experience. But now, the ladder, that is, the inspiration by which he transformed this old junk into poetry, has been taken away. He can't do the tricks or create the illusions anymore. Therefore, he must "lie down where all ladders start." The place from which all this creative energy and transforming power arose was himself, "the foul rag-and-bone shop of the heart." At the end of his career, he no longer presents his performing animals of legend and dreams; he deals more plainly with the realities of himself.

The poetry of Yeats is based on a complex set of symbols representing actual persons, legendary and historical events, and mystical experiences. Some critics claim that only one who has studied and mastered Yeats's symbolic systems can appreciate his poetry. However, many of his best poems require minimal background. The crucial images of the wild swans, the golden bird, and the scarecrow can impress any reader with their essential import. The more one reads Yeats, the more each poem is enriched.

In an era when the traditional body of images from classical culture and the Western tradition seemed to have become exhausted, Yeats invented new images and recombined old ones to create a fascinating and complex body of work. Yeats responded to historical events and to changes in literary fashion, but he was always essentially driven by his own visions and desires.

Selected Readings

Ellmann, Richard. *Yeats: The Man and the Masks*. London: Macmillan, 1949.

Liammboir, Michebal Mac, and Eavan Boland. *W. B. Yeats and His World*. New York: Viking, 1972.

Unterecker, John. *A Reader's Guide to William Butler Yeats*. New York: Noonday, 1959.

18

The New Novel—
James Joyce and
D. H. Lawrence

1900 Freud, *Interpretation of Dreams*

1901–1910 Reign of Edward VII

1904 Opening of the Abbey Theatre, Dublin

1905 Joyce leaves Dublin; Wilde, *De Profundis*

1906 Yeats, *Poetical Works*, vols. I and II

1907 Joyce, *Chamber Music*

1909 Lawrence's early poems and short stories reviewed in Ford Madox Ford's
English Review

1910 Lawrence, *The White Peacock*

1910–1936 Reign of George V

1912 Joyce, *Gas from a Burner*

1912–1913 Freud and Jung disagree, largely over the extent of sexuality's contribution
to the life force

1913 Lawrence, *Sons and Lovers* and *Love Poems and Others*

1914 Joyce, *Dubliners*; Lawrence and Frieda Von Richthofen return to England
and marry; World War I begins

1915 Lawrence, *The Rainbow*

1916 Joyce, *A Portrait of the Artist as a Young Man*

1918 Joyce, *Exiles*

1919 Lawrence expelled from Cornwall as suspected German spy, begins his restless travels

1921 Lawrence, *Women in Love* and *Sea and Sardinia*; Jung, *The Psychology of the Unconscious*

1922 Joyce, *Ulysses*; Lawrence, *Aaron's Rod*; Fitzgerald, *The Great Gatsby*

1923 Lawrence, *Kangaroo*

1924–1927 Lawrence and Frieda with Mabel Dodge in Taos, New Mexico

1926 Lawrence, *The Plumed Serpent*

1927 Joyce, *Pomes Pennyeach*; Lawrence, *Mornings in Mexico*

1928 Lawrence, *Lady Chatterley's Lover* and collection of short stories, *The Woman Who Rode Away*; Huxley, *Point Counter Point*; Brecht, *Three-Penny Opera*

1929 In the United States, the stock market crashes and the Great Depression begins

1930 Lawrence dies

1931 Lawrence, *Apocalypse* published posthumously

1932 Lawrence, *Last Poems* published posthumously; Mabel Dodge writes of the Lawrences' stay in New Mexico in *Lorenzo in Taos*

1933 Lawrence, *The Lovely Lady and Other Stories* published posthumously

1934 Ban on *Ulysses* lifted in Great Britain

1936 Joyce, *Collected Poems*; Spanish Civil War begins; Dos Passos, *U.S.A. Trilogy*

1936–1952 George VI reigns

1939 Joyce, *Finnegans Wake*; Yeats dies; World War II begins; Steinbeck, *The Grapes of Wrath*

1941 Joyce dies; United States enters war against Germany, Italy, and Japan

1959 Censorship on the publication of *Lady Chatterley's Lover* lifted in the United States

During the Victorian Age the novel had been the most popular and influential literary form, recreating the realities of economic power and social class and the stresses of social mobility, industrialization, and the disappearance of the agricultural base of English life.

In the twentieth century, novelists turned their attention to new realities of the individual's conscious and subconscious mind. The wise, companionable, omniscient narrator of Victorian fiction was replaced by a narrator who was uncertain and fallible, like Conrad's Marlow, who is not sure he fully understands the story he tells.

The American novelist Henry James, who lived and wrote in England, contrasted the American and European ways of seeing the world—two types of consciousness he saw as completely incompatible. It was James who first used the term "stream of consciousness" to describe the enactment of a character's mental experiences as a technique of fiction.

In the second decade of the twentieth century, the ideas of the great psychologist Sigmund Freud began to influence novelists. For the first time novelists suggested to their readers that dreams, fantasies, and obsessions were significant aspects of their characters. The new realism lay not in plot and incident but in complexities of individual psychology. The narration is not bound by a strictly chronological sequence; the dimension of time is manipulated as a part of the consciousness of character.

The novelists James Joyce and D. H. Lawrence advanced the modernist conception of fiction, experimenting in different ways with the fictional recreation of psychological existence. Each one ignored the Victorian limitations of subject matter that had forbidden any frank discussion of sexuality. Joyce and Lawrence both saw sexual desires and fantasies as integral parts of consciousness, which no authentic representation of mental life could omit. They both experimented with form as they explored the intellectual and psychological development of their young male protagonists.

JAMES JOYCE (1882–1941)

Joyce was born and raised in Dublin, Ireland. This single biographical fact is central to all his fiction. The world of Dublin is his only subject, and Dublin becomes the whole world, representing all experience.

Joyce's father, a failed businessman and skillful storyteller, sent James to Jesuit schools in preparation for the priesthood. James, however, gradually fell away from the Roman Catholic church and its teachings, although the culture and symbolism of Catholicism remained as a thread in his writings. Joyce went to the University College of Dublin to study languages. This aspect of his education gave him the vast multilinguistic knowledge of Western literature that his fiction displays.

Meanwhile, Joyce began to feel repelled by the narrow life of the middle-class Dubliner. Like Yeats, he found such an existence too commercial in its values and shot through with sentimental hypocrisy. These Dubliners became the characters Joyce explored and exposed in *Dubliners*, a collection of short stories published in 1914. Subsequently Joyce became alienated from his country and sought exile as a necessary precondition for creativity.

In 1904 Joyce left Ireland to teach English in Trieste. He only once briefly returned. He was accompanied by Nora Barnacle, with whom he lived for the rest of his life. They had two children but did not marry until 1930. In 1915 Joyce took another teaching post in Zurich. After World War I, he and his family moved to Paris, where he lived until his death.

Joyce was encouraged in his writing by Ezra Pound and William Butler Yeats, among other writers, and by patrons who gave him financial assistance. Despite this help, he was chronically short of money. He suffered from glaucoma, which diminished his eyesight, and he was depressed by the mental illness of his daughter. Furthermore, authorities in London and Dublin prevented the publication of Joyce's fiction on the ground of indecency. While the artistic and intellectual world championed Joyce as a great innovator, each of his major works was delayed or denied publication.

Joyce's great novel *Ulysses* was published first in Paris in 1922, having failed to find a publisher in an English-speaking country. In 1933 the U.S. Post Office, deciding that the book was obscene, refused to allow copies of *Ulysses* into the country. After a court challenge the ban was lifted. This challenge became a landmark trial in issues involving freedom of the press. A few years later, the ban was also lifted in England.

Joyce experimented more radically with fictional form in his final work, *Finnegans Wake*, a dream sequence with complex multiple levels of symbolism.

Ulysses and *Finnegans Wake* broke entirely with traditional forms of the realistic novel. Joyce introduced and extended the "stream of consciousness" technique, in which a character presents an unbroken stream of thoughts, feelings, memories, and reactions to the current moment, with no description or explanation by a separate narrator.

"The Dead"

This is the final story in *Dubliners*, Joyce's series of character studies of some of the middle-class citizens of his home city. Each story is an independent whole, but the collection shows complementary facets of the lives of Dubliners, their false piety and shallow respectability.

In this story the members of a social group gather for a Christmas party. The traditionally jolly time is beclouded, however, by anxiety and eventually by remorse. At the beginning, Joyce re-creates the bustle and excitement as the hostesses, two elderly sisters, and their niece, all music teachers, greet their arriving guests. The older ladies await their nephew Gabriel, who will act as master of ceremonies at the supper. Finally he arrives with his wife,

Gretta, as does Freddy Malin, a troublesome guest likely to get drunk ("screwed").

Joyce describes the party, the small talk and flirtatious banter, the dancing and singing, and the conversational maneuvering among the guests.

The climax of the evening is the lavishly served feast. Gabriel, having carved and served the Christmas goose, makes a complimentary speech about his hostesses as examples of old-fashioned Irish hospitality. Calling them the Three Graces, he proposes a toast in their honor. Gabriel's attitude toward his own performance is ambivalent. While he thinks of these ladies and their guests as rather common, perhaps even vulgar, and not likely to understand a fine quotation from Browning that he had thought of using in his speech, he is still eager to speak well and to make a good impression on them. He is relieved when the party begins to break up; his more relaxed frame of mind is evidenced by a humorous story he tells about his grandfather.

While other guests are leaving, Gabriel looks up the staircase to see his wife standing and listening to a lingering guest who is singing an old Irish song. Her mood seems strange. Gabriel feels sudden joy and desire as he watches her. These feelings intensify as Gabriel, Gretta, and two other guests walk back to a hotel where they will spend the night. Alone in their dark room, both Gabriel and Gretta are in unaccustomed moods. But while Gabriel wants to act on his intense desire for his wife, she seems absent.

In response to his questions, she reveals that the song she heard at the party reminded her of a boy she knew years ago in her home village. Gabriel's jealousy is aroused, but she tells him that the boy is dead. Actually, he died for love of her when she left the village to come to school in Dublin.

As she weeps for the dead boy who loved her, Gabriel feels envy for that great romance in her life. Let down, his desire faded, he watches from his bed as the snow falls against the windowpane. As the narrator points out, the snow is falling all over Ireland and on the grave of his wife's dead lover. A sense of his own mortality mingles with a sense of loss of his own identity.

A Portrait of the Artist as a Young Man

The most directly autobiographical of Joyce's works, *A Portrait of the Artist as a Young Man* was first published in 1916.

STEPHEN DEDALUS

The central character of "Portrait" is Stephen Dedalus, whose second name recalls the mythical Greek Daedalus, the inventor of the labyrinth and a craftsman who made wings out of feathers and wax for himself and his son Icarus. The name therefore suggests one who invents intricate structures and one who soars. Stephen was the name of the first Christian martyr. Joyce uses this name also for the young man in *Ulysses*.

Portrait follows the development of Stephen, a young man of intellectual and literary ambitions. It begins with the child Stephen listening to a story his father tells in baby talk, then shows the growth of Stephen's mind from his early school days, when he was bullied, and into his years at the university. Gradually, as Stephen's sense of himself develops, he feels increasingly alienated from his family, the church, and middle-class Dublin society. He is repelled by the vulgar and petty quarrels between the Irish nationalists and the narrow views of the Roman Catholic church in Ireland.

Eventually, during a lonely walk on the seashore, Stephen realizes that his vocation is to be a writer. In order to do so, he must leave Ireland so that he can write more objectively. He states that his goal is "to forge in the smithy of my own soul the uncreated conscience of my race."

JOYCE'S STYLE

The most outstanding formal innovation of this novel was Joyce's use of Stephen's actual language. The opening episodes are told in the childish words and limited concepts of a schoolboy, while later episodes are articulated in the sophisticated and abstract vocabulary of a scholarly young man. During the course of the book Stephen develops a theory of literary form that moves from the simple, direct expression of emotion in lyric forms, to the less personal forms of narrative, to the drama, which is the most objective and in which the author's own speaking voice is completely removed, allowing the characters to speak for themselves.

Ulysses

Joyce considered Ulysses, the hero of Homer's great epic *The Odyssey*, to be the most complete and perfect hero. Thus Joyce loosely patterned his own great novel on the episodes of the Homeric epic.

Ulysses depicts events in Dublin on one particular day, June 16, 1904, which has since become celebrated as "Bloomsday" in Dublin. The events are depicted as they are perceived by three main characters—Leopold Bloom, an Irish Jew who corresponds to Ulysses; Stephen Dedalus, who corresponds to Ulysses's son Telemachus; and Molly Bloom, the wife of Leopold, who corresponds to Ulysses's wife, Penelope.

For the most part the reader follows Bloom as he moves about Dublin, from the street to a restaurant to a newspaper office to a funeral. Details that enter Bloom's awareness are presented in his frame of reference and serve to trigger mental associations or memories. Bloom is an ordinary man but curious and humane. As an Irish Jew he is both citizen and alien. In his wanderings around Dublin he meets many people whom he knows, but their Catholicism makes them strangers even as they are familiar. Finding in Stephen a substitute for the son whom he has lost, he tries to protect Stephen from the effects of too much drinking.

At the end of the day, he brings Stephen home for a communal cup of chocolate, but no lasting tie is formed between the older and younger men. Stephen has been moving about the city also, several times nearly meeting Bloom. He has been getting drunk with some medical students and reaches a state where the images of his subconscious mind move toward the surface.

The novel ends with Molly Bloom's famous soliloquy. She is home in bed dreaming of her past life—her early courtship with Bloom, the loss of their son, and her recent infidelities with the singer Blaze Boylan. Molly provides a climactic view of sexuality and generative power.

STRUCTURE OF ULYSSES

Ulysses has no plot in the usual sense. Rather, it moves through a series of episodes, each more revealing of a pattern representing the cycles of life and death. The passage from morning through the day and into night suggests the complete and constantly recurring pattern of human existence. The novel is comprehensive and encyclopedic at the same time that it focuses on the ordinary events of a single day.

D. H. LAWRENCE (1885–1930)

Son of a coal miner and a genteel, socially ambitious mother, Lawrence grew up in the mining country of Nottinghamshire. Encouraged by his mother to rise out of the working class, he attended Nottingham University and became a teacher. Lawrence was also self-educated in literature and philosophy.

His first important novel was *Sons and Lovers*, published in 1913. This autobiographical novel reflects Lawrence's own close relationship with his mother and his alienation from his father. It also describes the encouragement of his friend Jessie Chambers, who appears as Miriam in the novel.

In 1912 Lawrence ran off to Germany with Frieda Von Richthofen, the wife of a professor at Nottingham. Following her divorce, the two were married after their return to England in 1914, at the start of World War I. Frieda's German nationality made life in England uncomfortable. At the same time, Lawrence found his next novel, *The Rainbow* (1915), banned for indecency because of its frank depiction of sexual relations. Disgusted with British society, Lawrence and Frieda left at the end of the war. They lived in Italy, Mexico, the United States, and Australia, eventually returning to Europe and settling in the south of France. The couple's unsettled life was complicated by Lawrence's ill health, quarrels, and a chronic lack of money.

After *The Rainbow*, Lawrence's next novel was a sequel, *Women in Love* (1921). These two novels are considered his greatest; in them he developed his new style. Breaking away from the conventional realism of *Sons and Lovers*, Lawrence created an intense and heavily symbolic prose, which he used in the rest of his fiction. He became notorious for the explicit sexual descriptions in *Lady Chatterley's Lover*, written in 1928 but banned from publication until 1959.

Lawrence produced not only novels but also dramas, poetry, travel books, and essays of literary criticism, as well as several collections of short stories.

One constant theme in his writings is the belief that the modern individual, living in a mechanical and artificial social world, has lost the essence and vitality of his or her genuine self. Images of nature, and especially the symbolic presentation of animals, contrast with the stifling constraints of family relationships and emotional demands.

In 1930 Lawrence died of tuberculosis in the south of France, where he had gone hoping that the warm, dry climate would improve his health. At the time of his death, his works were still controversial. Only later was he seen as a teacher and moralist and not merely as a rebel.

"Odor of Chrysanthemums"

Set in a coal-mining town in the midlands, this rather long short story reflects Lawrence's family situation as a youth. It focuses on the miner's wife, who, alienated from her husband, has redirected her feelings toward her children.

Elizabeth Bates is the wife of a coal miner and the mother of two young children. She is expecting a third child. Elizabeth strives to keep a clean and orderly home and to protect her children, but the environment they live in makes this difficult. Their small, dark house is near the mine; it is damp and low and the yard is full of rats. In addition, Elizabeth's husband, Walter, tends to drink. Several evenings a week, instead of coming home to supper, he passes by his own front door to go to a pub to drink, spending money they cannot afford to waste. Elizabeth's marriage has been a bitter disappointment to her. In contrast, her father, an engineer on the mine trains, has recently remarried, hoping to regain the pleasures of domestic company after the death of his first wife.

The story opens just before dusk on an autumn evening. Elizabeth calls her son in and prepares tea, the most substantial meal for the mining family, consisting of toast and pudding and boiled potatoes. The daughter returns from school. The impatient children persuade their mother to serve tea, even though their father has not yet come home. As Elizabeth raises her arms to light a lamp, the daughter is delighted to see a chrysanthemum blossom stuck in the waistband of her apron. The girl thinks it is beautiful, but Elizabeth remarks bitterly that she had chrysanthemums at her wedding and at the birth of her first child, and they had been present the first time her husband had been brought home drunk. She associates the flower with pain and disappointment. After tea the children play quietly. Elizabeth's anger at her husband's neglect grows more intense while she waits for him. She puts the children to bed. As the evening grows late, her anger begins to be mixed with fear.

In the second half of the story, Elizabeth begins to act on her fears. She visits a neighboring wife, Mrs. Rigley, who asks her husband to go out and look for Walter. Elizabeth returns to her own home to wait. Eventually, she hears someone coming. It is her mother-in-law, who comes in crying that there has been an accident in the mine. Walter is either badly injured or dead. While Walter's mother weeps and moans, Elizabeth quickly runs over the possibilities in her mind. If he is injured, she will have to nurse him back to health. If he is dead, how will she cope? Will she have enough money to take care of the children? Meanwhile, Mrs. Bates recalls what a good son Walter has been, what a good and happy young fellow. Finally, the pit manager and some miners carry Walter's body on a stretcher into Elizabeth's small and chilly parlor. The room is so small that they can scarcely maneuver, and one miner knocks down a vase of chrysanthemums. The children awake, so Elizabeth goes upstairs to quiet them. The men depart on tiptoe. Walter has been smothered by an avalanche of coal. His body is not damaged.

As the wife and mother begin to undress and clean the body, Mrs. Bates weeps over the loss of her son. She dwells on his physical beauty and hopes that he made his peace with God before his death. Elizabeth's reactions are different. As she washes him, she is amazed at how remote from him she feels. He and she had been strangers for a long time. Living together as husband and wife, sleeping together and begetting children, they had nevertheless been apart. He had been alien to her. Now she feels great shame and regret that she denied him the freedom to be what he was. She realizes his suffering and feels pity for him instead of her habitual anger and resentment. She will submit to the duties before her, to the care of her children, but she feels "fear and shame" as she thinks of her lost relationship with her husband.

Unlike most symbolic flowers, the chrysanthemums in this story are associated with sorrow and suffering. In this story chrysanthemums, which are autumn flowers, become funeral flowers. They are torn and broken and spilled on the floor, and their beauty is out of place in the dark lives of these characters. The climax of the story is not the death of Walter; that event takes place elsewhere, as in a Greek tragedy. The climax occurs in the mind of Elizabeth as she realizes her failure to her dead husband and the unbridgeable gap between them.

"The Horse Dealer's Daughter"

Mabel Pervin is the central figure of this short story. Until the age of twenty-seven she lived with her father and brothers in a modestly comfortable way. Now she suddenly finds herself confronted with poverty and homelessness. Her father, the horse dealer, has died, leaving many debts. Her three brothers cannot sustain the business.

The story opens a few days before they must vacate their home. At breakfast, the brothers try to discuss with Mabel what will become of her. Joe, the eldest, a coarse, animal-like man, will marry into a family that can provide him with a job. The two younger brothers will leave the neighborhood and, presumably, find work for themselves. But they have no way to provide for their sister. They suggest that she visit with their other sister, who is married, and then perhaps study to become a nurse. Mabel responds to neither of these ideas, maintaining a sullen calm. They are getting nowhere. Then they receive a visit from Jack Ferguson, a young Scottish physician who works in the town and who socializes evenings with the brothers. He has stopped by to find out when the younger brothers will be leaving. During his visit, he is aware of Mabel, but when he asks her what she plans to do, she barely replies. He feels uncomfortable in her presence; he is conscious of her eyes.

After this opening dialogue, the narrator explains that Mabel had acted as housekeeper for her father and brothers. She was proud of their affluence and after their fall into poverty she bitterly resented her loss of status. Now she feels relieved that the situation has come to an end.

Later, taking some clippers and cleaning implements, Mabel visits her mother's grave to trim the grass and clean the stone marker. Ferguson, the young doctor, watches her at this task. When she has finished and looks up, their eyes meet.

Later that afternoon, Ferguson is walking along a path above the town on his way to visit a patient. He looks across the fields and sees a dark figure leave the Pervins' house and walk down toward a pond. As he watches, he realizes that the person is Mabel. She walks deliberately into the pond. Realizing that she is about to commit suicide, he rushes across the fields and into the pond to rescue her. The water is dark and cold. Despite his fear and revulsion, he is determined to rescue her. He even loses his footing and falls. Finally, he finds her unconscious form floating on the surface. He drags her out of the pond, restores her breathing, and carries her back into her own house, taking her into the kitchen, where a fire is still burning. He leaves her on the hearth while he finds blankets. Then he removes her wet clothes and dries her, wrapping her in the blankets.

When she regains consciousness, she recognizes him and asks, "What did I do?" She questions him: Was she out of her mind? Did he rescue her from the pond? Why did he do it? Did he undress her? And finally, then, does he love her? Ferguson feels torn between keeping a professional attitude, wanting to go and find dry clothes for himself, and feeling held back by her presence. When she comes to the final question, "Do you love me?," he is afraid and bewildered, but as she moves toward him and clasps his legs, he feels it is both horrible and wonderful.

The narrator repeats several times that Ferguson "never intended to love her," but as he touches her bare shoulder, his heart gives way and he responds, "Yes." It is suddenly true that he does love her. After some kisses and some tears of relief, Mabel gathers her blankets about herself and goes upstairs to dress. She throws down some dry clothes for Ferguson. Coming down neatly dressed in her best dress, she offers to make tea, but Ferguson feels the pull of his obligations to his patients. As he leaves, Mabel complains that she must look horrible and that her hair still smells of the pond. But he reassures her, saying that they will marry as quickly as possible. She feels equally afraid of his passion for her and of the possibility that he does not want her.

This scene between Mabel and Ferguson shows how Lawrence treats the love between men and women in a new vein. This is not conventional romance. Each character feels conflicts between fear and desire. The lover behaves awkwardly and feels embarrassed and even absurd. Their passion seems terrible to themselves, but they must yield to its influence. Lawrence shows the ambivalence of lovers and the gritty realism of how sexual desire overcomes other feelings such as pride and duty. For a Lawrence character, falling in love may be horrible.

"Why the Novel Matters"

In this poetic essay, Lawrence states his essential belief in the total awareness of both body and mind, or soul. The whole body has intelligence, it knows. Lawrence separates everything in the world into two categories— the alive and the dead. He claims this insight as the special knowledge of novelists. Others, such as parsons, philosophers, and scientists, tend to analyze and dissect, separating the body from the mind or examining only the dead parts rather than the living whole.

For Lawrence, "nothing is important but life." He has no interest in an afterlife. The words and thoughts that flow from one person to another Lawrence calls "tremulations upon the ether." They pass between individuals like radio messages.

Lawrence declares that he, as a living man and as a novelist, is superior in knowledge to the saint, to the philosopher, and to the scientist, each of whom only partially studies the human being.

Lawrence believes that the novelist presents the individual as a dynamic whole, trembling with life. Therefore, the novel is important. He includes among novels such texts as the Bible and the works of Homer and Shakespeare—books that present the wholeness of the living person.

Characters in novels live in their full complexity and ability to change. The novel is a helpful guide because it does not present simple rules of right and wrong; rather, it helps one develop an instinct for life and to avoid being a "dead man" in life. In the full play of the novel, life emerges.

"Love on the Farm"

This poem displays the richly sensual, sexual imagery which derives from Lawrence's idea of the body as having its own knowledge. The speaker in the poem is a farm woman sitting alone in her house and thinking about her lover while she waits for his visit. Looking out she sees large leaves making shadows on the window; they look to her like large, grasping hands such as her lover has. Realizing that she is merely seeing leaves, she watches the red sunset. She notices the woodbine, a creeping flowered plant, visited by a pollinating moth. The flower and moth are described as two lovers; the receptive flower yields to the active, flirtatious moth. Then she imagines how her lover comes walking toward her home. As he passes through fields and past a shed the timid birds cower or shy away. The terrified rabbit first hides then starts to run at the man's approach, but the rabbit is caught in a snare; a wire ring tightens around its neck and it dies. The man takes this rabbit as a gift to the woman waiting in the house. The fate of the rabbit foreshadows the encounter of the lovers. Overpowered by his presence, the woman feels that his hand on her throat is like the entrapping wire. Her response of "sweet fire" she calls a sort of dying, but this metaphorical death is good. Her sense of being as a separate self is annihilated.

Joyce and Lawrence as innovative novelists show the liberating effects of modernism. They felt free to abandon the constraints of realism and to present narratives of the mind and feelings. The reader is thrust into a maze of conflicting and sometimes incoherent thoughts in a character's consciousness. This means freeing the narration from ordinary chronological sequence to accommodate the movements of memory and mental patterns of association. The focus of the novel shifts from characters' efforts to find their proper roles in society toward an examination of states of doubt, isolation, and self-absorption. The formal freedoms of the new novel are extended to include a more frank presentation of sex, which became a deglamorized force overriding other forces in awkward and not always happy ways. Both Joyce and Lawrence found that their fiction created controversy. Each felt that he had to live in exile from his homeland in order to write. As outsiders, they looked back and created powerful images of the fears and dilemmas of men and women emerging in a complex modern world.

Selected Readings

Ellmann, Richard. *The Consciousness of Joyce*. New York: Oxford University Press, 1977.

Gifford, Don. *Joyce Annotated: Notes for Dubliners and A Portrait of the Artist as a Young Man*. Berkeley: University of California Press, 1982.

Pinion, F. B. *A D. H. Lawrence Companion: Life, Thought and Works*. New York: Barnes, 1979.

Sagar, Keith. *The Art of D. H. Lawrence*. Cambridge: Cambridge University Press, 1966.

Tindall, William York. *A Reader's Guide to James Joyce*. New York: Noonday, 1959.

19

The Bloomsbury Group

1919   Woolf, *Night and Day*; Keynes, *Economic Consequences of the Peace*

1921   Strachey, *Queen Victoria*; Woolf, *Monday or Tuesday* and *A Haunted House and Other Stories*

1922   Forster, *Alexandria: A History and a Guide*; Strachey, *Books and Characters*; Woolf, *Jacob's Room*

1923   Germany experiences extreme inflation, as predicted by Keynes

1924   Forster, *A Passage to India*; Eliot, *Homage to John Dryden* published by Hogarth Press

1925   Strachey, *Pope*; Woolf, *Mrs. Dalloway* and *The Common Reader*, which included essay "Modern Fiction"

1927   Woolf, *To the Lighthouse*; Forster resident fellow of Kings College, Cambridge

1928   Forster, *The Eternal Moment*; Strachey, *Elizabeth and Essex*; Woolf, *Orlando*

1929   Woolf, *A Room of One's Own*

1929–1977   Graves's poetry, novels, and translations written

1930–1970   Auden's poetry written

1931   Strachey, *Characters and Commentaries*; Woolf, *The Waves*

1932   Woolf, *The Second Common Reader*

1933   Woolf, *Flush: A Biography*

1933–1949   O. Sitwell's poetry and prose written; Orwell's novels and essays written

1936   Forster, *Abinger Harvest*, collected essays; Keynes, *The General Theory of Employment, Interest, and Money*

1936–1952   George VI reigns

1937   Woolf, *The Years*

1938   Woolf, *Three Guineas*; in the United States, nuclear fission demonstrated

1939   Great Britain and France declare war on Germany

1940   Woolf, *Roger Fry: A Biography*; German *Luftwaffe* begins Battle of Britain

1941   Woolf, *Between the Acts*; Woolf commits suicide; United States enters World War II

1942   Woolf, *The Death of the Moth* published posthumously

1943   Battle of Stalingrad; Italy surrenders

1944   Western Allies launch D-day invasion of Normandy; Copland, *Appalachian Spring*

1945 Germany surrenders; United States drops atomic bombs on Japan; Japan surrenders, World War II ends

1946 Nuremberg War Criminal Trials

1949 Cold War begins; Miller, *Death of a Salesman*

1950 Woolf, *The Captain's Death Bed* published posthumously

1951 Forster, *Two Cheers for Democracy*; with Eric Crozier, Forster writes libretto for Benjamin Britten's opera *Billy Budd*

1952 Reign of Queen Elizabeth II begins

1953 Forster, *The Hill of Devi*; Woolf, *A Writer's Diary* published posthumously

1956 Forster, *Marianne Thornton: A Domestic Biography*; Woolf, *Letters* published posthumously; Suez Crisis

1958 Woolf, *Granite and Rainbow* published posthumously

1966 Woolf, *Collected Essays* published posthumously

1969 Forster awarded the Order of Merit

1970 Forster dies

1971 Forster, *Maurice* published posthumously

Bloomsbury is a residential section of London, near the British Museum, which became in the early twentieth century the center of activity of an influential group of writers, painters, and intellectuals that came to be known as the Bloomsbury group. They met in one author's homes and especially in the home of Virginia and Leonard Woolf.

The group was united by the belief, as articulated by G. E. Moore in his book Principia Ethica, *that the greatest goals of life are the pleasures of friendship and the enjoyment of art. Cultivating these goals, the group rejected the restraints of propriety and the sexual prudery of Victorian society. They were avant garde in art and literature and remarkably free in their interlocking personal lives. Marital fidelity was not honored, and several members of the group were bisexual. The circle included, in addition to the Woolfs, Virginia Woolf's sister, Vanessa Bell, a painter; and Bell's husband, Clive Bell, a writer and art critic. Other important members of the group were John Maynard Keynes, the economist; Douglas Grant, a painter; Roger Fry, a playwright; the novelist E. M. Forster; and Lytton Strachey, a writer whose book* Eminent Victorians *attacked the values of the previous age.*

The group came under criticism not only for the perceived immorality of their personal lives, but also for the aestheticism and sometimes for the obscurity of their literature. However, the Hogarth Press, founded in 1917

by Leonard and Virginia Woolf, was first to publish works by some of the major writers of the first half of the twentieth century. These works included the early poems of T. S. Eliot and translations of such great Continental writers as Chekhov, Dostoevsky, Tolstoy, and Rilke. The Woolfs presented new, experimental works that would not have found publishers elsewhere.

VIRGINIA WOOLF (1882–1941)

Born Virginia Stephen, Virginia was the daughter of Sir Leslie Stephen, a well-known Victorian intellectual and the editor of the *Dictionary of National Biography*. Stephen, who was an agnostic, oversaw a vigorously literary and philosophical household. Virginia received a rigorous education at home from private tutors and with the help of her father's substantial library. At the death of their father in 1904, the Stephen children settled in Bloomsbury. Their household became the center of an active circle of writers and artists.

Virginia was employed as a reviewer for the *Times Literary Supplement* and launched into fiction writing as well. Her first novels were in the realistic tradition and were not very successful. Meanwhile, in 1912, Virginia married the journalist and political writer Leonard Woolf.

Virginia suffered from bouts of mental depression that may have stemmed in part from the sexual abuse she suffered as a child at the hands of her older half-brother. Partly to provide Virginia with a kind of therapy, the Woolfs founded the Hogarth Press and undertook the publication of modern, experimental literary works. One of their most famous publications was *Poems* by T. S. Eliot, who was their friend but not a member of the Bloomsbury group.

Woolf's Style

Woolf's first novel in the modern style was *Jacob's Room* (1922), an impressionistic and poetic treatment of the death of a young man during World War I. This was followed by her greatest novels, *Mrs. Dalloway* (1925) and *To the Lighthouse* (1927). In these novels, Woolf developed the stream-of-consciousness technique as a means of exploring the inner lives of her characters. With the publication of *The Waves* in 1931, her reputation as a major innovative novelist was established. She had also continued to write essays on literary criticism, which were collected in two volumes, *The Common Reader* and *The Second Common Reader*. Modern feminists have popularized her lecture *A Room of One's Own* (1931) and its sequel, *Three Guineas* (1929). Despite recurring bouts of mental illness, Woolf continued to write essays and fiction as well as maintain a voluminous correspondence. During a period of severe depression, Woolf drowned herself in 1941.

"The Mark on the Wall"

This fanciful mental excursion was first published by the Hogarth Press in *A Haunted House and Other Stories* (1921). Here Woolf set down the stream of consciousness of the character (perhaps Woolf herself), who looks up from reading one winter afternoon to focus on a black spot on the white wall opposite. Her mind begins to speculate about the mark—What is it? What made it? Is it a nail, a hole, or a rose petal?

Each new possibility begins a new stream of thought. The thought of a nail provokes an image of the people who might have put the nail there. The hole suggests the contingencies of life—one never can know for certain how a thing came to be. One of life's mysteries is where lost things go, and the afterlife is even more open to speculation. If the mark is a substance, it indicates careless housekeeping. One thought leads on to another thought, shifts sometimes being indicated by the ellipses (...). It occurs to the character that novels of the future will deal with the reflection of individuals as shown in ordinary faces, that generalization and rules seem to create restrictions and a false ordering of reality, and that the "phantoms" of the past will be laughed away, yielding a new freedom. She then indulges in the fanciful creation of the life of an antiquary, an old colonel who digs up remnants of the primitive past and makes his life important by collecting and lecturing about these artifacts. But the sort of knowledge promoted by the antiquary is futile, the work of "specialists," and not conducive to "beauty and health of mind." She mocks the serious self-importance of "professors or specialists or housekeepers."

The final speculation is an imaginative re-creation of the lives of trees, their existence in nature and their later transformation into furniture. In the middle of this train of thought the character is suddenly interrupted by someone speaking to her, bringing her out of her reverie. He remarks casually, solving the puzzle, "I don't see why we should have a snail on our wall."

Instead of rendering reality by means of descriptive details, the story reenacts the pattern of mental life, the stream of thoughts and impressions that represent the self.

"Modern Fiction"

In this 1925 essay, Woolf tries to express her sense of what the modern novelist should be writing about. Drawing upon more than a decade of reviewing new works of fiction, Woolf proposes a new kind of subject matter. She rejects the work of such "materialists" as H. G. Wells, Arnold Bennett, and John Galsworthy, all novelists of skill and talent. She calls Wells a materialist "from sheer goodness of heart"—that is, he uses fiction to express useful social ideas. She cites the fine craftsmanship of Bennett, but somehow, she says, "life escapes" from his meticulous and authentic renderings of clothes and houses, his careful plots and maintenance of probability. Woolf believes that "the proper stuff of fiction" is to represent the mind as it receives impressions "from all sides" and responds to those impressions. She cites Thomas Hardy and Joseph Conrad as novelists who deserve gratitude for their experiments in writing a more modern kind of fiction. Among younger writers, she singles out James Joyce as one who comes closer to a valid depiction of "life" by showing the patterns and the incoherence of consciousness.

Woolf had read Joyce's *A Portrait of the Artist as a Young Man* and some of the first episodes of *Ulysses*, just then being published in installments. She praises Joyce for being "spiritual" rather than materialistic and for being courageous enough to disregard novelistic conventions in order to present "the flickerings of that innermost flame which flashes its message through the brain." However, she finds Joyce less masterful than Hardy and Conrad because of his comparative narrowness. She is also somewhat put off by what she calls his "indecency."

Woolf goes on to cite the modern Russian writer Anton Chekhov as a writer who breaks with the usual emphasis on plot to create a new kind of fiction, one not easily classified in the old categories of "comic" or "tragic." Indeed, she finds in the Russian writers great human sympathy expressed in almost saintly ways. The possibilities of fiction, she feels, are infinite; there is no one best way to compose it. Every method is permissible so long as it avoids pretense and falsity.

A Room of One's Own

In the fall of 1928, Woolf was invited to deliver two lectures on the subject of women and fiction. These lectures were expanded and published the following year by the Hogarth Press under the title *A Room of One's Own*, which refers to Woolf's observation that having a private room in which to think and write is a basic requirement for producing literature, a requirement that, along with economic independence, few women in history had ever enjoyed. Raising the question of why women had not produced much first-rate fiction, Woolf describes the poverty, social pressures, family demands, and lack of education that tended to prevent women from writing.

Creating an imaginary figure, the sister of Shakespeare, she follows the steps of Shakespeare's career to show how, at each step, a woman of the same talents would have been thwarted and opposed. Judith Shakespeare, a woman of great mental powers, would not have been sent to school. Instead she would have been kept at home and betrothed against her wishes to some local tradesman. If she had run away to avoid the marriage, she could not have found work in the theater; there were no actresses at that time. Unable to survive alone, she would have fallen into degradation and perhaps committed suicide. Woolf supposes that women of unusual gifts ended up isolated and despised, some of them surviving as village wise women or perishing as persecuted witches. Even if a woman had been allowed to write, her imagination would have been distorted and made morbid by the difficulties of keeping an independent existence.

Woolf pays tribute to those women of the nineteenth century who did manage to write, pointing out that the novel, a relatively new and flexible form, was their most natural genre. But looking at the present and future, she predicts that women poets will also emerge. Woolf ends the lectures hopefully, encouraging her young audience to write "exactly what [they] think," to have the courage to use their independence (500 pounds a year she thought would suffice) to "go it alone" and work for what is worthwhile.

E. M. FORSTER (1879–1970)

Although not one of the central members of the Bloomsbury group, Edward Morgan Forster was a friend to many of them. Like them, he believed that cultivating personal relationships is both difficult and essential in civilized life.

Son of an architect, Forster was raised mainly by his mother and his aunts. As a day student among boarders he was unhappy at Tonbridge School, but he enjoyed Cambridge university and established there those friendships that brought him into the Bloomsbury group.

After Cambridge, Forster traveled to Greece and Italy, countries that came to represent for him a freer, more spontaneous life than was permitted by the middle-class restraints he was accustomed to in England. He worked as a tutor and began to write for a liberal journal, *The Independent Review*. Among those whom he tutored was Syed Ross Masood, a young Indian who encouraged Forster to visit India in 1912 and again in 1922.

Unlike Joyce and Woolf, Forster wrote realistic novels in the formal tradition of the nineteenth century, criticizing the customs and social class barriers of English society. His best-known works are *A Room with a View* (1908), which depicts awkward English tourists in Italy; *Howards End* (1910), about the necessary connections of action and feeling; and his masterpiece, *A Passage to India* (1924), which uses his experiences in India to explore the possibility of cross-cultural friendships. This was Forster's last novel. His novel *Maurice* was published only in 1971, after his death, because of its treatment of homosexual love.

In the years after the publication of *A Passage to India*, Forster continued to write short stories, essays, biographies, and literary criticism. He was active in the campaign against censorship and wrote a popular discussion of the novel form, *Aspects of the Novel*. He was given a fellowship at

Cambridge in the 1940s. The University became his home, along with a country house in Surrey that he had inherited.

The Road from Colonus

In the ancient Greek tragedy *Oedipus at Colonus,* by Sophocles, Oedipus the king has banished himself from Thebes because he has murdered his father and committed incest with his mother. He arrives blind and poor at the village of Colonus, accompanied by his daughter Antigone. Theseus, king of the nearby city of Athens, offers Oedipus the hospitality of the city, but the son and daughter of Oedipus make other claims upon him. Finally, promising a boon to Athens, Oedipus retires to that city, where he dies and is buried.

In Forster's *The Road from Colonus,* the parallels between Mr. Lucas and Oedipus and between his daughter Ethel and Antigone are made explicit in a comment by Mrs. Forman. They are in a group of English tourists traveling by mule in rural Greece with the guidance of a dragoman, or interpreter. Moving ahead of the others, Mr. Lucas arrives at a grove of plane trees, where a spring gushes out from the base of one huge old tree. Mr. Lucas, old and disappointed by the trip, suddenly finds the place beautiful and peaceful. He steps inside the hollow tree trunk and feels its sacredness. When his daughter and the others arrive, he tries to tell them about the beauty and peace he feels, but he can speak only with his habitual calm understatement.

Mrs. Forman and Ethel, by contrast, are full of exclamations of pleasure. Ethel jokingly suggests that they should spend a week there, but Mr. Lucas takes her seriously and feels great joy in anticipating the stay. He feels that he will find peace and companionship at last among the simple folk who keep the Khan, or the inn. When he discovers that his daughter was joking and that she is determined to continue the journey as planned, Mr. Lucas tries to resist. However, he cannot convey how much it would mean to him to stay; he can only speak of the "inconvenience" of leaving. With the help of Mr. Graham, a younger man in their party, Ethel urges, bullies, and finally forces her father away, provoking an unsuccessful attempt at "rescue" by the family who runs the inn. They can sense how much staying there means to Mr. Lucas. Ironically, Ethel thanks Mr. Graham for "saving" her father. Mr. Lucas yields to their pressure, relapsing into his "old self" of discontent.

The final scene takes place some months later in London. Ethel and her father are at breakfast. She tries to distract him from his habitual petty complaints about the discomforts and noises of the house. He is particularly irritated by the sound of water running from a pipe. (He had enjoyed the sound of the gushing stream at Colonus.) Ethel receives a parcel, which turns out to be a gift of some flower bulbs from Mrs. Forman, who remains in Greece. The bulbs are wrapped in an old newspaper, which Ethel reads. She discovers that, by coincidence, the very Kahn her father had hoped to stay in has been destroyed by the falling of the great hollow tree. The family who kept the inn has been killed in the disaster. This catastrophe happened on the very night they would have stayed there. Ethel cannot resist pointing out to her father, "You would have been killed," not realizing that the remainder of his life is barren and full of irritation. Even he seems to have forgotten his wish to stay and die in that beautiful place.

The story presents a lost opportunity to die peacefully in a state of joy and companionship. Mr. Lucas lives on, but his life is a trial to himself and to his daughter.

Among the fiction writers of the Bloomsbury group, there existed a shared sense of being at the frontiers of a new kind of fiction, a fiction that presents the way the mind works. They all saw that a stream of consciousness is different from a flow of conversation or from a storyteller's narrative line. The mind has its own sequence, and while it moves in apparently random ways it also shows a pattern based on the individual's habits of associating one thought with another. This new fiction was more difficult for readers to follow. All the usual indicators of time and transition were absent. The customary plot line, by which a novel is held together and made to seem meaningful, was broken up or abandoned altogether. Nevertheless, stream of consciousness permitted close study of a character's inner life of thought and feeling. Its power became clear, and later novels incorporated more and more the techniques of this new way of composing fiction.

Selected Readings

Cavaliero, Glen. *A Reading of E. M. Forster.* Totowa, NJ: Rowman, 1979.

Crews, Frederick. *E. M. Forster: The Perils of Humanism.* Princeton: Princeton University Press, 1962.

Hafley, James. *The Glass Roof: Virginia Woolf as Novelist.* New York: Russell, 1963.

Johnstone, John Keith. *The Bloomsbury Group: A Study of E. M. Forster, Lytton Strachey, Virginia Woolf, and their Circle.* New York: Noonday, 1954.

Leaska, Mitchell A. *The Novels of Virginia Woolf: From Beginning to End.* New York: John Jay, 1977.

Trilling, Lionel. *E. M. Forster.* New York: New Directions, 1965.

20

Poetry and Literature Between the Wars

1901–1910 Reign of Edward VII

1901 Freud, *The Psychopathology of Everyday Life*

1903 Mansfield arrives in London; Pankhurst founds Women's Social and Political Union

1907 Picasso, *Les Demoiselles d'Avignon*

1908 Forster, *A Room with a View*; in the United States, first model-T Ford

1910–1936 Reign of George V

1911 Mansfield, *In a German Pension*; suffragette riots in London

1913 Braque, *Musical Forms*

1914 World War I begins; Panama Canal opens

1915 Eliot settles in London; Eliot, *The Love Song of J. Alfred Prufrock* appears in *Poetry* magazine

1915–1941 Woolf's novels, essays, and criticism written

1916–1921 E. Sitwell edits and contributes to *Wheels*

1916–1939 Joyce's novels and poetry written

1917 Eliot, *Prufrock and Other Observations*; in the United States, first jazz recording

1917–1919 Eliot assistant editor of *Egoist* magazine

1918 Germany agrees to armistice, ending World War I

1919   Eliot, "Gerontion"; in the United States, Eighteenth Amendment brings "Prohibition"

1920   Mansfield, *Bliss and Other Stories*; Eliot, *The Sacred Wood*; Modigliani, *The Reclining Nude*

1922   Eliot, "The Waste Land"; Mansfield, *The Garden Party and Other Stories*

1922–1927   Orwell serves in Burma police

1922–1939   Eliot founds and edits the *Criterion*

1923   Mansfield, *The Dove's Nest and Other Stories*; Mansfield dies; Mansfield, *Poems* published posthumously; Freud, *The Ego and the Id*

1924   Mansfield, *Something Childish and Other Stories* published posthumously; Eliot, *Homage to Dryden*; Ernst, *Two Children Are Menaced by a Nightingale*

1927   Graves with Riding, *A Survey of Modernist Poetry*; Mansfield, *The Journal of Katherine Mansfield* published posthumously

1928   Fleming discovers penicillin

1929   Graves, *Goodbye to All That*; Mansfield, *Selected Stories* and *The Letters of Katherine Mansfield* published posthumously; in the United States the Great Depression begins

1930   Eliot, "Ash Wednesday"; Mansfield, *The Aloe* published posthumously; Masefield named poet laureate

1930–1970   Auden's poetry written

1932   Eliot, *Selected Essays*

1933   Orwell, *Down and Out in Paris and London*; Eliot, *The Use of Poetry and the Use of Criticism*; O. Sitwell, *The English Eccentrics*; West, *Miss Lonelyhearts*

1934   Graves, *I, Claudius* and *Claudius the God*; Orwell, *Burmese Days*; Eliot, *After Strange Gods*

1935   Eliot, *Murder in the Cathedral*; Orwell, *A Clergyman's Daughter*

1936   Smith, *Novel on Yellow Paper*; Eliot, *Essays Ancient and Modern*; Orwell, *Keep the Aspidistra Flying*

1936–1952   George VI reigns; accession of Edward VIII, followed by his abdication and the succession of his brother to the throne

1937   Orwell, *The Road to Wigan Pier*; Smith, *A Good Time Was Had by All*

1938   Graves, *Count Belisarius*; Orwell, *Homage to Catalonia*

1939   Eliot, *The Family Reunion* and *Old Possum's Book of Practical Cats*; Orwell, *Coming Up for Air*; Great Britain and France declare war on Germany

1940 Orwell, *Inside the Whale*; German *Luftwaffe* begins Battle of Britain

1941 Orwell, *The Lion and the Unicorn: Socialism and the English Genius*

1943 Eliot, *Four Quartets*; Graves, *Wife to Mr. Milton*

1943–1945 Orwell literary editor for *The London Tribune*

1945 Orwell, *Animal Farm*; O. Sitwell, *Left Hand, Right Hand*; United States drops atomic bombs on Japan; World War II ends

1946 Graves, *King Jesus*; Orwell, *Politics and the English Language*; O. Sitwell, *The Secret Tree*; Chagall, *The Cow with a Parasol*

1948 Eliot receives Nobel Prize for literature and the Order of Merit; Graves, *The White Goddess*

1949 Graves, *The Golden Ass of Apuleius* and *The Common Asphodel*; Orwell, *Nineteen Eighty-four*

1950 Eliot, *The Cocktail Party*; Orwell, *Shooting an Elephant*; hydrogen super-bomb exploded

1952– Reign of Elizabeth II

1953 Eliot, *The Confidential Clerk*

1955 Graves, *Greek Myths* and *The Crowning Privilege*

1957 Eliot, *On Poetry and Poets*; Smith, *Not Waving but Drowning*; Kerouac, *On the Road*; interferon, substance produced by body to fight viruses, is discovered

1958 Eliot, *The Elder Statesman*

1961–1966 Graves professor of poetry, Oxford University

1962 E. Sitwell, *The Queens and the Hive*

1963 Eliot, *Collected Poems, 1909–1962*

1965 Eliot dies

1968 Orwell, *Collected Essays, Journalism and Letters* published posthumously

1969 Smith awarded Queen's Gold Medal for Poetry

1971 Smith dies

1975 Smith, *Collected Poems* published posthumously

1979 Margaret Thatcher becomes first woman prime minister of Great Britain

1983 Smith, *Me Again: Uncollected Writings* published posthumously

1985 Graves dies

In the 1920s the modernist breakthroughs made by Joyce, Lawrence, and Woolf in fiction began to affect poetry in obvious ways. Yeats's dreamily aesthetic style of the late nineteenth century began to shift to a more lean and conversational style. The technique of placing the voice of the poem within a character, a technique used earlier by Browning in the dramatic monologue, was now reinforced by the influence of Freudian psychology. The mind's distorted and fragmented perception, which the novelists were exploring with the stream-of-consciousness technique, also emerged as the poets' dominant focus. The most successful and widely read poet of the twenties and thirties was T. S. Eliot, whose poems began to change the way readers approached poetry. Eliot and his contemporaries were often considered difficult or obscure, but they created the new phrases and images that communicated the fatigue and disillusionment of the modern individual.

T. S. ELIOT (1888–1965)

Thomas Stearns Eliot was American-born, although his poetry career and his personal sympathies were English. Raised in St. Louis, Missouri, Eliot attended Harvard University, where he studied philosophy and literature. He continued his education in Paris and at Oxford University. By 1915 he had settled permanently in England. He took a position at Lloyd's Bank in London and married an Englishwoman, Vivienne Haight-Wood, whose poor health and mental instability placed impossible demands on the marriage. She was eventually committed to a mental institution, and Eliot obtained a divorce in 1933.

Meanwhile, Eliot had begun to publish poetry. His early success was *The Love Song of J. Alfred Prufrock*. Through his essays of literary criticism Eliot helped revive interest in the metaphysical poets and in the dramatists of the early seventeenth century. Eliot wrote for various literary journals, and in 1922 founded his own quarterly journal, the *Criterion*, which became an important publisher of literary essays and new poems and stories.

The Waste Land, Eliot's most famous work, was first published in the *Criterion* in 1922. Eliot left Lloyd's Bank and became an editor at Faber and Gwyer, a publishing house. In 1927 Eliot became a British citizen and a member of the Anglican church. He continued to write essays and poetry throughout the 1930s. He also wrote plays, none of which was particularly successful. The most notable of them were *Murder in the Cathedral* (1935) and the philosophical comedy *The Cocktail Party* (1950). Eliot's volume of poetry for children, *Old Possum's Book of Practical Cats* (1939), became the basis for *Cats*, a spectacularly successful musical show.

Eliot's first wife died in an institution in 1947. By this time Eliot was the most influential critic and poet in England. Some of his poetic phrases, such as "April is the cruelest month," had become familiar even to those who had not read his poetry. Eliot won the Nobel Prize for literature in 1948. In 1957 he married a second time, finding a happy domestic life only in old age.

The Love Song of J. Alfred Prufrock

The speaker in this ironic monologue is a modern, urban man who, like many of his kind, feels isolated and incapable of decisive action. Irony is apparent from the title, for this is not a conventional love song. Prufrock would like to speak of love to a woman, but he does not dare.

The poem opens with a quoted passage from Dante's *Inferno*, suggesting that Prufrock is one of the damned and that he speaks only because he is sure no one will listen. Since the reader is overhearing his thoughts, the poem seems at first rather incoherent. But Prufrock repeats certain phrases and returns to certain core ideas as the poem progresses. The "you and I" of the opening line includes the reader, suggesting that only by accompanying Prufrock can one understand his problems.

The images of the opening lines depict a drab neighborhood of cheap hotels and restaurants, where Prufrock lives in solitary gloom. In line 12 he suggests making a visit, and immediately his mind calls up an image of the place he and the reader will go—perhaps an afternoon tea at which various women drop in and engage in polite chitchat about Michelangelo, who was a man of great creative energy, unlike Prufrock.

The next stanza creates an image of the dull, damp autumn evening when the tea party will take place. In the rest of the poem Prufrock imagines his arrival, his attempt to converse intimately with the woman whose love he seeks, and his ultimate failure to make her understand him. Prufrock has attended such parties many times and knows how it will be, and this knowledge makes him hesitate out of fear that any attempt to push beyond mere polite conversation, to make some claim on the woman's affections, will meet with a frustratingly polite refusal.

So Prufrock simultaneously plans his approach and tells himself that he can put off action. The phrase "There will be time," repeated five times between lines 23 and 36, represents his hesitation and delay. When he says in lines 44 and 45 "Do I dare/ Disturb the universe?," the universe he is referring to is his small social circle of middle-class acquaintances. He would disturb its equilibrium if he actually tried to sing a "love song" to one of them. He already "knows them all" and knows that they do not expect much from him. He tries, starting at line 70, to rehearse a speech he might make to one particular woman, but he gives up almost as soon as he has started, saying that it would be better to be merely a crab rather than a human being who has to make love speeches and ask for affection.

Deciding not to try, Prufrock questions whether his efforts would have been worthwhile. He excuses his fear by rationalizing that his speaking to the woman would not have achieved any real response. In line 110 Prufrock contrasts himself to Hamlet, a hero who hesitated but finally acted decisively. But Prufrock sees himself as more like Polonius, the old fool from the same play. Prufrock will retreat into a solitary, dignified old age. He has gone past dreams of romance into the sober but empty existence of a passionless old man.

PRUFROCK AS MODERN MAN

For many readers in the 1920s, Prufrock seemed to epitomize the frustration and impotence of the modern individual. He seemed to represent thwarted desires and modern disillusionment. Such phrases as "I have measured out my life in coffee spoons" (line 51) capture the sense of the unheroic nature of life in the twentieth century. Prufrock's weaknesses could be mocked, but he is a pathetic figure, not grand enough to be tragic.

The Waste Land

Eliot believed that modern society lacked a vital sense of community and a spiritual center. The waste land of the poem is modern European culture, which had come too far from its spiritual roots.

Eliot alludes to various ancient religions as well as to the medieval legend of the Holy Grail, finding in them the common thread of the mythic cycle of the death and resurrection of gods. More specifically, he found in a book by Jessie Weston, *From Ritual to Romance* (1920), the story of the Fisher King, a mythic figure whose loss of power or fertility produces a corresponding blight or drought in his kingdom. Only through the death of this king and his replacement by a new, young, and vigorous knight can the land be restored to fertility.

Eliot's poem, depicts modern society as being in the infertile part of the cycle. Human beings are isolated, and sexual relations are sterile and meaningless. Because of the variety and relative obscurity of Eliot's allusions, readers must work through the poem's footnotes several times to appreciate it, but the general impression of isolation, decadence, and sterility comes through in every reading.

ELIOT'S STYLE

The poem presents a series of conversations or scenes that lead through the wasteland to a moment of hope, the expectation of rain, at the end. The sections are numbered to indicate shifts of scene and speaker.

Part 1. The first part, "The Burial of the Dead," presents the voice of a countess looking back on her pre–World War I youth as a lovelier, freer, more romantic time. Her voice is followed by a solemn description of present dryness when "the dead tree gives no shelter." Then the poem returns to a fragmentary love scene of the past, perhaps the countess's. The scene shifts to a fortune-teller who reads the tarot cards and warns of death. The final section of part 1 presents a contemporary image of London crowds moving along the streets blankly, as if dead. One pedestrian calls out to another, grotesquely asking if the corpse in his garden has sprouted yet, suggesting the necessity of death before rebirth can take place. In the final line of this section, the poet calls the reader a hypocrite who thinks he is any better off.

The subsequent parts of the poem are similarly complex, shifting unexpectedly to different locations and speakers.

Part 2. "A Game of Chess" presents a neurotic rich woman frustrated by her male companion's reserve. This is followed by a gossipy barroom conversation about a woman who was unfaithful to her soldier husband during the war and who had an abortion to hide her guilt.

Part 3. The third section, "The Fire Sermon," mingles snatches of an old marriage song celebrating the Thames River with a contemporary image of the filthy, trash-filled Thames. Then, starting at line 215, the ancient seer Tiresias narrates a banal and loveless scene of seduction of a typist by her "lover," a petty real estate agent. The scene is squalid and passionless; the sexual act is meaningless to both participants. This is followed by contrasting images of Queen Elizabeth I boating on the Thames with her lover, the earl of Leicester.

Part 4. The fourth section, "Death by Water," fulfills the prophecy made by the fortune-teller in part 1. It is a brief section, marking death as the end, or, in keeping with the whole poem's structure, death that must precede transformation and rebirth.

Part 5. The final section, "What the Thunder Said," begins with images of a journey over barren and rocky ground. The thunder is sterile, being unaccompanied by rain, but a mysterious sense of some compassionate spirit visits the traveler. Chaotic images of rot and of a crumbling city lead up to line 393, at which time a cock (a symbol of Christ) crows, announcing the coming of rain.

The poem ends with the exposition of three terms from Hindu lore: Datta (to give alms), Dayadhvam (to have compassion), and Damyata (to practice self-control). Then the poem seems to collapse into a rush of quotations and allusions—a flood of meanings and suggestions ending with the word *shanti* (peace).

"Little Gidding"

This poem is one of four poems Eliot published in 1943 under the title *Four Quartets*. The title alludes to the structure of a musical quartet. Each of these four poems—"Burnt Norton," "East Coker," "The Dry Salvages," and "Little Gidding"—refers to a place. Each one is an independent work, but together they share a concern with the past and the present and the changes that take place over time.

ELIOT'S STYLE

Little Gidding was the site of a religious community founded in the seventeenth century by Nicholas Ferrar. Eliot is said to have composed the poem while on duty as a civilian fire watcher during the bombing of London in World War II. Each of the poems features one of the four classical elements: air, earth, water, and fire. The element of fire, which is associated with battle, is featured in "Little Gidding."

Part 1. King Charles I is supposed to have visited Little Gidding after his defeat at the battle of Naseby (see line 26). In the present, bombs are raining fire on London. Fire destroys, but it also purifies. Little Gidding was and is a place for prayer and for receiving messages from the dead.

Part 2. Part 2 presents an encounter between the poet and a ghost who represents the spirits of Jonathan Swift and William Butler Yeats. The ghost discloses the gifts of old age: the loss of sensation, the rage against impotence, and the pain of reevaluation of all one's past deeds. Mentioning the "restoring fire" of spiritual purification, the ghost fades away as day breaks.

Part 3. In part 3, memory is celebrated as a means of liberation, of going beyond the attachments of the moment to a state of transformation, when "All shall be well" and the soul will be purified of temporary, factional desire.

Part 4. Part 4 contains images of fire and passion, love, and as torment, the love that consumes the soul.

Part 5. In the final part, the cyclical nature of all existence assures us of both death and rebirth, "for history is a pattern of timeless moments." Therefore, each traveler through life ends where he began, only now he will "know the place for the first time." The poem ends in reassurance that "all shall be well."

"Tradition and the Individual Talent"

This essay was influential in changing the way modern readers and literary critics viewed the relationships between poems and poets. Eliot begins by remarking that the word *tradition* is used negatively by critics who value most highly the individual and personal aspects of a poet's work. But Eliot argues that an historical sense is necessary to appreciate any poem fully. The poet must work to absorb the poetic tradition from which he or she has emerged. The whole body of Western poetry is a complete order, with dynamic relationships among all the significant works. When a new poem is created, it is added to that whole and modifies it, even if only slightly. Each new poem can be judged only by the standards that have been set by the poetry of the past.

Eliot believed that as a poet matures, his or her poetry leaves personality behind and becomes more aware of tradition. In the best poetry, the poet acts as a catalyst, an agent whose presence is needed to make the materials of poetry—the emotions, images, and phrases—come together in the best way to make a new poem.

Rejecting Wordsworth's definition of poetry as "the spontaneous overflow of powerful feeling," Eliot sees the person who experiences personal feelings as a different aspect of the poet, who combines experience and impressions in a new way to make poetry. The poet's own emotional life may be dull. As an artist, the poet is able to express emotions that he or she may never have felt. Poetry is "an escape from emotion" and "an escape from personality," because the emotion that is found in art is impersonal.

In this essay, Eliot shows his antiromantic perception of the sources and the role of poetry. He gives a theoretical foundation for a new, more modern concept of poetic value, and he provides the basis for a new appreciation of some poets who had been long neglected, the metaphysical poets of the seventeenth century in particular.

KATHERINE MANSFIELD (1888–1923)

Mansfield's full name was Katherine Mansfield Beauchamp. She was born in New Zealand but came to London in 1903 to complete her education at Queen's College. She returned briefly to New Zealand, but went back to London in 1908. She spent the remainder of her brief life in England and in continental Europe.

Mansfield began to write short stories during a stay in Germany in 1909. Her stories, which were influenced by the style of the Russian writer Chekhov, deal with the texture of everyday life. Most of them lack the conventional neat plot of the short story genre. Mansfield develops the story through the subtle use of telling details, giving symbolic significance to seemingly minor objects. She also experimented by using shifting time and flashbacks and multiple points of view.

In 1912 Mansfield met the literary critic John Middleton Murry, whom she married in 1918. He was editor of several literary journals in which her stories were published. During this time Mansfield was suffering from the early stages of tuberculosis; hoping to improve her health, she spent part of every year in Switzerland and in the south of France.

Mansfield published several collections of stories during her life: *In a German Pension* (1911), *Bliss and Other Stories* (1920), and *The Garden Party and Other Stories* (1922). Mansfield and Murry were associated with other important writers of the twenties. They spent some time in Cornwall, living near their friends D. H. Lawrence and his wife, Frieda. Leonard and Virginia Woolf published Mansfield's story "Prelude," although Virginia Woolf later became antagonistic toward Mansfield.

In January 1923, Mansfield died of tuberculosis in a sanitorium in France. After her death, her final collections of stories were published, including *The Dove's Nest and Other Stories* (1923) and *Something Childish and Other Stories* (1924).

"The Daughters of the Late Colonel"

The main characters of this rather long short story are two timid middle-aged women who were dominated by their father, a typical Victorian patriarch. Now he is dead, and the sisters, Josephine (called Jug) and Constantia (called Con), are afraid to admit to themselves or each other how much joy and relief they feel. Old habits of submission still linger, making them afraid to sort through their father's personal effects. They are hounded by the sense of his continuing disapproval of every action, even of their having him buried. The sisters hesitate to make demands on their young servant Kate, who treats them with cool insolence because she knows they dare not challenge her. Of the two sisters, Josephine seems to take the lead, but Constantia has the advantage in that she does not mind seeming weak and is therefore less plagued by doubts about what she must do.

Both sisters dote upon their nephew Cyril, the son of their brother, who is in India. When Cyril comes to tea, a "rare treat" for the lonely women, they have spent lavishly on cakes that he barely nibbles at. His brief and reluctant visits with their father, his grandfather, had been pointless and awkward. Now Josephine proposes giving Cyril their father's gold watch. But the more immediate decision they must face is whether to keep Kate on or let her go. They are full of suspicions and doubts about Kate.

In the midst of their indecision they hear the music of an organ grinder from the street. Their first reaction is to rush out with a coin to silence the music, but then they remember that their father, who used to be enraged by the music, is dead and can no longer insist on stopping the music. They sit quietly and listen. The music seems to sing of their freedom from their father's tyranny as the sunlight shines into their room. The sunlight strikes an old photograph of their mother, dead since their early childhood, and Josephine's thoughts wander over the few events of their restricted lives. She wonders if they might have found husbands if their mother had been alive to help them into society. Their father had quarreled with his friends, isolating his daughters from social contacts. Meanwhile Constantia is having sad memories of a life wasted in petty services to their father, only occasionally relieved by trips to the seashore and private fantasies in the moonlight. Each sister is even isolated from the other. At the end of the story, each one wants to say "something important" about their future, but neither can quite find the words.

MANSFIELD'S CHARACTERIZATION

While the silly, naive, and timid sisters are ridiculous in their preoccupation with trivia (while in mourning, should they wear black dressing gowns?) and in their foolish fears (can Kate overhear their talks?), the reader also gradually gathers a sense of the sad emptiness and frustration of their lives. Josephine might have been a happy wife and mother; perhaps Constantia would have been an artist or poet. Their lives have been wasted by a family system that pinched each one into a narrow and dowdy existence with no pleasures and no chances to express herself. By the time their father died, their capacity for joy and self-expression had been lost.

"Her First Ball"

One of Mansfield's best-known stories, "Her First Ball" is about Leila, a young girl from the country who has come up to London with her mother to attend her first dance party. She is full of excited anticipation in the cab with her cousins, three girls and their brother, who have been to such balls before and who take an amused but protective attitude toward Leila. They arrive with a great crowd, and the girls have to squeeze into a ladies' room among many others to adjust their dresses and smooth their hair. They each get a dance program, a little card listing the dances to be played with a space beside each for a partner's signature. The young men will ask to sign these cards, thus reserving each dance. All this is new and thrilling to Leila, and she forgets that only an hour ago she had been shy and full of fear, longing to go home to the country rather than face the ordeal of the ball. Now she finds the dance floor beautiful, the flowers and lanterns "heavenly." After some minutes of awkward hesitation, the young men approach the girls, asking to sign their programs. Various youths ask to sign Leila's program, as does a fat and slightly bald older man who seems out of place in this adolescent crowd.

The dancing begins. Full of enthusiasm, Leila is a little disappointed by the cool and routine small talk of her first two partners. She explains that this is her first ball, but none of her excitement is picked up by them. The third dance is claimed by the fat man, who instantly knows that this is her first ball. After telling her that he has been attending such balls for thirty years, an amazing length of time to Leila, he begins to talk more philosophically about the passage of time. He draws a picture for Leila of herself thirty years later, a staid matron who no longer dances but accompanies her daughter to balls. Hearing this, Leila feels suddenly depressed. She wants to stop dancing. Everything seems spoiled by the fat man's predictions. She gets a little angry at him for ruining her fun and she wants to be back home in the country. But when the music begins again, a new partner guides her on to the dance floor and the magic of the occasion returns. She forgets, for the evening at least, the mournful lesson of the fat man.

MANSFIELD'S STYLE

This story illustrates the modernism of Mansfield's short fiction. The plot is slight, if the story can be said to have any plot at all. The events are presented through the sensibility of the central character; her perceptions and anxieties shape the story. Visions of other places and states of being are thrust into the midst of the story as Leila thinks of her home in the country. The ending is the achievement of a state of feeling rather than a decisive event.

ROBERT GRAVES (1895–1985)

Like the poets of World War I, Robert Graves served in the British army during the war and wrote his first poetry while in service. He left the army in 1917 and married the next year. He then attended Oxford University but left before taking a degree; in 1925 he was given a degree on the basis of his critical writings.

His novel about the war, called *Goodbye to All That*, was published in 1929. Graves had been teaching English in Cairo, Egypt, but the success of this novel enabled him to leave teaching. For the rest of his life he worked as a writer, producing a vast number of essays, poems, novels, and stories. After his first marriage ended he settled in Majorca, an island in the Mediterranean near Spain, with the American poet Laura Riding. They never married but lived and worked together until World War II. Graves then left Majorca to return to England for the war's duration, and Riding went back to the United States. In 1946, with a second wife, he returned to Majorca. He made his home there until his death.

Although Graves thought of himself as a poet, he is best known for his novels, especially for the two historical works based on imperial Rome— *I, Claudius* and *Claudius the God* (1934), both of which were made into a popular television series.

Graves was also interested in biblical scholarship and myth. In *The White Goddess* (1948) he puts forward a theory that the world was originally governed by the female principle, imagined as a moon goddess, who was an inspiration to poets. Graves traces the weaknesses of modern poetry to the displacement of the muse, of the female principle, by the authoritative and patriarchal male principle, which deals in logic and reason only. He called for a return to the "worship" of the White Goddess of myth.

In 1955 and again in 1975, Graves published his *Collected Poems*, as he claims consideration as a major writer not only of historical fiction but also of modern poetry, one who uses colloquial language to explore relationships of love and personal conflicts. Much of his imagery is also drawn from classical myth and biblical and Celtic lore.

"The Devil's Advice to Story-tellers"

This short poem is spoken as if by the devil to a would-be writer of fiction. The advice is both ironic and valid. The modern writer should ignore the rules of the novel that call for coherence, probability, and a seeming authenticity. Instead, the writer should, like a grand liar, make up stories out of odd bits and pieces of observations and random characters, leaving the outcome of the story to work itself out by chance. If the resulting story is pointless and contradictory, that will be exactly right, because human life is without any coherent meaning or moral.

"The Cool Web"

This poem tells how language is a mediator of experience. It contrasts the state of young children, who do not have command of language, to the adult state of articulateness. Children experience physical sensations directly and forcefully because they have not developed language barriers between themselves and experiences. Adults use speech to dull and moderate sensations. In the last stanza, Graves imagines that at death, as the "cool web" of language fails or is cast off, the return of intensity of experience must drive the dying one mad.

"The White Goddess"

This poem celebrates the mythic figure that Graves had introduced in his book of the same title. The speaker is one of those ("we") who scorn to worship the god Apollo, a Greek and Roman god associated with calm and poised manly beauty and with classical order and discipline. Instead, they seek as inspiration an unruly and remote figure, the "sister of the mirage and echo"—that is, one who escapes any direct knowledge. They seek in wild and dangerous places, at the ends of the earth.

The second stanza contains an image of the wildly beautiful goddess as they imagine she would look if they could only find her. This image is strong enough to carry them through experiences of "cruelty" and "betrayal," still seeking her and shaking off all dangers. With shouts of joy they celebrate the Mountain Mother in spring and in a raw November.

"A Slice of Wedding Cake"

This short monologue presents a speaker, perhaps an old man at a wedding, who questions why young women seem to marry "impossible men" who are not worthy of them. He rejects the obvious answer to his question—that women make such marriages out of a "missionary" call to help the men or to improve them. The second and third stanzas describe these men, with their faults and bad behavior, as "dramatic foils," that is, as contrasting types who make the women look better. The last stanza rephrases the question. Perhaps the men are not so bad; perhaps the speaker merely tends to "over-value" women. The poem ends with that question and the answer "It might be so."

STEVIE SMITH (1902–1971)

Florence Margaret Smith wrote under the name Stevie, her childhood nickname. She lived an outwardly ordinary life, working as a secretary while living with and caring for her aunt in Palmer's Green, a London suburb. Smith was known as a clever conversationalist at literary parties in the city. She wrote three novels in the 1930s and 1940s, but she is best known for her poetry, which is original almost to the point of being eccentric. She also illustrated her poetry with unusual line drawings.

The first volume of her poems, *A Good Time Was Had by All* (1937), established her reputation. The best-known of her several later volumes is *Not Waving but Drowning* (1957). Smith's poetry deals with problems of religious belief, sexual anxiety, and suicide in an often comic or whimsical style.

"Not Waving but Drowning"

The two voices in this poem belong to the drowned man and the people on the shore who fail to hear his cry or understand his gesture. Like the people around us who are oblivious to our personal disasters, the people in this poem assumed that the desperate man's arm movements are a joke, a "lark," and that he really needs no help. But the drowned man was in earnest; all his life he had been trying to attract attention and to get help. The bland voice of the self-assured people contrasts with the mournful, despairing moans of the drowned man.

"Thoughts About the Person from Porlock"

This poem alludes to the poet Coleridge's explanation of why he did not complete his famous poetic fragment *Kubla Khan*. Coleridge claimed that the poem came to him in a dream. On awakening, he had begun to write it down, but he was interrupted by a visitor, a "person from Porlock," the neighboring village. After they had discussed some business, the visitor left and Coleridge returned to his writing. He found to his dismay that the memory of the dream was gone; he could make no further progress with the poem.

Smith takes a playful attitude toward Coleridge's story. She entertains some doubts of its validity, guessing that Coleridge was already stuck. She knows, as a poet, how that can happen. She says it is wrong to blame the person from Porlock, but that "often we all do wrong." Coleridge is forgiven. Smith turns her attention to the Person, to whom she gives the name Porson.

She imagines some biographical details and begins to wish that she had such a person to provide an excuse for not finishing her writing. She longs for him as a welcome distraction from her own thoughts. Everyone should welcome the person from Porlock.

In the last stanza, Smith reveals what sort of thoughts she wishes to be distracted from. She is depressed, thinking that God is merely experimenting with human beings and that all one can do is submit, smile, and "get some work to do."

"Pretty"

In this poem Smith plays with the overworked and trite word *pretty*, renewing it to freshness by using it to describe a scene not usually considered pretty. She presents a November landscape, with a pool where the old pike stalks his prey, the water rat survives along the shore, and the owl looks out across the fields. The upland field tilts toward the horizon. Nature does not intend to be pretty; in fact, it has no purpose at all. But the person who moves within the scene can "steal" a look, can see the prettiness and name it as "pretty."

In the final stanza, the speaker looks forward to a time when one is out of nature and done with "humanity." That, she states, would be the prettiest. Death is included among things that can be called pretty.

GEORGE ORWELL (1903–1950)

Born in India into a family of English civil servants, Eric Blair was sent back to England to be educated at Eton, a prestigious school for aristocratic boys. As a scholarship student, he felt the weight of his lower social status. After Eton he went to Burma, where he joined the Imperial Police. His discomfort in this service is captured in his "Shooting the Elephant" and in the novel *Burmese Days* (1934).

When he began to write, he adopted the pen name George Orwell. He retained his interest and sympathy for people of lower economic classes and for exploited people. He struggled to survive at low-paying jobs, first in Paris and later in London. Orwell was drawn to socialist causes and participated as a volunteer in the Spanish Civil War, on the side of the Republicans—that is, the antifascists. But Orwell was not a follower of any one party; he took an independent view and was skeptical of communism as well as of capitalism. He continued to write novels, essays, and political journalism during the 1930s and 1940s.

His most famous books are the political allegory about Stalinism, *Animal Farm* (1945) and his science fiction dystopia *1984* (1949), in which he pictures England under a dictatorship of mechanized bureaucracy. During the time he wrote these political satires, Orwell had been suffering from tuberculosis. He died of the disease in 1950.

"Politics and the English Language"

In 1946, just after the end of World War II, Orwell became dissatisfied with the language of essays and speeches, particularly on political topics. He urges the reader to do something about the vague and dishonest use of language, to reform one's own writing and to reject such language in public statements.

Orwell chose five examples of essays from recent publications by journalists, politicians, and professors. Then he analyzes what these five examples have in common, listing their faults under four main headings: dying metaphors, which create no clear mental image; operators, which substitute padded phrases for simple and direct nouns and verbs; pretentious diction, which dresses up simple statements in foreign or scientific-sounding words; and meaningless words, which have no precise definition but merely carry a vague approval or disapproval. Orwell calls his list "this catalogue of swindles and perversions." He illustrates how awful such language can be by translating a simple and direct passage from the Bible into debased modern English. Why do modern readers use vague and clumsy language? Orwell gives two main reasons. First, it is easier to write if one merely sticks together established, tired phrases, since they come to mind automatically. Second, vague and pretentious language can hide weak ideas or ugly truths and numb the mind, encouraging political conformity. In an example of the right way to write, Orwell observes that an insincere writer turns "to long words and exhausted idioms, like a cuttlefish squirting out ink."

But he insists that the reading and writing public can improve the English language by a conscious effort. One can choose to do better. Near the end of his essay he gives a short list of rules to help any reader who has been convinced that the effort should be made.

Animal Farm

In this modern fable, Orwell satirizes the events of the Russian revolution and the subsequent rise to power of the communist dictatorship.

The farm represents the land that was to become the Soviet Union. Farmer Jones is the czar, who frankly exploits the people (the farm animals) because he has always done so and feels that he has that right. When the animals are driven to revolt, they are led by the intelligent pigs, especially by Snowball (Leon Trotsky) and Napoleon (Joseph Stalin). The plot parallels historical events: the idealistic revolution; the displacement of Snowball by Napoleon; the establishment of a secret police force (the dogs) to enforce conformity to party rule; forced collectivization of the farm and the exploitation of the worker, as represented by the work horse Boxer; and the development of rule by terror. Napoleon, who has used Snowball as a scapegoat and has purged the farm of any possible rivals or dissenters through forced confessions and executions, gradually isolates himself and lives in increasing luxury while the other animals barely subsist. Ultimately, he sells Boxer for a supply of whiskey. He has become more and more like Farmer Jones, even walking on his hind legs, while the enslaved animals live in despair, unable to unite against this new threat. The revolutionary doctrine that "All animals are equal" has been corrupted to read "Some animals are more equal than others."

In the end, Napoleon and his agent Squealer live just like upper class humans, enjoying a banquet, while the starving general populace can hardly remember the old revolutionary ideals. The conclusion does not suggest any grounds for hope.

*T*he writers discussed in this chapter are highly individualistic. Each one pursues the aims of modernism in a different way. All feel free to experiment, to depart radically from the demands of formal realism. They are interested in how the human mind and emotions work in the private realms of thought, memory, and desire. The exception is Orwell, whose primary interest was in public speech, but who expressed that concern in original and idiosyncratic ways.

Selected Readings

Barbera, Jack, and William McBrien. *Stevie: A Biography of Stevie Smith.* New York: Oxford University Press, 1987.

Berkman, Sylvia. *Katherine Mansfield: A Critical Study.* New Haven: Yale University Press, 1951.

Kirkham, Michael. *The Poetry of Robert Graves.* New York: Oxford University Press, 1969.

Meyers, Jeffrey. *A Reader's Guide to George Orwell.* Totowa, NJ: Littlefield, 1977.

Southam, B. C. *A Guide to the Selected Poems of T. S. Eliot.* New York: Harcourt, Brace, Jovanovich, 1969.

Williamson, George. *A Reader's Guide to T. S. Eliot: A Poem-by-Poem Analysis.* New York: Noonday, 1953.

21

Poetry of the Thirties and Forties

1929 MacNeice, *Blind Fireworks*; Ortega y Gasset, *Revolt of the Masses*; in the United States the Great Depression begins

1930 Auden, *Poems*

1932 Auden, *The Orators*; Thomas moves to London; Thurber, *The Seal in the Bedroom and Other Predicaments*

1933 Auden, *The Dance of Death*

1934 Thomas, *Eighteen Poems*; Sayers, *The Nine Tailors*

1935 Auden, *Look, Stranger* and *The Dog Beneath the Skin*; MacNeice, *Poems*

1936 Auden with Christopher Isherwood, *The Ascent of F6*; Thomas, *Twenty-five Poems*; Spanish Civil War begins

1936–1952 George VI reigns

1937 Auden, *On This Island*; Picasso, *Guernica*; Tolkien, *The Hobbit*; Dinesen, *Out of Africa*; Auden leaves Spain to travel

1938 Auden, *Selected Poems* and *The Oxford Book of Light Verse*

1939 Auden becomes citizen of United States; MacNeice, *Autumn Journal*; Thomas, *The Map of Love*; Yeats dies; Great Britain and France declare war on Germany

1940 Auden, *Another Time*; MacNeice, *Selected Poems, 1940* and *Poems 1925–1940*; Thomas, *Portrait of the Artist as a Young Dog*; Germany begins Battle of Britain

1941 MacNeice works for BBC; Woolf commits suicide, Joyce dies; Japan attacks Pearl Harbor; United States enters war against Germany, Italy, and Japan

1943 Thomas, *New Poems*

1944 MacNeice, *Christopher Columbus* and *Springboard: Poems 1941–1944*; Western Allies launch "D-Day" invasion of Normandy

1945 Auden, *The Collected Poetry*; Orwell, *Animal Farm*; United States drops atomic bombs on Japan; World War II ends; United Nations established

1946 Thomas, *Selected Writings* and *Deaths and Entrances*; Auden becomes citizen of United States

1947 Auden, *The Age of Anxiety*; MacNeice, *The Dark Tower*; nationalization of coal industry

1949 MacNeice, *Collected Poems*; in China, Mao Tse-Tung deposes Chinese Nationalists

1951 Auden, *Nones*; Auden libretto for Stravinsky opera, *The Rake's Progress*; Salinger, *The Catcher in the Rye*

1952 MacNeice, *Ten Burnt Offerings*; Thomas, *In Country Sleep*

1952– Reign of Elizabeth II

1953 Thomas, *Collected Poems*; Thomas dies

1954 MacNeice, *Autumn Sequel*; Thomas, *Under Milk Wood* published posthumously; Golding, *Lord of the Flies*

1955 Thomas, unfinished novel *Adventures in the Skin Trade* published posthumously; Universal copyright convention

1956 Auden professor of poetry at Oxford; the Suez Crisis

1957 MacNeice, *Visitations*; Caitlin Thomas biography of Dylan Thomas, *Leftover Life to Kill*; Common Market founded

1960 Auden, *Homage to Clio*

1968 C. Day-Lewis named poet laureate

1972 Betjeman named poet laureate; direct rule by British government in Northern Ireland

1973 Auden dies

1974 Auden, *Thank You Fog* and *Last Poems* published posthumously

1975 Franco dies and monarchy is restored in Spain

The poets of the generation following T. S. Eliot tended to follow two lines of development. First, they were influenced by the political upheavals of the thirties and tended to be liberal in their sympathies. Auden especially became a voice of protest against exploitation and suffering. And second, in his later career, Auden turned toward more personal, autobiographic matters, abandoning the role of political spokesman. His friend MacNeice also left politics behind and focused on the intensity of private experience. MacNeice, like Dylan Thomas, indulged in the rich and rowdy play of language, leaving dry rationality behind in favor of an energetic and highly suggestive but often obscure and seemingly carefree flow of words. Actually, Thomas was a painstaking craftsman, but the lively, vigorous tone of his poems conceals this effort.

W. H. AUDEN (1907–1973)

Wystan Hugh Auden, whose father was a doctor, came from a middle class family in York. Auden went to Oxford University, where he studied and began to write poetry. After leaving Oxford he lived briefly in Germany, where he met his friend and frequent collaborator, the dramatist Christopher Isherwood.

Back in England in the early 1930s, Auden worked as a schoolteacher. He was deeply moved by the social problems in England during the economic depression of the thirties. Like many young intellectuals of that time, Auden was a liberal who saw capitalism as a faltering system of inequalities. He was influenced by the theories of Karl Marx as well as by Sigmund Freud's theories of the psychological basis of the discontents of modern civilization.

Auden volunteered to serve with the leftist Republicans in the Spanish Civil War. However, he became repelled by the excessive violence of both sides, and he left Spain to travel to Iceland, to China, and finally to the United States, where he settled and became a citizen in 1946.

By this time Auden had written a significant body of poetry, much of it dealing with the chaos of public life. He and Isherwood had also written several plays. The poetry of his American period became increasingly concerned with human isolation. Turning away from social and political issues, Auden regained an interest in Christian themes.

In 1956 Auden returned to England as a professor of poetry at Oxford, but after four years he came back to New York. He spent his last years in New York City and in his summer home in Austria.

"On This Island"

This is the title poem of Auden's 1937 volume of poems. It is a lyric poem expressing frank pleasure at the island image that England presents. Along the south, the cliffs rise up abruptly from the sea; the island seems to stand up distinct from the moving sea, which cannot wear it away. In the last stanza, the ships leaving England seem as small as "floating seeds" when seen from the cliffs. Then the point of view shifts and the poet looks back from a ship to see England seem to float away in the distance.

"Spain 1937"

In 1936 a left-wing Marxist government was elected in Spain. The rightist political faction reacted with a rebellion that developed into a full-scale civil war. Most European and American liberals were sympathetic to the Republican leftist group. They saw the war as a battle between the progressive, democratic forces of the new left and the old guard, rightist fascist forces. Many young intellectuals volunteered to fight in the war; Auden went as an ambulance attendant. However, he became disillusioned by the Republicans' corruption and misuse of power.

"Spain 1937" was written before Auden's brief stay in Spain. Auden places the conflict in a historical context, as a painful but necessary struggle marking the transition from the old order of the past to a new era of peace and progress. These three separate stages are called "yesterday" (the past from ancient times down to the twentieth century), "today" (the current struggle), and "to-morrow" (the uncertain future).

STRUCTURE OF THE POEM

The first twenty-four lines of the poem present a series of sequential historical glimpses of moments in the evolution of civilization: the development of writing and mathematics, mechanical inventions, navigation, and the gradual displacement of superstitions with rational explanations. Meanwhile, history seems to be falling into disorder and chaos; some new organizing power is needed.

In lines 40 through 44, humankind calls upon God, who has created the vast and impressive order of the natural world, to descend and create order. He is called upon as a "dove" (merciful spirit), a "furious papa" (vengeful spirit), and a "mild engineer" (the impersonal first cause).

In lines 47 through 56 God answers that people themselves must choose whether the future will be "the Just City" or a "suicide pact." Spain is the place and 1937 is the time for that decision to be made. Therefore, those who have hope for the future have come to "present their lives" in the struggle.

Glimpses of the possible future are shown in lines 69 through 80. It is a future of technical and scientific progress, making for a more peaceful and leisurely life. But the poet returns to the present struggle, describing both the risks of the battlefront and the efforts to mobilize support by writing pamphlets and attending meetings.

At the end of the poem, history's decision is still pending. The fighters are "left alone with [their] day," facing the possibility of defeat. In actuality, the fascists, led by Franco, did indeed win and continued in power until Franco's death in 1975.

"Musée des Beaux Arts"

In this short poem, the speaker is standing in a museum, looking at a well-known painting by the Flemish Renaissance painter Pieter Brueghel that shows the countryside with many human and animal figures and a portion of the sea with a small ship in the distance. The white legs of a young man are seen above the water, as if he has just fallen in.

This figure is Icarus, the son of the legendary Daedalus who made wings of wax and feathers so that both of them could fly. Icarus flew too near the sun and his wings melted, causing him to fall into the sea and drown. As the speaker contemplates this painting, he sees that the Old Master, the great Renaissance painter Brueghel, realized how little attention people pay to the sufferings of others. He notices that all the other creatures, adult and child, horse and dog, are unaware or unconcerned with the strange event of "a boy falling out of the sky." The sun shines on, just the same as before, and the little ship calmly sails on its way. Personal pain or martyrdom do not cause the rest of the world to stop in awe, or even to pause.

"Lullaby"

This song is not a mother's lullaby to a child but a lover's song to his beloved. It expresses disillusionment and full awareness that the present moment of love will surely not last. Eternal faithfulness is only a sweet dream, an illusion that lends enchantment to the moment, and cannot stand the light of day. But the truth that love will pass should not intrude upon the beauty of the present moment; the "noons of dryness" will come soon enough.

"In Memory of W. B. Yeats (d. Jan. 1939)"

This elegy is Auden's tribute to the great and influential Irish poet Yeats, whose long poetic career ended in 1939. Auden cites the moment of death as the moment when a poet is transformed from a living person into a body of poetry that lives on in the lives of his followers, those who continue to read the poet's works.

Auden begins by describing the cold and snowy day of Yeats's death. Then Auden imagines Yeats's last day alive and the gradual process by which death emptied his body of sensations. When all "feeling failed," Yeats "became his admirers," that is, he now exists in the world only in the attention that is paid to his works. His existence will scatter around the world, changing as readers reinterpret for themselves the images of Yeats's personal symbolic code.

In part 2, the speaker remarks on the independence of poetry. Yeats's poems survived all the various changes and problems of his own life. Now his poetry will go on among other lives, surviving as "a way of happening, a mouth" speaking to new generations.

Part 3 is a final funeral song in rhymed four-beat lines. It contrasts the present bleak times to the healing influence of Yeats's poetry, which will teach humankind to rejoice and praise.

"In Praise of Limestone"

This is a topographical poem, that is, one in praise of a particular place. Auden is looking back on the landscape of Yorkshire that he knew and enjoyed as a boy. Since limestone eventually dissolves as water runs over it, the countryside is pleasantly irregular, with softened edges and many pools, caves, gullies, and odd shapes that have been carved out by centuries of running water. The varied shapes are inviting to rambling boys and bands of hikers, who are never far from shade and a cool stream. Local boys are "born lucky" because they do not have to endure a neighborhood of rough volcanoes, barren hot desert, or damp jungle. If these boys "go bad" despite their good luck, it is "incomprehensible."

But the best as well as the worst local boys do leave this beautiful place for "immoderate soils." The best are lured away by the prospect of martyrdom in hard "granite wastes." The worst—ambitious—go off to lands of clay and gravel to fight and to construct huge monuments to themselves. And the truly reckless go to no soil at all; they go instead to sea, which "promises nothing."

In the final stanza the poet considers his own relationship with the limestone landscape. Although it seems "seedy" and "backward," and although the poet has tried to escape to realms more grand and unpredictable, he comes back eventually to this scene. When he tries to depict in a poem a "faultless lover" or "the life to come," the images to which he returns are of the shapes and sounds of the "limestone landscape."

LOUIS MACNEICE (1907–1963)

The son of a Protestant clergyman in Ireland, MacNeice was sent to England to study. At Oxford University he became friends with W. H. Auden; the two later traveled to Iceland together. MacNeice studied classical literature at Oxford and then taught for a few years at other colleges, but his main career was as a writer and producer of programs for the British Broadcasting Corporation (the BBC), Great Britain's public radio network. During the 1930s and 1940s he wrote radio dramas and documentaries for the BBC as well as poetry.

In his poetry he used the classical forms with which he was very familiar, but he also included some of the sound patterns he remembered from Irish folk literature. MacNeice's last volume of poetry was published in 1963, the year of his death.

"Sunday Morning"

This fourteen-line lyric with rhyming couplets is a variation on the sonnet form. The first part describes the pleasures of a morning off work spent playing music or tinkering with a car. These acts are ends in themselves; they exist apart from the ordinary obligations of the weekdays. The poet recommends that we enjoy such pleasures. But in the last four lines, the tolling of church bells seems to cancel out the pleasures of Sunday, reminding us of the dreary responsibilities of "weekday time."

"Carrickfergus"

In this autobiographical poem, MacNeice describes the small Irish coastal town where he lived as a boy. The town is a noisy industrial harbor and mill town, full of the Irish working poor. But it also contains a middle-class Scottish neighborhood and a walled Norman castle and church at the edge of the harbor. There as a boy the poet sat in the front row, under the gaze of the portraits of an ancient family of aristocratic rulers. This old order of society—the poor, the middle class, and the faded aristocracy—is invaded by a new force at the outbreak of World War I as a huge contingent of soldiers sets up camp at the edge of town and begins to train for war. As a boy of only eight, the poet observes them in wonder. When he goes away to school in England, he finds the boat and train full of soldiers. He imagines that the wartime conditions of rationing and total preoccupation with the war effort have become the normal way of life and will go on forever. At school the boy's world changes again, becoming restricted to the narrow routines of a boarding school. The worlds of the mill town and the noisy soldiers are far away. The poem traces the boy's transition from place to place and from infancy to boyhood. In each situation, he finds himself shut off from the vital centers of action.

"Bagpipe Music"

This rollicking lyric suggests rowdy Irish barroom songs. It is full of allusions to the ordinary experiences of people working, getting drunk, making love, and bearing children. The tone is jolly and irreverent. The newly delivered mother looks at her fifth child and declares, "I'm through with over-production." But underneath the flippant and joking tone, the idea emerges that all of life's apparent joys and satisfactions are brief and uncertain. After a life of effort, there is no "profit" but only a small pension or the poor relief.

In the final line, the "glass" is the barometer. The barometer falls, indicating rough weather to come. Even if one rebels by breaking the glass, the bad weather will still come. Life is made up of losses and accidents; all we can hope for are some moments of relief or pleasure along the way.

DYLAN THOMAS (1914–1953)

Thomas was born and educated in Wales, a mountainous and relatively uncultivated land to the west of England. His father was an English schoolmaster. After finishing school, Thomas worked as a journalist, first in Wales and later in London. He had begun to write poetry while still a student and published his first volume of poems in 1934. The poems were notable for their rich enthusiasm and what was seen as a wild romanticism, although Thomas was actually a careful and painstaking craftsman.

Thomas also wrote essays and short stories. He developed a reputation for heavy drinking and for being an effective, emotional reader of his own poems. Both his personality and his poems were imbued with exuberance and energy.

In 1950 Thomas began to make successful tours in the United States, reading his poems to enthusiastic audiences. In 1953, while on one of these tours, Thomas died suddenly from an overdose of alcohol.

"The Force That Through the Green Fuse Drives the Flower"

This poem provides a good example of Thomas's energetic style. The long first line, full of stressed monosyllables, imitates the forceful pressure of growth, both in a flower and in a person, such as the speaker. Thomas celebrates the unity of all forms of life; all are moved by the similar forces of birth, growth, aging, and ripening toward death.

In each stanza the poet compares a force of the natural world—plant, water, earth, or wind—with a force within himself. Also, in each stanza, he is "dumb to tell"—that is, he sees how his life and the motions of nature are the same, but there is no means of communication between himself and them. However, just as time brings death to all others, he senses the beginnings of death in himself.

"Poem in October"

Thomas had early success as a poet; his first two volumes were published while he was still in his twenties.

In this poem he looks at himself at the age of thirty, a point between the summer of youth and the autumn of maturity. In this richly descriptive poem, the poet sets out from a little seacoast town early in the morning, before the town is awake. It is raining in the town, but as he walks upward into the surrounding hills, he emerges into sunlight. Looking back, he sees the town small and misty in the distance. He is surrounded by singing birds. The air changes to summer; the clouds clear away. The return of sunny weather carries him back to the days of his childhood, to the joyous walks with his mother through the same landscape, when the abundance of nature spoke to his boyish imagination.

He becomes that boy again: "his tears burned my cheeks and his heart moved in mine" (line 52). The joy that he felt as a child has come back to him with the change of weather. He hopes for a similar return next year to the "heart's truth" of childhood.

"Fern Hill"

This, one of Thomas's most famous poems, is named for the Welsh farm of his aunt where he spent his summers during boyhood and where he was "happy as the grass was green."

The farm is presented with extreme subjectivity as the memory of his boyhood experience. Childlike, he sees himself as the ruler of the farm, as its prince and lord, as its "huntsman and herdsman." When he went to sleep at night, the farm vanished, and when he awoke, it reappeared.

The farm is his paradise, fresh and innocent as the Garden of Eden. The days spent roaming and playing among the fields and barns seemed to be timeless; the boy was oblivious to any passage of time or to the possibility that this experience would ever end.

"Do Not Go Gentle into That Good Night"

This poem is in the form of a *vilanelle*, a French form of five three-line stanzas and a concluding four-line stanza. The first and third lines of the first stanza are repeated in the second through the fifth stanzas, and the last stanza repeats both of them. So much repetition creates a mood of great intensity.

Thomas uses this intensity to create the emotion of raging resistance to death, which is seen from the point of view of the one dying, who is Thomas's father, as "the dying of the light." Even though the night of death may be gentle, the dying person should hold on to life and live it fully until its last moment, grasping for insight or wisdom. The "fierce tears" of the final stanza capture the poem's violent yoking together of rage and gentleness.

"A Refusal to Mourn the Death, by Fire, of a Child in London"

Thomas begins this anti-elegy by presenting his concept of the continuous flow and change of all creatures. Each "bird beast and flower" comes out of darkness, lives, and returns in a constant cycle. He himself will return to take on the form of a drop of water or a grain of corn. Therefore, he does not mourn the child's death. Her death is human and innocent, not to be degraded by any utterances of grief. She, "London's daughter," has merely rejoined the vital earth, the "dark veins of her mother" earth, over which the Thames River glides.

In the final line, the consolation of traditional elegies is stated as a promise of new and continuous existence, because "After the first death, there is no other."

*T*he poetry of the 1930s and 1940s, influenced by the earlier experiments of T. S. Eliot and William Butler Yeats, became more privately allusive and more private and idiosyncratic in its imagery. Poets were accused of being deliberately obscure or too difficult because readers found themselves plunged into strange, illogical realms with no familiar landmarks or narrative line. Although Auden, MacNeice, and Thomas were all liberals and, to some extent, critics of political and social conditions, they also retreated into highly personal formulations of their own experiences.

In the poems of this era, the speaking voice is often tough and cynical and never sentimental. When the speakers are cheerful, there is often an accompanying rowdiness, as if they are daring to go on living in a world that God has apparently forgotten.

Selected Readings

Callan, Edward. *Auden: A Carnival of Intellect*. New York: Oxford University Press, 1983.

Marsack, Robyn. *The Cave of Making: The Poetry of Louis MacNeice*. Oxford: Clarendon, 1982.

Maud, Ralph N. *Entrances to Dylan Thomas' Poetry*. Pittsburgh: University of Pittsburgh Press, 1963.

McKinnon, William T. *Apollo's Blended Dream: A Study of the Poetry of Louis MacNeice*. London: Oxford University Press, 1971.

Moynihan, William T. *The Craft and Art of Dylan Thomas*. Ithaca: Cornell University Press, 1966.

Spears, Monroe K. *Auden: A Collection of Critical Essays*. Englewood Cliffs, NJ: Prentice-Hall, 1964.

22

Modern Drama

1944 Beckett, *Watt*; Western Allies launch "D-Day" invasion of Normandy

1945 Orwell, *Animal Farm*; United States drops atomic bombs on Japan; World War II ends; United Nations established

1951 Beckett, *Molloy*

1952– Reign of Elizabeth II; Beckett, *Waiting for Godot*

1956 Beckett, *Malone Dies*; Osborne, *Look Back in Anger*; the Hungarian revolt

1957 Pinter, *The Room* and *The Dumb Waiter*; Osborne, *The Entertainer*; Soviet Union launches *Sputnik*

1958 Beckett, *Endgame*; Pinter, *The Birthday Party*

1959 Beckett, *Krapp's Last Tape*; Castro takes power in Cuba

1960 Beckett, *The Unnameable*; Pinter, *A Night Out* and *The Caretaker*; first birth control pills

1961 Beckett, *Happy Days*; Soviets put first man in space

1963 Beckett, *Play*

1964 Pinter, *The Homecoming*; Dr. Martin Luther King, Jr., receives Nobel Peace Prize

1966 Beckett, *Imagination Dead Imagine* and *Eh Foe*; Stoppard, *Rosencrantz and Guildenstern Are Dead*

1968 Stoppard, *The Real Inspector Hound*; student uprisings in France; in the United States, Dr. King assassinated

1969 Beckett awarded Nobel Prize for literature

1971 Pinter, *Old Times*

1972 Beckett, *The Lost Ones* and *Breath and Other Short Plays*; Stoppard, *Jumpers*

1973 Beckett, *First Love* and *Not I*; Vietnam war ends

1974 Stoppard, *Travesties*

1975 Pinter, *No Man's Land*

1976 Beckett, *That Time*, *Footfalls,* and *Ghost Trio*; Stoppard, *Dirty Linen*

1977 Beckett, *But the Clouds*; Stoppard, *Every Good Boy Deserves Favour*

1978 Pinter, *Betrayal*; Stoppard, *Night and Day*

1980 Beckett, *Rockaby*; in the United States, John Lennon is murdered

1981 Stoppard, *On the Razzle*; Egyptian President Sadat is assassinated

1982 Beckett, *Quad* and *Catastrophe*; Pinter, *A Kind of Alaska*; Stoppard, *The Real Thing*; war with Argentina in Falkland Islands

1983 Beckett, *What Where*

1985 Ted Hughes named poet laureate; Stoppard, *Rough Crossing*; Gorbachev becomes First Secretary of the Soviet Union

1987 Stoppard, *Hapgood*

1988 Pinter, *Mountain Language*

1989 Beckett dies; Berlin Wall falls; *Voyager 2* encounters Neptune

Early in the twentieth century, George Bernard Shaw attempted to make the English theater into an arena for the play of ideas. Plays about social and political issues, however were unable to hold a mainstream audience. Radical and experimental dramas remained on the fringes, while commercially successful plays followed conventional formulaic plots. The financially successful theater offered comedies of middle class life, while the influence of continental expressionist drama was felt only in small, independent antiestablishment theater companies.

After World War II, however, things began to change. Government financing of small repertory companies made possible a wider range of productions. While commercial plays continued to be produced in London, provincial theaters opened possibilities for young, protesting playwrights.

One of the group known as the "angry young men," John Osborne wrote plays about the alienation of young men from the petty respectabilities of middle class society. His play Look Back in Anger *(1956) is the most notable play of this type. On the other hand, some more experimental playwrights, such as Samuel Beckett, Harold Pinter, and Tom Stoppard, influenced by existentialism and the concept of life as absurd, wrote plays that attempted to dramatize the elemental psychological forces and absurd situations of modern life. In either case, mere entertainment gave way to a more forceful, ironic, and provocative drama.*

SAMUEL BECKETT (1906–1989)

An Irishman, Beckett was born near Dublin and educated there, attending Trinity College. Like his predecessor James Joyce, he studied languages. Beckett taught English in Paris and then French in Dublin. In the meantime he traveled in Europe, living frugally on a small annuity. He met James Joyce in Paris in 1929 and became the older man's devoted friend and assistant.

Beckett settled permanently in Paris and began to write in French, later translating his novels and plays into English. His novels of the early 1950s, *Molloy, Malone Dies*, and *The Unnameable* did not attract many readers, being obscure and difficult monologues that mingled comic absurdity and despair. But in 1952 Beckett's play *Waiting for Godot* made him famous as a witty and powerful writer of the Theater of the Absurd. His subsequent dramas continued in the same mode, featuring weary, grotesque, and beaten figures who retell obsessively the events and frustrations of their lives. Many, such as *Krapp's Last Tape* and *Happy Days*, are monologues of characters in extreme situations, pushed to the edge. Beckett's dramatic pieces of recent decades have been brief and minimal. In *Not I*, for example, the audience sees only a lighted mouth speaking out of a totally dark stage.

This sparing use of theatrical means influenced later playwrights, including Harold Pinter and Tom Stoppard. Beckett was awarded the Nobel Prize for literature in 1969. He continued to write, including radio plays, into old age.

Waiting for Godot

Written in French as *En attendant Godot*, this was Beckett's first play. It revolutionized the expectations of the British theater audience.

On a bare stage two tramps, Estrogon and Vladimir, are waiting on a road for the arrival of a mysterious but important person named Godot. They are not sure why they are waiting or what will happen when he arrives. Godot's identity is not to be pinned down. When asked who Godot is, Beckett is said to have answered, "If I knew, I would have said so in the play." Their state of continued uncertainty causes Estrogon and Vladimir to alternate between moods of hope and despair. They try to pass the time by making jokes and playing word games.

At the end of each of the two acts a boy comes to deliver the message that Godot will not come until tomorrow. Estrogon and Vladimir agree to leave, but they do not. Much of the stage business and verbal cross-talk follows the style of a vaudeville stage comedian or circus clown.

The personalities of the two tramps are complementary. Vladimir is the more practical and confident of the two; he holds out more hope that Godot will come. Estrogon is more dreamy and forgetful.

In each act the tramps meet two other characters passing along the road. These are Pozzo, the rich master, and his slave, Lucky. The slave is burdened by a load of his master's possessions. While he is submissive, Lucky is also more clever and intelligent than his master. In Act 1 they are on their way to a fair where Pozzo will sell Lucky. When they return in Act 2, Pozzo is blind and Lucky is without speech. Lucky has not been sold, and Pozzo complains of the burden of his mere presence. They are locked into a sadomasochistic relationship that makes the relationship of Vladimir and Estrogon look much superior. They are at least joined in waiting, and waiting is what life is all about, at least in this play by Beckett.

Happy Days   The main character in *Happy Days* is the middle-aged woman Winnie, who in Act 1, is buried to just above her waist in a barren mound of earth. The second character is Willie, her husband, the top of whose head is seen behind the mound. Winnie's long and rambling speech of reminiscence and idle comment is addressed to Willie, but she is not sure he's always listening. Though he responds only occasionally and briefly, each response makes her happy to know that he is still there and at least sometimes paying attention. She can see him only with difficulty by twisting backward and toward the right. Winnie brushes her teeth and examines the miscellaneous contents of her huge handbag which lies nearby on the mound. It holds, among other things, a gun with which Willie had intended to kill himself. Now he reads bits from a newspaper while she recalls past days of courtship and romance.

Winnie's actions and speech seem to be a routine or ritual, as if she has said these things and examined this bag the same way many times. Minor pleasures make her day happy; for example, Willie's jokes or a pleasant memory of her youth, when she was beautiful and lovable. Her mind is full of garbled bits of old poems and songs. She longs for something to happen, but she does not really expect it to. She recalls that once a strange couple walked by, and the man asked why Willie didn't dig her out. As the day ends, she is happy and intends to sing, but then she decides to pray. But she neither sings nor prays.

In Act 2, Winnie is buried in the same mound, now up to her neck. Her bag is still nearby, but she cannot reach for it. Her motions are mostly of the eyes, from side to side or to the front. Willie is not in sight at first, and she is concerned for him. The gun is lying conspicuously on her mound. She frets about losing her mind. She tells a childish story of a girl and her wax doll, but interrupts herself, saying anxiously, "I hope nothing is amiss."

When Willie appears, he crawls on all fours partway up her mound, but then slides back. His presence cheers and reassures Winnie; she finally sings her song. It has been another happy day. No matter how much her life is reduced, Winnie keeps alive on her memories and imaginings.

HAROLD PINTER (1930–)

The son of a Jewish tailor, Harold Pinter was born in London, where he studied to become an actor. He began an acting career as a member of a touring company that performed Shakespearian plays. He later became part of a repertory company. His first play, *The Room* (1957), was written for performance at the University of Bristol. This was quickly followed by another one-act play, *The Dumb Waiter*. In these first plays, Pinter established his essential form: two people together in a room talk absurdly, with no effective communication, while they await some threatening arrival from outside the room.

Pinter's first great success was *The Birthday Party* (1958), a three-act play that was produced in a commercial theater in London. Its audiences were puzzled at first, but soon became fascinated. Subsequently, Pinter wrote plays for television and radio, as well as screenplays.

His most important stage dramas are *The Caretaker* (1960) and *The Homecoming* (1964). He has received many drama awards. Though at first Pinter's plays appear to be more realistic than Beckett's, the closed room in which Pinter's characters exist is suggestive of multiple allegorical interpretations. The dialogue, usually consisting of seemingly trivial chatter and random remarks, comes to be perceived as concealing an unspoken range of fears and neurotic fantasies, so that even the pauses and silences resonate with anxiety and dread. The comic turns horrible and tragic.

The Dumb Waiter

A dumb waiter is a small elevator once used to carry dishes and food between a downstairs kitchen and an upstairs dining room. It is called "dumb" because it cannot speak.

As the play begins, two men are waiting in a room furnished with two beds on either side of the shaft and the opening for the dumb waiter. The men are two paid assassins who have come to do a "job" and expect their orders at any moment. Ben, the more confident of the two occupies himself by reading a newspaper. Gus, is trying to make tea, but he has no coin to put into the meter that provides gas to heat the teakettle. The men argue absurdly about whether one says "Light the gas" or "Light the kettle." Their silly quarrels seem to mask a growing tension and anxiety about the "job." Ben examines and prepares his gun. Suddenly noises come from the shaft as the dumb waiter descends. It contains written orders, but these are for food, not for a killing. Baffled, they send up the bits of food that Gus has brought in his bag, Soon more elaborate orders for food come down. They do not know what to do.

Gus discovers a speaking tube beside the shaft. Ben talks to someone above, who is complaining about the food. Then Ben rehearses Gus in the procedure they will use to assassinate the victim when he comes through the door. Gus seems inattentive and distracted. As Gus goes out to the lavatory, Ben reads the final order, which has come down in the dumb waiter. Ben is then instructed through the speaking tube to employ the "normal method." When the door opens, it is Gus who enters. He is to be the victim. The curtain falls as the two men stare at each other in recognition.

TOM STOPPARD (1937–)

Born in Czechoslovakia, the son of a physician, Stoppard came to England with his mother after his father's death. When his mother remarried, he took the last name of his stepfather. Stoppard worked first as a journalist but began to write plays in the early 1960s.

His important early success was *Rosencrantz and Guildenstern Are Dead* (1966). Using two minor characters from Shakespeare's *Hamlet*, Stoppard explored the workings of chance in the lives of two ordinary men who are unknowingly caught up in the plots and counterplots of the powerful. In later comedies, including *Travesties* and *The Real Inspector Hound*, Stoppard used established plays as points of departure.

Stoppard has more recently written plays for radio and television, as well as screenplays. His later dramas deal with more serious philosophical and political issues while remaining comic in tone.

The Real Inspector Hound

The Mousetrap, a clever play by the famous mystery writer Agatha Christie, has been performed in London for decades. In his farce *The Real Inspector Hound* Stoppard parodies some of the style and plotting of that play, as well as conventionally written mystery stories in general. At the start of the play two theater critics, Moon and Birdboot, have joined to watch and review *The Real Inspector Hound*, which will be interrupted at regular intervals while they share their comments with the audience. Moon is a substitute reviewer, a second to the regular reviewer, Higgs. Moon is preoccupied with his rivalry with Higgs and with his desire to take over as the first-string critic. Birdboot is preoccupied with his desire to have an affair with one of the young actresses; he intends to praise the play to promote her career and win her gratitude and affection. Meanwhile, Birdboot proclaims his fidelity to his wife, Myrtle, and claims to be shocked by scandal-mongers who accuse him of an undue interest in young and pretty actresses.

On the stage, a dead body lies near a settee, but none of the characters notices it until the play-within-a-play is considerably advanced.

The setting is an aristocratic country house that is, implausibly, located on a remote spit of land frequently shrouded by fog. The mechanics of the mystery plot are obvious and the dialogue is trite. Radio messages report a madman on the loose. The servant overhears characters threatening to kill each other. The two leading ladies are rivals for the love of one young man who has popped in unexpectedly. A wheelchair-bound brother-in-law goes off to clean his gun. Yet Moon and Birdboot, talking in the arty jargon of the literary critics, praise the play as subtle and deep. When Inspector Hound, the local policeman, shows up, no one is aware of any crime, but before leaving he happens to step on the dead body, quite to everyone's surprise and embarrassment.

During the intermission of the play-within-a-play, Moon is contemplating murdering his superior, Higgs, when the stage phone rings. Birdboot's wife is calling to complain of neglect. Having entered the stage to speak with his wife, Birdboot is caught up in the action as a preceding scene begins again. He is being thrust into the role of the young man. He goes through the scene again, with variations that indicate he is playing both himself, the flirtatious critic, and the play's hero Simon, who had already been shot at the end of the preceding act.

At a crucial moment, Birdboot discovers that the original corpse is the dead Higgs, thus involving Moon in the play. When Moon tries to retreat to his front row seat, he finds Inspector Hound and the murdered hero Simon. All semblance of separating art and reality breaks down as the brother-in-law stands up from his wheelchair, and takes off a mask, revealing himself as the real Inspector Hound. He shoots the fleeing Moon, then further reveals that he is also the long lost husband of the leading lady, newly recovered from years of amnesia. Moon dies, convinced that he has been murdered by the next substitute in line for the job of drama critic.

The whole farce involves several layers of illusion and the intermingling of different kinds of artifice, with very funny results.

The revival of the drama in England in the 1950s and 1960s was largely the work of playwrights who were willing to depart from the prevailing realism or naturalism of social class conflict and from the artificial conventions of drawing room comedy. The playwrights were influenced by experimental drama in Germany, Norway, and France. They tended to pare down situations to those involving a few desperate characters and to deal with elemental feelings of grief, anxiety, and regret. Their plays puzzled audiences. These playwrights did not cater to popular tastes but made demands on the audience's powers of perception and concentration. Beckett and Pinter presented scenes of bleak agony, depicting life reduced to its minimum drives and frustrations. Stoppard, more playful than Beckett, mocked conventional ideas of plotting, turning the conventions of cause and effect into an absurd game.

Selected Readings

Cahn, Victor L. *Beyond Absurdity: The Plays of Tom Stoppard*. Rutherford, NJ: Fairleigh Dickinson University Press, 1979.

Fletcher, Beryl S. *A Student's Guide to the Plays of Samuel Beckett*. London: Faber, 1978.

Friedman, Melvin J., ed. *Samuel Beckett Now: Critical Approaches to His Novels, Poetry, and Plays*. Chicago: University of Chicago Press, 1970.

Gale, Steven H. *Butter's Going Up: A Critical Analysis of Harold Pinter's Work.* Durham, NC: Duke University Press, 1977.

Ganz, Arthur, ed. *Pinter: A Collection of Critical Essays.* Englewood Cliffs, NJ: Prentice-Hall, 1972.

Hayman, Ronald. *Tom Stoppard.* London: Heinemann, 1977.

Kenner, Hugh. *A Reader's Guide to Samuel Beckett.* New York: Farrar, Straus, 1973.

Smith, Elton Edward. *The Angry Young Men of the Thirties.* Carbondale: Southern Illinois University Press, 1975.

Trussler, Simon. *The Plays of Harold Pinter: An Assessment.* London: Gollancz, 1973.

23

Contemporary Trends

1945 Larkin, *The North Ship*; United States drops atomic bombs on Japan; World War II ends

1946 Larkin, *Jill*; Lessing moves to London

1947 Larkin, *A Girl in Winter*; India becomes independent

1949 Orwell, *1984*; Soviet Union explodes atomic bomb

1950 Lessing, *The Grass Is Singing*

1952 Reign of Elizabeth II begins; Lessing, first of *Children of Violence: Martha Quest*

1954 Gunn studies at Stanford University, California; Gunn, *Fighting Terms* and *Poems*; Lessing, second of *The Children of Violence: A Proper Marriage*; in United States, Supreme Court outlaws school segregation

1955 Larkin, *The Less Deceived*; polio vaccine developed

1956 *New Lines* anthology edited by Conquest includes poems by Larkin; group of poets come to be known as "the Movement"; in the United States, Elvis Presley's first TV appearance

1957 Gunn, *The Sense of Movement*; Hughes, *The Hawk in the Rain*

1958 Lessing, third of *The Children of Violence: A Ripple from the Storm*

1960 Hughes, *Lupercal*; first successful laser developed

1961 Hill, *The Enclosure*; Hughes, *Meet My Folks*

1962 Lessing, *The Golden Notebook*

1963 Hill, *Do Me a Favour*; Hughes, *Earth Owl and Other Moon People*; in the United States, President Kennedy assassinated; Beatles tour U.S.A.

1964 Larkin, *The Whitsun Weddings*

1965 Lessing, fourth of *The Children of Violence: Landlocked*; first space walk

1967 Hughes, *Wodwo*; Arab-Israeli "Six-Day War"

1968 Hill, *Gentlemen and Ladies*; in United States, Dr. Martin Luther King, Jr., and Robert Kennedy assassinated

1969 Hill, *A Change for the Better*; Lessing, *The Four Gated City*; Americans land on the Moon

1970 Hill, *I'm The King of The Castle*; Hughes, *Crow*

1971 Gunn, *Moly*; Hill, *Strange Meeting* and *The Albatross*; Hughes, *Poems* and *Eat Crow*; Lessing, *Briefing for a Descent into Hell*

1972 Hill, *The Bird of Night* and *The Custodian*

1973 Hill, *A Bit of Singing and Dancing*; Hughes, *Prometheus on his Crag*; Larkin Editor, *The Oxford Book of Twentieth-Century English Verse*; Vietnam war ends

1974 Hill, *In the Springtime of the Year*; Hughes, *Spring Summer Autumn Winter*; Larkin, *High Windows*; Lessing, *A Small Personal Voice: Essays, Reviews, Interviews*

1975 Hughes, *Cavebirds*; International Women's Year

1976 Gunn, *Jack Straw's Castle* and *My Sad Captains*; *Viking II* lands on Mars

1977 Hughes, *Gaudete*

1979 Gunn, *Selected Poems, 1950–1975*; Hughes, *Remains of Elmet* and *Moortown*; Margaret Thatcher first woman prime minister of Great Britain; Americans taken hostage in Iran

1982 Gunn, *Passages of Joy*

1983 Hill, *The Woman in Black: A Ghost Story*; Hughes, *River*; Larkin, *Required Writing*

1984 Lessing, *The Diary of Jane Somers*; Ted Hughes named poet laureate; AIDS virus identified

1985 Hughes, *Season Songs*; Larkin dies

1986 Hughes, *Flowers and Insects*; American space shuttle *Challenger* explodes; Soviet nuclear disaster at Chernobyl

1988 Lessing, *The Making of the Representative for Planet 8* made into an opera with music by Philip Glass

1990 Reunification of Germany

1991 Persian Gulf war; Union of Soviet Socialist Republic (USSR) dissolves

*I*n the second half of the twentieth century, poets and novelists have tended to move away from the wild excitement generated by such poets of the forties as Dylan Thomas. Contemporary poets see the state of the world as precarious and threatened. One earlier group of writers at Oxford, headed by Philip Larkin and Kingsley Amis and known as "the Movement," faced the global conflicts and uncertainties of the Cold War era by trying to regain a sense of rational control. In their restraint and formal convention they were similar to the neoclassical poets of the eighteenth century. "The Movement" soon disbanded as its members began to explore their individual paths.

The contemporary poet Ted Hughes focuses on the violence of nature, while prose writer Doris Lessing depicts the violence of social conflict. Thus writers of this era do not form a coherent group, except that all take a pessimistic, and rather sardonic view of contemporary life.

DORIS LESSING (1919–)

Born in Persia, now Iran, Doris Taylor moved in childhood to a farm in southern Rhodesia, now Zimbabwe. As an adolescent she worked at several low-level jobs. By the time she was thirty, she had become a political activist, married, divorced, remarried, borne several children, and written her first novel. (She writes under the surname of her second husband.) After divorcing once again and moving to England, where she published her novel, Lessing began a prolific writing career, producing novels, short stories, and essays.

Lessing again remarried, this time to a liberal and a feminist. She wrote a series of five semiautobiographical novels known collectively as *The Children of Violence*, describing the development of Martha Quest, a young white woman growing up in Africa.

Her experimental novel *The Golden Notebook* (1962) explores the lives of single women in England, using the device of a writer who records several versions of her own life in several different notebooks. Lessing continues to be a productive and innovative writer. She has turned to the genres of science fiction and horror to study the psychological experiences of people in the modern age—mental fragmentation, suffering, breakdown, and survival.

"To Room Nineteen"

In this rather long short story, Lessing studies the effects of modern life on a woman who does not successfully deal with the stresses it causes. The story's opening sentences announce the topic as "a failure in intelligence" of a marriage. Marriage is seen not as an intense emotional or sexual bond but as a relationship based on intelligence—on being "sensible."

The story is told in a cool, abstract, and analytical tone, as if it could describe any number of middle class marriages or modern marriage in general. The narrator follows the thoughts of Susan, a young professional cartoonist, during her marriage to Matthew Rawlings. Early in the marriage they sensibly move out of their city apartment to a suburban house, where over a period of time Susan gives birth to four children. She puts her career aside to raise the children (with the assistance of Mrs. Parkes, a daily domestic helper) in the big, comfortable white house with a pleasant garden. Susan and her husband seem to have achieved the ideal: an understanding and loving marriage enhanced by creature comforts.

But when the younger children start school and Susan has time for herself, instead of feeling liberated as she expected, she feels restless, irritated, and still tied down by the obligations of running the household. Knowing that her discontent is irrational, Susan nevertheless develops strategies to gain more freedom from the obligations that come with being a wife and mother and the organizer of a household.

At first she sets aside a private room for herself, but this arrangement is too artificial; she is still in the house. More and more she feels that her sensible, rational self is going through the motions of being Mrs. Rawlings while another, secret self is being pursued by a demon. She next arranges for the help of a German au pair girl—that is, a young woman, usually European, who trades child care services for room, board, and the chance to learn English. Sophie, the au pair, gradually becomes the substitute mother, while Matthew discreetly takes a mistress in the city. In a search for solitude Susan escapes to first one and then another cheap hotel. At the second, called Fred's Hotel, she peacefully spends the daytime hours alone and isolated, returning home each evening to superficially play the role of wife and mother. She feels that she has two separate selves, but that the real one exists in Room 19 of Fred's Hotel.

The crisis comes when Matthew, upset and suspicious, has a private detective seek out the hotel. He wonders if Susan is having an affair or if she is leaving the house daily for some stranger, more disturbing reason.

When he asks for an explanation, Susan suggests that she merely has a lover, feeling this to be the more rational and "sensible" motivation for her actions. But when Matthew suggests that they and their two lovers make up a foursome, Susan is caught. She cannot back up her lie.

Seeing her situation as hopeless and herself as undoubtedly mad, Susan returns one last time to Fred's Hotel. She spends a few last hours in the pleasure of complete solitude and then commits suicide by turning on the gas of the room's heater. She drifts quietly into death.

The story shows how the apparently civilized and sensible personal relationships of modern, middle-class society starve the soul, making irrelevant such concepts as faithfulness, guilt, confession, and forgiveness. Only emptiness and a sense that life is absurd remain. Intelligence alone fails to sustain life.

PHILIP LARKIN (1922–1985)

Larkin was born in Coventry in the English midlands. After attending school there he went on to Oxford University, where he became associated with the writers of "the Movement." This was a group of young poets and novelists who took a rather sardonic, antiromantic view of modern life. While Larkin's early poetry was influenced by William Butler Yeats, as he matured he found Thomas Hardy a more stimulating influence. Like Hardy, Larkin has a strain of ironic fatalism. He casts a cold eye on contemporary society and does not find much to celebrate. His style attempts to recreate modern, casual speech, but each word is placed with surgical precision.

Larkin became a leading example of the postwar school of poetry exemplified by "the Movement," which tried to counter the threats and chaos of modern politics and society by returning to the quiet, rational restraint of classicism.

"Church Going"

While the loss of religious faith tended to cause the Victorian poets to suffer, many modernists take the loss for granted. The speaker in this poem is a man who comes upon a small old village church while out bicycle riding and, on impulse, goes in to explore it. Remnants of respect for the place are indicated by his removing his hat and the clips that hold the bottoms of his pant legs. The church, while unoccupied at the moment, is still in use. The flowers and holy articles are all in place. The speaker explores the church not as a believer but as a tourist, trying out the lectern and examining the condition of the roof. He finds nothing remarkable, but he admits that he often stops at old churches out of an inexplicable curiosity. He begins to speculate about what will become of these old church buildings, the relics of the past, when the last believers have died off. Will a few be kept as museums and most be left to go to ruin?

In the fourth stanza, the speaker imagines the time when the local churches will have been abandoned. He supposes that among the uneducated, the Church ruins will retain their reputations as holy places where special herbs might be gathered or ghosts might linger. Some fragments of faith will survive as superstitions. Meanwhile, antiquarians will come to study the remains. The remnants of the church buildings will retain thus their association with things spiritual, and people who feel the need will impulsively seek out the still-holy ground, just as the speaker himself does. That is, even without the discipline, ritual, and teachings of religion, some inward tendency to find a sacred place will persist.

"MCMXIV"

The title of the poem is made up of the Roman numerals for 1914, the year World War I began. Those numerals are engraved on many monuments throughout England. The monuments serve the next generation, Larkin's generation, as reminders of the war. Larkin and his contemporaries know the war mainly as a series of photographic images.

The poem describes these as typical snapshots or newspaper photos. In one, soldiers stand in line waiting to be shipped off, while the shop's along the street display the advertisements and the prices of the time. In another, the peaceful countryside looks the same as ever, except that the people are dressed in old-fashioned clothes and the cars look antique.

In the last stanza, the speaker looks back on the years just before 1914 as a time of innocence, the last moment of simple, orderly life before the great disillusionment brought about by the useless slaughter of the war.

"High Windows"

This poem is written from the point of view of a middle-aged man during the 1960s, the era of sexual liberation. Looking at young couples, he envies their sexual freedom, contrasting it to the fears and inhibitions he felt as a youth, when the church still had authority to declare sexual promiscuity a sin. Now in the 1960s, he sees all young people "going down the long slide to happiness." They seem to have found freedom with no effort and have not suffered to win it. But "the long slide" image has a second connotation. In the last stanza, the speaker thinks of the high church windows being opened up, to let in the open blue sky that leads nowhere. The same freedom from restraint that gives happiness in life also deprives us of any sense of an afterlife, of something beyond ourselves other than infinite empty space.

"The Explosion"

Modern industrial England was built on coal power, and coal miners were an important force in the early labor movement.

In this poem Larkin pictures a group of cheerful and convivial miners as they walk on an early spring morning down a lane toward work. In the third stanza, one lively man steps aside to chase a rabbit and returns with a nest full of lark's eggs that he has come upon in the field.

In the fifth stanza, the scene shifts. At noon the men are down in the mine when a sudden tremor shakes the earth. There has been an underground explosion. (In early, poorly ventilated mines, coal dust could build up in the air, and any spark might ignite it.) In the sixth stanza, the minister offers pious consolations at the funeral of the dead miners. As he speaks, the grieving widows imagine seeing their lost men again in heaven as splendid shining figures. The one who found the lark's eggs will still be holding them, unbroken. The women's simple faith gives them visions of glory and salvation.

THOM GUNN (1929–)

Thom Gunn was born in England and educated at Cambridge University. In 1954 he came to the United States to continue his studies at Stanford University in California. He has since settled in the United States permanently. Although he was first associated with Larkin and the other poets of "the Movement," Gunn gradually adopted a more energetic style. He is fascinated with such icons of pop culture as Elvis Presley and motorcycle gangs.

Gunn has published six volumes of poetry between 1954 and 1976. His *Selected Poems, 1950–1975* was published in 1979 and his *Passages of Joy* in 1982.

"A Map of the City"

This early poem, set in rhymed tetrameter, is written from the point of view of a person standing on a height above a city. As he looks down he sees the streets and buildings laid out in a complex pattern that to a person drunk at night might seem like a maze. The speaker feels that the city belongs to him. The irregular and broken pattern of lights that come from the buildings and streets is pleasing to him. The complex pattern suggests that more is to come, that the city has potential and at the same time risk, because the pattern, being unfinished, is still open to possibilities.

"Black Jackets"

The central figure of this poem is a young member of a motorcycle gang. During the week he has a dull job driving a van, but the poem depicts him in his weekend mode of existence. Dressed in black leather, he hangs out in a bar with his fellow gang members, drinking beer and listening to loud music.

The regularity of the poem's form—quatrains with an *a b a b* rhyme pattern—seems to contain and diminish the banal existence of the gang. The "heroic fall or climb" of line twelve is ironic; these men are not confronting fate but merely climbing (or failing to climb) steep banks on their motorcycles. They sit around now "concocting selves," that is, creating a sense of identity by talking of their cycling exploits. Meanwhile, the central figure, the red-haired boy, drinks beer and peers across the dim and flickering lights of the barroom. He lives entirely in the present. His only thoughts are memories of his rite of initiation into the gang. They had him get two tattoos on his shoulders, one showing the name of the gang, The Knights, and the other the gang's motto, "Born to Lose." Both of these tattoos are ironic. These modern, motorized Knights have no courtly ideals, no ennobling quests. They resemble knights only in their wandering. They are all losers, banded together in the hope of making a sense of self out of their mutual belonging.

"My Sad Captains"

This is the title poem of Gunn's 1976 collection of poetry. The captains are the poet's heroes, the men—some personal friends and some public "historical" figures—whom he found attractive and fascinating. They have faded now and they have become distant figures. But as he looks back at what they were, their weaknesses or failures drop away and reveal the men themselves, distilled to images of hard, clear, energetic actions. It does not matter that the actions were wasteful or futile. They remain as bright in the memory as stars in the darkness.

"From the Wave"

This poem describes surfers on a California beach. The opening stanza presents an image of a huge wave, the type of wave that surfers covet for a long ride. In the next stanza the surfers, poised on surfboards, move in harmony with the force of the wave and blend into it, "half wave, half men." The climax of their ride is the balanced, slicing cut across the face of the wave just before it hits the beach. The surfers triumph, while the wave breaks and ceases to be. After that grand moment, the surfers walk about or paddle in the shallow water of the beach. Finally, they all turn and simultaneously swim out into the sea, to await the next big wave.

The poem is written in stanzas of alternating four-foot and three-foot lines, but the meter is irregular, like the rhythm of the waves. Two lines can be read together, making a long, seven-foot line to suggest the longer rise and fall of a big wave, as in stanza two. Elsewhere, the smaller units of phrasing suggest smaller waves.

TED HUGHES (1930–)

Ted Hughes was born in West Yorkshire, an area in the north of England where he and his brother spent many holidays fishing and hunting for game. Images of these experiences appear frequently in his poetry. Hughes attended Cambridge University, where he met the American poet and novelist Sylvia Plath. After marrying in 1956, the couple came to the United States for a year to teach, and then returned to London. In 1961 they moved to a country home in Devon. Plath's increasing mental instability put a strain on the marriage. She committed suicide in 1963.

Hughes's first volume of poetry, *The Hawk in the Rain*, was published in 1957. In the 1960s and 1970s he brought out six more volumes of poems as well as children's books, plays, and two books of topographical poems in collaboration with photographers. Hughes frequently uses a bird, especially the crow, to symbolize the wild and predatory forces of nature. In 1985 Hughes was named poet laureate.

"Wind"

This early poem shows Hughes's treatment of a natural force, in this case the wind, as violent and overpowering. In unrhymed quatrains he describes how the wind feels to the inhabitants of a battered house. At the opening of the poem, the house has been buffeted all night by a strong wind, as if it were a ship on the open sea. The air has been filled with the sound of the wind shrieking through the woods and booming over the hills. The sun rises in clear, luminous air, but the wind keeps blowing. At noon the speaker ventures out into the wind to fetch more coal to heat the house. As he looks around, he thinks that the fields and hillsides are like the flaps of a tent that might blow away at any moment. Back inside, he feels the vibrations of the house like the vibrations of a fine glass that will shatter if just the right pitch is sounded. He and his companion in the house feel dominated by this threatening wind. Instead of going on with their normal activities, they huddle by the fireplace, listening to the cry of the wind.

"Relic"

This sixteen-line poem has a two-part structure suggestive of the sonnet, but like most of Hughes's poetry, it does not rhyme.

The relic is the jawbone of some large fish or sea creature that the speaker has found washed up on the shore. Viewing the bits and remnants of various creatures, he thinks about the tough, competitive lives of beings who survive in the sea. This jaw was used to devour some prey, as each creature preys on another in the evolutionary struggle. The remnants that wash up on shore are the castoffs of that timeless competition in which "none grow rich." This jawbone gripped its victims while it was part of a living creature; now it remains as the evidence of and memorial to the fight.

"Pike"

The pike is a freshwater game fish that eats smaller fish. From the point of view of a human being it is beautifully delicate: from the point of view of its prey, it is a monstrous horror. Thus it appears to be either three inches long (stanza 1) or "a hundred feet" (stanza 2). The speaker observes the pike's efficient jaws, which are well adapted as an instrument of killing. He tells of keeping in an aquarium tank three pike of slightly different sizes—three inches, four inches, and four and one-half inches. Even though they were fed, the largest ate the other two. This reminds him of having seen on a riverbank two pike washed up together. The head of one was jammed into the mouth of the other, who tried to but could not swallow it. Thus, they both died.

The speaker thinks also of the huge old pike in an ancient pond where he fishes. As he casts his line the thought of pike makes his hair stand on end. He feels that these old and powerful fish are watching him as they watch for other prey.

"The Seven Sorrows"

This descriptive poem consists of a six-line stanza for each of the consecutive "sorrows" or images that tell that autumn has come and winter is approaching. The second and the sixth sorrows have to do with the autumn sport of the hunt. The pheasants have been shot and the sorrowful fox has been hunted down to provide "joy" for the huntsmen and their hounds. The other images are more tranquil. The dead flowers, the golden sunlight, the black-looking pond, the bare trees, and the litter of dead leaves on the ground all bespeak a cold and sparse season. In the last stanza, winter has arrived. The point of view shifts indoors, where the frost on the outside of the windowpane resembles a wintry face looking in.

SUSAN HILL (1942–)

Born in Scarborough and educated at the University of London, Susan Hill has been a broadcaster, a journalist, and a writer of plays for radio and television. Presently she writes novels and short stories. Her fiction, which is based on the conventional forms of the social novel, often explores relationships of dependence and isolation. She has written ten novels since 1968.

How Soon Can I Leave?

This story examines the relationship of two middle-aged women. The elder, Miss Roscommon, is more capable, more widely experienced, and more financially secure. She has a comfortable home on a hillside above a seacoast resort town. The younger woman, Miss Bartlett, is forty when the story begins. She is less stable and thinks of herself as artistic. She lives in a beach cottage and barely supports herself by selling handcrafted items, most of which she makes herself, to the summer visitors. But Miss Bartlett thinks of her present arrangements as temporary; she imagines that life still holds many possibilities. While Miss Roscommon talks about her active and interesting past, Miss Bartlett dreams vaguely about her future.

When a storm swamps Miss Bartlett's cottage, she is rescued by the hospitality of Miss Roscommon. Gradually the two settle into a relationship, and live together for seven years. Miss Roscommon plays the role of maternal caretaker; she looks after Miss Bartlett and handles her business affairs, eventually helping her set up a shop. While Miss Bartlett enjoys the cozy comforts of living with Miss Roscommon, she always keeps a mental reservation that this relationship is temporary. She resists the idea of being settled while she also imagines that she is helping Miss Roscommon by allowing the older woman to act as her caretaker.

A crisis comes after a visit from Miss Roscommon's newly married niece and her husband. Their youthful and self-satisfied presence makes Miss Bartlett take stock of herself. She resents being thought of as old, like Miss Roscommon. Miss Bartlett moves back to her cold and damp beach cottage, but the next bad storm invades the ground floor. She swallows her pride and climbs up the hill to rejoin Miss Roscommon, rehearsing her humble speech of apology and helplessness. But she is too late. Discovering Miss Roscommon lying dead in her living room, she realizes only at that moment the full extent of her need and her loss.

While the story has an omniscient narrator, it follows closely the thoughts and feelings of Miss Bartlett and conveys her fears and petty resentments as well as her self-deception about her age and her independence. Miss Bartlett's emotional maturity seems to have been arrested in late adolescence, when the desire for freedom from parental control is still in conflict with the fear of action and the need for protection. Miss Bartlett has lived to be forty-seven without having made the leap into adulthood.

The writers of the late twentieth century do not form a group that is marking out any definite trend. The anxieties and apparent chaos of the post-World War II years are depicted in literature as the trials and defeats of isolated individuals. Ordinary social ties and relationships do not bring satisfaction; rather, they grate on and depress the individual. Outside, nature is wild and predatory rather than benign. Joy and pleasure are either transitory or shallow.

These writers seem to be saying that hope and confidence are naive in a world dominated by the conflicts of superpowers. We readers have yet to see what a post-Cold-War era will bring about in literature.

Selected Readings

Kuby, Lolette. *An Uncommon Poet for the Common Man: A Study of Philip Larkin's Poetry*. The Hague: Mouton, 1974.

Motion, Andrew. *Philip Larkin*. London: Methuen, 1982.

Pratt, Annis and L. S. Dembo, eds. *Doris Lessing: Critical Studies*. Madison: University of Wisconsin Press, 1974.

Sagar, Keith. *The Art of Ted Hughes*. Cambridge: Cambridge University Press, 1975.

Singleton, Mary Ann. *The City and the Veld: The Fiction of Doris Lessing*. Lewisburg, PA: Bucknell University Press, 1977.

24

Literary Names and Terms: Literary Forms

TABLE OF FORMS

Narrative	*Lyric*	*Dramatic*
narrator speaks:	poet speaks:	characters speak:
epic	song	drama
fable	ode	farce
tale	elegy	comedy
novella	complaint	tragedy
romance	sonnet	comedy of manners
novel		dramatic monologue
short story		

Each literary genre and subgenre falls into one of three major categories: narrative, lyric, and dramatic. In each case the major generic form is determined by the person or persons speaking the words that make up the literary work.

NARRATIVE FORMS

Narratives are written in both poetry and prose. In a narrative, the person speaking describes the thoughts and actions of other characters.

Narrative Speaker

Narrators can comment on the characters and their behavior or on the events surrounding them. The narrator stands *between* the characters in the story and the reader, interpreting and revealing as he or she sees fit but not participating in or affecting the events being narrated.

Narrative Strategy

The narrator thus controls what the reader knows, when the reader knows it, and to some extent how the reader feels about it. The narrator's personality influences the reader's perception of story events. If the narrator seems to be distorting the story, the reader may conclude that the narrator is not always to be trusted to give the most appropriate emphasis or the correct interpretation of events. If this occurs, the narrator is said to be "unreliable." He or she thus takes on some of the qualities of a character but still occupies the position of narrator in relationship to the other characters and to the reader.

LYRIC FORMS

Although prose may contain lyrical-sounding passages, almost all lyrics are in verse.

Lyric Speaker

In a lyric, the person speaking seems to be the poet. The lyrical speaker tells of his or her own actions, thoughts, and feelings in such a way as to seem to be talking to him- or herself, to some unknown other person who may be present or absent or directly to the reader. In a formal lyric such as an ode, the speaker may be addressing the public in general or some large segment of it. Whatever the audience, the speaker is primarily creating a feeling. He or she may relate brief stories or bits of conversation (dialogue), but the speaker's own feelings are the focus of the poem.

As the speaker of a lyric, the poet may project a version of self that does not exactly represent his or her whole self or perhaps reflects that self only as it was at a given moment in the past. To the extent that the poet creates a somewhat separate personality for the speaker, the poem moves away from being a lyric and becomes more like a dramatic monologue.

Lyric Strategy

Because it presents a feeling, the lyric is ordinarily written in the present tense. The essence of a lyric poem is "I feel"—that is, first person, present tense. The lyric poet creates images and metaphors that suggest the feelings rather than stating flatly what they are.

DRAMATIC FORMS

In dramatic literature, the only speakers are the characters. One or more of the characters may represent the attitudes or values of the playwright, but the playwright does not appear on stage.

Dramatic Speaker

Each speaker or character in a drama sees the situation from his or her own point of view and engages in dialogue with the other characters, each character expressing his or her own thoughts and feelings in conflict with each other.

Dramatic Strategy

The reader of the play or its audience must comprehend and evaluate each character's statements and actions as a part of the whole work and then come to an understanding of the meaning of the play. The conflict of values acted out by the characters needs to be resolved by the end of the play, or else the audience feels puzzled and unsatisfied. Usually, the playwright guides the audience by showing that the characters who represent the "right way" are those who succeed in the end, but this is not always so. In a tragedy, the hero may be destroyed even though his values are the most praiseworthy.

25

Literary Names and Terms: Glossary

Aesthetic Movement   In England during the 1880s and 1890s, a group of artists and writers, heavily influenced by French symbolist poets, adopted the artistic credo that art is, or should be, separate from all considerations of social and moral issues. Art exists for art's sake, they said. Its purpose is to create artistic sensations in the reader or the viewer. These artists rejected the moral earnestness of the major Victorian poets and the "high seriousness" of such critics as Matthew Arnold. Their leading critic was Walter Pater; the best-known writer of the movement was Oscar Wilde, whose flamboyant dress and behavior epitomized the "aesthete." Their concept of the independence of literature from all other values but its own influenced in the poetry of T. S. Eliot and William Butler Yeats and formed the unifying concept of The Rhymers' Club in the 1890s.

Allegory   In an allegorical form of narrative, the characters, places, and actions represent abstract ideas at the same time that they operate as parts of the story. In an allegory, characters may, for instance, stand for the good or bad traits of humankind, places may represent the status or the goals of the characters, actions may represent right or wrong choices. For example, in an allegorical story, a road may stand for the way, right or wrong, along which a character proceeds on during his or her journey through life. The goal of that journey may be represented as a splendid castle, a city of light, or a beautiful garden. In allegories, the names of the characters may indicate the traits or abstractions the characters represent. If, for instance, a character is called Mankind or Everyman, the character stands for the universal condition of human beings in relationship to the moral forces at work in the narrative. In his allegory of Stalinism, *Animal Farm*, Orwell calls the tyrant pig Napoleon to indicate the nature of the pigs' gradual consolidation of power under the guise of carrying out democratic reforms. The depiction of the ruling class as pigs is an allegorical comment on their greed and gluttony as well as on their shrewd intelligence.

In working out an allegorical narrative, the shifting relationships between the characters are intended to show the reader how these qualities or traits function in relationship to each other. The final victory of the characters who stand for "the best way" or the "right" qualities produces the meaning of the narrative.

In interpreting an allegory, however, it is usually best to assume that not all the traits of every character are translatable into abstractions. Certain details may be included merely to advance the story or to make it more exciting.

Alliteration   Two or more words are said to alliterate if they have the same initial sound. "Lovely lilies lying along a lonely lane" alliterates on the *l* sound; five of the words start with *l*. Notice also that the word *along*, while it does not start with *l*, has that letter as the first sound of its stressed syllable; therefore, it is also part of the alliterative pattern. Sounds used to create alliteration are ordinarily consonants, but in Old English poetry, initial vowel sounds were also used to alliterate.

Alliteration is a way of giving emphasis, but it can also be used merely to create a pleasant, singing effect. In his fragmentary poem *Kubla Khan*, Coleridge uses alliteration to describe the sacred river: "Five miles meandering with a mazy motion." The alliteration on the *m* sound creates a murmuring effect, imitating the sound of the moving water.

Allusion   When a writer refers indirectly to some well-known person or event expecting that the reader or audience will recognize the reference although it has not been specifically named, that writer is making an allusion. To mention, for example, "the fall of our first father" is a way of bringing to the reader's mind the story of Adam and his expulsion from the Garden of Eden without digressing into a complete retelling of Adam's story. The author expects the reader to catch the reference and to understand its relevance to the present text. Of course, allusion requires that both the writer and the reader are familiar with the same body of literature and information; otherwise the allusion does not work. The reference will not be recognized and the additional meaning will be lost. In a Christian culture, for example, allusions to the Bible will be frequent, but allusions to Islam's Koran will be almost nonexistent.

In Yeats's poem "The Second Coming," the speaker asks "what rough beast" is approaching birth at Bethlehem. Yeats assumes that his readers will know that the birth of Christ was a great history-making event and that he is comparing that event to one which is soon to occur.

Topical allusions, those that refer to recent and local events, cause a literary work to become dated and difficult to read by a new generation of readers. It thus becomes the work of scholars and editors to seek out the sources and meanings of the allusions and to add explanations, in the form of notes, to literature of a past era or different culture.

Autobiography

An autobiography is a personal narrative about the author's own life. The writer presents his or her own life story as he or she sees it and recollects it. An autobiography differs from a diary, which is written daily or almost daily over a long time, because in an autobiography, the writer has the benefit of hindsight and can show how certain early events or conditions led up to later ones. The autobiographer thus presents his or her life as a unified whole and traces one or more themes through its development. Wordsworth wrote a poetic autobiography, *The Prelude*.

The autobiographical form is sometimes borrowed for novels. In a fictional autobiography, the author pretends that the narrator is telling his or her own story. The novel is told in the first person, as in Charlotte Brontë's *Jane Eyre*.

Ballad

A ballad is a song that tells a story. This poetic form is both narrative and lyric. The narrative ballad usually focuses on some single striking incident or event, often the violent crisis of a sequence of actions not fully explained. The characters of the narrative ballad are usually described sketchily in conventional formulaic phrases; their motivations are implied rather than stated. The story told in the ballad may be developed through dialogue between the central characters. Love, treachery, betrayal, and death are common themes of ballads. In love ballads, rejection and infidelity are found more often than sincerity and truth. A good example of a literary ballad is Keats's "La Belle Dame sans Merci."

Folk ballads were transmitted orally in the early stages of their development. As they were repeated, minor variations were introduced. The less dramatic stanzas often were forgotten, so that various versions of a ballad sometimes came into existence. Later, when the ballads were written down, it was not possible to retrieve the "original" version or even to say which version was the most authentic one.

Beast Fable

A fable is a brief narrative that illustrates a legendary story or a moral. If the characters are animals with human characteristics, the story is called a beast fable. The animals allegorically represent various human traits or weaknesses. Thus, a fox is often used to illustrate slyness or trickery, a lamb often represents innocence or meekness, and a pig usually stands for greed or gluttony. Beast fables are found in many cultures. The famous beast fables of Aesop, an ancient Greek, have been popular since their creation. In the best beast fables, human qualities or motivations are blended with details of actual animal behavior so that the character is both beastlike and human at the same time. The most famous modern beast fable is Orwell's *Animal Farm*.

Bildungsroman   This German term is used to name the novel of personal development that describes the process by which a sensitive young person grows up. It presents a series of educational experiences and describes deepening self-awareness. The central character ultimately declares his or her own values, which are usually not the same as the society in which he or she lives, and makes a decisive choice or performs an act that marks the beginning of maturity. In English literature, two of the best known *bildungsromans* are James Joyce's *Portrait of the Artist as a Young Man* and Charles Dickens's *Great Expectations*. A female bildungsroman is Charlotte Brontë's *Jane Eyre*.

Biography   Biography is the narrative account of a person's life. The term implies that the writer has investigated the person's life and that the authenticity of the events recounted can be vouched for. The biographer may have consulted written records, letters, diaries, journals, and even account books and may also have gathered anecdotes or gossip. However, as a biographer, he or she is obliged to have weighed the relative accuracy of all such materials and exercised judgment about what to include. Thus a biography is more historical than literary. It can also be considered a literary work if it is well written: if the biographer brings to the subject sufficient imagination, sympathy, and perception, and if the biographer has developed a theme or idea that the life illustrates.

Blank Verse   A poem written in iambic pentameter (a line of five iambic feet) with no rhyme is said to be written in blank verse. This form, rarely found in lyric poetry, is used most commonly in narrative, dramatic or philosophical poetry because the relatively long and open line it provides gives the poet freedom and flexibility to imitate speech and to discuss ideas at length. Blank verse was the dominant form in the drama of the Renaissance. In more recent times, Wordsworth used it in such narrative poems as "Michael" and "The Ruined Cottage." Some of Browning's dramatic monologues, such as *Fra Lippo Lippi*, are also in blank verse.

A wide variety of effects can be achieved in blank verse by making the lines either end-stopped or run on. Also, a pause within the line (a caesura) can be placed at the end of any one of the five poetic feet. The poem's pace and smoothness can thus be adjusted to suit the subject matter and mood.

Caesura   A caesura is a stop or a pause within a line of poetry. The pause may be indicated by punctuation or simply by the natural grouping of words that would occur if the line were spoken. For example, in Tennyson's "The Lotos-Eaters," the following descriptive lines contain pauses not indicated by commas but by the word order. The caesura is marked by a /.

Music that brings sweet sleep / down from the blissful skies.

Here are cool mosses deep,

And through the moss / the ivies creep. (lines 52–54)

Canto   A canto is a section of a long narrative poem. It is similar to a chapter in a prose narrative. Cantos are usually numbered, as in Lord Byron's mock epic poem, *Don Juan*.

Chivalry   During the Middle Ages, the aristocracy in England and other European countries was organized into a system of mutual protection, service, and obligation based on the honor of each individual knight. The knight vowed obedience to his king, loyalty to his fellow knights, and faithful love to a single maiden, whose protector and champion he became. The knight followed, or tried to follow, a lofty code of conduct.

As a literary character, the knight was the hero of the medieval romance. Although actual knights were often less than ideal, the chivalrous knight of romance sought glory in self-sacrifice and heroic risk-taking against any odds. He was a devout Christian, chaste and humble before God and a defender of Christianity against pagans. On the other hand, the knight would undertake seemingly impossible tasks in service to his chosen lady. He would go on long journeys and wait years for the fulfillment of his desires. The code of chivalry blended Christian morality with military honor to provide a comprehensive set of standards for action. The knights of King Arthur's Round Table, as described in Tennyson's *Idylls of the King*, illustrate the decline of chivalry.

Comedy   In the most general sense, any literary work that ends happily for its major characters is a comedy. More specifically, the term "comedy" applies to a kind of play that makes fun of human weaknesses and follies. Comedy shows the less-than-ideal aspects of human nature and makes them the objects of laughter. Often the characters of a comedy are of low social rank, rustic fellows or simple folk, but modern comedy ridicules the middle class or aristocracy.

Comedy of Manners   Plays whose main object was to criticize manners dominated the stage during the Restoration and have been revived from time to time since then. In a comedy of manners, the courtship customs, social behavior, and superficial values of a fashionable and style-dominated set of characters are shown to be artificial and false. Hypocrisy and pretense are exposed to ridicule. Characters for whom the play ends happily have somehow risen above the general level of affectation and found a way to express their feelings sincerely or to maintain genuine honor rather than merely holding on to reputation or avoiding scandal. The appeal of a comedy of manners lies often in the quick wit of the dialogue, or repartee. The characters, despite the artificiality of their charm or glamour, are nevertheless appealing. The best example of a modern comedy of manners is Oscar Wilde's *The Importance of Being Earnest.*

Convention   A writer who uses the forms, devices, and techniques that were used by earlier writers within a certain genre is following the conventions of the genre. The advantage of a writer's adhering to literary conventions is that his or her readers or audience will be familiar with the conventions and will therefore understand the new work more readily and react to it in somewhat predictable ways. The reader of a romantic ode, for example, expects to find rising intensity of emotion that reaches a climax and turning point late in the poem. Of course, every writer uses conventions to suit the individual work. George Bernard Shaw used the style and structure of an ordinary drawing room comedy to discuss serious social problems in plays such as *Mrs. Warren's Profession.* Conventions provide familiar signposts to experienced readers, helping them recognize the structure and strategies of the literary work and enabling them to put it into a context of other works of the same kind.

Couplet   Two lines of poetry that end with the same rhyme sound comprise a couplet. Ordinarily, both lines of a couplet are the same length—that is, they have the same numbers of metrical feet and the same meter. The most common couplet in English is made up of two rhyming lines of iambic pentameter with the sentence or sentences within the couplet having a complete grammatical structure—that is, not running forward into the first line of the next couplet. Such couplets are called heroic couplets. However, in Browning's famous dramatic monologue *My Last Duchess*, the lines are run on to de-emphasize the couplet form:

> That's my last Duchess painted on the wall,
>
> Looking as if she were alive. I call
>
> That piece a wonder, now: . . . (lines 1–3)

In Tennyson's "Lockesley Hall," the couplets are closed; each one makes a complete statement and a separate stanza:

> Am I mad, that I should cherish that which bears but bitter fruit?
>
> I will pluck it from my bosom, though my heart be at the root.
> (lines 65–66)

The lines are unusually long, each having seven feet.

Courtly Love   In the Middle Ages, the relationships of men and women were governed, in literature at least, by a code of conduct and set of ideals called courtly love. Based on ideas found in writings of the poet Ovid, the courtly love ideal was a part of the knight's life of chivalry. Courtly romances follow a conventional pattern: lovers fall in love completely, at first sight; they feel so absolutely overwhelmed by emotion that they become restless, sick, pale, and distracted; they sigh, weep or complain about their state, feeling weak and helpless from the effects of love and from despairing of ever being worthy to be loved in return. If the lady recognizes the courtly lover, he is joyous and inspired with hope; he undertakes to perform some difficult or dangerous task to prove his worthiness. Thus, courtly love combines an idealization of the lady with sensuous, even illicit, pleasure. The courtly lover is, above all, absolutely faithful despite all obstacles and delays. The origin of many ideas about courtly love in England was the twelfth-century treatise *The Art of Love* by the Italian writer Andreas Capellanus.

In nineteenth-century romantic poetry, remnants of the courtly lover can be seen in Keats's hero Porphyro in "The Eve of Saint Agnes." The courtly lover is mocked in the situation of Byron's hero, Don Juan.

Deconstruction   In the mid-twentieth century there arose a concept of language and a method of handling texts derived from the works of the French philosopher Jacques Derrida.

Deconstruction accepts the structuralist premise that language and culture achieve meaning by way of the relationships between all sorts of "representations," including words. Meaning is not inherent but depends on systems of relationships. Pictures or texts have value and significance according to their place in a structure that is in the mind, not because they represent something outside the mind. The text contains "signifiers" that point to the "signifieds" outside the text. This is the basic model of structuralism, but deconstruction destabilizes this model by refusing to accept the idea that structures have a center because that would imply that one part of the structure is independent, not a function of relationship. Thus the deconstructionists see a universal indeterminacy or what they call the "free play" of the signifiers. Ultimately, meaning cannot be determined or pinned down.

Didactic   This adjective can be applied to any literary work whose purpose is to teach a lesson or illustrate a moral. The message of a didactic work is usually unambiguous. Unlike fables, which may be ironic, didactic stories provide clear examples of the wrong way and/or the right way to act or think. Didactic works tend to rank rather low artistically because they do not deal imaginatively with the complexities of human behavior. However, since every effective piece of literature expresses some values, it is not possible to say what is or is not didactic in any absolute sense. Rather, the term "didactic" is applied to those poems, stories, and plays that teach a lesson in an obvious or heavy-handed way. The term has negative connotations of narrowness of view or dullness of presentation.

Doggerel   A form of verse that is below the level of poetry, doggerel is crude, jogging, and trite. It is full of clichés and tired phrases. Doggerel is sometimes used for satiric purposes, to make fun of ideas or to mock sentiments by putting them into low, undignified form. Written for comic effect, doggerel uses obvious rhymes, but sometimes the rhythm or meter is grossly out of order, creating false emphasis and awkward phrasing. One fixed form of doggerel is the limerick, but almost any verse form, if exaggerated and poorly executed, can become doggerel. Lewis Carroll exemplifies the satiric use of doggerel in "Jabberwocky" and other poems.

Dramatic Monologue   In this poetic form, the speaker of the poem is a character who has a distinct and often strange or corrupt personality. This character is, as it seems, overheard talking to himself or herself or to some other character who does not speak, but merely listens. The speaker usually starts in the midst of a situation that is not explained; the reader must piece it together by inference from various clues in the speaker's discourse. Thus a dramatic monologue may be baffling at the first reading. This complaint was made of the dramatic monologues of Robert Browning, one of the greatest users of this form. Other Victorian poets, including Tennyson and Arnold, also wrote dramatic monologues, and the form continues to be used by modern poets.

Dystopia   This is a kind of satire that describes a bad society. It is the opposite of a utopia, which describes a good or ideal society. In a dystopia, faulty doctrines or flawed concepts of human nature determine the power structure and distort the relationships between people. Characters may mistakenly admire the orderly dystopia at first, but more experience reveals that it somehow violates basic concepts of fairness or individual integrity. One of the most famous dystopias of English literature is Orwell's novel *1984*.

Elegy   A type of lyric poem, the elegy expresses serious or mournful feelings. It is usually a meditation on death. Many elegies are written to mourn the death of a particular person. For example, Tennyson's long elegy "In Memoriam" is an expression of his grief over the death of his college friend Arthur Henry Hallam. In the twentieth century, W. H. Auden responded to the death of Yeats with an elegy, *In Memory of W. B. Yeats*. In this poem, Auden follows the elegiac convention of finding consolation in the lasting influence of the dead poet, declaring that Yeats still lives in the minds of his readers. *See also* Pastoral

Empiricism   In the early development of scientific thought, the English philosophers Francis Bacon and John Locke both advocated an examination of actual objects and events. This approach contrasted with that of the rationalist philosopher Descartes, who started with abstractions and made deductions from them. The empiricists believed that a broad and systematic examination of nature would reveal natural laws, the principles by which the universe operates. In the twentieth century, poets of "the Movement" felt that poetry ought to focus on real objects in the world, thus becoming empirical.

End-stopped Line   When the end of a grammatical unit of expression—a clause, a phrase, or a sentence—coincides with the end of a line of poetry, that line is said to be end-stopped. Reading aloud, one would pause slightly at the end of such a line, even if no punctuation is given. This line from Wordsworth's *Ode: Intimations of Immortality* is end-stopped;

> Earth fills her lap with pleasures of her own. (line 77)

The term "enjambement" describes lines that are not end-stopped.

Enjambement   Enjambement results when a line of poetry does not contain a complete meaning, and the reader must proceed to the next line to grasp the sense. Here is an example from Wordsworth's "Ode":

> O joy! that in our embers
>
> Is something that doth live. (lines 130–131)

Enlightenment   A philosophical movement commonly called the Enlightenment developed during the seventeenth and early eighteenth centuries in England and western Europe. Its name refers to its basic premise that many beliefs of the past had been dark, that is, mere superstitions or false systems of thought based on faulty authority. The new philosophers tried to free their minds of all established and traditional explanations of humanity and nature, getting down to essential, directly observable or self-evident propositions. They laid the foundations for the modern scientific method and at the same time tended to undermine religious faith by seeking rational explanations for all phenomena. However, many individual Enlightenment thinkers retained their faith in God even as they came into conflict with church authorities who feared the effects of their new ideas. France was the center of Enlightenment thinking, but its influence was felt in all the major European cities. Enlightenment philosophers undertook to reexamine the laws of nature and the foundations of human nature. Their studies led them to political theory, mathematics, physics, psychology, astronomy, and new theories of education, as well as many other fields. The new ideas generated in the Enlightenment are often cited as one cause of the social unrest that culminated at the end of the eighteenth century in the French Revolution. While Enlightenment thinkers were not revolutionaries, their writings tended to undermine traditional sources of authority and to stress the essential equality of human beings. These ideas underlie the English Romantic Movement, with its rejection of authority and emphasis on individual freedom.

Envoy   Sometimes spelled *envoi*, this term has the root meaning of "to send." It refers to a final stanza that "sends" or directs a poem to a specific person. However, sometimes the term merely indicates a conclusion or a repetition of a refrain found earlier in the poem.

Eolian Harp   Also written as *aeolian harp*, this stringed instrument is named for Aeolus, the Greek god of the winds. It has a wooden framework of rectangular shape and can be mounted in the opening of a window. When breezes blow, the force of the moving air plays upon a series of strings, causing a sound that varies with the variations in the wind. This instrument was a favorite romantic symbol for the force of nature and for the inspiration of natural forces working upon the poet. For example, Coleridge wrote an early poem to his wife called "The Eolian Harp" and used the harp again in "Dejection: An Ode," in which he calls it "this Aeolian lute."

Epic   A long, narrative poem, the epic was considered the highest form of literature in classical and Renaissance critical theory. Expressing the values and the legendary history of a culture or national group, the epic focuses on the deeds of a central hero who embodies those qualities most admired and worthy of imitation. The narrator of the epic poem comments on the hero's actions, maintaining a tone of objectivity but also pointing out certain truths about human experience illustrated by the hero's fate. The style of an epic poem is serious, lofty, and dignified. Characters make lengthy speeches. Some other conventions of the epic poem are: the poet calls upon a muse or deity for help or inspiration in telling the epic story; the action begins in the middle of things (*in medias res*) and the earlier episodes are added later; supernatural beings oversee and sometimes direct events that either help or hinder the hero's progress; extended metaphors (epic similes) and allusions extend the range of reference of the epic to include other actions or situations from other literary sources. The conventional epic has not survived in modern literature, but modified use of epic structures underlie some novels, which are also lengthy narratives centered on the adventures of a hero. James Joyce made use of Homer's *Odyssey* as a pattern on which to build his novel *Ulysses*.

Essay   An essay is a short prose work loosely organized around a unifying topic but admitting many variations in form and digressions in content. The essay gives the personal thoughts, notions, recollections, and anecdotes of the essayist in an informal or conversational style. The father of the essay is the French writer Montaigne, whose *Essais* were published between 1580 and 1595. The word *essay* means to try or to attempt, indicating that the essay was not a finished treatise but rather a sketch or preliminary thought. In England in the eighteenth century, series of essays were published in daily, weekly, or thrice-weekly periodicals. The best known of these periodical essays were Addison and Steele's *The Tatler* and *The Spectator*.

In the nineteenth century, imaginative romantic essays were written by Charles Lamb, who begins each of his "Essays of Elia" with some trivial personal detail and expands it with gentle wit and humor. Later in the same century, many essays of critical, philosophical, and political ideas were written for intellectual and literary periodicals.

Farce   A farce is a short play that provokes laughter by means of physical humor such as slaps and falls or low-level verbal games that are sometimes merely pointless repetitions. Plot is minimal, situations are absurd, and characters are stock types. Elements of farce are used in the theater of the absurd, in such plays as Samuel Beckett's *Waiting for Godot* and Harold Pinter's *The Dumb Waiter*, but these plays lack the light and silly tone of traditional farce.

Foil   In drama, a foil is a character who contrasts with the central character. The foil character highlights the hero's traits by being different or opposite. Thus in George Bernard Shaw's *Mrs. Warren's Profession*, the character Frank is too morally correct to marry the daughter of a prostitute; he is a foil for the more corrupt but less hypocritical suitor, Sir George Crofts.

   The term "foil" has also been used to describe a contrasting character in a novel, one who is used to help define or set off the traits of the central character. The wicked Sydney Carton in Charles Dickens's *A Tale of Two Cities*, who is the opposite of the heroic Charles Darnay, is an example.

Foot   A foot is a standard unit of meter or rhythm in a poetic line. In the line, a pattern of accented and unaccented syllables (or stressed and unstressed syllables) is divided into a number of similar units, each called a foot. In English, the most commonly used foot is the iamb, which consists of two syllables, the first unstressed and the second stressed. The words *forget* and *begin* make iambic feet, as does the phrase "to grieve." Five such feet in one line results in iambic pentameter, the most frequently used line in narrative and dramatic poetry. Here is a line of five iambic feet:

   The picture of the mind revives again:

Other types of feet commonly found in English poetry are these:

   Trochee: two syllables, stress on the first—*reason*

   Spondee: two syllables, both stressed—*May day*

   Anapest: three syllables, stress on the last—*for a while*

   Dactyl: three syllables, stress on the first—*heavenly*

   It is usual for a poet to vary meter by substituting an occasional foot of a different kind into lines written primarily in one foot. Another common variation is to omit the unstressed syllable at the beginning or end of a line of poetry, leaving a foot of just one syllable.

Gothic   Gothic style is a medieval style named after the Goths, a Germanic tribe that prevailed in Europe between the ancient classical era and the Renaissance. The word describes the architectural style of the medieval cathedral, with its tall and narrow spaces, pointed arches, and elaborate stained glass windows. In a literary context, Gothic may have negative connotations, implying a crude and old-fashioned style as judged by later, neoclassical critics. In the era of Alexander Pope and Joseph Addison, Gothic style was considered irregular and barbaric, without essential discipline, unity or restraint. Toward the end of the eighteenth century, the Gothic novel was one that neglected realism is favor of suspense, horror, and mysterious incidents. Anne Radcliffe's novel *The Mysteries of Udolpho* (1794) is a prominent example of this type of fiction. In the romantic era that followed, "Gothic" became a term of praise, suggesting what was free, wild, primitive, and unspoiled by too much civilization.

Gothic Novel   A form developed and made popular in the late eighteenth century, the Gothic novel does not observe the conventional realism of the mainstream English novel but borrows some of the techniques and devices of the medieval romance. It exploits the supernatural and the grotesque. It contains highly improbable incidents set in remote and threatening locales such as ancient, isolated castles. The characters of a Gothic novel tend to be stock figures; the emphasis is on mysterious situations and shocking events rather than on subtlety of characterization. The famous Gothic novel by Anne Radcliffe, *The Mysteries of Udolpho*, was satirized by Jane Austin in *Northanger Abbey*, a mock-Gothic novel.

Hack Writer   A hack writer is one who writes to order, producing pages of fiction, poetry, or essays on demand at a fixed rate of pay per page or, if poetry, per line. The term arose in the early eighteenth century when publishing became an industry and books became a commodity sold to a mass market. Many hack writers survived by doing translations, abridgements, or reviews of more complex original works by others. Most hack writers remained poor and obscure; they were standard objects of satiric scorn.

Hero   A hero is the central character of a literary work whose choices or actions determine the outcome of events. (If such a character is female, she may be called a heroine.) In classical dramatic theory, the tragic hero must be a person of high rank, and he must suffer from a flaw or weakness that causes his downfall. However, the term is also used more broadly to apply to any main character whose fortunes and struggles are central to the plot of a fiction or drama. In heroic literature, such as the epic, romance or heroic play, the hero exemplifies admirable conduct; courage and self-sacrifice are among his prominent traits. He represents an ideal, the best that human capacities can accomplish. But in more realistic genre, the novel, for instance, the hero is shown as developing from a state of immature and mistaken behavior to a better, wiser, and more capable condition. His heroism consists partly in discarding childish or inadequate ways; he is rewarded by being received as a full member of established society. In romantic literature of the late eighteenth and early nineteenth centuries, the hero is a sensitive person, a man of feeling, perhaps a poet. The idea of a hero thus changes according to the dominating values of the society in which he is created and for which he stands as an example of the right way. In modern literature, the hero may be isolated, excited, or alienated from society, isolated or an exile.

Heroine *See* Hero

Humanism Humanism was a broad artistic and philosophical movement that was a major aspect of the Renaissance. Starting in Italy in the fourteenth century and developing in England in the late fifteenth century, humanism was a reaction against the spiritual, ascetic, and otherworldly emphasis of medieval thought. European humanists studied the languages and the literatures of ancient Greece and Rome, wherein they found an emphasis on the earthly life of human beings rather than the medieval assumption that life on earth is merely a trial and preparation for life after death. Humanists celebrated the dignity of the individual and a person's capacity to learn and to enjoy a full moral life governed by reason. They sought to combine the dignity and restraint of classical culture with Christian idealism. In the Victorian Period, the poet and critic Matthew Arnold called for a revival of humanism. In this era of declining influence of religion, Arnold argued in "The Function of Criticism at the Present Time" that one should learn "the best that is known and thought in the world" in order to revive the spiritual vigor of the English nation.

Iambic Pentameter A poetic line of five iambic feet, this is the most common verse line of English narrative and dramatic poetry. It is used in some lyric poetry as well. The reason for the popularity of this line is said to be that it most nearly approximates the rhythm of prose speech. *See also* Meter

Lyric One of the major forms of poetry, the lyric is a poem of emotion, expressing directly the feelings of the speaker. The term "lyric" comes from the ancient custom of accompanying a song with the music of a lyre. A lyric poem may contain some narrative elements, some brief story or incident related to the feeling, but the primary emphasis is on conveying that feeling by image, metaphors, and modulations of tone. Lyric poems are written in a wide variety of verse forms. Some of the major kinds of lyrics are sonnets, songs, odes, and elegies. The lyric modes are dominant in poetry of the romantic period.

Metaphor This is a general term for figures of speech that compare two essentially unlike things. One or more qualities of the thing described (called the tenor) are said to be like qualities of the thing that makes the metaphor (the vehicle). For example, when Shelley says in his "Ode to the West Wind," "I fall upon the thorns of life:" (line 54), he compares life's difficulties and travails with thorns, which pierce and give pain. If the comparison is made explicit by the use of a word such as *like* or *as*, the metaphor is called a simile. When a lover says that his mistress is like a flower (a common simile), he suggests that the qualities of beauty, freshness, and fragility that are found in a flower are also traits of the lady he loves. Metaphors are used extensively in poetry because of their emotional suggestiveness.

Metaphysical   This term names a group of poets of the early seventeenth century, but these poets did not use the term to describe themselves. It was applied to them in the next century by the poet and critic Samuel Johnson. In philosophy, metaphysics deals with what is beyond (meta) the physical, that is, with the incorporeal, supernatural, or transcendental. In a general sense, many philosophical poems can be called metaphysical, but in literary discussions, the term usually applies to those poets of the seventeenth century, John Donne and his followers, who challenged the conventions of the Renaissance lyric and wrote poems that questioned and probed the meaning of human existence the individual's place in the universe, and his or her relationship to God. Perhaps because of its difficulty, metaphysical poetry was not much read during the eighteenth and nineteenth centuries, but in the early twentieth century interest in this poetry was revived by an influential essay by T. S. Eliot on the metaphysical poets. He and other modernists responded to the probing wit and intellectuality of this poetry.

Meter   The basic sound pattern in English poetry is created by repetition and alternation of stressed and unstressed syllables (or accented and unaccented syllables). The overall pattern of a poem is called its meter (measure). In a poetic line, the pattern of stressed and unstressed syllables is divided into units of nearly the same length and arrangement of stresses; each such unit is called a foot. For example, in this line from Coleridge's "The Rime of the Ancient Mariner"

A sadder and a wiser man (line 625)

stresses fall on the second, fourth, sixth, and eighth syllables, resulting in a very regular meter that has four feet, each foot containing one unstressed followed by one stressed syllable. (The fourth syllable, "and," is perhaps not much stressed, but it is more so than the syllables just before and just after it.) The meter of a line is named according to the number of feet. These are the usual names:

Monometer (seldom used): one foot

Dimeter: two feet

Trimeter: three feet

Tetrameter: four feet

Pentameter: five feet

Hexameter: six feet

Heptameter: seven feet

Various kinds of feet can be used to make up the poetic line, but one kind tends to predominate. (*See* Foot, for a list of the different kinds of poetic feet.)

In English poetry, the shorter lines, trimeter and tetrameter, are found mostly in lyrics, while the longer lines, pentameter and hexameter, are used in dramatic, narrative and philosophical poetry. *See also* Blank Verse

Middle English   Middle English was the language spoken in England from the early twelfth through the late fifteenth century.

Mock Epic   A mock epic is a satirical poem that uses the structure and style of an epic poem but deals with nonheroic or antiheroic materials. The term "mock-heroic" refers to the style or to the whole poem. In a mock epic, the hero may be a low character, representing what is base, foolish, or trivial, perhaps to show how far from ideal the culture has become. The conventions of the epic are parodied. The purpose of a mock epic is usually to make fun of the nonheroic subjects of the poem, to show by contrast to heroic norms how weak, superficial or degenerate these characters are. In Byron's mock epic *Don Juan* the hero is admirable but too naive; he is seduced rather than being the seducer. Byron uses the epic form very loosely, with many digressions.

Modernism   This is a broad term used to refer collectively to a number of related tendencies in literature and the arts since the early twentieth century. Generally, modernism is relativistic and experimental, focusing on the psychological, nonrational, and nonmoralistic representations of experience. Rejecting traditional forms and conventions, much of modernist writing seems disorganized and obscure to the uninitiated reader. Much is suggested but little is explained. The most influential modernist poem is probably T. S. Eliot's *The Waste Land*, which reflects the disarray and sense of loss of its period. It incorporates allusions and fragments of literary works of the past; it is arranged as a series of discontinuous scenes and monologues around a central concept of a land laid waste, sterile, and dry, without purpose or hope.

Narrator   The narrator is the person who seems to be telling a story. This person can stand in various relationships to the author and to the characters of the story. In the simplest arrangement, the narrator may be identified with the author; such a narrator is not a character in the story but knows all about the characters and can describe their actions and even their thoughts. This narrator is omniscient (all-knowing). On the other hand, a narrator who is presented as one of the characters in the story can plausibly know only what is observable from his or her own point of view. This type of narrator has limited perceptions, but he or she may be either very acute or somewhat biased and limited. If such a narrator is naive or mistaken, telling of situations that he or she seems not fully to understand, the narrator is said to be unreliable, and the reader may draw meanings from the story that the narrator appears to have missed or avoided.

In first-person narration, the narrator refers to herself or himself as "I" and recounts the story from a limited point of view. In third-person narration, there is no "I"; the telling is done impersonally, and all characters are "he" or "she," distinct from the narrator.

Nature   This broad term is difficult to define because its meaning changes as the concept of art and its purpose change. Nature always has positive connotations; it is the thing that art, including literature, is about, the basic subject that all literary works are supposed to explore. In classical literary theory, literature imitates nature. In this conception, nature is the universal and unchanging way that things are in the world. Human nature especially is the subject, and since basic truths about human life and characters are assumed to be the same for all times and all places, a play or poem of ancient Greece or Rome will have relevance for modern life as well. Readers can judge the quality or value of a literary work by holding it up to the standard of nature, that is, to what they know about life from their own learning and experience. Nature is contrasted to art.

However, nature has other meanings as well. Sometimes it refers to the material world. In such cases what is human is contrasted to the realm of nature, the physical world. Nature is also contrasted to the spiritual realm, the supernatural. The laws of nature are orderly restrictions, but the supernatural can break those laws, creating visions, ghosts, and miracles.

In the late eighteenth century, a concept of nature arose that tended to fuse the physical and the spiritual definitions of nature. To the poets of romanticism nature embodied the uncultivated or rural world, the mountains, rocks, trees, flowers, and birds. But to these poets nature also contained spiritual force, so that the individual in a natural setting received impulses toward goodness by sympathetic association with nature.

Generally, then, nature is a value term, used to name whatever the writer values most highly and tries to present in the works he or she creates. The adjective "natural" is a general term of praise suggesting simplicity, sincerity, and truth.

Novel   The novel is a long prose narrative that traces the development of a main character or a group of characters through a series of events, situations or actions that may or may not be told in chronological order. Unlike a romance, a novel tries to give the impression of recreating real life, the ordinary day-to-day existence of believable people. Thus the novelist tends not to use highly improbable events or idealized characters. The novel emerged in the early eighteenth century and is not essentially a development of earlier romances or Renaissance narratives. The novel's roots lie in subliterary forms such as diaries, spiritual autobiographies, confessions, letters, and journalistic accounts of actual events. In the 1740s the novel became popular among the middle class as both a guide and an entertainment. It was particularly read and written by women, because reading a novel did not require a university education (women did not attend universities). However, the novel's appeal was very broad, and in the nineteenth century novels became the predominant form of literature in England.

The great novelists of the Victorian Era wrote long narratives that tended to show the effects of social restraints and inequalities upon the struggling central characters. They examined society of all classes, from top to bottom, in panoramic novels of contemporary life. However, in the twentieth century, the focus of the novel has shifted toward the inner life of one or a few characters. The psychological novel examines the tensions, motivations, memories, and anxieties of the characters and their effects or expression in action. One of the most widely used techniques of the modern psychological novel is the stream-of-consciousness. *See also* Gothic Novel

Occasional Poetry   The term "occasional" refers to poems written to celebrate or commemorate a special occasion such as a coronation, a birthday, a marriage, a great victory, or the anniversary of some significant historical moment. "Easter 1916" is Yeats's occasional poem about the Irish nationalist uprising on that day. It honors the nationalists as heroes.

Ode   The ode is an extended and lofty lyric poem expressing emotions about a significant occasion or a person to whom the ode is dedicated. As a dignified and inspiring work, the ode contains images of grandeur, creating a feeling of awe in the audience. The ode is derived from a Greek form of lyric that was part of the Greek play. This was a lyric passage separating the episodes of the drama and expressing the feelings of the chorus. Thus, unlike most lyric forms, the ode may be public and general, expressing the feelings of all rather than private or personal emotions.

Greek odes were separated into stanzas marked as the strophe, the antistrophe, and the epode, indicating different movements of emotions. These stanza terms are less common in English odes. The major types of odes written in English are: the Pindaric ode (named for the Greek poet Pindar), the Horatian ode (after the poet Horace), and the irregular ode developed by the English poet Abraham Cowley. Briefly, the Pindaric ode uses varied stanza forms, while the Horatian ode keeps the same stanza form throughout. The irregular ode varies even more than the Pindaric; each stanza may use a unique form. This is the kind of ode used by the major romantic poets. Some primary examples include Wordsworth's "Ode: Intimations of Immortality," Coleridge's "Dejection: An Ode," Shelley's "Ode to the West Wind," and Keats's "Ode on a Grecian Urn." These romantic odes tend to be more personal in their tone and subject matter. They build up to a climax of personal emotion, then return to relative calm.

Omniscient Narrator   A story told by a narrator who knows all about everything, including the inner thoughts of the characters, has an omniscient narrator. Use of such a narrative point of view gives great flexibility; the narrator can shift easily in time and place and can arrange the events of the story to fit any strategy of revelation.

Ottava Rima   This stanza form consists of eight lines of iambic pentameter with a rhyme pattern of a b a b a b c c. This is an Italian form, as its name indicates. It was used by Byron in his narrative poem *Don Juan*.

Paradox   A paradox is a statement that seems to contain its own contradiction. It seems that a paradox cannot logically be true, yet the poet asserts the paradox as an essentially true statement. The seventeenth-century metaphysical poets used paradox to state mysterious truths. Modern poets find paradox a fitting expression of the contradictions of modern life.

Parody   Parody is a technique used in satire. In it, the writer closely imitates some of the conventional elements and the actual wording of a known and familiar literary work in order to mock that work or to make a ludicrous application of the style of the work to other, less dignified subject matter. The humor of the parody lies in the disparity between the serious style of the original and its application to trivial or low material. One of the most parodied speeches from Shakespeare's plays, for example, is the famous soliloquy from *Hamlet* that begins, "To be or not to be, that is the question." One such silly parody begins: "Toupee or not toupee, that is the question." Another: "To sneeze or not to sneeze, that is congestion." In the Victorian era, Lewis Carroll mocked the seriousness of moralistic poetry in many parodies—the nonsense poems found in *Alice in Wonderland*.

Pastoral   *Pastor* in Latin means a shepherd. Therefore, any literary work that has shepherds as its main characters can be called pastoral. In this broad sense, *pastoral* is an adjective modifying another literary form, as a pastoral drama, a pastoral elegy, or a pastoral romance. The main characters in a pastoral are idealized rather than realistic shepherds. They may speak in cultivated diction and sing elegant, even courtly, songs.

Two important pastoral elegies of the nineteenth century are Shelley's elegy on the death of Keats, "Adonais," and Arnold's elegy on the death of his friend Arthur Hugh Clough, "Thyrsis." In each case, the dead poet is addressed as a lost shepherd whose songs will be missed within the country landscape.

One idea common to all types of pastorals is that of the goodness of a simple and rustic life, in contrast to the evils of the sophisticated life of the court or the great city. The pastoral idealizes rural life as simple and pure, free of ambition and corruption.

Patronage   Before the full development of the printing and book-selling industry in the eighteenth century, writers who were not financially independent needed the gifts or support of wealthy patrons. These were men, and occasionally women, who were interested enough in literature to help support promising or established writers. In return, the writer often dedicated many of his works to his patron, writing prefaces of dedication in praise of the patron's good taste and generosity. The patronage system died out when a large reading public and a well-organized printing industry made the sale of printed books lucrative enough to support writers by buying their manuscripts, hiring them as hack writers, and paying them royalties. Royal patronage lasted long after other forms of patronage had declined. In England, the poet laureateship is the current remainder of the patronage system.

Pentameter   A five-foot line. *See* Meter

Periodical Essay   In the eighteenth century, before the development of the modern magazine or journal, individual prose essays were published in series under a unifying title. Two of the best-known early series were by Richard Steele and Joseph Addison: *The Tatler* (1709–1711) and *The Spectator* (1711–1712 and 1714). Essayists wrote on topics of current interest: matters of taste, fashion, manners, the arts, and public life.

    In the nineteenth century, literary and artistic journals or reviews carried articles by a number of different contributors on various topics, but the periodical had some unity based on the philosophical or aesthetic position of its editors. Much of the influential prose of the Victorian Era, literary criticism and social commentary, was published in periodicals.

Persona   The speaker of a literary work has a more or less well-developed personality or style. If the speaker's personality becomes a character clearly unlike the author's personality, this character is called the persona. The term literally means a mask. The author is conceived of as putting on the mask of another self for the purpose of the story he or she is telling. In several of the stories of Joseph Conrad, the storyteller is an old seaman of wry wit and broad experience, a captain called Marlow, who may represent Conrad's attitudes and values, but who is a separate, created person having had many experiences that Conrad never had. Any narrator who projects another self into the story can be said to create a persona.

Personification   This is a figure of speech in which something that is not a person—for example, the sea, a sheep, or a season—is presented as having human emotions or human responses to situations. The thing personified may be an object, an animal or a concept. Poets who use personification are suggesting that nature is in harmony with or participates in people's mental lives. Trees that weep, windows that yawn, and rocks that stand guard are obvious personifications. In pastoral poetry, the whole landscape is full of sympathetic, personified objects and forces. In allegorical forms such as the morality play and the masque, the characters are personifications of concepts or ideas.

Philistines   This term is from the Bible. The Philistines were a crude and corrupt tribe who opposed the Israelites. Matthew Arnold introduced the term to describe dull and humorless persons of the middle class who are more concerned with respectability than with essential morality, who are narrow and unimaginative. They lack culture and oppose any new ideas.

Poetic Justice   The dramatist who arranges matters so that at the end of a play the good characters, those whom we admire and sympathize with, are rewarded and made happy, while the bad characters, the villains, are punished, has created poetic justice.

Portmanteau Words   A portmanteau is a large suitcase or traveling bag, so called from its French origins, *port* (to carry) and *manteau* (a coat or cloak). Lewis Carroll coined the term "portmanteau word" to name the invented words he used in some of his poems, most notably in "Jabberwocky," in which the word *slithy*, for example, is a combination of elements from the two words *lithe* and *slimy*. It is a way of saying two words at once and uniting the suggestive power of both words. In his novel *Ulysses*, James Joyce also makes such word combinations. In the Proteus episode, Stephen is thinking about Arius, the *heresiarch* or the arch heretic.

Pre-Raphaelite   Raphael was an Italian painter of the fifteenth century whose works came to represent the defiance of rules in art to a group of English writers and painters of the 1840s and early 1850s. The group, which called itself the Pre-Raphaelite Brotherhood, aimed at the creation of spiritual beauty and the close observation of nature. The members held joint exhibitions and started their own literary journal, *Germ*. The founding members included the poet Dante Gabriel Rossetti and his brother, William Michael Rossetti, who edited *Germ*.

Prosody   Appearances notwithstanding, prosody has nothing to do with prose. It is the study of versification, a general term for all principles of meter, rhyme, and stanza form. All the various patterns of sound in a poem constitute its prosody. The term also names the rules and models that provide guidance and set up standards of making poetry.

Quatrain   A quatrain is a stanza consisting of four lines. The most common rhyme pattern in a quatrain is a b a b. This is found, for example, in Wordsworth's Lucy poems, including "She Dwelt Among the Untrodden Ways" and "A Slumber Did My Spirit Seal." Poets use other rhyme patterns as well, of course. The famous "In Memoriam" stanza of Tennyson uses a rhyme pattern of a b b a. The English sonnet is composed of four quatrains and a couplet.

Romance   A romance is a kind of long fictional narrative that is more imaginative than realistic. Such a work is called a romance because early narratives of this sort were composed in French, a language derived from the Latin language spoken by the inhabitants of the ancient Roman Empire. Medieval romances, mostly written in verse, were fantastic stories about the adventures of princes, knights, and their ladies. Lighter and more fanciful than the epic, the romance shows characters who are motivated by love and lofty notions of honor and who move in a landscape of castles and towers, caves and dungeons. The ultimate medieval romance in English is *Sir Gawain and the Green Knight.*

The term "romance" was also used in the eighteenth century to distinguish between two types of long prose narrative. In contrast to the novel, which proposed to describe real people in authentic or realistic settings and plots, the prose romance was less bound by the constraints of realism and could include ghosts, magical events, and remote, exotic settings. Emphasis in such a romance was on ingenuity of plot and on suspense rather than on character development or examination of manners.

Other forms of literature that use the same imaginative approach and show similar characters motivated by love are often called romantic; for example, romantic comedy or romantic epic. Romantic poetry, however, derives from a different set of ideas and practices that developed from Wordsworth and Coleridge's new poetic theories of the early nineteenth century. Keats's poem "The Eve of Saint Agnes" is a romantic romance.

Satire   A satire is a literary work that criticizes or attacks the values or behavior of its characters. Satires can be written in a wide range of genres. Satires work by showing in clear or exaggerated detail the foolish or wicked ways in which society or one social group conducts its affairs. In so doing, satire often causes laughter. It is witty or funny because it shows the disparity between the characters' pretensions and their real attitudes or actions.

In direct satire, the speaker is the satirist, describing with scorn and sarcasm the debased world that he or she observes. In formal verse satire, a genre developed in Rome by Juvenal and Horace, the satirist remains aloof from the society described and comments on it with the hope of awakening the people to their wrong-headed ways. The Juvenalian satires are rough and bitter, containing obscene and disgusting detail. The satires of Horace are milder and more humane. Horace mocks the excesses of society, but he can also mock himself because he realizes that human nature is inclined to be weak and easily corrupted. The terms "Juvenalian" and "Horatian" are used to classify more modern satires according to the violence or mildness of their style.

In England the great age of satire was the early eighteenth century. Poets of the romantic era, except for Byron, avoided satire. The late nineteenth century produced such satiric playwrights as Oscar Wilde and George

Bernard Shaw. In the twentieth century, satire is mainly found in the theater of the absurd.

Simile   A simile is a kind of metaphor that compares two things that are basically dissimilar but that have one or more traits in common. In this figure of speech, the word *like* or *as* makes the comparison explicit. When the poet Robert Burns says, "My love is like a red, red rose," he suggests the freshness, beauty, and delicacy of his beloved. A lady and a flower can have these traits in common, even though they are really very different from each other. *See also* Metaphor

Sonnet   A fixed form of lyric poem, the sonnet has fourteen lines of iambic pentameter. Several kinds of sonnet are distinguished by different rhyme patterns. The Italian sonnet has two parts: an octave (eight lines) rhyming a b b a a b b a; and a sestet (six lines) rhyming c d e c d e or c d c d c d. The English sonnet is arranged differently. The Spenserian sonnet has three quatrains (four lines) rhyming a b a b b c b c c d c d and a final couplet rhyming e e. The Shakespearean sonnet also uses three quatrains, but the rhyme sounds are different in each one: a b a b c d c d e f e f. The couplet follows, g g. Both Spenser's and Shakespeare's sonnets are called English sonnets to distinguish them from Italian sonnets. The English sonnet tends to emphasize the climactic ending of the couplet, while the Italian sonnet, with its two-part structure, emphasizes the contrast or contradiction from the octave to the sestet.

The sonnet was originally a vehicle for love poetry. Renaissance poets wrote long series or cycles of love sonnets tracing the development of their love relationships with a single idealized woman. Since the seventeenth century, however, the sonnet form began to be used for a wider range of subjects, including religious and political statements. Both Wordsworth and Keats wrote a variety of sonnets.

Speaker   When a reader begins to read a literary work, whether poem or prose, the words seem to be the utterances of a voice, of one who is speaking to the reader, to himself or herself, or to a character. This voice is identified as the speaker, in distinction from the author, who may or may not be the same person. In fiction, the main speaker is called the narrator.

Stream-of-Consciousness   This modern narrative technique attempts to create the illusion that the reader is experiencing the unstructured flow of observations, ideas, memories, and associations that occur in the mind of the fictional character. The stream is often illogical and puzzling in its apparent disorganization, but some patterns of association, habits of thought or recurrent images begin to emerge, providing indications of the overriding fears, preoccupations, and interests of the character. The stream-of-consciousness tries to get at the elemental, emotional life, the hidden psychological life of the character.

Major novels of stream-of-consciousness are James Joyce's *Ulysses* and Virginia Woolf's *To the Lighthouse.*

Structuralism   In the modern study of how language works to create meanings, structural linguists argue that all language is an arbitrary set of signs that gain their ability to convey meaning not from their inherent qualities but from the positions they hold in conventional structures of meaning (phrases and sentences) in specific contexts. Literary forms are one important kind of conventional structures that permit meanings to be conveyed. Such forms are "codes" or systems of signification. They are not maps of reality but self-contained sets of rules that the reader uses to decode the written work.

Symbols   Although words are symbols in that they stand for the things, concepts, or relationships they name, in a work of literature a symbol is something that not only exists as itself but also suggests other ideas or refers to other situations. A symbol such as the cross is widely understood and carries a similar significance in many different contexts. Other symbols are more specific to a single literary work. In Tennyson's poem "The Lady of Shallot," for example, the mirror in which the lady sees images of life passing beneath her window represents the artist's isolation from reality. In the later poetry of Yeats, such isolation is represented by a stone tower.

Topographical Poem   A topographical poem is one written to describe, and usually to praise, a particular place. The poet views a landscape and creates images of its visual features and also suggests the feeling of the place, its quality of dignity or restfulness. Thus, while the topographical poem is lyrical, it also has a philosophical aspect. Early important topographical poems include "Cooper's Hill" by John Denham and "Windsor Forest" by Alexander Pope. Matthew Arnold celebrates the countryside around Oxford in "The Scholar Gypsy," and more recently, W. H. Auden had described his native Yorkshire in "In Praise of Limestone."

Tragedy   One of the major forms of drama, a tragedy is a serious play that shows the central character, the hero or heroine, striving against overwhelming forces to carry out a significant action. The efforts of the hero ultimately destroy him; however, the action he has undertaken will make the moral status of his state or community better in some way or rid it of an evil. The essence of a tragedy is not that it is sad; passive victims are sad. Tragedy has more inspiring elements; it shows the dignity of human nature in making moral decisions and bearing the consequences. Many critics question whether tragedy can be written in the modern era, when the destiny of the individual is seen to be less meaningful and more absurd.

Utopia   A utopia is an ideal place. In literature, it is a fictional narrative or description of an ideal society supposed to exist in some remote location. The term was used by Thomas More as the title of his philosophical story

(1516) about a communal society established for the fulfillment of ideals of human justice, sharing of goods in common, and cultivation of harmony. Since then, the term "utopia" has been applied to any such fictional society that sets up an ideal set of social arrangements; it applies as well to the fiction in which the ideal is described. A negative utopia, one describing a bad or corrupt place, is called a dystopia.

Wit   The term "wit" can refer either to the intellectual quality of the author or to the witty quality found in the literary work. Derived from the Anglo-Saxon word for knowledge, wit is always associated with mental quickness and acute perception. The wit of the metaphysical poets, for example, was shown in their clever and ingenious conceits and extended metaphors. The association of wit with laughter came later. Wit is sharper, quicker, and more biting than humor and lacks its good-natured, clowning quality. The revival of wit as a positive quality in poetry was promoted by T. S. Eliot and other modern, anti-sentimental poets.

26

Literary Names and Terms: People and Places

THE ROMANTIC AGE (1785 to 1832)

Deism

Eighteenth-century deism based its doctrine on the evidences of God in nature or in the "natural" world. Deism opposed the scripture-based Christian conventions.

Industrial Revolution

Historians have labeled the decades between 1760 and 1830 as "The Age of the Industrial Revolution." This was a period of unprecedented economic growth in England that also created major changes in the nation's economic structure, transforming it from a nation with a rural work force engaged in agriculture to one with a mainly urban work force engaged in industry (including some nonurban mining and construction).

The invention of large machines that were housed in factories and mills increased production while urbanizing the areas around them. The development of steam-powered equipment freed the factories from the need to be near water. Canals and the development of the steam-powered railway trains and steam-powered ships advanced the development of consumer markets. The expansion of consumer markets and the concentration of markets in towns encouraged the refinement of distribution and retailing. Finally banking, financial institutions, and the communications industry developed in response to these changes.

EARLY ROMANTICS: BLAKE, BURNS, AND WOLLSTONECRAFT

Highlands

The Highlands are the region of the north and west of Scotland. The Highlands are predominantly Celtic, and the Celtic language of Gaelic once was dominant there. Highlanders lived under the "Clan" system, and while they were always poorer economically than the "lowlanders" of the south and east of Scotland, they maintained strong family traditions and pride in past glories.

Although the parliaments of England and Scotland were merged in 1707, the poets and writers of the Highlands continued to react against the perceived diminishment of Scotland. Robert Burns of Ayrshire, a county in the southwestern part of Scotland, wrote in Scots or Celtic in *Poems, Chiefly in the Scottish Dialect* as an act of patriotism as well as to describe and commemorate the Scottish Highlands culture. Walter Scott, while more readily accepting of the union, nonetheless cherished the ballads of the border country to which his family belonged. Scott considered himself to be a celebrator of both the legendary and the heroic elements of the Scottish past both in his early *Minstrelsy of the Scottish Border* and in the later Waverley novels.

THE MAJOR ROMANTIC POETS: WORDSWORTH AND COLERIDGE

Lake Country, Lake District

The Lake District is in the hilly northwestern Cumberland-Westmoreland region of England, below the border with Scotland and just off the Irish Sea. Wordsworth, born and educated on the banks of the Esthwaite, lived most of his life in the area surrounding the lakes. He died at Rydal Mount close to Rydal Lake.

Lake School Poets

The term "Lake Poets" or "Lake School" was first used in 1817 in the *Edinburgh Review* to describe Wordsworth, Coleridge, and Southey, poets who lived in and drew inspiration from the Lake District.

Southey, Robert

Poet laureate from 1813 until 1843, Southey was closely associated with Wordsworth and Coleridge. The three poets lived in the northern Lake District. Southey holds his place in the group more by personal friendship than by his literary talent. He left Oxford to join Coleridge in his scheme of a utopian pantisocracy. Then, refusing to consider any other occupation,

Southey labored at literature for more than fifty years. He set himself the task of writing something every working day; he could not wait for inspiration as he was compelled to support his own large family and also, in large measure, that of his friend Coleridge.

SECOND-GENERATION ROMANTIC POETS: BYRON, SHELLEY

Clairmont, Claire

Claire was the daughter of Mary Jane Clairmont. In 1801 Mary Jane became the second wife of William Godwin. In 1816 Claire accompanied her stepsister, Mary Wollstonecraft Shelley, and Shelley to Switzerland. While Byron visited the Shelleys, Claire seduced him. In 1817 she bore Byron a daughter, Allegra.

SECOND-GENERATION ROMANTIC POETS: KEATS

Brawne, Fanny

Fanny was the young girl of eighteen with whom Keats fell in love and became engaged to wed. They never married because of his poverty and his fatal illness.

Clarke, Charles Cowden

Charles Clarke, son of the Reverend John Clarke, headmaster of Enfield private school, was first the teacher and then the long-time friend of John Keats. Clarke encouraged Keats in his studies and his writing both in school and during their later friendship. It was Clarke who introduced Keats to the poetry of Spenser and to other poets such as Homer. By late in his life, Clarke and his wife, Mary, were acknowledged Shakespearean scholars.

Hunt, Leigh

While always considering himself to be a poet and critic, for more than thirty years Leigh Hunt worked continuously as an editor and essayist. His chief object seems to have been to "discover" and encourage writers of good literature such as Shelley, Keats, Tennyson, Browning, and Dickens. Dickens caricatured Hunt as Harold Skimpole in *Bleak House*. Keats was condemned by the critic Hazlitt as a poet of the "Cockney school of poetry" of which Leigh Hunt was considered the chief. In 1812 Hunt was sentenced and imprisoned for two years for libeling George, the prince regent. Hunt was also a close friend of Shelley and had joined the Shelleys and Byron in Italy to prepare the new magazine *The Liberal* when Shelley died. Hunt's *Autobiography* (1850) provides illuminating descriptions of his friends and of the milestones of his life.

MINOR ROMANTICISTS: LAMB, HAZLITT, DE QUINCEY

The Temple

In the heart of old London is an enormous, rambling structure, originally a chapter house of the Knights Templars, that still has about it a suggestion of the Crusades of the Middle Ages. For the last four hundred years at least, the buildings have housed the offices and lodgings of lawyers and barristers. Charles Lamb was born there, and it was the setting for many lectures by nineteenth-century writers. It is associated with Tommy Traddle of Dickens's *David Copperfield* and with the characters of Gilbert and Sullivan's operetta *Trial by Jury*. The Temple received extensive bomb damage during World War II but was restored so artfully that now it is not possible to distinguish the restored from the original areas.

East India Company

English trade with India began about 1591. The East India Company was chartered in 1600 by Queen Elizabeth I and given the monopoly for the eastern trade: silk, calico, cotton, and tea were principal imports despite high duties. During the eighteenth century the company's extensive commercial influence developed into political power. In 1784 the British government shared with the East India Company virtual rule of India. After the Indian Mutiny of 1857 the company was taken over by the British government.

The East India Company was extremely important in the lives of several writers of the early nineteenth century. About 1790, when he was only fifteen years old, Charles Lamb joined the company. He soon became a clerk in the accounting department, where he remained for thirty-three years. In 1806 James Mill, father of John Stuart, began writing his *History of British India*; its publication in 1817 secured him a post at India House, the London office of the East India Company. After reading for the law, John Stuart Mill took a position under his father at the company. He rose rapidly to become chief examiner and remained in this post until 1858, when the governance of India was transferred to the Crown.

THE VICTORIAN AGE (1837 to 1901)

Queen Victoria

Victoria was the granddaughter of George III and the Queen of the United Kingdom from 1837 to 1901. She was made Empress of India in 1876. In 1840 she married her cousin Albert, by whom she had nine children. Victoria demanded to be kept informed on all government matters, especially foreign affairs, and took particular interest in the 1854–1856 Crimean War. After Prince Albert died in 1861 the Queen spent a decade in seclusion and mourning. Her popularity recovered when she once again began to appear frequently in public. Victoria's reign was enthusiastically celebrated with the Golden Jubilee of 1887 and the Diamond Jubilee of 1897.

Disraeli, Benjamin, Earl of Beaconsfield

Disraeli was both a politician and an author. As a politician, he led the Conservative Party (Tories) in the 1860s and 1870s and twice was prime minister (1868, 1874–1880). Disraeli is credited with the development and passage of the Great Reform Bill of 1867, which added to the rolls 2 million voters, primarily factory workers. In addition, he bought Britain a controlling interest in the Suez Canal, had the Queen made Empress of India, and annexed the South African Transvaal in 1877.

Disraeli's early literary talents won him the friendship of Byron, Scott, and Southey. His first novel, *Vivian Grey*, written when he was only twenty-two, gained him immediate acclaim. Flamboyant and considered by some to be opportunistic, Disraeli used his money and popularity to win a seat in Parliament, where he advocated the ideas for social reform he later embodied in his political novels *Coningsby* and *Sybil*. Using a phrase borrowed from an American preacher in *Sybil*, Disraeli made famous the economic divisions of a nation's people between "the rich and the poor."

EARLY VICTORIAN ESSAYISTS: CARLYLE, NEWMAN, MILL

Emerson, Ralph Waldo

An American essayist, poet, and abolitionist, Emerson visited England in 1833 at the start of his career. During that trip he made the acquaintance of Wordsworth and Coleridge, and developed a friendship with Thomas Carlyle. Carlyle's letters to Emerson over their lifetimes generated many of Emerson's "human Portraits, faithfully drawn."

Chartism

Lasting from 1837 to 1848, Chartism was the movement to extend voting rights to the working class. The name of the movement came from the 1838 "six-point People's Charter," which demanded universal suffrage (for men), secret-ballot voting, annual elections, equal electoral districts, no property qualifications for members of Parliament, and payment for service as a member of Parliament. Three "Charter" petitions (1839, 1842, 1848) were presented to Parliament for approval, but the petitions made no impact on the government.

Oxford Movement/ Tractarianism

A religious force within the Church of England, the Oxford Movement generally dates from Keble's 1833 sermon at Oxford titled "National Apostasy." The movement preached that the Church had an independent spiritual status, was a direct descendant of the medieval Catholic church, and represented a "middle way" between "Roman" Catholicism and Protestantism.

Tracts for the Times, were the treatises of the movement. Many of them were written by John Henry Newman, then vicar of St. Mary's, Oxford. The issues discussed in the tracts had a great influence on religious and intellectual life in Britain. In literature, the revival of interest in the medieval church profoundly influenced the Pre-Raphaelites and Tennyson.

Clapham Sect

Taking their name from that of the London suburb where they lived, the Clapham Sect was a group of wealthy Church of England businessmen and their families. The Clapham Sect were conspicuous defenders of the poor, the oppressed, and the unfortunate. The sect's influence on British culture and on the establishment of charitable acts in the Anglican church far outlasted the Evangelicalism of the period.

William Wilberforce, who fought to abolish slavery, Edwin Chadwick whose specialty was public health, and the earl of Shaftesbury who led the campaign to reform factory conditions and limit working hours were all Clapham Sect members. Distinguished twentieth-century writers such as Virginia Woolf and E. M. Forster were descendants of Clapham Sect members.

Evangelicalism

The Evangelical Movement began in the eighteenth-century Church of England as a reaction against spiritual complacency and the emotional coolness of an easygoing religious deism. It manifested a spirit of Christian philanthropy inspired by John Wesley's work among the poor. Anglican Evangelicalism is chiefly important in the history of English culture for the moral tone it lent society. The Evangelicals undertook to reform the morality of the middle class to which they belonged, the working class over whose morals they exercised a special guardianship, and most of all the aristocracy, which was felt to be worldly, cynical, and immoral.

**Bentham,
Jeremy**

Bentham was an influential philosopher, economist, and political theorist. Though he was active in parliamentary reform, he is most widely known as the founder of utilitarianism.

Utilitarianism

Utilitarianism is a system of ethics wherein "it is the greatest happiness of the greatest number that is the measure of right and wrong." This ethical system contends that the rightness or wrongness of an action must be judged by its consequences. Jeremy Bentham was the founder of this school of thought, and James and John Stuart Mill became its best-known advocates.

MAJOR VICTORIAN POETS: TENNYSON, BROWNING, ARNOLD

Hallam, Arthur

One of the happiest aspects of Tennyson's student life at Cambridge was becoming a member of The Apostles, a group of intellectual undergraduates who questioned conventional beliefs and ideas. One member, Arthur Hallam, a brilliant Eton graduate, befriended Tennyson, who was the student-poet of the group. When Tennyson left Cambridge in 1831 without taking his degree, Hallam remained his friend. In 1833, while visiting in Vienna, Hallam suddenly and unexpectedly died. Tennyson was plunged into a period of grief and sorrow during which he published nothing. Although he was silent, it was during this time that Tennyson began to write his elegy to his friend. Though Hallam lived only twenty-two years, because of his friendship with Tennyson and because of the poem "In Memoriam" that Tennyson wrote to honor him, he is given a place in English cultural history.

MINOR VICTORIAN POETS: BARRETT, FITZGERALD, BRONTË, CLOUGH, MEREDITH, AND HOPKINS

Wimpole Street

The address 50 Wimpole Street, London, is synonymous with both the semiseclusion of the gifted poet Elizabeth Barrett and with the romantic story of the love between Barrett and Robert Browning.

In 1835 the Barrett family moved to Wimpole Street. While living there Elizabeth gained a literary reputation with the publication in 1838 of *The Seraphin and Other Poems*. Then illness and the shock of her brother's death placed her frail life at risk, and for the next six years she was confined to her room, where she continued to write. A reference to Browning in her poem "Lady Geraldine's Courtship" is supposed to have first led Browning to write to Barrett in 1845. Soon afterward he visited the invalid, and during the following year they fell in love, apparently against the wishes of her father. They eloped to Italy from Wimpole Street.

MID-VICTORIAN ESSAYISTS: RUSKIN, HUXLEY, AND ELIOT

Social Darwinism

Social Darwinism is an ideology that applies Darwin's principle of natural selection to social and political analysis.

Whistler, James McNeill

Though born in the United States, from the 1860s on Whistler lived mostly in the Chelsea section of London. Among his more famous portraits are those of his mother and of Thomas Carlyle (1873). Whistler had a reputation for wit and sophistication and was a friend of both Swinburne and Wilde.

In his famous *Nocturnes* series of paintings, Whistler was more concerned with tone values than with the direct representation of nature. He sued Ruskin for describing *Nocturne in Black and Gold: The Falling Rocket* as "flinging a pot of paint in the public's face." Whistler won the case but was awarded only a farthing in damages. In 1890 he wrote *The Gentle Art of Making Enemies*, in which he chronicled the trial.

THE PRE-RAPHAELITES AND AESTHETICISM: THE ROSSETTIS, SWINBURNE, AND PATER

Burne-Jones, Sir Edward

While a student at Oxford, Burne-Jones formed a friendship with William Morris. Together they decided to take up art. Both were attracted to Dante Rossetti's theories and were associated with but not members of the Pre-Raphaelite Brotherhood. Burne-Jones admired the Pre-Raphaelites' highly polished techniques founded on the medieval paintings they all admired.

Burne-Jones's paintings explore the Arthurian cycle and mythological scenes. He and William Morris later designed stained-glass windows and tapestries.

Morris, William   A poet, designer, printer, and entrepreneur, Morris was one of the most important artists of his day. As a poet he published *The Defense of Guenevere and Other Poems* in 1858. In association with Burne-Jones, Dante Rossetti, and others, in 1860 Morris established the firm of Morris, Marshall, Faulkner and Co., for the design and manufacture of artistic furniture and household decorations; subsequently the company added tapestries and other textiles, wallpapers, book illustrations, and printing to its list of products and services. Morris found the time to write and publish between 1867 and 1870 *The Life and Death of Jason* and *The Earthly Paradise*. Morris's original design firm dissolved in 1871 and in 1881 he transferred his business to Merton in Surrey.

In 1890 Morris founded the now famous Kelmscott Press, for which he designed type fonts, ornamental letters, and borders. Morris became an active socialist during the 1880s. Later in life, he was a leader in the Socialist League of England.

VICTORIAN HUMANISTS AND SATIRISTS: LEAR, CARROLL, AND WILDE

Tenniel, Sir John   Tenniel is the well-known illustrator of Lewis Carroll's two books, *Alice in Wonderland* and *Through the Looking Glass*. It is less well known that Tenniel joined the staff of *Punch* magazine in 1851. He worked with the magazine for over fifty years, primarily as a political cartoonist. He was knighted in 1893.

THE TWENTIETH CENTURY (1897 to PRESENT)

The Crown, Lords, and Commons   After the death of Queen Victoria the monarchy continued to flourish but the Court of Lords and Ladies faded.

The Parliament Act of 1911 took from the House of Lords the power to veto legislation and substituted a power of delay only. The apparent anomaly of this chamber has several times in the twentieth century been discussed, notably in 1949, when the Labour government tried to reduce further the ability of the House of Lords to delay legislation. In 1958 life peers were created and they began to play a larger part in the political activities of the chamber. In spite of discussion, a way to make the "Lords" more "representative" has not been found.

Thus the monarchy, the House of Lords, and the House of Commons have remained intact. This institutional continuity is unmatched by any other major European country.

The Aliens Act of 1905

The British Empire at the turn of the century was made up of a great diversity of territories and peoples: India, Malaya, Ceylon, Borneo, and Hong Kong; the extensive dependencies of Gibraltar, Cyprus, Malta, and Egypt in the Middle East; the "undeveloped estate" of vast areas of Africa; as well as the self-governing Canada, Australia, and New Zealand. While the Empire did not reach its greatest extent until after World War I, the strains of growth began to be felt much earlier. Slowly but steadily, a substantial and growing population either born in or descended from non-English parents began to call England home. The 1905 Aliens Act was the first substantial legislation aimed at restricting immigration.

The Conservative, Labour, and Liberal Parties

The names of the three major political parties are the same today as at the start of the twentieth century: Conservative, Labour, and Liberal. New parties such as the British Communist party and the British Union of Fascists party have appeared and disappeared. For most of the century the governing politics has been a two-party system, with a third party attracting the fringe of political sentiment.

TRANSITION TO THE NEW CENTURY: HARDY, SHAW, CONRAD, AND HOUSMAN

The Congo

The Congo originally was the name of the area in central Africa on both sides of the Congo River. The territory to the east and south of the river came under Belgian control in 1885 and officially became known as the Belgian Congo in 1908. Independence came in 1960, and the country was renamed Zaire later in the decade.

The territory on the west of the river was called the French Congo. It achieved independence from France in 1960 and is now known as The People's Republic of the Congo. Brazzaville is its capital.

Fabian Society

The Fabian Society was a political society founded in 1884. The membership consisted primarily of middle class intellectuals who lived around London. The Fabian Society advocated gradual social reform. George Bernard Shaw was a leading member.

Wessex	The Wessex in Thomas Hardy's novels and poems is the thinly disguised area around Dorchester, Dorset, and the West Country where Hardy was born and lived. The area was the fictional setting in his novels and poems known as "Wessex."

POETRY OF WORLD WAR I: BROOKE, SASSOON, GURNEY, AND OWEN

Battle of the Argonne Forest	The Battle of the Argonne Forest was fought during September and October 1918. It was the allied forces' final offensive against the Germans.
Gallipoli	The devastating campaign in Turkey began in February 1915 with landings by the allies. The allies suffered heavy losses and began to evacuate in 1916. In 1915 Rupert Brooke died of blood poisoning in Skyros in the Dardanelles while on his way to take part in the campaign.
Trench Warfare	British military chiefs believed that a small professional mobile offensive utilizing the newly invented British tanks would be sufficient to win World War I, which was anticipated to be a brief war that would not require massive mobilization. The use of tanks as effective shock weapons on the battlefields of France and Belgium, known as "Flanders," was prevented when the Germans dug in to miles of barbed-wire-lined trenches. The Germans' newly improved machine guns and long-range recoil artillery gave them strong advantage in battle.
Verdun and the Battles of the Somme	For almost ten months during 1915 the allies battled to repel a German attack at Verdun, France. Ultimately the Germans lost, but both sides suffered heavy losses. For his courageous fighting in that first Battle of the Somme, Siegfried Sassoon received the Military Cross.

From July to November 1916 the allies fought using British tanks in the Battle of the Somme to relieve Verdun. It has been estimated that the battle cost 400,000 British lives, 200,000 French lives, and about 400,000 to 500,000 German lives to gain the allied forces 125 square miles of no particular strategic importance. The Somme River was the setting used by Ivor Gurney in his first book of poetry, *Severn and Somme*. Wilfred Owen fought from January to May 1917 as an officer in the Battle of the Somme. Subsequently he was "invalided" out of the military with shell shock.

The final Battle of the Somme took place in the spring of 1918. During this battle the Germans tried unsuccessfully to split the allied forces. Once again, the battle caused a great number of deaths and casualties.

Ypres

Ypres, in "Flanders," Belgium, near the border of France, was the site of three major battles in World War I. At the first battle in the autumn of 1914 the German offensive in Belgium was halted by the British troops. The second battle in the spring of 1915 marked the first time that the poison gas chlorine was used in combat by the Germans. The third battle, called the "Passchendaele offensive," was fought from July through November 1917. During this battle the British advance of five miles was made at the cost of 400,000 British lives and the demoralization of the army. In the third battle Ivor Gurney, on his second tour to the front lines suffered from the effects of poison gas during the summer of 1917. He was returned to a mental hospital in England.

WILLIAM BUTLER YEATS

Abbey Theatre and Lady Augusta Gregory

Lady Gregory met Yeats in 1898. Gregory was the widow of the member of Parliament from Coole, Dublin. Her husband had also been the former governor of Ceylon. While editing her husband's autobiography, Lady Gregory developed an interest in Irish history and folklore. Gregory became so deeply a part of the Celtic literary renaissance, and particularly of the renaissance of Irish theater, that she became known as the godmother of the Abbey Theatre.

Yeats and Gregory first founded the Irish Literary Theatre which in 1904 became the Abbey Theatre, and the Irish Academy. While Lady Gregory was a director of the Abbey, there was no task she did not perform for the theater, from writing brief comedies used "to close the performances" to traveling with the company when it took its repertory abroad. Lady Gregory translated Molière from French into the Gaelic idiom of western Ireland that she, Synge, and Yeats made familiar to readers and theater-goers. Yeats both wrote and produced plays for the Abbey Theatre, and until 1909 was the theater manager.

Celtic Myths, Magic, and the Celtic Literary Renaissance

Celts, especially in Ireland, maintained a mysterious imaginative and almost pagan folklore. Historians speculate that the development and maintenance of native Celtic Irish legends and mythology were possible because the Germanic invasions that took place in fifth-century Britain never reached Ireland. In ancient Celtic mythology Oisin filled the gap between paganism and Irish Christianity.

Yeats and other Irish poets used the idea of the Celtic national characteristic as a weapon in the cause of Irish nationalism. They intensified the ancient Irish legends in order to build up a distinctly Irish literary consciousness that would replace the dominant English culture. Yeats risked (and incurred) scorn, for instance, by stating without explanation that he believed in fairies.

Coole Park

Coole Park was the name of the Gregory estate in County Galway, the area west of Dublin near the Irish Sea. One of Yeats's principal works, *The Wild Swans of Coole*, is set at the estate.

Fenians

Named for the Old Gaelic word for Irish warriors, the Fenians were a secret revolutionary group founded in 1858. The organization had strong links with the Irish-American community. In Dublin in 1867 an attempted Fenian insurrection failed. The league was reorganized as the Irish Republican Brotherhood in 1873. When Yeats returned to Ireland from London in 1896 and became caught up in the Irish Revolution, he called himself a Socialist and he was undoubtedly a Fenian.

Gonne, Maude

Maud Gonne, a beautiful actress and a fervent Irish revolutionary, was the love of Yeats's life.

Rhymers' Club

Formed in the 1890s by Ernest Rhys and Yeats, the preeminent poets of the Rhymers' Club were Ernest Dowson, Lionel Johnson, and Arthur Symons. The club met at the Cheshire Cheese Cafe on Fleet Street in London. The Rhymers' Club publication, an illustrated quarterly review, was called *The Yellow Book*.

THE NEW NOVEL: JOYCE AND LAWRENCE

Adventures in Publishing Joyce's Works

In 1914 Ezra Pound asked Joyce's permission to include a poem from *Chamber Music* in Pound's first published collection, *Imagist Anthology*. Along with his permission, Joyce sent to Pound his manuscript of *A Portrait of the Artist as a Young Man*. Pound was able immediately to arrange the manuscript's serial publication in the vanguard English magazine *The Egoist*. The Egoist Press attempted to publish this novel in book form, but no printer in Britain would even "entertain the idea of printing such a production." Ultimately the Egoist Press had to import sheets from the United States, where Ben. W. Huebsch published the book in 1916.

In England, *The Egoist* serialized those parts of the novel *Ulysses* that the printer would agree to set up; in the United States, *The Little Review* published twenty-three installments of the novel in 1918 through 1920. Three of the installments caused the magazine to be confiscated by the U.S. Post Office for alleged obscenity. The editors were fingerprinted and fined

$100. In Paris, Sylvia Beach decided to publish *Ulysses* under the imprint of Shakespeare & Co. Joyce himself edited the book. The 1,000 numbered copies of the first edition were sold within a month.

Of the second printing of 2,000 copies, 500 copies were burned in New York City by the U.S. Post Office. The English customs authorities confiscated 499 copies of the third edition of 500 copies. Wherever *Ulysses* was banned it was smuggled in. It was not until 1933 that Americans were legally permitted to read the book, when U.S. District Judge Woolsey ruled in a now famous decision that "while in many places . . . *Ulysses* . . . is somewhat emetic, nowhere does it tend to be an aphrodisiac." The 1934 Random House edition of *Ulysses* was the first legally printed edition in any English-speaking country. The 35,000 copies sold out almost immediately.

Dodge (Evans, Sterne, Luhan), Mabel

A literary-diarist, the four-times-wed Mabel was known among the "literary" international set primarily as Mabel Dodge (the surname of her second husband). Dodge's home in Venice became the first of her many salons. After her second divorce she returned to New York City and started another salon whose frequenters this time were not only artists but also liberals and radicals of all persuasions. Following a notorious love affair with John Reed, Mrs. Dodge married the artist Maurice Sterne. The couple went to New Mexico to establish a new art colony in Taos. They divorced, and in 1923 Mabel married Tony Luhan, a full-blooded Pueblo Indian. She described herself as "a patron of art and artists and poets, congregating those famous artists, writers, and musicians in my home salon." Dodge was also described by critic Malcolm Cowley as "a species of head-hunter. She collected people in exactly the same spirit as she collected china dogs for her mantelpiece." It was Mabel Dodge who first introduced the painter Georgia O'Keeffe to New Mexico. Often Dodge became deeply emotionally involved with the artists she patronized; for example, with D. H. Lawrence, about whom she wrote *Lorenzo in Taos*.

THE BLOOMSBURY GROUP: WOOLF AND FORSTER

Bloomsbury

The Bloomsbury district is a "neighborhood" a short distance from the British Museum where the Stephen children—Vanessa, Virginia, and their brothers—made their home following the death of their father. The house at 46 Gordon Square became the gathering place of a group of writers who were all personal friends. After Virginia married Leonard Woolf, the group met in or around the couple's home in Tavistock Square, Bloomsbury.

Hogarth Press

In 1917 Leonard and Virginia Woolf started, as a hobby, the Hogarth Press, an amateur publishing business in which they did everything, including the printing. The press was so successful that it eventually became a regular publishing business. It took so much of Virginia's time to help manage the company that she retired from it. John Lehmann came in as Leonard's partner.

The first publication of the Hogarth Press was *Two Stories* by L. and V. Woolf. In 1918 they published *Poems* by their friend T. S. Eliot and *Prelude* by Katherine Mansfield, who was then unknown. In 1920 Hogarth published E. M. Forster's *The Story of the Siren*. Their policy was to publish "the best and the most original." They favored obscure young authors—who, however, did not remain obscure very long. Virginia Woolf's older sister, Vanessa, a painter who had married Clive Bell, illustrated and designed the distinctive dust jackets of Hogarth Press books.

The Reform Act of 1918 and the "Flapper Vote"

The Reform Act of 1918 gave voting rights to women over the age of thirty who fulfilled certain occupancy qualifications. The enfranchisement was given largely in recognition of women's contributions to the war effort. However, the reform could not have been won without the long campaign by the women's suffrage movement.

The 1928 Equal Franchise Act, known as the "Flapper Vote," reduced the voting age for women to twenty-one and established the same residence qualifications for women as for men.

POETRY AND LITERATURE BETWEEN THE WARS: ELIOT, MANSFIELD, GRAVES, SMITH, AND ORWELL

The British Commonwealth of Nations

The 1931 Statute of Westminster established the former colonies as a federation of equal and autonomous partners with Great Britain in the British Commonwealth.

Pound, Ezra

Ezra Pound was an American poet and critic. Besides composing his own original poetry, he published books on literature, music, art, and economics and translated and edited authors and poets in those same fields from the Italian, French, Chinese, and Japanese languages.

Pound lived in London from 1908 through 1920. Immediately following World War I Pound became the leader of the new postwar Imagist Movement, a "revolutionary" movement of writers (including Wyndham Lewis,

Hilda Doolittle, Amy Lowell, and T. S. Eliot) who wished to "blast" out the stuffiness of the Edwardian period. Pound's writings were obscure to many readers because they included content from his vast readings in a variety of languages. Pound moved to Paris in 1920 and to Italy in 1924.

For many years Pound was engaged in writing a long series of esoteric and argumentative "cantos" which opposing camps of critics regarded as either the apex of his achievement or the ultimate in absurdity.

While in Italy, Pound became increasingly supportive of fascism. In January 1941 Pound began broadcasting fascist propaganda by shortwave radio from Rome to the United States. He continued to make broadcasts throughout World War II. At the end of the war Pound was jailed by American forces on charges of treason. He was found mentally unfit to stand trial. Pound was committed to St. Elizabeth's Hospital, Washington, D.C. After his release in 1958 he left the United States for Italy, where he resided until his death in 1972.

Riding, Laura

An American, Riding began writing poetry while a scholarship student at Cornell University. In 1925 she went to Europe. While there she met Robert Graves. The two lived together for thirteen years in Egypt, England, Majorca, and France. She often collaborated with Graves on scholarly works. Riding returned to the United States in 1939.

Spanish Civil War

The Spanish Civil War, which lasted from 1936 to 1939, was fought between the conservative Nationalists, composed of the Spanish aristocracy, the fascist Falange party, church leaders, and the military, led by General Francisco Franco; and the Loyalists, supported by those Spaniards loyal to the deposed Republican government.

The Soviet Union sent aid to the Loyalists, some of whom were communists; the German and Italian fascist governments of Adolf Hitler and Benito Mussolini supported the Nationalists. The British government followed a policy of nonintervention, aiding neither side, but about 2,000 Britons joined International Brigades to fight with the Loyalists. The Nationalist forces won the war.

Many British writers and intellectuals were affected by the civil war. Stephen Spender worked as a Republican propagandist, and W. H. Auden joined the war effort as an ambulance driver. George Orwell served four months on the front with the Republican militia and was badly wounded. He later stated, "What I saw in Spain, and what I have seen since of the inner workings of the left-wing political parties, have given me a horror of politics."

POETRY OF THE THIRTIES AND FORTIES: AUDEN, MACNEICE, AND THOMAS

Battle of Britain and "The Blitz"

During the first stage of the invasion of Britain, the German military plan was to eliminate British air superiority and to bomb British cities into submission. The plan began with attacks on the merchant shipping that was supplying the British Isles with both military and domestic materiels.

From July 1940 through October 1940 the Royal Air Force (RAF) airfields were bombed constantly. The RAF lost over 1,000 planes and many airmen. In an intensive campaign to destroy civilian morale, in early September the German's began to bomb London with day and night *blitzkrieg* (German for "lightning") tactics, using the V-1 jet-powered flying bomb. Each day between 300 and 600 civilians were killed, and between 1,000 and 3,000 were injured.

From October 1940 to April 1941, German attacks included key industrial facilities from Plymouth to Glasgow.

The RAF Spitfire fighter planes ultimately enabled British fliers to defeat the German *Luftwaffe*'s offensive, forcing Hitler to call off his planned invasion of Great Britain.

Prime Minister Winston Churchill, known for his oratory, said of the British airmen who fought in the Battle of Britain, "Never in the field of human conflict was so much owed by so many to so few."

British Broadcasting Corporation

The British Broadcasting Corporation, a group financed by radio manufacturers, became a public corporation established by royal charter in 1926 after the government endorsed the principle of monopoly for broadcasting. The BBC thus became a public-service corporation empowered to act in the "national interest." Both Louis MacNeice and Dylan Thomas worked for the BBC.

Day-Lewis, C. (Cecil)

Day-Lewis, poet and scholar, was a friend and associate of his Oxford classmates Auden, Spender, MacNeice, and Isherwood. In the 1930s his poetry became more and more reflective of his political leanings and concerns with the class struggle and communist-cause sympathies. Day-Lewis joined the British Communist party in 1936. During the 1940s and later, his poetry became more personal and more tranquil. In the late 1930s, writing under the pseudonym Nicholas Blake, he published many detective books. From 1951 to 1956 he was professor of poetry at Oxford.

Isherwood, Christopher

British-born, Oxford educated, and later a naturalized United States citizen, Isherwood spent ten years in Germany (1923–1933). Although these were the years just before Hitler came to power, Isherwood was one of the first prose writers to feel the full build-up and impact of the fascist movement in Germany. This era in Germany provided the background for his two largely autobiographical novels, *Mr. Norris Changes Trains* (1935) and *Goodbye to Berlin* (1939). Part of *Goodbye to Berlin* was dramatized in 1951 as *I Am a Camera*. In 1968 the same section was transformed into the musical *Cabaret*. Isherwood and Auden coauthored several works, including *The Ascent of F6*.

Spender, Stephen

Educated at Oxford, Spender was a member of the "Auden" group in the 1930s. He was a distinguished critic and literary journalist as well as a poet. From 1939 to 1941 he was coeditor with Cyril Connolly of the monthly *Horizon*, and in 1953 he was editor of *Encounter*. *The Thirties and After*, a volume of memoirs (1978), his *Collected Poems 1982–1985*, and his *Journals 1939–1983*, both published in 1985, are his most recent works.

Wales

Wales is a mountainous country to the west of England where Celtic society survived Roman occupation. The Normans made their first foray into Wales within a year after the Battle of Hastings (1066), but it took them 200 years to complete the conquest. After two devastating campaigns in Wales (1276–1277 and 1282–1283) King Edward I of England defeated the lords of Wales. He confiscated the lands of Prince Llewelyn at Gruffudd and bestowed these lands on his eldest son, giving him also the title Prince of Wales, a custom often since followed by the monarchs of England.

In 1634 Cromwell began the policy of incorporating Wales into England. Since the 1636 Act of Union, Wales has been politically united with England. Only the unsuccessful revolt of Owain Glyndwr, which swept Wales from 1400 to 1408, ever presented a challenge to English control. Despite its union with England, Welsh literature, largely poetry, has been primarily written in the Welsh language.

MODERN DRAMA: BECKETT, PINTER, AND STOPPARD

Camus, Albert

Born in Algeria, Camus was a French writer of novels, dramas, and essays. He worked as a journalist, an actor, and a manager of a theatrical company. Toward the end of World War II he worked for the French resistance movement against the Germans, and with Jean-Paul Sartre he coedited the left-wing newspaper *Combat*. In the midst of the war, while with the underground resistance press, Camus published his philosophical essay *The Myth of Sisyphus*. His writings revealed his discouragement at civilization's failure to cope with major moral issues. Camus was unable to accept the existence of God but constantly tried to find significant values in a meaningless world. His thought was often centered on the idea that the individual's position in the world was absurd. He won the Nobel Prize for literature in 1957.

Existentialism

A twentieth-century school of philosophy, existentialism first stresses that individuals are entirely free and thus entirely responsible for what they make of themselves. With this responsibility comes a profound sense of anguish and dread. Second, the philosophy stresses the absurdity of reality.

Theatre of the Absurd

The Theatre of the Absurd is a term used to characterize plays that stress the illogical or irrational aspects of experience. Usually these plays show the pointlessness of life.

CONTEMPORARY TRENDS: LESSING, LARKIN, GUNN, HUGHES, AND HILL

Plath, Sylvia

An American poet and novelist, Plath was educated at Smith College, Massachusetts, and Cambridge University. In 1956 she married the English poet Ted Hughes. After teaching at Smith for a time, she settled in England. Her works include the poetry collections *The Colossus* (1960) and *Ariel* (1965) and her only novel, *The Bell Jar* (1963). Sylvia Plath committed suicide in 1963.

Rhodesia (now Zimbabwe)

In 1965 the government of Rhodesia issued a Unilateral Declaration of Independence from Britain after Britain refused to grant independence without introducing black majority rule. Black guerrilla warfare in Rhodesia forced the Rhodesian government to negotiate, resulting in the establishment of a transitional government in 1979. After elections in Rhodesia in 1980, Zimbabwe emerged as an independent nation.

Wain, John

A British novelist, poet, and critic, Wain has been associated with "the Movement," a group of novelists who concern themselves with post–World War II social changes.

Index

OTHER BOOKS IN THE HARPERCOLLINS COLLEGE OUTLINE SERIES

ART
History of Art 0-06-467131-3
Introduction to Art 0-06-467122-4

BUSINESS
Business Calculus 0-06-467136-4
Business Communications 0-06-467155-0
Introduction to Business 0-06-467104-6
Introduction to Management 0-06-467127-5
Introduction to Marketing 0-06-467130-5

CHEMISTRY
College Chemistry 0-06-467120-8
Organic Chemistry 0-06-467126-7

COMPUTERS
Computers and Information Processing 0-06-467176-3
Introduction to Computer Science and Programming
    0-06-467145-3
Understanding Computers 0-06-467163-1

ECONOMICS
Introduction to Economics 0-06-467113-5
Managerial Economics 0-06-467172-0

ENGLISH LANGUAGE AND LITERATURE
English Grammar 0-06-467109-7
English Literature From 1785 0-06-467150-X
English Literature To 1785 0-06-467114-3
Persuasive Writing 0-06-467175-5

FOREIGN LANGUAGE
French Grammar 0-06-467128-3
German Grammar 0-06-467159-3
Spanish Grammar 0-06-467129-1
Wheelock's Latin Grammar 0-06-467177-1
Workbook for Wheelock's Latin Grammar
    0-06-467171-2

HISTORY
Ancient History 0-06-467119-4
British History 0-06-467110-0
Modern European History 0-06-467112-7
Russian History 0-06-467117-8
20th Century United States History 0-06-467132-1
United States History From 1865 0-06-467100-3
United States History to 1877 0-06-467111-9
Western Civilization From 1500 0-06-467102-X

Western Civilization To 1500 0-06-467101-1
World History From 1500 0-06-467138-0
World History to 1648 0-06-467123-2

MATHEMATICS
Advanced Calculus 0-06-467139-9
Advanced Math for Engineers and Scientists
    0-06-467151-8
Applied Complex Variables 0-06-467152-6
Basic Mathematics 0-06-467143-7
Calculus with Analytic Geometry 0-06-467161-5
College Algebra 0-06-467140-2
Elementary Algebra 0-06-467118-6
Finite Mathematics with Calculus 0-06-467164-X
Intermediate Algebra 0-06-467137-2
Introduction to Calculus 0-06-467125-9
Introduction to Statistics 0-06-467134-8
Ordinary Differential Equations 0-06-467133-X
Precalculus Mathematics: Functions & Graphs
    0-06-467165-8
Survey of Mathematics 0-06-467135-6

MUSIC
Harmony and Voice Leading 0-06-467148-8
History of Western Music 0-06-467107-7
Introduction to Music 0-06-467108-9
Music Theory 0-06-467168-2

PHILOSOPHY
Ethics 0-06-467166-6
History of Philosophy 0-06-467142-9
Introduction to Philosophy 0-06-467124-0

POLITICAL SCIENCE
The Constitution of the United States 0-06-467105-4
Introduction to Government 0-06-467156-9

PSYCHOLOGY
Abnormal Psychology 0-06-467121-6
Child Development 0-06-467149-6
Introduction to Psychology 0-06-467103-8
Personality: Theories and Processes 0-06-467115-1
Social Psychology 0-06-467157-7

SOCIOLOGY
Introduction to Sociology 0-06-467106-2
Marriage and the Family 0-06-467147-X

Available at your local bookstore or directly from HarperCollins at 1-800-331-3761.